Volkswagen Beetle 1300/1500 Owners Workshop Manual

by J H Haynes

Member of the Guild of Motoring Writers

and D H Stead

Models covered
Volkswagen Beetle 1285 cc (78.3 cu in)
Volkswagen Beetle 1493 cc (91.1 cu in)

*Does not cover 1302/1303 Super Beetles, 1300A or any model
with 1200 or 1600 cc engine*

(039-5S7)

ABCDE
FGHIJ
KLMNO
PQ

3

Haynes Publishing Group
Sparkford Nr Yeovil
Somerset BA22 7JJ England

Haynes Publications, Inc
861 Lawrence Drive
Newbury Park
California 91320 USA

Restoring and Preserving our Motoring Heritage

Few people can have had the luck to realise their dreams to quite the same extent and in such a remarkable fashion as John Haynes, Founder and Chairman of the Haynes Publishing Group.

Since 1965 his unique approach to workshop manual publishing has proved so successful that millions of Haynes Manuals are now sold every year throughout the world, covering literally thousands of different makes and models of cars, vans and motorcycles.

A continuing passion for cars and motoring led to the founding in 1985 of a Charitable Trust dedicated to the restoration and preservation of our motoring heritage. To inaugurate the new Museum, John Haynes donated virtually his entire private collection of 52 cars.

Now with an unrivalled international collection of over 210 veteran, vintage and classic cars and motorcycles, the Haynes Motor Museum in Somerset is well on the way to becoming one of the most interesting Motor Museums in the world.

A 70 seat video cinema, a cafe and an extensive motoring bookshop, together with a specially constructed one kilometre motor circuit, make a visit to the Haynes Motor Museum a truly unforgettable experience.

Every vehicle in the museum is preserved in as near as possible mint condition and each car is run every six months on the motor circuit.

Enjoy the picnic area set amongst the rolling Somerset hills. Peer through the William Morris workshop windows at cars being restored, and browse through the extensive displays of fascinating motoring memorabilia.

From the 1903 Oldsmobile through such classics as an MG Midget to the mighty 'E' type Jaguar, Lamborghini, Ferrari Berlinetta Boxer, and Graham Hill's Lola Cosworth, there is something for everyone, young and old alike, at this Somerset Museum.

Haynes Motor Museum

Situated mid-way between London and Penzance, the Haynes Motor Museum is located just off the A303 at Sparkford, Somerset (home of the Haynes Manual) and is open to the public 7 days a week all year round, except Christmas Day and Boxing Day.

Telephone 01963 440804.

Acknowledgements

Thanks are due to the Champion Sparking Plug Company Limited who supplied the illustrations showing spark plug conditions, to Holt Lloyd Limited who supplied the illustrations showing bodywork repair, and to Duckhams Oils who provided lubrication data. Thanks are also due to all the staff at Sparkford who helped in the production of this manual.

© Haynes Publishing Group 1991

A book in the **Haynes Owners Workshop Manual Series**

Printed in the USA

ISBN 0 85696 494 8

Whilst every care is taken to ensure that the information in this manual is correct, no liability can be accepted by the authors or publishers for loss, damage or injury caused by any errors in, or omissions from, the information given.

Contents

About this manual

Its aim

The aim of this manual is to help you get the best value from your car. It can do so in several ways. It can help you decide what work must be done (even should you choose to get it done by a garage), provide information on routine maintenance and servicing, and give a logical course of action and diagnosis when random faults occur. However, it is hoped that you will use the manual by tackling the work yourself. On simpler jobs it may even be quicker than booking the car into a garage, and going there twice to leave and collect it. Perhaps most important, a lot of money can be saved by avoiding the costs the garage must charge to cover its labour and overheads.

The manual has drawings and descriptions to show the function of the various components so that their layout can be understood. Then the tasks are described and photographed in a step-by-step sequence so that even a novice can do the work.

Its arrangement

The manual is divided into thirteen Chapters, each covering a logical sub-division of the vehicle. The Chapters are divided into Sections, numbered with single figures, eg 5; and the Sections into paragraphs (or sub-sections), with decimal numbers following on from the Section they are in, eg 5.1, 5.2, 5.3 etc.

It is freely illustrated, especially in those parts where there is a detailed sequence of operations to be carried out. There are two forms of illustration: figures and photographs. The figures are numbered in sequence with decimal numbers, according to their position in the Chapter: eg Fig. 6.4 is the 4th drawing/illustration in Chapter 6. Photographs are numbered (either individually or in related groups) the same as the Section or subsection of the text where the operation they show is described.

There is an alphabetical index at the back of the manual as well as a contents list at the front.

References to the 'left' or 'right' of the vehicle are in the sense of a person in the driver's seat facing forwards.

Unless otherwise stated, nuts and bolts are removed by turning anti-clockwise, and tightened by turning clockwise.

This manual is not a direct reproduction of the vehicle manufacturers' data, and its publication should not be taken as implying any technical approval by the vehicle manufacturers or importers.

Whilst every care is taken to ensure that the information in this manual is correct no liability can be accepted by the authors or publishers for loss, damage or injury caused by any errors in, or omissions from, the information given.

Introduction to the 1300 and 1500 Beetle

When the 1300 Beetle was introduced in August 1965 the tradition of a one model 'Beetle' was finally broken after 30 years. Prior to that time every improvement or increase in engine size had been a development of the one model. Now an alternative model was offered with a larger engine and other refinements putting it in the de luxe category. The 1200 was to carry on the original concept of a basic 'people's car' — until 1977. In 1966 yet another alternative emerged in the same body shell — the 1500. This had a somewhat larger engine again and the added refinement of disc brakes as standard on the front wheels.

Both of these alternatives in the 'Beetle' range varied very little and the basic design was identical. Body style changes, when made, were made for all three Beetle models. Further engine development was not significant until 1969/70 by which time the 1500 model was being phased out in the U.K. to make way for the 'Super Beetle' — a quite different animal altogether. From then on developments of the flat four air cooled engine in larger capacities for other models have all had a reflective effect on the smaller version. Improvements in oil circulation and cooling and increase in valve size have all come about because of lessons learnt from the larger engines. Standardisation of parts is also of some considerable account, one assumes.

In 1967 an optional extra was offered in the form of an 'automatic stickshift transmission'. This was a sort of compromise between a normal gearbox and an automatic and details are given in Chapter 7. It was received with mixed feelings and this is understandable as the idea did not really fit the 'Beetle' image. However, one bonus of the system is a trailing link rear suspension with double jointed driveshafts. There can be no doubt that this system is superior in roadholding to that of the swinging arm design.

The double joint rear axle is available only on 1300 and 1500 automatic transmission versions and there are doubtless many who speculate whether the 'basic' Beetle will in the future be available with the new rear suspension, either with or without the automatic option.

Early type 1967 Volkswagen 1500 Beetle Saloon

Tools and working facilities

Introduction

A selection of good tools is a fundamental requirement for anyone contemplating the maintenance and repair of a motor vehicle. For the owner who does not possess any, their purchase will prove a considerable expense, offsetting some of the savings made by doing-it-yourself. However, provided that the tools purchased meet the relevant national safety standards and are of good quality, they will last for many years and prove an extremely worthwhile investment.

To help the average owner to decide which tools are needed to carry out the various tasks detailed in this manual, we have compiled three lists of tools under the following headings: *Maintenance and minor repair, Repair and overhaul* and *Special*. The newcomer to practical mechanics should start off with the *Maintenance and minor repair* tool kit and confine himself to the simpler jobs around the vehicle. Then, as his confidence and experience grows, he can undertake more difficult tasks, buying extra tools as, and when, they are needed. In this way, a *Maintenance and minor repair* tool kit can be built-up into a *Repair and overhaul* tool kit over a considerable period of time without any major cash outlays. The experienced do-it-yourselfer will have a tool kit good enough for most repair and overhaul procedures and will add tools from the *Special* category when he feels the expense is justified by the amount of use to which these tools will be put.

It is obviously not possible to cover the subject of tools fully here. For those who wish to learn more about tools and their use there is a book entitled *How to Choose and Use Car Tools* available from the publishers of this manual.

Maintenance and minor repair tool kit

The tools given in this list should be considered as a minimum requirement if routine maintenance, servicing and minor repair operations are to be undertaken. We recommend the purchase of combination spanners (ring one end, open-ended the other); although more expensive than open-ended ones, they do give the advantages of both types of spanner.

Combination spanners — 10, 11, 12, 13, 14, 17 mm
Adjustable spanner — 9 inch
Engine sump/gearbox drain plug key
Spark plug spanner (with rubber insert)
Spark plug gap adjustment tool
Set of feeler gauges
Brake bleed nipple spanner
Screwdriver — 4 in long x ¼ in dia (flat blade)
Screwdriver — 4 in long x ¼ in dia (cross blade)
Combination pliers – 6 inch
Hacksaw (junior)
Tyre pump
Tyre pressure gauge
Grease gun
Oil can
Fine emery cloth (1 sheet)
Wire brush (small)
Funnel (medium size)

Repair and overhaul tool kit

These tools are virtually essential for anyone undertaking any major repairs to a motor vehicle, and are additional to those given in the *Maintenance and minor repair* list. Included in this list is a comprehensive set of sockets. Although these are expensive they will be found invaluable as they are so versatile — particularly if various drives are included in the set. We recommend the ½ in square-drive type, as this can be used with most proprietary torque wrenches. If you cannot afford a socket set, even bought piecemeal, then inexpensive tubular box spanners are a useful alternative.

The tools in this list will occasionally need to be supplemented by tools from the *Special* list.

Sockets (or box spanners) to cover range in previous list
Reversible ratchet drive (for use with sockets)
Extension piece, 10 inch (for use with sockets)
Universal joint (for use with sockets)
Torque wrench (for use with sockets)
'Mole' wrench — 8 inch
Ball pein hammer
Soft-faced hammer, plastic or rubber
Screwdriver — 6 in long x 5/16 in dia (flat blade)
Screwdriver — 2 in long x 5/16 in square (flat blade)
Screwdriver — 1½ in long x ¼ in dia (cross blade)
Screwdriver — 3 in long x 1/8 in dia (electricians)
Pliers — electricians side cutters
Pliers — needle nosed
Pliers — circlip (internal and external)
Cold chisel — ½ inch
Scriber
Scraper
Centre punch
Pin punch
Hacksaw
Valve grinding tool
Steel rule/straight-edge
Allen keys
Selection of files
Wire brush (large)
Axle-stands
Jack (strong scissor or hydraulic type)

Special tools

The tools in this list are those which are not used regularly, are expensive to buy, or which need to be used in accordance with their manufacturers' instructions. Unless relatively difficult mechanical jobs are undertaken frequently, it will not be economical to buy many of these tools. Where this is the case, you could consider clubbing together with friends (or joining a motorists' club) to make a joint purchase, or borrowing the tools against a deposit from a local garage or tool hire specialist.

The following list contains only those tools and instruments freely available to the public, and not those special tools produced by the vehicle manufacturer specifically for its dealer network. You will find occasional references to these manufacturers' special tools in the text of this manual. Generally, an alternative method of doing the job without the vehicle manufacturer's special tool is given. However, sometimes, there is no alternative to using them. Where this is the case and the relevant tool cannot be bought or borrowed, you will have to entrust the work to a franchised garage.

Valve spring compressor
Piston ring compressor
Balljoint separator
Universal hub/bearing puller
Impact screwdriver
Micrometer and/or vernier gauge
Dial gauge
Stroboscopic timing light
Dwell angle meter/tachometer
Universal electrical multi-meter
Cylinder compression gauge
Lifting tackle
Trolley jack
Light with extension lead

Buying tools

For practically all tools, a tool factor is the best source since he will have a very comprehensive range compared with the average garage or accessory shop. Having said that, accessory shops often offer excellent quality tools at discount prices, so it pays to shop around.

There are plenty of good tools around at reasonable prices, but always aim to purchase items which meet the relevant national safety standards. If in doubt, ask the proprietor or manager of the shop for advice before making a purchase.

Care and maintenance of tools

Having purchased a reasonable tool kit, it is necessary to keep the tools in a clean serviceable condition. After use, always wipe off any dirt, grease and metal particles using a clean, dry cloth, before putting the tools away. Never leave them lying around after they have been used. A simple tool rack on the garage or workshop wall, for items such as screwdrivers and pliers is a good idea. Store all normal spanners and sockets in a metal box. Any measuring instruments, gauges, meters, etc, must be carefully stored where they cannot be damaged or become rusty.

Take a little care when tools are used. Hammer heads inevitably become marked and screwdrivers lose the keen edge on their blades from time to time. A little timely attention with emery cloth or a file will soon restore items like this to a good serviceable finish.

Working facilities

Not to be forgotten when discussing tools, is the workshop itself. If anything more than routine maintenance is to be carried out, some form of suitable working area becomes essential.

It is appreciated that many an owner mechanic is forced by circumstances to remove an engine or similar item, without the benefit of a garage or workshop. Having done this, any repairs should always be done under the cover of a roof.

Wherever possible, any dismantling should be done on a clean, flat workbench or table at a suitable working height.

Any workbench needs a vice: one with a jaw opening of 4 in (100 mm) is suitable for most jobs. As mentioned previously, some clean dry storage space is also required for tools, as well as for lubricants, cleaning fluids, touch-up paints and so on which become necessary.

Another item which may be required, and which has a much more general usage, is an electric drill with a chuck capacity of at least 5/16 in (8 mm). This, together with a good range of twist drills, is virtually essential for fitting accessories such as mirrors and reversing lights.

Last, but not least, always keep a supply of old newspapers and clean, lint-free rags available, and try to keep any working area as clean as possible.

Spanner jaw gap comparison table

Jaw gap (in)	Spanner size
0.250	¼ in AF
0.276	7 mm
0.313	5/16 in AF
0.315	8 mm
0.344	11/32 in AF; 1/8 in Whitworth
0.354	9 mm
0.375	3/8 in AF
0.394	10 mm
0.433	11 mm
0.438	7/16 in AF
0.445	3/16 in Whitworth; ¼ in BSF
0.472	12 mm
0.500	½ in AF
0.512	13 mm
0.525	¼ in Whitworth; 5/16 in BSF
0.551	14 mm
0.563	9/16 in AF
0.591	15 mm
0.600	5/16 in Whitworth; 3/8 in BSF
0.625	5/8 in AF
0.630	16 mm
0.669	17 mm
0.686	11/16 in AF
0.709	18 mm
0.710	3/8 in Whitworth; 7/16 in BSF
0.748	19 mm
0.750	¾ in AF
0.813	13/16 in AF
0.820	7/16 in Whitworth; ½ in BSF
0.866	22 mm
0.875	7/8 in AF
0.920	½ in Whitworth; 9/16 in BSF
0.938	15/16 in AF
0.945	24 mm
1.000	1 in AF
1.010	9/16 in Whitworth; 5/8 in BSF
1.024	26 mm
1.063	1.1/16 in AF; 27 mm
1.100	5/8 in Whitworth; 11/16 in BSF
1.125	1.1/8 in AF
1.181	30 mm
1.200	11/16 in Whitworth; ¾ in BSF
1.250	1¼ in AF
1.260	32 mm
1.300	¾ in Whitworth; 7/8 in BSF
1.313	1.5/16 in AF
1.390	13/16 in Whitworth; 15/16 in BSF
1.417	36 mm
1.438	1.7/16 in AF
1.480	7/8 in Whitworth; 1 in BSF
1.500	1½ in AF
1.575	40 mm; 15/16 in Whitworth
1.614	41 mm
1.625	1.5/8 in AF
1.670	1 in Whitworth; 1.1/8 in BSF
1.688	1.11/16 in AF
1.811	46 mm
1.813	1.13/16 in AF
1.860	1.1/8 in Whitworth; 1¼ in BSF
1.875	1.7/8 in AF
1.969	50 mm
2.000	2 in AF
2.050	1¼ in Whitworth; 1.3/8 in BSF
2.165	55 mm
2.362	60 mm

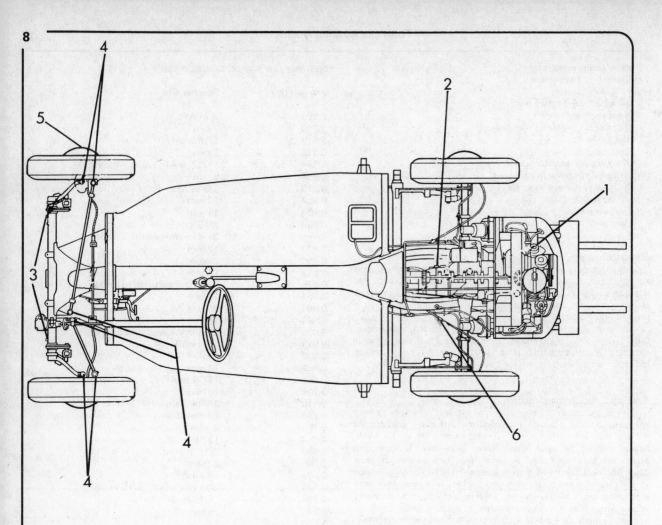

Recommended lubricants and fluids

Component or system	Lubricant type/specification	Duckhams recommendation
1 Engine	Multigrade engine oil, viscosity SAE 20W/50	Duckhams QXR or Hypergrade
2 Transmission and final drive	Hypoid gear oil, viscosity SAE 80EP	Duckhams Hypoid 80
3 Front axle torsion arm bushes	Multi-purpose lithium based grease	Duckhams LB 10
4 Steering and suspension balljoints – where applicable	Multi-purpose lithium based grease	Duckhams LB 10
5 Front wheel bearings	Multi-purpose lithium based grease	Duckhams LB 10
6 Handbrake cables – where applicable	Multi-purpose lithium based grease	Duckhams LB 10
Brake hydraulic system	Hydraulic fluid to SAE J1703 or DOT 3	Duckhams Universal Brake and Clutch Fluid
Torque converter	Dexron type ATF	Duckhams D-Matic

Buying spare parts and vehicle identification numbers

Buying spare parts

Spare parts are available from many sources. VW have many dealers throughout the UK and the USA, and other dealers, accessory stores and motor factors will also stock VW spare parts.

Our advice regarding spare part sources is as follows:

Officially appointed vehicle main dealers — This is the best source of parts which are peculiar to your vehicle and are otherwise not generally available (eg complete cylinder heads, internal transmission components, badges, interior trim etc). It is also the only place at which you should buy parts if your vehicle is still under warranty. To be sure of obtaining the correct parts it will always be necessary to give the storeman your vehicle's engine and chassis number, and if possible, to take the 'old' part along for positive identification. Remember that many parts are available on a factory exchange scheme — any parts returned should always be clean! It obviously makes good sense to go straight to the specialists on your vehicle for this type of part, for they are best equipped to supply you.

Other dealers and auto accessory stores — These are often very good places to buy materials and components needed for the maintenance of your vehicle (eg oil filters, sparking plugs, bulbs, fan belts, oils and greases, touch-up paint, filler paste etc). They also sell general accessories, usually have convenient opening hours, charge lower prices and can often be found not far from home.

Motor factors — Good factors will stock all of the more important components which wear out relatively quickly (eg clutch components, pistons, valves, exhaust systems, brake cylinders/pipes/hoses/seals/shoes and pads etc). Motor factors will often provide new or reconditioned components on a part exchange basis — this can save a considerable amount of money.

Vehicle identification numbers

Modifications are a continuing and unpublicised process in vehicle manufacture. Spare parts manuals and lists are compiled on a numerical basis, the individual vehicle numbers being essential to identify correctly the component required.

Chassis number — The chassis number is stamped on the frame tunnel under the back seat or in the front compartment on a plate behind the spare wheel.

Engine number — The engine number is stamped on the crankcase at the base of the generator pedestal.

Routine maintenance

Introduction

Because of their inherent toughness and reputation for reliability and long life there is a tendency for owner's to be a bit sketchy on VW maintenance - particularly with vehicles not in the first flush of youth.

The VW will put up with neglect for a much longer time than most cars but when the crunch eventually does come it is likely to be drastic.

Regular maintenance therefore, is just as important as on any other vehicle. If it is not neglected the Beetle is very much a long term investment with a low rate of depreciation in value.

The service procedures listed hereafter cover all the points of required regular service. The frequency of service tends to vary according to changes in design of various components, the conditions under which the vehicle is used, and the way in which it is driven. The frequencies given are based on a mileage of 12000 per year in a temperate climate which is mainly non dusty. Variations from this will be taken into account by VW service agencies in different conditions. Variations in driving style must be the responsibility of the driver where servicing requirements could be affected.

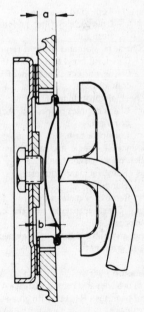

Engine oil filter and suction pipe
cross-section

Dimension (a) = 10 mm ± 1 mm (from top of suction pipe to flange face on crankcase)
Dimension (b) = 6 mm ± 1 mm (strainer flange to bottom of strainer)

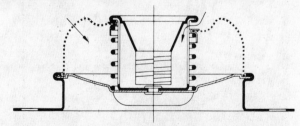

Filter fitted to later 1500 engines incorporating relief valve. Left arrow indicates normal oil flow. Right arrow shows how oil by-passes the screen which is pulled down against the spring if the mesh is blocked.

Where maintenance is solely a matter of inspection (rather than lubrication, cleaning or adjustment) the findings from such inspections will determine whether or not further action is required. Such further action is no longer within the scope of Routine Maintenance. It is a workshop procedure requiring repair or renewal. How to do the maintenance is detailed after the schedules. If the details are already in the main chapters then reference is made appropriately.

Topping up engine oil

1 Safety maintenance
a) Steering
Front suspension arm ball joints - Check for wear.	3 months
Steering tie rod ball joints - Check for wear.	3 months
Steering gear - Check worm to roller play and worm shaft bearings. Adjust if necessary.	3 months
Front wheel bearings - Check end play and adjust if necessary.	3 months

b) Brakes
Hydraulic fluid reservoir level.	1 month
Efficiency and foot pedal free play - Check and adjust as required.	3 months
Handbrake efficiency - Check and adjust as required	
Brake friction lining material - Check thickness.	6 months
Hydraulic lines, hoses, master cylinder and wheel cylinders - Examine exteriors for leaks or corrosion.	6 months
Renew all seals and fluid.	3 years

Note: A significant drop in fluid reservoir level or any other indication of fluid leakage is a danger signal. A complete and thorough examination of the hydraulic system should be made.

c) Suspension
Tyres - Inflation pressure check.	Weekly
Tyres - Wear and damage check.	As suspect
Front suspension arm ball joints - Check for wear.	3 months
Dampers - Check for leakage and malfunction.	3 months

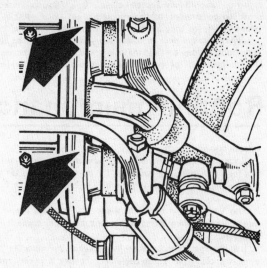
Front suspension torsion arm bearing grease nipples.

2. Efficiency and performance maintenance
a) Engine
Lubricating oil - Top up to level.	Weekly
- Drain, clean filter and refill with fresh oil.	3 months
Fan belt - Check tension and adjust if required.	1 month
Air cleaner - Clean out bowl and refill with oil.	1 month
- Check correct operation of warm air control flaps.	1 month
Battery - Check electrolyte level.	Weekly
Distributor - Check contact points gap. Adjust and/ or renew.	3 months
- Lubricate cam.	3 months
Valve clearances - Check and adjust as required (renew rocker cover gaskets).	6 months
Spark plugs - Removal clean and reset.	3 months
- Renew.	12 months
Fuel pump - Remove and clean filter.	6 months
Carburettor - Check setting of throttle cable and lubricate linkage.	6 months
Cover plates and fan housing - Check security of screws and all grommets.	3 months

b) Front suspension
Torsion arm bearings and bushes - Grease 4 nipples.	6 months
Front wheel bearings - Repack with grease.	2 years

c) Transmission and final drive
Gearbox oil - Check level and top up as needed.	3 months
- Drain and refill with fresh oil.	2 years
Clutch pedal free play - Check movement and adjust.	As necessary

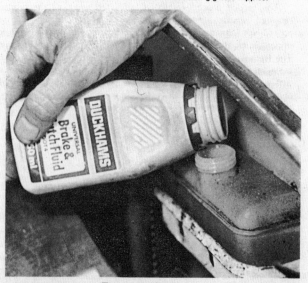
Topping up brake fluid

Axle tube flexible gaiters - Check for leaks or impending splits.   3 months

d) Automatic transmission
Refer to Chapter 7.

Maintenance procedures

1. Safety maintenance
a) Steering
See Chapter 11.

b) Brakes
Hydraulic fluid reservoir level - Raise the front compartment lid. The fluid reservoir is either behind the spare wheel or mounted at the left hand side. The latter type is indicative that a dual circuit braking system is fitted (1967 on).
Clean round the filler cap before removing it and top up to the indicated level with approved fluid as required.
Remaining items - See Chapter 9.

c) Suspension
See Chapter 11.

2. Efficiency and performance maintenance
a) Engine
Lubricating oil.
Top up the oil, remove the filler cap from the filler pipe at the right hand side of the engine. Remove the dipstick to prevent possible blow back up the filler pipe when pouring oil in. A funnel is necessary when using certain containers if spillage is to be avoided.
When changing the engine oil the filter screen - which is a simple wire gauze - should also be flushed out with paraffin to clear the gauze. This entails removing the circular retaining plate in the centre of the bottom of the crankcase. Before starting, you must obtain two new gaskets for it, and it is also desirable to get six new copper washers for the stud nuts.
First drain the oil by removing the centre plug and then remove the cover plate. Take care when removing the strainer. Do not distort it.
The oil suction pipe which goes into the centre of the strainer gauze must be quite firm. If it is loose then it is likely that suction is being lost and the oil circulation is not 100% efficient. (The engine needs completely stripping to put this right).
On 1500 models from 1968 the strainer incorporates a relief valve in case the filter mesh should get completely blocked up.
Having thoroughly cleaned everything refit the strainer with a gasket in each side of the flange. See that the suction pipe is properly located in the strainer. Fit new copper washers followed by the cap nuts. Do not overtighten the cap nuts - otherwise the threads may strip and the plates distort.
Replace the drain plug and refill with 4½ pints of approved engine oil.
Fan belt - See Chapter 2.
Air cleaner - See Chapter 3.
Battery - See Chapter 10.
Distributor - See Chapter 4.
Valve clearances - See Chapter 1.
Spark plugs - See Chapter 4.
Fuel pump - See Chapter 3.
Carburettor - See Chapter 3.
Cover plates - See Chapters 1 and 2.

b) Front suspension
Torsion arm bearings - Greasing.
On the upper and lower front axle tubes there is a grease nipple at each end. Clean the nipple and surrounds and give each one 2 or 3 shots from a grease gun filled with recommended lubricant. Do

not overgrease or the seals will be damaged.
Front wheel bearings - See Chapter 11.

c) Gearbox oil
To check the level stand the car on level ground and undo the level plug which is halfway up the side of the casing on the left - just ahead of the axle shafts. This plug is a recessed hexagon which could be very difficult to undo. It may be necessary to weld a suitably sized hexagon bolt head to a piece of bar to use as a special tool.
Add oil through from a suitable oil gun or squeeze pack with flexible filler spout. Add oil slowly until it runs out from the filler/level hole. Clean the plug and replace it tightly.
When changing the transmission oil it is best to run it warm first. Then undo the two magnetic drain plugs in the bottom of the casing. Here again a specially prepared tool may be needed. Let the oil drain out for at least 15 minutes. Clean the magnetic drain plugs and replace them. Before beginning to refill get the exact amount of oil needed ready, and then start to fill up through the filler/level plug. It is possible that oil will overflow before you have put it all in. Wait so that the air pockets have time to bubble out and then continue until all the oil is put in.
Clutch pedal free play - See Chapter 5.
Axle tube gaiters - See Chapter 8.

Check the clutch pedal free play

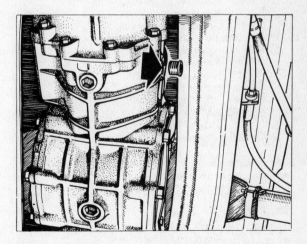

Filling the transmission with oil (using a pressure oil line)

Chapter 1 Engine

For modifications, and information applicable to later models, see Supplement at end of manual

Contents

Specifications

Engine specifications and data — 1289 cc 40 DIN bhp 1965 on
— 1493 cc 44 DIN bhp 1966—1970

Engine - General	1300 (Code F)	1500 (Code H)
Type...	4 cylinder horizontally opposed flat	Pushrod o.h.v.
Weight (approx)	237 lbs (108 kgs)	
Bore...	77 mm	83 mm
Stroke	69 mm	69 mm
Cubic capacity	1285 cc	1493 cc
Compression ratio	7.3 : 1*	7.5 : 1
Power output	40 DIN bhp at 4000 rpm*	44 DIN bhp at 4000 rpm
Torque	69 lb.ft at 2600 rpm*	78 lb.ft at 2600 rpm
Compression pressure..	106—135 p.s.i.	114—142 p.s.i.
Location of No.1 cylinder	Right hand pair - front	
Firing order	1 (R. front) 4 (L. rear) 3 (L. front) 2 (R. rear) **See Fig. 4.1.**	
Engine mountings	Bolted direct to transmission casing, 2 bolts, 2 studs	

*NOTE: With effect from August 1970 the engine output was uprated (bhp) and the engine number prefix code letter changed from F to AB. The main differences are:

Compression ratio...	7.5 : 1	
Power output (DIN bhp)..	44 bhp at 4100 rpm	
Torque	68.7 lb.ft at 3500 rpm	

Camshaft and camshaft bearings

Camshaft drive...	Lightweight alloy gear direct from crankshaft
Camshaft bearings..	Steel backed white metal shells
Camshaft journal diameters...	24.99 — 25.00 mm (.9837 — .9842 in)
Journal/bearing radial clearance	.02 — .12 mm (.0008 — .0047 in)
End float.	.04 — .16 mm (.0016 — .0063 in)
Gear backlash	0 — .05 mm (0 — .0019 in)

Connecting rods and bearings

Type...	Forged steel
Big end bearings	Three layer thin wall shells
Crankpin (big end) diameter..	54.98 — 55.00 mm (2.1644 — 2.1648 in)
Small end bush	Pressed in steel bush with lead/bronze coating
Undersize big end shells available	.25 mm, .50 mm and .75 mm
Crankpin to bearing clearance limits	.02 — .15 mm (.0008 — .006 in)
Crankpin end float	.1 — .7 mm (.004 — .028 in)
Gudgeon pin / bush radial clearance limit..	.01 — .04 (.004 — .0016 in)
Gudgeon pin diameter	21.996 — 22 mm (.8658 — .8661 in)
Connecting rod weight - brown or white	580 — 588 grams
- grey or black	592 — 600 grams
Maximum crankpin ovality	.03 mm (.0011 in)

Crankshaft and main bearings

Number of bearings	4
Main bearing journal diameters Nos 1, 2 and 3	54.97 — 54.99 mm (2.164 — 2.1648 in)
No 4	39.98 — 40.00 mm (1.5739 — 1.5748 in)
Regrind diameters undersize	.25 mm, .50 mm, .75 mm
Bearing shells - type Nos 1, 3 and 4	Aluminium, lead coated 1 piece
No 2	Split - 3 layer steel backed
Journal/bearing radial clearance limit	
Nos 1 and 3	.04 — .18 mm (.0016 — .007 in)
No 2	.03 — .17 mm (.0011 — .0066 in)
No 4	.05 — .19 mm (.0019 — .0074 in)
Crankshaft end float	Taken by flange of No.1 main bearing and adjusted by shims
End float limits	.07 — .13 mm (.0027 — .0051 in)
Main journal maximum ovality...	.03 mm (.0011 in)

Crankcase

Main bearing bore diameters Nos 1, 2 and 3	65.00 — 65.03 mm (2.559 — 2.5601 in)
No 4	50.00 — 50.04 mm (1.9685 — 1.9700 in)
Oil seal bore diameter (flywheel end)...	90.00 — 90.05 mm (3.5433 — 3.5452 in)
Camshaft bearing bore diameter	27.5 — 27.52 mm (1.0825 — 1.0852 in)
Oil pump housing bore diameter	70.00 — 70.03 mm (2.756 — 2.758 in)
Tappet (cam follower) bore diameters	19.00 — 19.05 mm (.748 — .750 in)

Cylinders

Type...	Single barrels - finned - cast iron
Distance between pair centres	112 mm (4.41 in)

Cylinder heads

Type...	Aluminium - 1 per pair of cylinders
Port arrangement	Common inlet port per pair of cylinders. One exhaust port for each cylinder.

Gudgeon pins

Type...	Fully floating, steel tube retained by circlips
Diameter	21.996 — 22.00 mm (.8658 — .8661 in)

Lubrication system

Type...	Wet sump — pressure and splash
Oil filter	Wire gauze suction strainer in sump
Oil type/specification	Multigrade engine oil, viscosity SAE 20W/50 (Duckhams QXR or Hypergrade)
Sump capacity	2½ litres (4.4 Imp. pints)
Oil pump type	Twin gear
Oil pressure (SAE 30, 70°C at 2500 rpm)	42 p.s.i. (min 28 p.s.i.)
Oil pressure warning light	Comes on between 2—6 p.s.i.
Oil cooler	Pressure fed multitube type in cooling fan housing

Oil pump

Gear/body end clearance (no gasket)	.1 mm (.004 in) max.
Gear backlash	0 — .2 mm (.008 in)

Oil pressure relief valve

Spring length loaded at 7.75 kg (17 lbs) ... ...   23.6 mm (.928 in)

Pistons

Type...	Light alloy with steel inserts and flat crown
Clearance in cylinder limits	.04 — .20 mm (.0015 — .008 in)
Number of rings	3 — Two compression, one oil control
Ring/groove side clearance - Top compression	.07 — .12 mm (.0027 — .0047 in)
- Lower compression	.05 — .10 mm (.0019 — .0039 in)
- Oil control	.03 — .10 mm (.0012 — .0039 in)
Piston oversizes available	.5 mm and 1.0 mm (.020 and .040 in)
Piston pin bore offset..	1.5 mm (.060 in)

Piston rings

Top compression:

Thickness	2.5 mm (.10 in)
Gap limit...	.3 — .9 mm (.012 — .035 in)
Bearing face	Bevelled, angle facing top of piston

Lower compression:

Thickness	2.5 mm (.10 in)
Gap limit...	.3 — .9 mm (.012 — .035 in)
Bearing face	Parallel, lower edge cut back

Oil control:

Gap	.25 — .95 mm (.010 — .037 in)

Tappets - (Cam followers)

Type...	Cylindrical flat based
Diameter	18.96 — 18.89 mm (.7463 — .7471 in)

Pushrods and rocker arms

Pushrod type	Tube with hemispherical ends
Length	272.5 mm
Rocker arm bore size limits...	18.00 — 18.04 mm (.7086 — .7093 in)
Rocker shaft diameter size limits	17.97 — 17.95 mm (.7073 — .7066 in)

Valves

	1300 (F)	1500 (H)
Inlet - head diameter	33 mm (1.299 in)*	35.5 mm (1.397 in)
- stem diameter		7.94-7.9 mm (.3125-.3109 in)
- seat width		1.3 — 1.6 mm (.05 — .06 in)
- seat angle		45°
- guide bore diameter		8.00 - 8.06 mm (.3149-.3156 in)
- maximum rock in guide		.8 mm (.031 in)
Exhaust - head diameter...	30 mm (1.181 in)*	32 mm (1.259 in)
- stem diameter		7.91 - 7.87 mm (.3114 - .3098 in)
- seat width		1.7 — 2.0 mm (.066 — .08 in)
- seat angle		45°
- guide bore diameter		8.00 - 8.06 mm (.3149 - .3156 in)
- maximum rock in guide...		.8 mm (.031 in)
- seat width correction angle - inner		75°
- outer		15°

*NOTE: Engines code AB (August 1970 on) were uprated and the valve dimensions altered.

Exhaust valve head diameter..	30.1 mm
Inlet valve head diameter..	35.6 mm

The exhaust valve stem diameter was also increased to between 8.91 and 8.92 mm

Timing

Inlet opens	7° 30'	BTDC
Inlet closes	37°	ABDC
Exhaust opens...	44° 30'	BBDC
Exhaust closes...	4°	ATDC

NOTE: Rocker arm to valve clearances are set at 1 mm (.040 in) for the purpose of valve timing only.

Rocker arm/valve clearance... ... ...   .15 mm (.006 in) all - cold

Valve springs

Type...	Single coil spring
Loaded length	31 mm at 53—61 kg (116 — 134 lbs)

Torque wrench settings

Crankshaft pulley nut	33	lb.ft (4.5 mkg)
Oil pump nuts	14	lb.ft (2.0 mkg)
Oil drain plug	33	lb.ft (4.5 mkg)
Oil strainer conver nuts	5	lb.ft (0.7 mkg)
Rocker shaft nuts...	18	lb.ft (2.5 mkg)
Cylinder head nuts	23	lb.ft (3.2 mkg) See text
Flywheel screw	217	lb.ft (30 mkg)
Crankcase nuts and screws M8	14	lb.ft (2.0 mkg)
M10 or 12	25	lb.ft (3.5 mkg)
Connecting rod cap nuts or screws	24	lb.ft (3.3 mkg)
Engine securing nuts	22	lb.ft (3.0 mkg)

1. Engine - general description and engine numbers

The 1300 and 1500 Volkswagen Beetle engines are a direct and very close descendent of the 1200 versions which they resemble in all but the most minor details.

As a guide to identification the engines, have prefix letters in front of their 7 figure serial numbers and these are 'F' for 1300 engines from August 65 to July 1970 and 'AB' for the uprated (44 bhp) 1300 thereafter.

1500 engines are denoted by the prefix letter 'H'.

The engine is an air-cooled horizontally opposed flat four cylinder design. The short crankshaft runs in aluminium alloy shell bearings located between the two halves of a magnesium alloy crankcase which join vertically. The camshaft runs centrally below the crankshaft and is gear driven from the rear end of the crankshaft. The camshaft is also located between the crankcase halves and runs in removable split shell bearings.

The distributor is driven by a removable shaft from a gear mounted on the rear end of the crankshaft. The same shaft incorporates a cam which operates the fuel pump operating plunger rod.

The gear type oil pump is mounted in the rear of the crankcase, held between the two halves and driven by a horizontal shaft. A tongue on the inner end of the shaft engages in a slot in the end of the camshaft.

The four, finned cylinder barrels are separately mounted and each pair has a common cylinder head containing the valves and rocker gear. The pushrods locate in cylindrical flat faced cam followers at the camshaft end and pass through sealed cylindrical tubes clamped between the head and crankcase outside the cylinder barrels. Each rocker cover is held to the head by spring hoops locating in a recess in the cover.

The flywheel is located on the front of the crankshaft by four dowel pegs and secured by a single central bolt which also incorporates needle roller bearings for the gearbox input shaft. The front crankcase oil seal bears on the centre hub land of the flywheel. The rear end of the crankshaft has an oil thrower plate and a helical groove machined in the pulley wheel hub to contain the oil. An oil filter screen is mounted in the bottom centre of the crankcase and the oil suction pipe for the pump comes from the centre of it. There is no other form of oil filter incorporated. The generator, which is mounted on a pedestal above the engine, is driven by a V-belt from the crankshaft pulley. On the forward end of the generator shaft the cooling fan is mounted. This runs in a sheet steel housing which ducts air down to the cylinder barrels.

There is no separate oil sump - the crankcase acting as an oil reservoir of just under 4½ pints.

Engine cooling is regulated by a bellows type thermostat which is mounted in the air flow under the right hand pair of cylinders. The thermostat operates two linked control flaps in the fan housing lower ducting section at left and right.

The car heating system is integral with the engine cooling and is achieved by directing air through ducts which shroud the exhaust pipes. Two flexible ducts lead from the fan housing to the heat exchangers - and then via 2 more ducts to the car interior.

The cooling system also incorporates an oil cooler which is a multitube heat exchanger mounted vertically on the crankcase and projecting into the air stream inside the fan housing.

Modifications were made in 1969 to the lubrication system when a second oil pressure regulating valve was added to keep main bearing pressures more even. At the same time the oil cooler apertures were increased in size.

In 1970 further modifications to the lubrication system involved the fitting of an aluminium oil cooler which was moved forward on the crankcase and given a more direct air stream which exhausted immediately through the front cover plate. The oil pump capacity was increased at the same time.

2. Repair and overhaul procedures - dismantling necessary

Although it may be possible to do more than remove and replace items listed below when the engine is installed no recommendations are made which are considered bad basic practice. Maintaining cleanliness is the main reason for limiting the amount of work done with the engine installed.

a) Engine in car
Rocker box covers
Oil cooler
Crankshaft pulley wheel
Oil pressure relief valve(s)
Oil filter screen
Distributor drive shaft.

b) Engine removed but crankcase not split
Cylinders
Piston rings
Pistons
Connecting rods
Big end bearing shells
Flywheel
Oil pump
Crankshaft oil seal.
Cylinder heads and valves

c) Crankcase split
Camshaft
Cam followers
Crankshaft
Main bearings
Distributor drive worm gear
Camshaft bearings.

3. Engine removal - preparation

Removal of the Beetle engine is quite straightforward and speedy provided that the correct tools and lifting tackle are assembled beforehand. The engine is held to the transmission unit by two studs and two bolts - nothing more. It has to be drawn back from these and lowered out of the car. If you have a pit or raised ramp, a firm stand or platform will be needed to support the engine as soon as it is detached. It weighs 200 lbs and attempts to draw it off without providing support under the ramp or in the pit will result in disaster.

Without a pit or ramp a method must be devised to support the engine as soon as it is detached so that the supports may then be removed and the engine readily lowered to ground level. The car body is then lifted up at the rear and the engine drawn out from under - or the car rolled forward over the engine. Four strong men can lift the car the required three feet to clear the engine. Alternatively a conventional hoist can be used to lift the car with the sling fastened between the rear bumper support brackets. If no hoist is available then at least two conventional scissor jacks or hydraulic jacks will be needed together with suitable wooden or concrete blocks, to raise and support the car at each side near the jacking points.

A 17 mm ring spanner - of the non-cranked sort you get on a combination - is essential for undoing the mounting nuts and bolts as there is no space to get a socket on. A second 17 mm open-ended spanner will also be needed.

If the car is very dirty underneath it would be well worthwhile getting it thoroughly cleaned off away from the removal area first. The lower mounting stud nuts are exposed to the elements and the top bolts and nuts call for a certain amount of reaching around. If you are working on your back at floor level, dirt falling in the eyes can be a major irritation.

It is possible to get the engine out and clear single-handed if all the foregoing equipment is available but the trickiest part is lowering the engine to floor level. Assistance is insurance against dropping it. Even a few inches fall could crack the aluminium crankcase - there being no conventional sump. Note that the engine is back-to-front as compared with a conventional layout so that the flywheel is at the front. All references to front and rear of the engine will, therefore, be in relation to its position in the car.

4. Engine - removal

1 Stand the car on a level hard surface with sufficient room to roll it forward about six feet if you wish to lift the car over the engine rather than drag the engine back from under the car. Disconnect the battery. Now is the time to drain the engine oil into a container - whilst you are disconnecting the ancillaries described next.
2 Open the engine compartment cover and then remove the carburettor air cleaner by slackening the clamp, removing also the pre-heater hose from the air duct end and the oil breather pipe from the filler neck. The air cleaner, complete with hoses, is then lifted off.
3 Remove the cheese headed screws which hold the rear cover plate in position and then lift the cover plate out.
4 Next disconnect the electrics. Starting at the right there are two heavy cables to a common screw clamp terminal on the voltage regulator on top of the generator. Disconnect these. Then disconnect the smaller gauge wire from the voltage regulator; then the wire from the automatic choke on the right side of the carburettor. There is another lead to the carburettor underneath the auto choke which operates the electric pilot jet. Remove this too. If the voltage regulator is mounted under the back seat remove the two leads from the generator that run down to it. Disconnect the lead from the coil (which is connected to the automatic choke lead) and finally remove the wire leading to the oil pressure gauge sender unit at the side of the crankcase. All leads to the engine are now detached and they

can be pushed to one side or held to the sides of the engine compartment with sticky tape.
5 The accelerator cable connected to the carburettor is the next item to be detached. This is somewhat unusual arrangement as the cable has to pass through the fan housing en route to the carburettor. First undo the locking screw which clamps the end of the cable to the link pin on the operating lever. Pull the cable out and do not lose the link. Early models had a slightly more elaborate return spring arrangement. On the cable, behind the rigid end piece, there is a sleeve containing a spring and this is held in position by a dished washer with a slot in it. This washer should be pulled off the cable whilst holding the spring tension so that it does not fly off and get lost. The sleeve and spring can then be drawn off the end of the cable. This leaves the front of the guide tube projecting through the front of the fan housing and it can now be pulled out over the cable. On later models this connection is modified. The throttle cable simply comes through the tube and connects to the throttle lever. The return spring is connected from the lever to the carburettor body. The cable itself need not be pulled through from the back of the fan housing until the engine has been disengaged from the transmission.
6 Now jack up the car, using the vehicle jack to enable you to get underneath the rear end comfortably but keep the tyres touching the ground. Replace the oil drain plug. From underneath, first disconnect the control wires that run to the heater flaps, one on each side. They are held to the flap control arms by cable clamps as used on the carburettor but are quite likely to be dirty and rusted up so be prepared with penetrating oil and suitable self-grip wrenches as necessary. If you have difficulty in identifying them get someone to operate the heater control while you are underneath. You will see them move. The fuel pipe runs along on the left side of the engine and if you feel around you will be able to locate the point where the flexible hose connection occurs. This should be pulled off at the end of the hose nearest the engine so that the end of the flexible pipe can be clamped, or plugged with a pencil stub, to prevent the fuel leaking out. If the fuel level in the tank is fairly low it may not be necessary to do this. Next unclip and pull off the flexible concertina hoses which fit onto the heat exchangers on the side of the engine.
7 The two lower mounting nuts can now be removed and this is where the 17 mm ring spanner mentioned earlier is needed. The nuts are positioned about four inches from each side of the engine centre line and about two inches up from the bottom of the flange where the engine joins the transmission unit. Remove the two nuts and washers (if any). Then lower the car and remove the vehicle jack. The ease or difficulty of removing the top two mounting bolts and nuts depends on whether they are rusted or not. The point is, you cannot see either the bolt head or the nut so you will have to feel for them. The nuts are behind (in front of!) the fan housing and you can get an arm round and put a 17 mm ring spanner on. Strictly speaking, it is safer to support the engine underneath now before the last two mounting bolts are removed although in fact the likelihood of the engine moving 3 to 4 inches rearward and falling down of its own accord is fairly remote. If the bolts turn when the nuts are being undone there are two ways to hold the bolt heads. The most sure way in the long run is to jack the car up a little way so that you can get underneath once more and get another 17 mm spanner on the bolt head. It is easier to do this with two people. If you are on your own an open-ended spanner can be put on in such a way that it will jam against the car when the nut is turned. Alternatively, the bolts can be jammed by drawing the engine back now so that the bolt heads bind against the transmission casing. This will mean putting the engine support arrangements under the engine straight away. A stout piece of plank about 18" x 12" should be put under the crankcase so that the jacks can be placed to support the whole unit firmly and evenly. If a trolley jack with a large lifting head is used it can be placed centrally. Later models have a round headed bolt with a flat on it which engages a recess in the casing. Provided the bolt is held in position the nut is easily removed. In 1970 modifications to the oil cooler position were made which

4.4(a) Disconnect the two leads to the carburettor ...

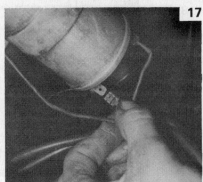

4.4(b) .... and the generator ....

4.4(c) .... and the coil.

4.5(a) Early type throttle cable return spring assembly. Note slotted dished washer (arrowed).

4.5(b) With the washer removed the retainer tube, spring and cable tube may be drawn off over the cable.

4.6(a) Detach the heater flap cables, ...

4.6(b) ... The heater air hoses ...

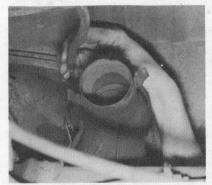

4.6(c) ... and the fuel line.

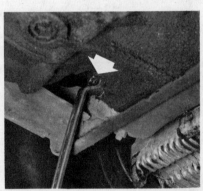

4.7. Undoing the lower left engine mounting nut.

4.8. Drawing the engine back off the transmission.

4.9(a) Lift the car in the air ...

4.9(b) ... and draw the engine out from under

18

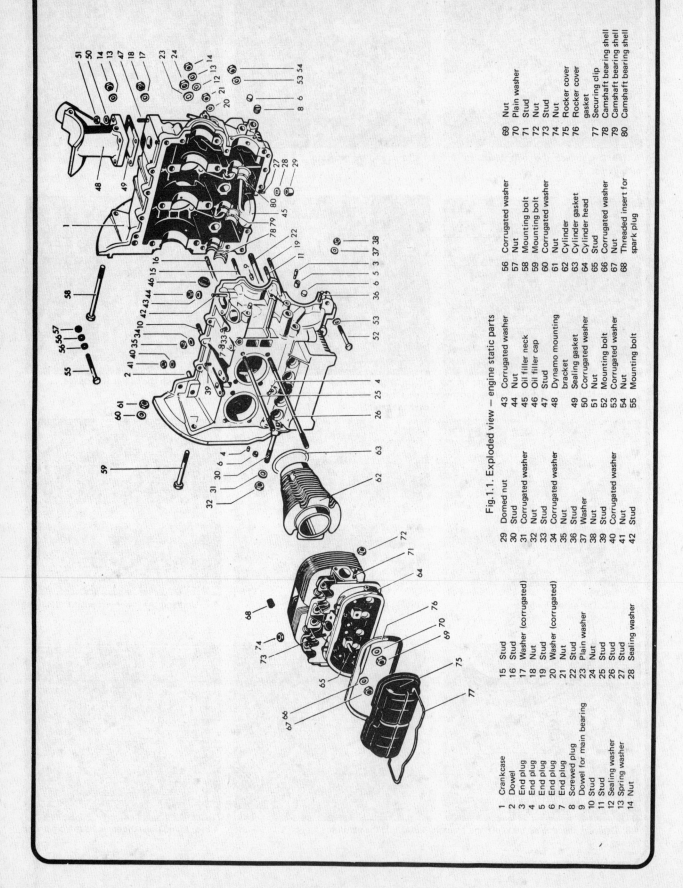

Fig.1.1. Exploded view – engine static parts

1 Crankcase	43 Corrugated washer
2 Dowel	44 Nut
3 End plug	45 Oil filler neck
4 End plug	46 Oil filler cap
5 End plug	47 Stud
6 End plug	48 Dynamo mounting bracket
7 End plug	49 Sealing gasket
8 Screwed plug	50 Corrugated washer
9 Dowel for main bearing	51 Nut
10 Stud	52 Mounting bolt
11 Stud	53 Corrugated washer
12 Sealing washer	54 Nut
13 Spring washer	55 Mounting bolt
14 Nut	56 Corrugated washer
15 Stud	57 Nut
16 Stud	58 Mounting bolt
17 Washer (corrugated)	59 Mounting bolt
18 Nut	60 Corrugated washer
19 Nut	61 Nut
20 Washer (corrugated)	62 Cylinder
21 Nut	63 Cylinder gasket
22 Stud	64 Cylinder head
23 Plain washer	65 Stud
24 Nut	66 Corrugated washer
25 Stud	67 Nut
26 Stud	68 Threaded insert for spark plug
27 Stud	69 Nut
28 Sealing washer	70 Plain washer
29 Domed nut	71 Stud
30 Stud	72 Nut
31 Corrugated washer	73 Stud
32 Nut	74 Stud
33 Nut	75 Rocker cover
34 Corrugated washer	76 Rocker cover gasket
35 Nut	77 Securing clip
36 Stud	78 Camshaft bearing shell
37 Washer	79 Camshaft bearing shell
38 Nut	80 Camshaft bearing shell
39 Stud	
40 Corrugated washer	
41 Nut	
42 Stud	

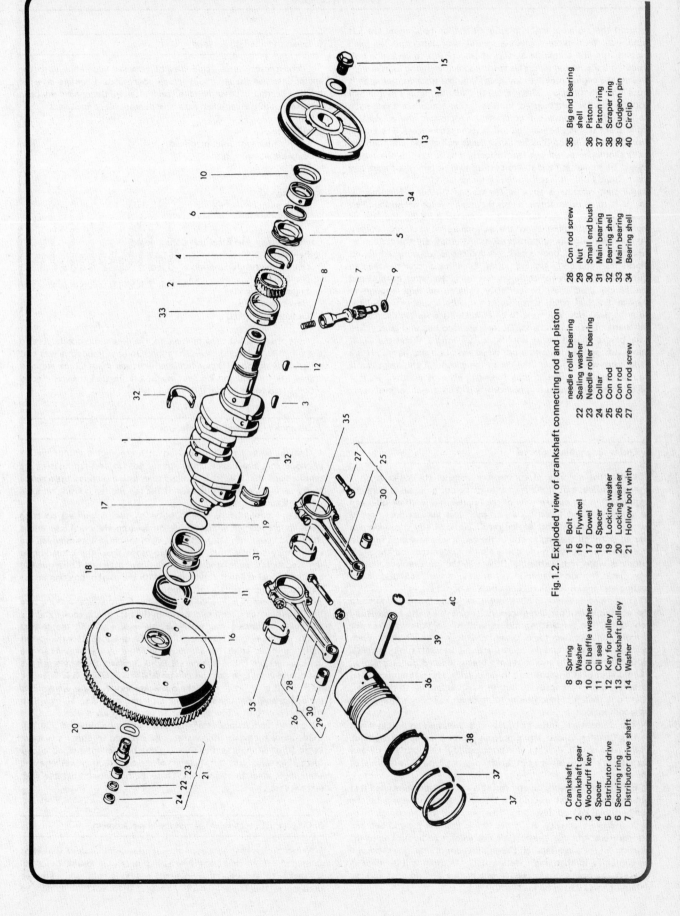

Fig. 1.2. Exploded view of crankshaft connecting rod and piston

1 Crankshaft	8 Spring
2 Crankshaft gear	9 Washer
3 Woodruff key	10 Oil baffle washer
4 Spacer	11 Oil seal
5 Distributor drive	12 Key for pulley
6 Securing ring	13 Crankshaft pulley
7 Distributor drive shaft	14 Washer

15 Bolt	needle roller bearing
16 Flywheel	22 Sealing washer
17 Dowel	23 Needle roller bearing
18 Spacer	24 Collar
19 Locking washer	25 Con rod
20 Locking washer	26 Con rod
21 Hollow bolt with	27 Con rod screw

28 Con rod screw	35 Big end bearing shell
29 Nut	36 Piston
30 Small end bush	37 Piston ring
31 Main bearing	38 Scraper ring
32 Bearing shell	39 Gudgeon pin
33 Main bearing	40 Circlip
34 Bearing shell	

reduced the available space in front of the fan housing on the left hand side. With these engines a special shouldered nut has been pressed into the crankcase at top left so one has to undo the bolt from the transmission side. This needs a socket and long extension.

8 Pull the engine back. It may need jiggling a little to disengage it from the transmission. Grip it by the silencer unit and the fan housing for this purpose. As soon as the top nuts are undone the engine may be drawn off completely. Disconnect the accelerator cable from the fan housing before lowering the engine. The engine should then be lowered as far as the jacks will permit and then the jacks should be pulled out from underneath. To do this the engine should be tipped as carefully as possible and be prevented from any sharp knocks until it is resting flat on the ground.

9 All that remains is to raise the rear of the car sufficiently to enable it to be rolled forward over the engine or for the engine to be drawn out from underneath. This can be achieved by four strong men or by hoisting the rear of the car with a sling stretched between the two rear bumper support brackets. Alternatively the car can be raised on two jacks, one on each side and supported progressively on blocks near the body jacking points. Great care must be taken to chock the front wheels securely when using this latter method and the blocks used must be perfectly square and large enough to provide a stable 'pillar' when stacked up. Each support under the body at each side will have to be at least 2ft 6 ins high so collect sufficient blocks beforehand. Do not use odd bits and pieces. The base blocks should be at least 9'' x 12'' square. When the car is raised sufficiently the engine can be pulled out from the rear. It is a little more work to lower the car to the ground at this stage but if you are going to leave it then the extra effort is worthwhile. It is better to be sure than sorry, particularly if there are children about.

5. Engine dismantling - general

1 Unlike the majority of conventional engines the Volkswagen is one which does not make it easy to carry out most tasks with the engine still in the car. In view of the relative ease with which it can be taken out and lifted on to a bench this manual does not, in general, recommend that engine repair work of any significance is carried out with the engine still in the car. If you have a pit or ramp that enables you to work conveniently under the car there are instances when it is justifiable. Otherwise the inconvenient 'flat on your back' method is far too risky in view of the likelihood of dirt getting into the wrong places and mistakes occurring.

2 For an engine which is obviously in need of a complete overhaul the economies against a replacement engine must also be carefully considered. The dismantling and reassembly of a Volkswagen engine is more complex than for a conventional four cylinder block. Each cylinder is separate and the crankshaft and camshaft run in bearings mounted between the two halves of a precision faced, split crankcase. The number of individual parts is far greater. It is not our intention to put you off - far from it - but we must, in fairness to the owner, point out that it is much easier to make an assembly mistake than on a conventional engine.

3 The dismantling, inspection, repair and reassembly as described in this Chapter follows the procedure as for a complete overhaul. Each section will indicate the practicability and method of any partial work to be carried out which may not justify the removal of the engine.

4 Before starting work on any part it is strongly recommended that time is spent in first reading the whole Chapter. It would be too cumbersome and confusing to cross reference the implications of each and every activity. So if you think that the big end bearings are your problem, for example, do not think that by turning to the heading 'Big end bearings' all the implications of repairing them will be contained in that single section alone. Mention will be made in brief of the operations necessary which may lead up to it and the details of these should be read first.

6. Engine ancillaries - removal

Although the items listed may be removed separately with the engine installed (as described in the appropriate Chapters referred to) it is normal practice to take them off after the engine has been removed from the car when extensive dismantling is envisaged.

Fuel System
    Carburettor with inlet manifold
    Exhaust silencer unit
    Fuel pump

Ignition System
    Spark plugs
    Distributor

Cooling System and Electrical Components
    Fan belt
    Generator with fan assembly
    Fan housing
    Engine cover plates
    Heat exchangers
    Generator pedestal

Note that the last item referred to, the generator pedestal, is also the oil filler and crankcase vent tube. On early models it was cast integrally with the crankcase but later on it was made a separate item and is held in position by four studs. Ensure that there is a good gasket fitted between it and the crankcase.

7. Oil cooler - removal and replacement

1 The oil cooler may be removed with the engine still in the car provided that the engine compartment lid, fan and fan housing are removed and that a suitable cranked spanner is available to gain access to the securing nuts. The details of the fan and fan housing removal may be found in Chapter 2.

2 The oil cooler is held in position by two downward pointing studs in the cooler which locate on lugs on the crankcase and a third stud fixed into the crankcase. With the three nuts removed the cooler may be lifted off. The photographs show the cooler being removed with the left hand top cylinder cowl detached. Consequently a conventional spanner can be used. With the cowl in position access and spanner movement is restricted.

3 Replacement is a reversal of the removal procedure, making sure that two new seals are fitted between the base of the cooler and the crankcase oil passageway openings. Make sure you fit the correct pair of sealing rings. There are others in the gasket set (for the rocker shaft mounting studs) which could be fitted by mistake. When the correct ones are fitted it is necessary to compress them between the cooler and crankcase and this can be felt.

4 In 1970 modifications to the crankcase and oil cooler were made, increasing the aperture size of the oil ports from 8 to 10 mm. It is still possible to fit a new cooler or an old crankcase or vice versa, but the correct conversion kit of special seals must be obtained. Fig.1.5. shows how the seals and washers are arranged in either situation. Later, further modifications moved the position of the oil cooler further forward and the material of its construction was changed from sheet steel to aluminium. These are not interchangeable with earlier types.

8. Oil pressure relief valve - removal and replacement

1 When overhauling an engine the oil pressure relief valve should be examined. If it does not function properly it could cause oil starvation to the bearings when the engine is cold, and excessive pressure in the cooler (possibly causing it to leak). It could also

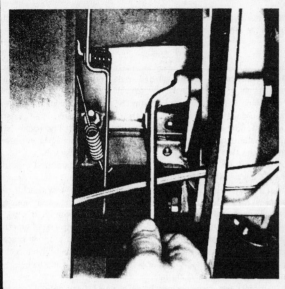

Fig.1.3. Undoing the upper engine mounting bolts

Fig.1.4. Undoing the lower engine mounting nuts

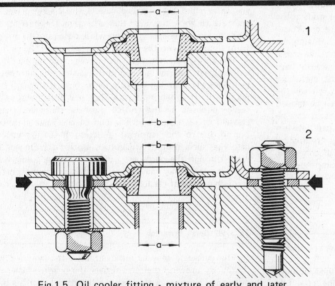

Fig.1.5. Oil cooler fitting - mixture of early and later types of cooler or crankcase showing adaptor washers

Top - New cooler, old crankcase a = 10 mm
Bottom - Old cooler, new crankcase b = 8 mm

7.3(a) Positioning the oil cooler seals.

7.3(b) Tightening the oil cooler lower nuts.

8.2. Oil pressure relief valve and spring.

8.3. Oil pressure relief valve sealing plug.

cause, at the other extreme, overheating of the oil and inadequate oil pressure. Later models had a second valve fitted to regulate pressure after the oil has passed through the cooler (see Fig.1.10).

2 The valve is positioned in the underside of the crankcase to the left of the oil pump at the rear. A slotted retaining plug can be removed with a large screwdriver and the spring and piston should then fall out. If the engine is cold and the piston sticks it will be forced out if the engine is turned over (this assumes of course that the engine is in the car and has oil in it). If the piston is stuck because of dirt or seizure it may be necessary to drill and tap a hole in it to draw it from the bore in the crankcase. This is only likely in cases of extreme neglect. If the bore of the crankcase is also damaged then the crankcase may have to be scrapped.

3 Replacement of the piston and spring is a reversal of the removal procedure. When fitting the plug use a new compressible sealing washer and make sure that the spring sits snugly in the recess of the plug.

9. Oil pump - removal

1 The oil pump gears may be removed relatively easily because once the oil pump cover plate (situated on the end of the crankcase under the crankshaft pulley) has been released by removing the four retaining nuts, the gears may be drawn out of the pump body.

2 The pump body itself is mounted over the same four studs at the cover plate and is clamped between the two halves of the crankcase. To remove the pump body from the engine without splitting the crankcase it is best done with a special tool which fits over the studs, locks to the inside of the body and draws it out. If you do not have such a tool then the best way is first to slacken the crankcase clamping stud nuts above and below the pump. This relieves the pressure on the body. A suitable pointed tool can then be tapped against the edge of the pump body and, in easy stages, it can be eased out over the studs. Do not force a tool into the gap between the pump body and the crankcase as this could damage the mating faces and upset the correct alignment of the pump on replacement.

If the crankcase is to be split anyway leave the pump body to be taken out then.

10. Cylinder heads - removal

1 Before starting work, ensure that all external grease and dirt is cleaned from the engine.

2 Remove the exhaust system, heat exchangers and upper cylinder cover plates as described in the Fuel and Cooling Chapters. The inlet manifold together with carburettor should also be taken off. See the Fuel System Chapter for details.

3 Prise off the spring clip, downwards, which clamps the rocker cover to the head. Take off the cover.

4 Undo the two nuts, evenly, which secure the rocker shaft standards and then pull off the standards, shaft and rockers as a complete assembly. Pull out the four pushrods and push them through a piece of cardboard so that the location of each one is known and which is the top and bottom end.

5 Before starting to undo the eight nuts which hold the cylinder head down onto the cylinder barrels it must be appreciated that when the head is released the four pushrod tubes will be freed and the cylinder barrels also. If the cylinder barrels are not being taken off the pistons they will rest in position but the engine must not be turned. If the engine is to be turned the barrels should be temporarily tied down to the crankcase with string or wire.

6 Using a socket spanner, the cylinder head stud nuts should be slackened ¼ to ½ turn each only, in the reverse order of the final tightening sequence as given in Fig.1.18. Continue releasing each nut a little at a time until they are all slack. When all are removed the head may be drawn back a little way.

7 Remove the pushrod tubes from between the head and crankcase

and make sure the cylinders are disengaged from the head before pulling the head right off.

11. Cylinder heads - dismantling of rocker gears, valves and springs

1 To remove the rocker arms from the shaft the spring clips at each end should be removed and the thrust washers and wave washers taken off. The end rockers may then be removed. The rocker shaft support standards may need tapping off if they are tight in order to remove the two inner rocker arms, clips and washers. If possible lay out the parts in the order in which they were dismantled in a place where they need not be disturbed.

2 To remove the valves it is necessary to use a proper tool to compress the valve springs. The tops of the springs are almost level with the edge of the head casting. If you are unable to obtain a G clamp with extended ends (to clear the edge of the head when the spring is compressed) it will be necessary to use a short piece of tube, with an aperture cut in the side, in conjunction with a conventional spring compressor. The aperture is to enable one to get at the split collars on the valve stem.

3 Compress the spring using the clamp and if the tubular spacer is being used make sure that the pressure is applied squarely and that the tube cannot slip. As soon as the two split conical collars round the valve stem are revealed, use a small screwdriver through the aperture to hook them off the valve stem. It is advisable to maintain one's hold on the spring clamp while doing this to prevent anything from slipping. When the collars are clear release the spring clamp.

4 The spring retainer collar and spring may then be lifted off. There will be small sealing rings round the valve stems and these too should be taken off. The valve can now be pushed through the guide and taken out. If it tends to stick then it will be because of carbon or sludge deposits on the end of the valve stems and these should be cleaned off as necessary. The end of the valve stem could also be burred due to the 'hammering' action of the rocker arm; in which case the burrs should be carefully stoned off. Do not force a tight valve through the guide or you will score the guide. Keep valves in order so that they may be replaced in the same port. Push them through a piece of cardboard to avoid getting them mixed up.

12. Cylinders - removal

The cylinders may be removed, after the cylinder heads are off, simply by drawing them from over the pistons. Make sure that the piston and rings are not damaged after the cylinder has been removed. It must also be remembered that if the crankshaft is turned after removing the cylinder the piston skirts can foul the crankcase unless they are guided at the bottom of the stroke.

13. Crankshaft pulley wheel - removal and replacement

1 The crankshaft pulley wheel is keyed to the rear end of the crankshaft and is a straight keyed fit. It is secured by a single, central bolt. To lock the pulley when undoing or tightening the bolt push a suitable article through one of the holes in the pulley and jam it against the crankcase flange.

2 If, when the nut has been removed, the pulley is a very tight fit, do not apply force at the edges or you are likely to distort it. Soak the boss with penetrating oil and hook something through the two holes if any leverage is necessary.

3 If the pulley has been removed during the course of an overhaul remember that the lower rear engine plate has to be re-fixed before the pulley. There is no access to the two securing screws after the pulley is in position.

4 The nut should be tightened to a torque of 33 ft/lbs when the pulley has been replaced.

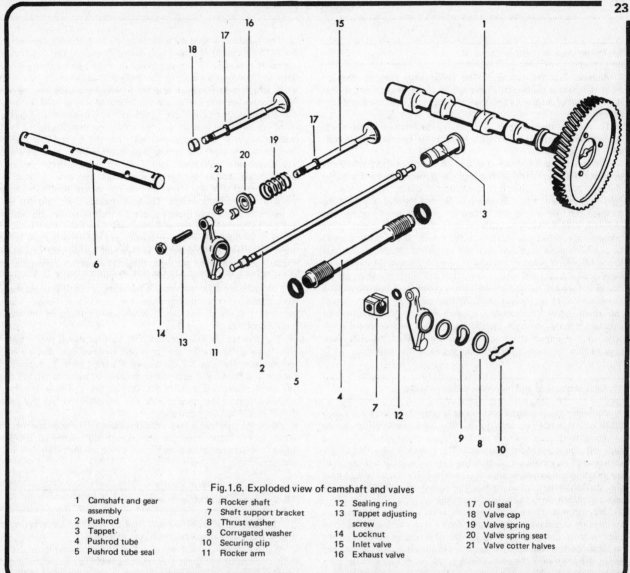

Fig.1.6. Exploded view of camshaft and valves

1	Camshaft and gear assembly	6	Rocker shaft	12	Sealing ring	17	Oil seal
2	Pushrod	7	Shaft support bracket	13	Tappet adjusting screw	18	Valve cap
3	Tappet	8	Thrust washer	14	Locknut	19	Valve spring
4	Pushrod tube	9	Corrugated washer	15	Inlet valve	20	Valve spring seat
5	Pushrod tube seal	10	Securing clip	16	Exhaust valve	21	Valve cotter halves
		11	Rocker arm				

13.3. Fitting lower rear engine plate before the crankshaft pulley.

13.4 Tightening crankshaft pulley nut.

14. Piston rings and pistons - removal

1 Remove first the cylinders. The piston rings may be removed from the pistons by carefully spreading the ends of each ring so that it comes out of its groove and then drawing it off over the top of the piston.

2 To remove the piston it is necessary to separate it from the connecting rod as it is not possible to get at the connecting rod bolts with the piston fitted.

3 Remove the circlip from one side of the piston boss where the gudgeon pin is retained and it will be possible to push out the gudgeon pin. If it resists then warm up the piston with an electric light bulb held next to it for a while. Do not try and drive out the gudgeon pin from a cold piston. You will possibly bend a connecting rod. It is only necessary to push out the pin far enough to enable the connecting rod to be released from the piston. If the pistons are to be put back make sure that each one is marked suitably so that you know (a) which number cylinder it came from and (b) which way faces forward. A good way is to scratch the number and an arrow, pointing forward, on the crown before removal. If you do make a nonsense and forget how it came off then carefully clean the top of the crown and look for identifying marks which indicate the front or flywheel side. Volkswagen pistons are stamped with an arrow at the edge of the crown pointing towards the flywheel. British made pistons have the word 'flywheel' stamped on in that position.

15. Connecting rods and big end bearings - removal

1 Connecting rods may be removed only after the pistons have been taken off. It is not necessary to split the crankcase although if you are going to do so anyway it will be simpler to take the connecting rods off the crankshaft afterwards. Start with No.1 and, using a socket with an extension, slacken the two connecting rod cap bolts by inserting the extension into the crankcase. It is important to have the crankshaft positioned so that the socket spanner fits squarely and completely onto the head of each bolt.

2 Once both bolts are loose, carefully undo each one and draw the connecting rod back at the same time so that you can bring them back with it. On later models, instead of a bolt going through the shoulder of the rod into the cap there are captive studs in the cap secured by nuts on the rod shoulders. Where nuts are used, keep them captive in the socket when undoing them so as not to drop them in the crankcase. You can easily see what is fitted before starting dismantling. The cap will be left behind and may be awkward to retrieve. Tip the engine to shake it out if necessary. Retrieve both halves of the bearing shells also. Loosely refit the cap to the connecting rod noting the two matching numbers on the shoulders of the rod and cap which must line up on replacement. It is a good idea to note on a piece of paper which serial number applies to which cylinder number. This avoids the need to mark the connecting rods further. If the same rods and pistons are being put back it is very desirable that they should go back in the same position as they came out.

3 If you have by chance ignored our advice and decided to go as far as removing the connecting rods with the engine still in the car do not blame us if you find yourself unable to retrieve some big end bearing caps or shells from inside the crankcase!

16. Camshaft and tappets - removal

1 See under Crankshaft - removal.

17. Flywheel - removal

1 With the engine removed from the car the flywheel may be removed once the clutch cover has been taken off (as described in Chapter 5.

2 The flywheel is held by a single centre bolt which is tightened up to 227 ft/lbs so do not think you can get it undone just like that. We found it necessary to obtain a piece of angle iron so that we could lock the flywheel by putting the angle iron across two of the clutch bolts which were put back into the flywheel and clamping the other end of this locking bar in the vice. This, of course, was done with the engine on the bench, the flywheel facing towards the front and lined up with the vice so that the angle iron was positioned firmly and squarely. A 36 mm socket was then put on the bolt with the longest handle from our socket set (do not under any circumstances try to use anything other than a correct sized socket - you could easily cause serious damage or even hurt yourself). A four foot piece of steel pipe was then put over the socket handle and leaned on with considerable weight. The bolt slackened with no fuss at all. It may cost you a little money to get the stuff to do this job properly but we cannot recommend any other way.

3 Remove the bolt and large washer and before going any further make an identifiable mark on the flywheel hub so that you can relocate the flywheel in the same place. The matching mark on the crankshaft cannot be made until the flywheel is off, so remember not to move the flywheel when it has come off until you can make a corresponding line up mark on the crankshaft flange. This is important as there may be no other way of knowing the correct position of balance.

4 The flywheel is now located only by four dowel pegs which fit into holes in the crankshaft flange and flywheel boss. Put a piece of wood under the edge of the flywheel starter teeth to support the weight and then use a soft mallet or block of wood to tap the edges of the flywheel and draw it off. Do not try and lever it off with anything against the crankcase or you are likely to crack the casting and that will be very expensive.

5 When the flywheel is free, hold it steady, and remove the metal or paper gasket fitted over the four dowel pegs in the flange. Then make the second line-up mark on the crankshaft referred to in paragraph 3.

18. Crankshaft front oil seal - removal

1 The crankshaft front oil seal may be removed after taking the engine from the car and removing the flywheel.

2 The oil seal may be levered out of the crankcase with a screwdriver or similar but great care must be taken to avoid damaging the crankcase where the seal seats. This means that the point of the tool used must not be allowed to dig into the crankcase.

3 When the oil seal is removed a number of shims which fit between the flywheel hub and the flange on the front main bearing will be observed. There should be three of them normally. These govern the amount of crankshaft end float. Make sure they are kept safely and not damaged.

4 If the crankcase is being split anyway it is simpler to wait until this is done when the oil seal may be easily lifted out.

19. Crankshaft - removal

1 In order to remove the crankshaft, camshaft and cam followers (tappets) the two halves of the crankcase will need to be separated. Unless you are quite sure that this is essential do not do it. It is not worth opening the crankcase up just to 'have a look'. Remember also that the main bearing shells are much more expensive than on conventional cars (three of the four are not split) and before you can remove one of them two gears must be removed from the crankshaft. These gears are on very tight and are difficult to draw off.

2 Having decided to split the crankcase, remove the oil filler and generator pedestal casing and prop the crankcase on its left side. All pistons and cylinders should already have been removed as should the flywheel. If the flywheel is left on it will add to the difficulty of controlling the weight of the crankshaft when the two halves

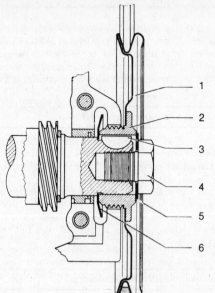

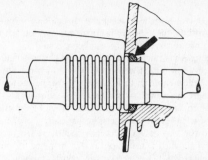

Fig 1.8 Push rods and tappets - early models
Showing adjustable guide plates in crankcase which
locate cam followers at the end of the pushrods

Fig.1.7. Crankshaft pulley wheel - cross section

1 Pulley   4 Crankshaft bolt
2 Oil return scroll thread   5 Spring washer
3 Woodruff key   6 Oil thrower disc

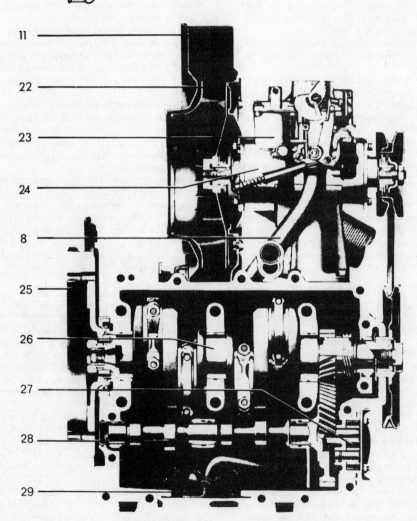

Fig.1.9. Sectional view of an assembled engine

8 Inlet manifold   23 Carburettor   26 Crankshaft   29 Oil strainer
11 Fan housing   24 Generator   27 Oil pump
22 Fan   25 Flywheel   28 Camshaft

release it. It will also be much more difficult to remove from the crankshaft afterwards. The connecting rods may be left on as these will be easier to remove after the crankcase is split.

3 The two halves are held together by large and small studs and nuts and two bolts and nuts. Slacken all the smaller nuts followed by the large nuts. Before starting to separate the two halves remember that the crankshaft and camshaft are held between them and you do not want either to fall out haphazardly. So if you keep the crankcase tilted to the left they will both rest in that half.

4 Separate the two halves by tapping lightly at the projecting lugs of the left half with a soft faced mallet or piece of wood. Do not hit anything hard. This progressive gentle tapping at the four corners will gradually increase the gap between the two until the right hand half will be free enough to lift off the studs. If you have a second pair of hands to help so much the better. When the right hand half has moved out a little way there will probably be a light clatter as one or more of the four cam followers in the right hand half fall out. If possible try and get hold of these and arrange them somewhere (in an egg box or numbered row on a shelf) so that they may be put back in the same bores.

5 Put the crankcase half in a safe place where it cannot fall or be damaged.

6 Lift out the camshaft from the other half of the crankcase. The bearing shells should be left in position. If they fall out note where they came from. If being renewed anyway take them out.

7 The tappets from the left hand half of the crankcase may now be taken out. Keep them in order like the others so they may be replaced in the same bores.

8 The crankshaft can now be lifted out and should be carefully put somewhere safe. The bearing shell halves for No.2 main bearing should be removed from their locations in each half of the crankcase. Note that the location of each main bearing is by a dowel peg which locates each bearing shell. These normally remain in the crankcase but if any have come out with the bearings retrieve them now before they get lost.

20. Distributor drive shaft - removal

1 The procedure for removing and replacing the distributor drive shaft from an assembled engine is given in Chapter 4. It is mentioned here because it is in order to leave it in position right up until the time when the crankcase is divided. It should, however, be removed before the crankcase is reassembled.

21. Crankshaft main bearings - removal

1 Three of the four main bearings may be removed as soon as the crankshaft is taken from the crankcase. No.1 is a circular flanged shell which is drawn off the flywheel end, No.2 is the split bearing and No.4 is a narrow circular bearing which can be drawn off the crankshaft pulley end. No. 3 however, is trapped by the helical gear which drives the camshaft. In front of this gear is a spacer and the distributor drive shaft worm gear, an oil thrower disc and Woodruff key.

2 To remove No. 3 main bearing first tap the Woodruff key out of the shaft and keep it safe. Take off the oil thrower disc. The two gears are a tight keyed fit onto the shaft and the only way to get them off is by using a proper sprocket puller which grips which will fit snugly and completely behind the helical gear so that both the gears and the spacer can be drawn off together. If you have difficulty in fitting the puller in the small gap between the bearing and gear do not try and pull off the gear gripping only against the gear teeth. You will either chip them or break them off. If you are committed to new bearings anyhow, cut the old bearing off to enable you to get the puller properly seated behind the gear.

3 If, when you start putting the pressure on it is obvious that considerable force is going to be needed it is best to clamp the legs of the puller to prevent them spreading and possibly flying off and

causing damage to the gear. Some pullers have a clamp incorporated for such a purpose. If you have press facilities available so much the better but on no account should you try to hammer the gears off. It is virtually impossible to do this without damaging the gears.

4 With the two gears removed the bearing can be taken off the shaft.

22. Engine components - examination for wear

Whatever degree of dismantling is carried out, components can only be examined properly after they have been thoroughly cleaned. This is best carried out using paraffin and a stiff bristled brush. Some engines can be particularly bad, with a stubborn coating of hard sludgy deposits - generally denoting neglect of regular oil changing - and it can take some time and effort to get this off. Afterwards, the paraffin can be hosed off with a water jet. Cleaning may sometimes seem to take a disproportionate amount of time but there is no doubt that it is time well spent.

23. Crankcase - examination and renovation

The crankcase should be free from cracks or any other form of damage and the two mating edges must be quite free from dents, scratches and burrs which could in any way affect their precise alignment when both are clamped together. The crankshaft bearing locations should also be examined for any signs of damage or distortion. In an engine which has been permitted to run on with worn out main bearings it is possible that the bearing shells themselves will have been 'hammered' by the vibration of the crankshaft into the crankcase. This will mean that new bearings will not be a tight fit in their crankcase locations. In such instances the crankcase must be scrapped. In these circumstances the best action would be to abandon ideas of renovating the engine and obtain a complete replacement. Make sure that the camshaft bearing surfaces are in good condition.

The studs in the crankcase, both for attaching the cylinder heads and for the two halves, must be tight in their threads. Any sign of looseness which may be due to worn threads in the alloy crankcase is reparable. It will mean drilling and fitting a 'Helicoil' insert - which is a new thread in effect. This can be done at the Volkswagen agents for certain and at many other places where aluminium engines and castings are often being repaired. In any case check the economics before buying a lot of other parts.

24. Crankshaft - examination and renovation

1 It is possible to examine the connecting rod big end journals after removing the pistons and connecting rods without splitting the crankcase, but only visually. They cannot be measured satisfactorily. Provided there is no good reason to suspect that the big end bearings were seriously worn and that the surfaces of the journal are bright and smooth with no signs of pitting or scoring then there should be no need to proceed further.

2 The main crankshaft bearing journals may be examined only when the crankcase has been split and the crankshaft taken out. An indication of serious wear in these bearings can be obtained by checking the crankshaft for signs of slackness in the bearings before the crankcase is split. A wooden lever put through one of the cylinder apertures can be used to test for any indications of rocking in the bearings. If there is any then the bearing shells will almost certainly need renewal, even though the crankshaft journals themselves may be serviceable. The journals should be perfectly smooth with a bright mirror finish. They should be measured with a micrometer across the diameter for signs of ovality. If any measurement should differ by more than 0.03 mm (0.0011 inch) from any other the crankshaft should be reground. This means taking it to a specialist engineering firm who can grind it to the undersizes permissible and supply the matching new bearing shells. In view of the need to remove the two

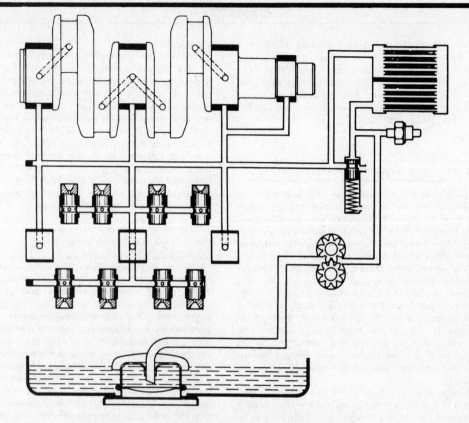

Fig.1.10a. Lubrication system diagram showing oil flow — (up to 1969)

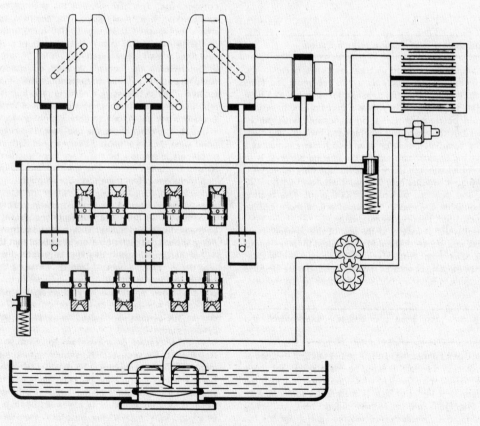

Fig 1.10b Lubrication system diagram showing two pressure valves (1969 onwards)

gears in order to examine No.3 main bearing journal the condition of the gears should also be checked, in conjunction with their respective mating gears on the camshaft and distributor drive spindle. The bronze worm gear which drives the distributor drive spindle is the most likely to show signs of wear. Any noticeable ridging or 'feathering' and variations in thickness of each spiral tooth indicate wear and renewal is probably justifiable.

25. Main and big end bearings - examination and renovation

1 When connecting rods are removed from the crankshaft the bearing shells will be released and even though the crankshaft journals are in good condition the bearings may need renewal. Certainly if their bearing surfaces are anything other than an even, matt grey colour they should be renewed. Any scores, pitting or discoloration is an indication of damage by metal particles or the top bearing surface wearing away. If there is any doubt it is always a good idea to replace them anyway unless there is a definite record that they have only been fitted for a small mileage. The backs of the shells are marked with serial numbers and an indication of whether or not they are undersized due to the crankshaft having been reground previously. If in doubt take them to your supplier who will be able to ensure that you are sold new ones of the correct type. If the crankshaft is being reground new bearings will be required anyhow and these are always available from the firm which does the regrinding.

2 The same principles apply to renewal of the main bearing. If they are to be renewed it should be remembered that the No.3 bearing will require removal of the helical and worm gears before it may be taken off. Do not replace three only out of the four - it is a waste of time and effort.

26. Camshaft and tappets - examination and renovation

1 The tappets should be checked in their respective bores in the crankcase and no excessive side-play should be apparent. The faces of the tappets which bear against the camshaft lobes should also have a clear, smooth shiny surface. If they show signs of pitting or serious wear they should be renewed. Re-facing is possible with proper grinding facilities but the economics of this need investigating first. The lobes of the camshaft should be examined for any indications of flat spots, pitting or extreme wear on the bearing surfaces. If in doubt get the profiles checked against specification dimensions with a micrometer. Minor blemishes may be smoothed down with a 120 grain oil stone and polished with one of 300 grain. The bearing journals also should be checked in the same way as those on the crankshaft. The camshaft bearings are renewable.

2 The gear wheel which is riveted to the end of the camshaft must be perfectly tight and the teeth should be examined for any signs of breakage or excessive wear. It may be possible to have a new gear-wheel fitted to the existing camshaft - much depends on the facilities available in your area. It is not a job to be attempted by the owner.

27. Connecting rods and small end bushes - examination and renovation

1 It is unlikely that a connecting rod will be bent except in cases of severe piston damage and seizure. It is not normally within the scope of the owner to check the alignment of a connecting rod with the necessary accuracy so if in doubt have it checked by someone with the proper facilities. It is in order to have slightly bent connecting rods straightened - the manufacturers provide special jigs for the purpose. If a rod needs replacement, care should be taken to ensure that it is within 10 grams in weight of the others. If too heavy, connecting rods may be lightened by removing metal from the shoulders near the big end of the wider parts where the bearing cap

mates up to it.

2 The small end bushes are also subject to wear. At a temperature of 70°F the piston (gudgeon) pin should be a push fit. No axial or rocking movement should be apparent. The fitting of new bushes is a specialist task and although the bushes themselves may be easily pressed in it is necessary to ream them to fit the gudgeon pins. Unless you have reamers readily available and the knowledge of how to use them this should be done by a firm (or individual) specialising in engine reconditioning. Remember that if you are fitting new pistons it may be necessary to fit new connecting rod bushes. If you are lucky the new gudgeon pins may fit the old bushes properly however. Make sure that the new bushes have been drilled to match the oil holes in the connecting rod. This should be done before reaming so that there are no burrs on the bush bore.

28. Pistons, rings and cylinders - examination and renovation

1 Piston and cylinder bore wear are contributory factors to excessive oil consumption (over 1 pint to 300 miles) and general engine noise. They also affect engine power output due to loss of compression. If you have been able to check the individual cylinder pressures before dismantling so much the better. They will indicate whether one or more is losing compression which may be due to cylinders and pistons if the valves are satisfactory.

2 The piston rings should be removed from the pistons first by carefully spreading the open ends and easing them from their grooves over the crown of the piston. Each one should then be pushed into the cylinder bore from the bottom, using the head of the piston to make sure they rest square in position about 5 mm from the bottom edge. The gap between the ends of the ring can then be measured with a feeler gauge. For the two compression rings it should not exceed 0.90 mm (0.035 inch) and for the oil scraper ring 0.95 mm (0.037 inch). If the gaps are greater you know that new rings at least are required.

3 Determining the degree of wear on pistons and cylinders is complementary. In some circumstances the pistons alone may need renewal - the cylinders not needing reboring. If the cylinders need reboring then new pistons must be fitted. First check the cylinders. A preliminary check can be done simply by feeling the inside walls about ½ inch down from the top edge. If a ridge can be felt at any point then the bores should be measured with an inside micrometer or calipers to see how far they vary from standard. The measurement should be taken across the bore of the cylinder about 15 mm (0.6 inch) down from the top edge at right angles to the axis of the gudgeon pin. Depending on whether or not the cylinders have already been rebored once the measurement should be 77 mm, 77.5 mm or 78 mm. Then measure the piston, also at right angles to the gudgeon pin across the skirt at the bottom. The two measurements should not differ by more than 0.20 mm (0.008 inch).

4 Further measurement of the cylinder across the bore will indicate whether or not the wear is mostly on the piston. If the cylinder bore is uniform in size fitting new pistons in the original bore size is possible. However, it is a very short sighted policy. If new pistons are needed anyway the cost or reboring will add 20–25% to the cost of the pistons so it would be as well to get it done whilst the cylinders are off.

5 Another feature of the pistons to check is the piston ring side clearance in the grooves. This should not exceed 0.12 mm (0.0047 inch) for the top ring and 0.10 mm (0.004 inch) for the other two. Usually however, this wear is proportionate to the rest of the piston and will not occur in a piston which is otherwise apparently little worn. If you think that only a new set of rings is required it would be a good idea to take your pistons to the supplier of the new rings and check the new rings in the gaps. You may change your mind about how worn the pistons really are! Once a cylinder has been rebored twice (to 78 mm diameter) it must not be rebored again and new cylinders must be obtained.

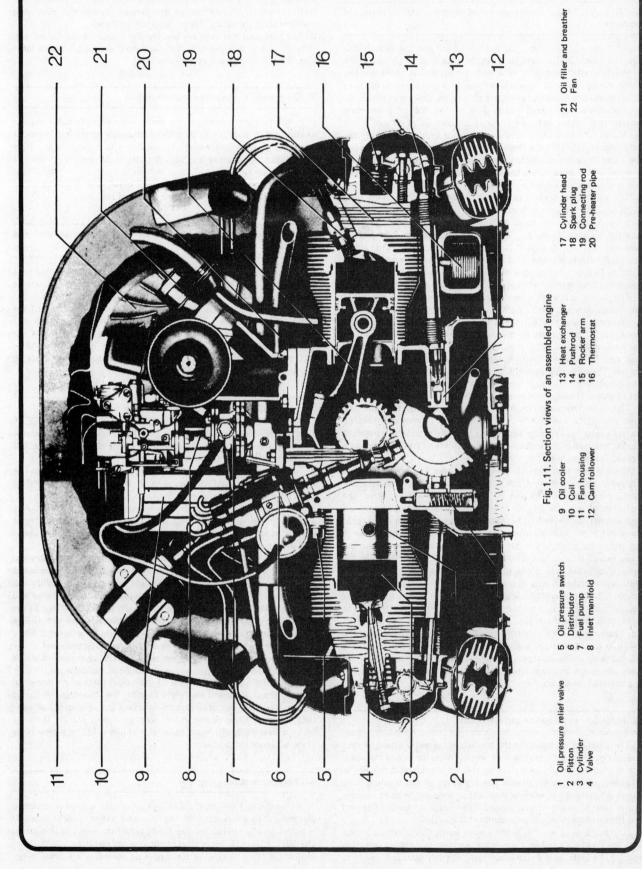

Fig.1.11. Section views of an assembled engine

1	Oil pressure relief valve	5	Oil pressure switch	9	Oil cooler	13	Heat exchanger	17	Cylinder head
2	Piston	6	Distributor	10	Coil	14	Pushrod	18	Spark plug
3	Cylinder	7	Fuel pump	11	Fan housing	15	Rocker arm	19	Connecting rod
4	Valve	8	Inlet manifold	12	Cam follower	16	Thermostat	20	Pre-heater pipe
								21	Oil filler and breather
								22	Fan

29. Cylinder heads, rocker gear and valves - examination and renovation

1 After the cylinder head has been removed and the valves taken out, the head itself should be thoroughly cleaned of carbon in the combustion chambers and examined for cracks. If there are any visible cracks the head should be scrapped. Cracks are most likely to occur round the valve seats or spark plug holes. Bearing in mind that one head will cost (new) nearly 20% of the cost of a complete replacement engine economies should be considered as well as the likelihood of obtaining a used head from a breaker's yard. If the latter, make sure that the head you get is the same type as the old one - and in better condition! There were differences in valve layout in other VW engines before the 1300 so don't be caught by someone telling you that they were all the same.

2 The valve seats should be examined for signs of burning away or pitting and ridging. If there is slight pitting the refacing of the seats by grinding in the valve with carborundum paste will probably cure the problem. If the seat needs re-cutting, due to severe pitting, then the seat width should not exceed specification. Fitting new valve seat inserts is a specialist task as they are chilled and shrunk in order to fit them. Check with the nearest Volkswagen dealer because you could have difficulty in getting this problem solved cheaply.

3 The rocker gear should be dismantled and thoroughly cleaned of the sludge deposits which normally tend to accumulate on it. The rocker arms should be a smooth fit on the shaft with no play. If there is any play it is up to the owner to decide whether it is worth the cost of renewal. The effects on engine performance and noise may not be serious although wear tends to accelerate once it is started. The valve clearance adjusting screws should also be examined. The domed ends that bear on the valve stems tend to get hammered out of shape. If bad, replacement is relatively cheap and easy.

4 The valves themselves must be thoroughly cleaned of carbon. The head should be completely free of cracks or pitting and must be perfectly circular. The edge which seats in to the cylinder head should also be unpitted and unridged although very minor blemishes may be ground out when re-seating the valve face.

5 Replace the valve into its guide in the head and note if there is any sideways movement which denotes wear between the stem and guide. Here again the degree of wear can vary. If excessive, the performance of the engine can be noticeably affected and oil consumption increased. The maximum tolerable sideways rock, measured at the valve head with the end of the valve stem flush with the end of the guide, is 0.8 mm (0.031 inch). Wear is normally in the guide rather than on the valve stem but check a new valve in the guide if possible first. Valve guide renewal is a tricky operation in these cylinder heads and you may find it difficult to get it done. Check with the nearest Volkswagen dealer first. Do not attempt it yourself. One final part of the examination involves the end of the valve stem where the rocker arm bears. It should be flat but often gets 'hammered' into a concave shape or ridged. Special caps are available to put over the ends. Alternatively the ends can be ground off flat with a fine oil stone. Remember that it is difficult to set the valve clearances accurately with the adjusting screw and valve stem in a battered condition.

30. Flywheel - examination and renovation

1 The flywheel is aligned to the crankshaft flange by means of four dowel pegs which are a precision fit into both the flange and flywheel. If any of these should be a slack fit there is considerable risk of the flywheel working loose, despite the tightness of the securing bolt. Where a flywheel has worked loose and caused the holes to become oval a new flywheel will be needed. (The precision work of boring and fitting oversize dowel pegs would cost more).

2 Another area of wear is in the starter teeth. These are machined into the flywheel itself so there is no question of fitting a new ring gear. If the teeth have become seriously chewed up it is in order to

have up to 2 mm (0.08 inch) machined off on the clutch side of the teeth. The teeth should then be chamfered and de-burred. Any good machine shop should be able to carry out this work.

3 Examine also the land on the flywheel boss where the oil seal runs. If this is severely ridged it may need cleaning up on a lathe also. Any such ridging is very exceptional.

31. Oil cooler - examination and renovation

It will be fairly obvious if the cooler leaks severely but if there is no apparent damage it may be difficult to decide whether it functions correctly. If suspect it should be subjected to a pressure test by a Volkswagen agent equipped with the proper equipment. If there is any doubt about it the only sure remedy is a new one. If the cooler is found to be leaking the oil pressure relief valve should also be checked as it could have caused the failure of the cooler.

32. Oil pressure relief and regulator valves - examination and renovation

1 The piston of the relief valve is perfectly plain and should be a free sliding fit in the bore of the crankcase. Minor signs of seizure may be cleaned up but if severe a new piston should be fitted.

2 The spring should be cleaned and examined. The length of the spring under a load of 7.75 kgs. (17 lbs) should be 23.6 mm (0.9 ins.)

3 Where a pressure regulating valve is also fitted (1970 on) the length of that spring under a load of 4.35 kgs (9.6 lbs) should be 16.8 mm (0.7 inches). If you have no way of conveniently measuring the springs then buy new ones.

33. Oil pump - examination and renovation

1 It is possible to check the pump fairly comprehensively without removing the body from the crankcase but it is, of course, far less convenient and liable to cause measurement inaccuracies.

2 First check the cover plate. If it is very badly scored it should be renewed anyway. Light scoring can be ground out using carborundum paste on a piece of plate glass.

3 Check that the driving spindle is a good fit in the body. Any apparent rocking indicates that the inside of the pump body must also be worn. The driven gear spindle should be tight in the body. The gear should be a good fit on it with no play.

4 Provided both gear spindles are in good shape refit the gears and measure the end clearance between them and the end of the pump body. This is done by putting a straight edge across the body and using a feeler gauge to measure the gap between the straight edge and the gears. Make sure no traces of gasket remain on the flange of the body when doing this. The gap should not exceed 0.1 mm (0.004 inch) or inadequate oil pressure will result. The wear is most likely to be in the pump body in this case and this will need renewal.

5 The backlash between the gear teeth can also be measured with a feeler blade and this should not exceed 0.2 mm (0.008 inch).

6 Depending on the availability of individual parts any renewals to parts of the pump must be weighed against the advantages of having a complete unit. If only the body shows signs of scoring or wear take the gears along to the Volkswagen parts store and try them for fit in a new body. In most cases of sloppiness fitting a new body alone will cure the problem.

34. Engine reassembly - general

1 As mentioned earlier, the Volkswagen engine is more complex in assembly than a conventional engine with a single cylinder block. It is therefore essential to get everything right first time and this means DO NOT RUSH IT. More than likely you will not have assembled an engine like this before so the order of assembly on other types

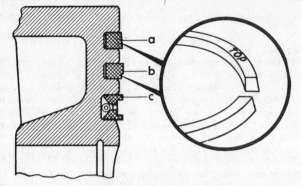

Fig.1.12. Piston rings

(a)   Top compression ring with bevelled face
(b)   Lower compression ring with stepped lower edge
(c)   Oil scraper control ring

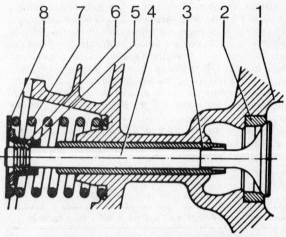

Fig.1.15. Valve assembly - cross section of valve,
spring and guide in assembled position

1	Cylinder head	5	Oil seal ring
2	Seat insert	6	Split collar
3	Guide	7	Valve spring
4	Valve	8	Spring retaining collar

Fig.1.13. Oil pump measuring gear end float

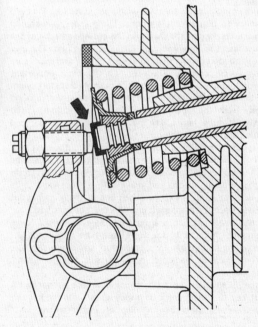

Fig.1.15A. Cap to rectify worn valve
stem end face (Part No. 113 109 621)

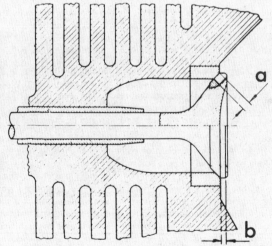

Fig.1.14. Valves - cross section of valve and seat
Dimension 'A' is seat width. Dimension 'B' is margin required
above seat
'A' Exhaust 1.7 - 2 mm Inlet 1.25 - 1.65 mm
'B' Minimum 1 mm (all valves)

cannot be relied upon for experience.

2 Before starting work clear the bench and arrange all the components nearby. The assembly surface must be particularly clean and it is a good idea to cover the working surface with sheets of strong paper. Have all the necessary gaskets and seals available together with clean oil in a can or convenient dispenser pack. If you are replacing bearing shells, cam followers and various other parts make sure the old parts are kept away from the assembly area in a carton or something. It is very easy to pick up an old cam follower for instance by mistake. At each stage, get the relevant batch of nuts and bolts ready - having cleaned the grit from them in a paraffin bath. A plentiful supply of clean cloths is the final requirement. Do not forget to clean the tools you will use as well. It is easy to transfer grit from a spanner to the engine with your hands and any small pieces of grit can ruin many hours and pounds worth of work, and again finally, take your time!

35. Crankshaft - assembly of gears and nos.3 and 4 main bearings

1 With the crankshaft thoroughly clean and the oilways blown out lubricate No.3 journal with clean engine oil. No.3 main bearing is one of the two largest one-piece circular shells. It does not have a flange on it. This bearing goes on to the journal one way only - that is with the small dowel peg hole (which is not central) towards the flywheel end of the crankshaft. Do not get this wrong or assembly will grind to a halt when you try and locate the bearing in the crankcase halves.

2 Next replace the camshaft drive gear. Before putting it on examine the surfaces of the crankshaft and key and the bore of the gear. If there are signs of slight scoring as a result of seizure when the gear was drawn off, clean them up with a very fine file. This will avoid a tendency to bind on replacement. The gear keyway should be lined up with the key in the shaft and the chamfered edge of the gear bore must face the flywheel end - i.e. it goes on first. The gear may be difficult to start on the shaft so keep it square and make sure that the keyway is precisely lined up. This is most important because if wrong you will have to draw the gear off and start again. It can then be drifted on with firm evenly spaced strikes around the gear (away from the teeth). Keep it square, particularly at the start, and drive it fully home. The crankshaft should be clamped between padded vice jaws for this operation.

3 Next the spacer ring followed by the spiral distributor drive gear are fitted. They can go on either way round and the gear should be carefully drifted up to the spacer without damaging the spiral teeth. Finally, fit the retaining circlip and make sure it fits snugly in its groove. If it will not go in the groove then one of the gears has not been fully driven onto the crankshaft and this must be rectified.

4 Next fit the small circular bearing over the end journal, once again making sure that the offset dowel peg hole is towards the flywheel end of the crankshaft. Do not confuse the dowel peg hole with the circular groove machined in the outside of this bearing. Lubricate the journal.

5 Next fit the oil thrower disc with the concave face outwards. Fit the Woodruff key (for the crankshaft pulley wheel) into the keyway now as this will prevent the disc from falling off inadvertently.

36. Connecting rods - assembly to crankshaft

1 If the crankcase has been split the connecting rods (without the pistons) should first be fitted to the crankshaft. Check that the gudgeon pins fit correctly in their respective small end bushes, otherwise difficulty will be encountered in fitting the pistons later. If you are refitting the connecting rods to the crankshaft in the assembled crankcase, note the additional information at the end of this section.

2 Lay the crankshaft down on the bench with the flywheel flange end away from you.

3 Arrange the connecting rods, two on each side of the crankshaft with Nos.1 and 2 on the right, No.1 nearest the flywheel end and No.3 and 4 on the left with No.3 nearest the flywheel end. The numbers on each connecting rod and cap must face downward for each cylinder. There is a forging mark on each rod on the opposite side which obviously faces upwards. If you are fitting new connecting rods check with the supplier first about any changes which may possibly have occurred in this principle of marking. Later rods have fixed bolts in the caps and nuts. These should not be mixed with earlier rods having bolts fitted through the rods into the caps. The first crank on the crankshaft, from the flywheel end, is No.3, left. Pick up the connecting rod and after wiping the bearing surface perfectly clean, fit the bearing shell with the notch engaging in the corresponding notch in the rod. Fit the other half of the shell bearing to the cap in the same fashion. Next, liberally oil the bearing journal with clean oil and assemble the rod to the crankshaft. Match the two numbers on the shoulders and with the rod pointing to the left face them downwards. Replace the cap bolts (or nuts) finger tight so that the assembly is not loose on the crankshaft.

4 Repeat this for No.1, right, which is the second crank from the flywheel end followed by No.4, left, and No.2, right. It is easy to get confused while doing this. If your crankshaft assembly does not look like the one in the photograph rotate the crankshaft 180° but keep the connecting rods pointing the same way. Then it should look familiar! Above all, think and do not rush.

5 Once the rods are correctly fitted to the crankshaft the bolts will need tightening to the correct torque of 3.3 mkg (24 ft lbs). The best way to do this is to mount the crankshaft vertically in the vice, clamping the No.4 bearing journal firmly between two pieces of wood. All the connecting rod bolts can then be tightened. It is advisable to tap the shoulders of each rod with a hammer to relieve any pre-tension which can be set up between the mating surfaces of the cap and the rod. When the cap bolts are fully tightened the connecting rods should be able to rotate around the journals under their own weight. There should be no tight or 'free' spots anywhere although if you are fitting new shells to an un-reground crankshaft this is possible. If very noticeable however, it indicates that the journal is out of round. If rods on a reground crankshaft are slightly tight the engine will need running-in. If very tight then the regrinding tolerances are wrong and it should be returned to the machinists for correction.

6 Place the assembled crankshaft on the bench once more, as before, with each connecting rod facing its proper cylinder position.

7 If you are fitting the connecting rods to an assembled crankcase/crankshaft lay out the rods alongside their respective cylinder positions as already explained and fit the shells into the rods and caps. Turn the crankshaft so that the journal for the rod to be fitted is nearest its crankcase opening. The cap must then be placed on the journal and the rod fitted to it. This is easy if you have four hands and fingers ten inches long! It is helpful to have a piece of bent metal rod which can be put through from the opposite side of the crankcase to hold the cap on the journal whilst the rod and bolts are being fitted. A certain amount of patience is essential as it is more than likely that you will drop a bolt or bearing cap into the crankcase at some stage and have to shake it out. The most important thing to ensure is that a bearing shell/s does not drop out unnoticed while you are fiddling about and get trapped and damaged. So if a shell drops in the crankcase go easy on rotating the crankshaft until you get it out. Needless to say, this operation is made even more difficult if attempted with the engine in the car. This is why we do not recommend it. As soon as the first connecting rod is fitted tighten the bolts to the correct torque and check that it moves freely but without any clearance. You will be refitting new shells to the original journal sizes so if something seems amiss - bearing too tight or too loose - make sure you have bought the correct shells by comparing the numbers and oversize (if any) with the old ones removed.

35.1(a) Clean oilways and lubricate No.3 journal.

35.1(b) No.3 bearing shell with dowel peg hole (indicated) towards the flywheel.

35.2(a) Replacing the camshaft gear.

35.2(b) Line up the camshaft drive gear keyway

35.2(c) Drifting on the camshaft drive gear.

35.3(a) Fitting the spacer collar.

35.3(b) Fitting the distributor drive gear.

35.3(c) Line up the distributor drive gear keyway

35.3(d) Fit the retaining circlip.

35.4. Position the end bearing shell with the dowel peg hole towards the flywheel.

35.5(a) Position the oil thrower disc

35.5(b) Tap the Woodruff key into the keyway.

37. Crankcase, crankshaft, camshaft and cam followers - reassembly

1 The items in the section heading are grouped together for the very good reason that they all have to be assembled together. None may be omitted. (See Figs 1.16 and 1.17).

2 Both crankcase halves must be perfectly clean, inside and out. All traces of jointing compound must be removed from the mating faces, the roots of the studs, and the chamfers in the stud hole mating faces. Use a solvent such as carbon tetrachloride to remove sealing compound and not a scraper which could damage the aluminium surfaces. The distributor drive gear should have been removed. The oil pump suction pipe must be tightly fitted. If loose it must be peened in position as necessary.

3 Place the left hand half of the crankcase on the bench with the flywheel end away from you and leaning over so that it rests on the cylinder head studs.

4 Oil the four cam followers for the left half and place them in their bores. If new followers are being fitted it is possible that their heads may be slightly thicker than the originals so compare them. If they are thicker then it is essential to check the clearance between them and the crankcase with the cam lift at its highest point. So having placed the cam followers in position replace the camshaft temporarily, with its shell bearings and revolve it. If any of the cam lobes should jam the followers against the crankcase then clearance will have to be provided by relieving the crankcase by about 1-2 mm behind each cam follower head. This can be done by a small, end face grindstone in a power drill by a competent handyman. Great precision is not important provided that there is no damage to the actual cam follower bore and the resulting clearance is adequate to permit full unobstructed movement of the cam and follower. Be sure to remove all traces of metal after such work. Repeat this check for the four cam followers in the right hand half of the crankcase.

5 Fit the flanged No.1 bearing shell at the flywheel end of the crankshaft. Once again make sure that the off-centre locating dowel peg hole goes towards the flywheel end. Look to see that the corresponding dowel pegs in the crankcase will mate up. The bearing surfaces of the journal should be well lubricated with clean oil but keep the outside surfaces of the bearing shell clean and dry.

6 Place one half of the split shell in position at No.2 bearing in the crankcase, engaging the dowel pin in the hole. Lubricate the bearing with clean oil.

7 The crankshaft assembly should now be placed into position in the left hand crankcase half. The three dowel holes in the circular bearings will need lining up so that they will locate snugly and Nos.3 and 4 connecting rods must pass through their respective apertures. It is a good idea to lift the assembly up by Nos.1 and 2 connecting rods for this operation. Do not force anything into place. The circular bearings may need rotating a little until you can feel the pegs engage. Ensure the thrower disc locates within the oil thrower recess in the casting. Once all the bearing pegs are located a little pressure will ensure that the assembly and bearings are completely seated. If it is stubborn for any reason lift it out, pause, look, think and have another go.

8 Next fit the camshaft bearing shells into clean locations, engaging the notches in the crankcase. Then oil the bearings in readiness for the camshaft.

9 Turn the crankshaft carefully until two teeth, each marked with a centre punch, are visible and well clear of the edge of the crankcase. There is a single tooth on the camshaft gear similarly marked which must mesh between them. Engage the teeth and roll the camshaft round, in mesh still, into its bearing location. Then turn the gears again to check that the timing marks are still correctly aligned.

10 Now fit the four tappets (cam followers) into the right hand half of the crankcase and if it seems as though they might fall out when it is lifted and tilted then put a dab of grease behind the lip of each one to help stick it in position.

11 Fit the other half of No.2 bearing shell into the right hand half of the crankcase locating it over its dowel peg correctly.

12 Now thinly coat the two clean, smooth mating surfaces of the

crankcase halves with aluminium alloy jointing compound. Use a good quality product such as Volkswagen themselves recommend or 'Hylomar'. Neither is cheap but then you do not want your crankcase to leak oil when it gets hot. Make sure the two surfaces are coated completely but thinly and evenly. Take care to cover round the base of the studs. Do not let any compound get into oilways or other places where it is not wanted and may cause obstruction or binding. Later models of the 1500 (Engine No.H0398526 on) were fitted with rubber sealing rings over the M12 crankcase studs. It will be seen that the stud holes have been countersunk in both halves of the crankcase to accept them. Place these in position over all six studs sized M12, pushing them down to the roots of the studs.

13 Place the right hand half of the crankcase over the studs of the left and carefully slide it down until it just touches the crankshaft bearings.

14 Coat the circular camshaft sealing plug with jointing compound and place it in position in its groove in the left hand half at the flywheel end of the camshaft, with the recess facing inwards, except on automatic stickshift when the recess should face out.

15 Move the two halves together, tapping lightly with a block of wood if necessary. Use no force - none should be necessary.

16 Now stop and check:

1 Are all the connecting rods protruding from their proper holes? Cap bolts tight?
2 Are all four bearings, two gears and oil thrower disc fitted to the crankshaft?
3 Are all eight cam followers in position?
4 You did not forget the camshaft? (It has been known!). Did you mesh the timing properly?
5 Camshaft sealer plug?

All in order, replace all the nuts on the studs finger tight. Revolve the crankshaft just to make sure that everything moves freely at this stage at least.

17 It is important to tighten down the stud nuts evenly and in the correct order. Tighten first the six large nuts to a torque of 1.5 mkg (11 ft lbs) only, followed by all the smaller nuts to the same torques. Then tighten the small nut near the lower large stud clamping round No.1 main bearing to its full torque of 2 mkg (14 ft lbs).

18 Tighten the large nuts progressively to a torque of 20 ft lbs and then to 25 ft lbs. Finally tighten the smaller nuts to 14 ft lbs. On some 1500 engines made prior to those fitted with sealing rings on the studs, the two centre stud nuts had plastic sealing rings incorporated in them. These should be installed with the sealing inserts against the crankcase and tightened to 18 ft lbs only instead of the 25 ft lbs of the other four. The engine numbers having this arrangement were H0230323-398525.

19 Now rotate the crankshaft - it should revolve smoothly without any stiffness. If there is stiffness however, slacken all the crankcase nuts. If it then turns freely something is wrong and you should separate the crankcase again. Then check that all the bearings have been properly located on their dowel pegs and that the split bearings of the camshaft are seated properly. Any pressure spots on bearings will be visible. The cause is normally due to dirt or burrs behind them, particularly on the corners of the bearing bore corners and mating face edges. These can be chamfered lightly if necessary. Whatever happens do not press on until you have found the reason for any tightness. Start again from the beginning if necessary.

38. Pistons, piston rings and connecting rods - reassembly

1 If you are only fitting new rings to existing pistons make sure you have examined the pistons properly as detailed in Section 28 and checked the new ring gaps in the cylinder bores.

2 The new rings should be fitted over the piston crown replacing the bottom ring first. If you do not have a proper ring expander tool spread the ends of the ring so that it goes over the top of the piston. Then carefully ease it down over the other grooves a little at a time. The blade of a feeler gauge or some shim steel will be of great

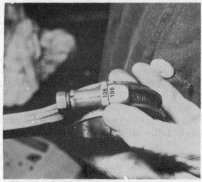

36.3(a) Match the numbers on the rod and cap.

36.3(b) Fit the connecting rod to the crankshaft.

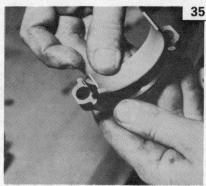

36.3(c) Put the shell bearing into the cap.

36.3(d) Assemble the cap to the rod

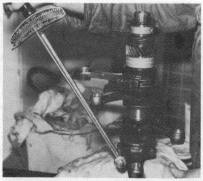

36.5. Tighten cap bolts (or nuts) to the correct torque.

37.3(a) Compare new tappets (cam followers) with old.

37.4(b) Fit the tappets into the crankcase

37.4(c) Check the cam lobe clearance.

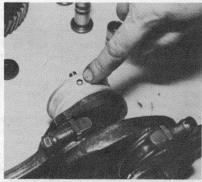

37.5. Position No.1 bearing (flanged) with the dowel peg hole towards the flywheel.

37.6. Fit No.2 (split) main bearing shells.

37.7. Placing the crankshaft assembly into the left half of the crankcase.

37.9. Meshing the crankshaft and camshaft gears at the valve timing marks.

assistance in sliding it over the grooves. Do not bend the ring in any way more than necessary to move it. It breaks easily. The top two rings are different. The lower of the two has a cut-away lower edge and the top ring is chamfered on its outer face. Both rings will be marked 'oben' or 'top' which denotes which way up they go. The lower of the two is fitted first. (See Fig.1.12).

3 When new pistons are supplied for rebored cylinders the rings are already fitted and the gaps should automatically be correct. It does no harm however to take the top ring off each piston and check it in the bore to make sure.

4 Assuming the small end bushes have been correctly sized for the gudgeon pins remove one circlip from each piston - if not already done - and push out the gudgeon pin until the piston boss is clear to permit the end of the connecting rod to be positioned. If the pins are too tight to push out do not force them. Warm up the pistons in front of the fire or on a radiator or next to an electric light bulb. Do not play over them with a blow lamp or gas torch. They only need warming - not heating.

5 If new pistons are being fitted they can go to any connecting rod and all that matters is that the side of the piston marked on the crown 'flywheel' or with a pointing arrow goes towards the flywheel end of the engine. Push the gudgeon pin back into place and replace the circlip. Make sure that you use only the circlips supplied with the pistons. Do not use the old circlips just because they are easier to contract. (Volkswagen pistons have wire circlips with long legs. English pistons have spring steel clips with small eyes needing proper circlip pliers to release them).

6 As soon as one piston has been fitted **take care** because when the crankshaft is rotated the skirt of the piston can foul the crankcase at bottom dead centre unless it is guided into the cylinder aperture. This could break it. Watch too that the piston rings do not get snagged up on anything which could break them.

39. Cylinders - replacement

1 Cylinders should normally go back in their original locations unless new pistons are being fitted or they have been rebored, in which case it does not matter.

2 It is a good idea to turn the engine upside down for the fitting of the cylinders as this will make the next step of fitting the cylinder heads so much easier also.

3 Make sure that the mating faces at both top and bottom of the cylinders are perfectly clean and clear of old gaskets. Select the new thin, cylinder base gaskets from the set and separate them. It is easy for two to stick together. Hang one over each connecting rod now so you do not forget to put them on. Before fitting the cylinders you may wish to lightly grind them into the seats in the cylinder head. This can be done using fine carborundum paste. Make sure that all traces of paste are flushed away afterwards. Light grinding in this way helps to ensure a gastight seal but do not overdo it.

4 Cylinders will only go on one way, that is with the narrow fins at the base and the flat fin edges of a pair of cylinders facing each other. This should be remembered for the first cylinder of each pair. You could get it wrong and have to take it off again when the second one is ready to go on!

5 The piston ring gaps should be spaced equally round the circumference of each piston with the gap in the oil control ring facing the top of the engine. Remember that the engine is upside down when positioning it.

6 The rings must be compressed into the piston grooves in order to get the cylinder over them. The type of compressor used must be such that it will split and come off round the piston because once the cylinder is on it will not be possible to lift it off over the top of the piston. In the instance illustrated a 'Jubilee' hose clip was used quite satisfactorily. The cylinder bore is chamfered at the bottom which also facilitates assembly.

7 Fit the clip round the rings and tighten it so that all three are compressed. Take care to see that no ring slips out from under the clip. This can easily happen, particularly when first tightening up the

clip screw.

8 Tighten the clip until the rings are flush with the piston but do not tighten it so much that the clip grips the piston tightly. Otherwise it will be difficult to slide the clip down the piston when the cylinder barrel takes over.

9 Not forgetting the lower cylinder gasket, place the cylinder over the piston crown narrow end first and with the fin flats facing the adjacent cylinder position and with the four studs aligned in the passages in the fins.

10 Press the base of the cylinder against the piston ring compressor or clip and tap it down with a wooden block of soft hammer. If the clip does not move slacken it a fraction and try again. Do not let the cylinder 'bounce' off the clip when tapping it otherwise you are likely to release an otherwise captive ring. If a ring does escape it will be necessary to start again. If you break a ring you will probably have to buy a set of three for that piston - rarely can you buy a single ring unless you are lucky and a supplier has a part set or is prepared to split a set.

11 Once all rings are inside the cylinder remove the compressor. With the 'Jubilee' clip this means unscrewing it until the end can be drawn out to release it.

12 Next, carefully position the base gasket onto the bottom of the cylinder barrel. Then move the barrel down and locate it into the crankcase. It will not be a tight fit. It is important to make sure that the gasket is not dislodged and trapped incorrectly. If it is, the joint may leak and, worse, the cylinder tilt fractionally out of line.

13 It may be found convenient to rotate the crankshaft as each cylinder is fitted. When this is done, precautions must be taken to keep the other cylinders in position, otherwise you will have to keep checking the gasket seating. Also guard against the pistons jamming the crankcase at bottom dead centre. The cylinders may be tied down with string to prevent them moving.

40. Cylinder heads, valve and springs - reassembly

1 The valves removed should be refitted in their original positions unless, of course, new ones are being fitted.

2 If possible treat the valve stem with molybdenum disulphide or some other form of anti-scuffing paste to prevent excessive initial wear in the guide.

3 Place the valve in the guide. Fit the oil seal round the valve stem and then the spring and spring collar. Note that the close coils of the spring go against the head.

4 Next arrange the valve spring compressor with the spacer tube fitted if required and carefully compress the spring. Watch that there is no likelihood of the spring flying out. Often the spring tends to tilt on compression and this can impede the fitting of the split collars. If you can straighten the spring up without risk of releasing it all is well. Sometimes it may be necessary to find another spring compressor.

5 Compress the spring far enough to expose the grooves into which the split collars locate.

6 It will be necessary to fit the split collars through the slot in the tube if you have used this method. Fingers will be found to be too fat so put a blob of grease on the end of a screwdriver and use this to pick up the collett and put it in position with the narrow end downwards. You may have difficulty with the second half because of the spring not being centrally spaced round the valve stem. This can be overcome by carefully tipping the spring with the compressor or by a little extra compression.

7 When both split collars are properly located in the grooves in the valve stems slowly release the compressor tool making sure that neither of the split collars is pushed out of position. When the spring compressor is fully released the two halves of the split collar should be flush. If not, one is not properly bedded in the grooves of the valve stem.

8 Repeat the procedure for each valve in turn.

37.13. Placing the crankcase right half into position.

37.15. Tap the two halves together lightly.

37.17(a) Torque down the large nuts to 11 ft/lbs.

37.17(b) Torque down the small nut near No.1 bearing to its full amount.

38.5(a) Positioning the piston over the connecting rod small end.

38.5(b) Push the gudgeon pin fully home.

38.5(c) Fit the retaining circlip.

39.6. Put the clamp round the piston rings.

39.8(a) Position the cylinder base gasket.

39.8(b) Put the cylinder in position.

39.9. Push the cylinder down over the piston rings.

Fig.1.16. Engine components displayed prior to assembly (see Section 37)

Fig.1.17. Crankshaft positioned in left half of crankcase (see Section 37)

39.10. Release the ring clamp.

40.3(a) Placing a valve in the guide.

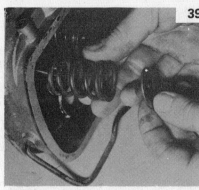

40.3(b) Replace the spring and collar.

40.4. Suitable spring compressor with hooked ends.

40.5. Compressing the valve spring with a conventional compressor tool and piece of tube with an aperture.

40.6. Use a blob of grease on a screwdriver to place the collet.

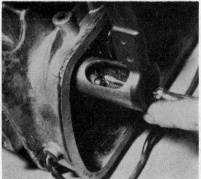

40.7. Collets put in place.

41.2. Fitting a seal to a pushrod tube.

41.3. Clipping the air deflector plate to the cylinder head studs and over the cylinders.

41.4(a) Offering up the cylinder head.

41.4(b) Putting the cylinder head over the studs.

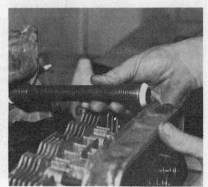

41.4(c) Positioning the pushrod tubes.

41.7. Tightening the cylinder head nuts.

42.2. Fitting the seals over the rocker shaft mounting studs.

42.3. Fitting the rocker shaft assembly.

43.4. Setting the valve rocker clearances.

44.2. Fitting the oil pump body into the crankcase.

44.5(a) Fitting the oil pump driving spindle and gear.

41. Cylinder heads - replacement

1 It is best for the engine to be inverted when fitting the cylinder heads as in this way the pushrod tubes will be much easier to assemble between the head and crankcase.

2 First check the pushrod tubes. They have compressible concertina ends and these should be stretched out a little by pulling them so that the distance between the outer ends of the concertina sections is no less than 181 mm. A new sealing ring should be fitted over each end so that the radiused face will go into the head or crankcase as appropriate. When stretching the tubes pull straight so as to avoid any possibility of cracking them. If they are fractured a positive oil leak will result so check their condition carefully. (Fig.1.19).

3 Next fit the sheet steel air deflector plate, of which there is one to each pair of cylinders. It is a spring fit to the two centre studs and to make sure it is tight, the clip flanges may be bent out a little. Note that these deflectors (which guide air into the cooling fins) are on the lower side, i.e. the same side as the pushrod tubes. They follow the contour of the cooling fins when installed so make sure they are the right way round. They cannot be fitted after putting the cylinder heads and tubes in position.

4 One head should now be put on to the eight head studs just far enough to be secure. Then place the four pushrod tubes into position in their recesses in the crankcase and move the head further on so that the other ends of the tubes locate in the corresponding holes in the head. Make sure that the pushrod seals seat firm and square and that the recesses are clean. The seams in the tube should face the cylinders.

5 The cylinder head studs should not be touching any of the cylinder barrel fins so if necessary turn the barrels a little to achieve this. A piece of postcard placed behind each stud will establish the presence of a gap.

6 Replace the stud washers and nuts and tighten them lightly and evenly as far as is possible with a socket and extension using no lever bar.

7 The tightening progression of the nuts is important and is in two stages. First tighten the nuts to 1 mgk (7 ft lbs) in the order shown in Fig.1.18(a). Then tighten them to 3.2 mkg (23 ft lbs) in the final diagonal pattern sequence as shown in Fig.1.18(b). There is a temptation to overtighten these head nuts. Resist it! Otherwise you will distort the head.

8 Repeat the operation for the second head.

42. Rocker gear and pushrods - replacement

1 With the cylinder heads replaced, put the pushrods into position making sure that the lower end engages in the recess in the cam follower.

2 Place a new seal over each rocker assembly mounting stud and then place the rocker shaft support blocks over the studs so that the socketed ends of the rocker arms will line up with the pushrods and the adjusters over the valve stems. The support blocks are chamfered and slotted. They are fitted with the chamfers outwards and slots upwards.

3 Replace the washers and nuts and tighten the two nuts down evenly ensuring that the pushrods are properly engaged in the rocker arms. Tightening torque is 2.5 mkg (18 ft lbs). Slacken all the rocker adjuster screws for later adjustment.

43. Valve to rocker clearances - adjustment

1 Valve clearances are important. If they should be too great the

valves will not open as fully as they should. They will also open late and close early. This will affect engine performance. Similarly, if the clearances are too small the valves may not close completely which will result in lack of compression and power. It will cause damage to valves and seatings.

2 The valve clearances should be set for each cylinder when the piston is at the firing point. With the engine in the car this may be first found on No. 1 cylinder (right, front) by removing the distributor cap and turning the engine so that the timing notch on the crankshaft pulley lines up with the centre of the crankcase and the rotor arm points to the notch in the edge of the distributor body.

3 With the engine out of the car and distributor not yet installed the easiest method is to turn the crankshaft pulley wheel clockwise up to the mark and at the same time keep a finger over No.1 cylinder plug hole to check that there is compression. This indicates that you are on the firing stroke.

4 Both valves on No.1 cylinder may then be adjusted. First slacken the locknut on each rocker arm adjusting screw. Then put a feeler blade of the appropriate thickness between the adjuster and the end of the valve stem and turn the adjusting screw until a light drag can be felt when the blade is moved. Tighten the locknut, holding the adjuster simultaneously with a screwdriver. Check the gap once again.

5 Continue with the subsequent cylinders; the order is 2, 3, 4 and the crankshaft pulley wheel should be rotated ½ turn (180°) anticlockwise. The distributor rotor arm will turn ¼ turn (90°). The valve clearances for No.2 cylinder may then be set. Continue the same way for cylinders 3 and 4 in that order.

44. Oil pump - replacement

1 Make sure that the mating faces of the crankcase and pump body are perfectly clean and unmarked.

2 Using a new gasket fit the pump body over the studs so that the fixed spindle is towards the bottom of the crankcase.

3 Carefully tap the body fully home over the studs, taking care that the gasket does not get trapped incorrectly.

4 When the body is fully home tighten the two crankcase stud nuts, above and below, to the correct torque.

5 Next fit the two gears, turning the driving spindle so that the tongue engages in the slot in the end of the camshaft. With both gears fully home the engine should now be turned through at least two complete revolutions. This ensures that the pump body is correctly centred by the revolving gears. The body should not be disturbed again after this has been done. Fit a new cover plate gasket followed by the cover plate. Replace the four nuts. Whilst tightening up the nuts to the recommended torque of 14 ft lbs it is worthwhile rotating the engine once or twice more in case the pump body should inadvertently have moved during tightening.

45. Crankshaft front oil seal - replacement

1 The seal must be replaced (if it has been removed) before the flywheel is fitted. Do not fit it however, until the crankshaft endfloat has been checked as this involves temporary replacement of the flywheel and the movement of shims.

2 Before fitting the seal, place the necessary circular shims over the crankshaft flange and make sure they are perfectly clean and lightly oiled.

3 Coat the outer metal edge of the new oil seal with jointing compound and place it squarely in position into the crankcase with the inner lip of the seal facing inwards. It may then be tapped

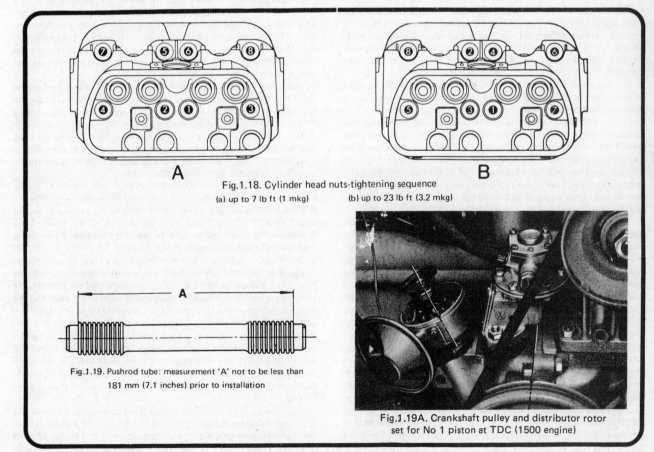

Fig.1.18. Cylinder head nuts-tightening sequence
(a) up to 7 lb ft (1 mkg)   (b) up to 23 lb ft (3.2 mkg)

Fig.1.19. Pushrod tube: measurement 'A' not to be less than 181 mm (7.1 inches) prior to installation

Fig.1.19A. Crankshaft pulley and distributor rotor set for No 1 piston at TDC (1500 engine)

squarely home using a flat piece of wood.

46. Flywheel - replacement

1 If you have taken the flywheel off you will presumably have the same equipment still available for replacing it. You will need it.

2 If you have overhauled the complete engine it will be advisable to check the crankshaft endfloat. This is governed by the gap between the inner face of the flywheel boss and the flange of the rear main bearing shell. Shims are introduced to reduce the gap and these shims need to be fitted before the oil seal. Although it is possible for them to be pushed in past the oil seal it is very difficult to get them out again without buckling or kinking them. If the main bearing shell has been renewed it is most likely that the shims originally fitted will be correct as the main wear takes place on the bearing shell flange. Three shims are always used to make up the required total thickness and they come in six thicknesses (0.24 mm, 0.30 mm, 0.32 mm, 0.34 mm, 0.36 mm, 0.38 mm). Fit two shims to start with, when the thickness of the third may then be calculated.

3 The four dowel pegs should all be placed in the crankshaft flange after having been checked for fitting in both the flange and the flywheel. If any of these should be slack there is considerable risk of the flywheel working loose, despite the tightness of the nut, and this could be disasterous.

4 Over the dowel pegs a metal or paper gasket is placed - fit a new one the same as the one you took off - both should be provided in the gasket set. Note the position of your lining up mark made before removal before putting the gasket in position.

5 Grip the flywheel firmly and, with the marks lined up, locate it over the dowel pegs. It is most important for the flywheel to be kept square. If it proves a bit of a strain and a fiddle to get in position find a piece of wood of a thickness suitable to support it at the right height. Once the flywheel is positively located on the pegs replace the centre bolt and washer and take it up as far as it will go finger tight. Then very carefully tighten the bolt to draw the flywheel on, at the same time keeping it perfectly square by tapping the rim as necessary with a soft faced mallet. If the bolt is tightened with the flywheel out of square the dowel pegs and holes will be seriously damaged.

6 It will be necessary to tighten the centre bolt to at least 75 ft lbs in order that the crankshaft endfloat may be accurately read. To do this a dial gauge micrometer is used against the face of the flywheel. The crankshaft is then moved in and out and the float measured. The thickness of the third shim is the measured float less 0.10 mm. Any three shims will do of course provided they add up in total thickness to the sum of the two in position and the calculated third.

7 Once the correct shims have been selected the flywheel should be removed and the three shims put in position and the oil seal fitted as described in Section 45. The flywheel is then replaced in the same fashion.

8 Final tightening of the centre bolt involves a torque of 217 ft lbs (30 mkg) and the locking of the flywheel for this purpose should be arranged in the same way as for removal. It is important to get this torque as accurate as possible because the flywheel may vibrate loose if it is insufficient. Too much, on the other hand, could cause unwanted stresses.

9 It should also be remembered that the flywheel bolt has a built-in roller bearing which supports the transmission input shaft. This bearing should be in good condition and not over-greased.

47. Engine - final assembly

Before the engine is replaced into the car it is normal to replace all the ancillary components. However, as it is not essential and as these various items may be removed whilst the engine is still in the car, they are dealt with in the appropriate chapters. Thus, the replacement of the inlet manifold and exhaust manifold is detailed in Chapter 3 and the fan housing heat exchangers, thermostat and associated 'tinware'

(as it is affectionately referred to!) is covered in Chapter 2. However, various items should be fitted in the correct order otherwise a lot of time may be wasted taking things off again. The list below gives a summary of what that order is although each item is dealt with under the appropriate chapter heading. Assuming that the crankcase oil pump, cylinders and heads have been assembled the order is:

Flywheel
Lower rear cover plate
Crankshaft pulley wheel
Oil cooler
Upper cylinder cover plates
Lower cover plates and pre-heater pipes
Front cover plate
Heat exchangers (do not tighten down)
Induction manifold (do not tighten down)
Generator pedestal
Fan housing (do not tighten)
Fan/generator assembly
Silencer assembly (connect up with heat exchangers and induction manifold (do not tighten down)
Carburettor
Fuel pump
Distributor

Those items which are not tightened down immediately are assembled and connected to other components as well as the main body of the engine so it is important to get them all lined up first.

48. Engine - replacement

1 Engine replacement is best done when the whole unit, including fan housing, has been assembled. However, it is possible to do the replacement before the ancillaries have been refitted. A slight advantage is that the car need be raised at the rear about a foot less. Also the top mounting bolts are more easily seen and accessible. If the starter motor has been taken out it is a good idea to connect the cables and put it in position with the top mounting bolt through the transmission casing before fitting the engine.

2 Note that if you put the engine back with the fan and fan housing off it will be necessary to remove the engine compartment cover to get them on afterwards. Details will be found in the section dealing with fan housing removal in Chapter 2.

3 It is much easier generally if you can raise the engine on a trolley jack as this permits easy forward and backward movement. Otherwise you will have to make a stable platform with conventional jacks as described in the removal procedure.

4 Make sure the clutch has been refitted and the friction disc centralised (see Chapter 5).

5 If the fan housing is already assembled to the crankcase do not forget to fit the front cover plate which clips to the front of the crankcase. You will not be able to get this on when the engine is installed and the fan housing fitted.

6 See that the clutch and accelerator cables are correctly in position where they will not get trapped. The accelerator cable should be in an unrestricted straight line and not caught round the clutch cable or anything else. It has to pass through the front cover plate and the fan housing in due course. It should be prevented from getting kinked or bent.

7 As soon as the engine has been raised sufficiently to line up the gearbox shaft with the centre of the clutch cover, move it forward into position. The two top mounting bolts should be placed loosely in position but make quite sure that their respecitve nuts are an easy run on the threads first. This will make tightening up a great deal easier.

8 If difficulty is encountered when trying to mate up the engine to the transmission unit check that it is not tilted out of alignment with the transmission input shaft. A certain amount of sideways juggling may be necessary but if the clutch plate has been centred with

44.5(b) Replacing the oil pump cover plate.

45.2. Crankshaft end float shims which must be calculated and inserted before fitting the oil seal.

45.3(a) Placing the oil seal in position.

45.3(b) Tapping the oil seal home.

46.3. Positioning flywheel dowel pegs into the crankshaft.

46.4. Fitting the flywheel gasket.

46.5. Positioning the flywheel.

46.8. Flywheel locked using a length of angle iron on two of the clutch mounting bolts.

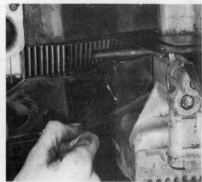

47.1(a) Fitting a lower cylinder cover plate.

47.1(b) Positioning the engine front cover plate.

47.1(c) Fitting the generator pedestal gasket.

47.1(d) .... and pedestal.

reasonable accuracy there should be no difficulty whatsoever.

9 When in position replace the nuts on the lower studs and on the upper bolts. For the latter you will have to feel around the fan housing and this is where preparation by cleaning the bolt threads will pay off. With luck you should be able to tighten the nut without the bolt itself needing to be held with another spanner.

10 Feed the accelerator cable through the hole in the cover plate and small hole in the fan housing. (The large holes in the fan housing are for the rubber grommets which support the H.T. leads).

11 With the engine and all ancillaries refitted the following check list should be used as a final check to ensure a first-time start without problems:

Fuel line connected to fuel pump inlet
Fuel line connected - pump to carburettor
Oil drain plug replaced and oil replenished

L.T. wires connected to coil, automatic choke and regulator box
Spark plugs tight
H.T. leads connected to coil, distributor and spark plugs
Rotor arm and contact points correct
Throttle cable connected
Starter motor leads connected (1 heavy, 1 light)
Two main feed cables connected to clamp terminal on control box
Battery leads securely and cleanly connected
All 'tinware' cheese head screws tight
Generator mounting strap and fan backplate bolts tight
Fan belt correctly tensioned and pulley bolt tight

12 As soon as the engine fires watch it running for some time - at least until fully warmed up - to ensure nothing is leaking or loose. Check and adjust if necessary the clutch pedal free travel.

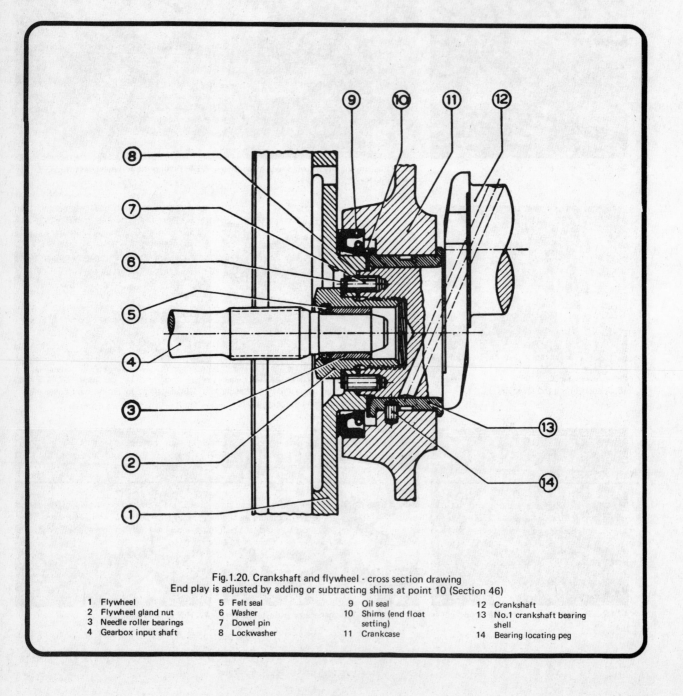

Fig.1.20. Crankshaft and flywheel - cross section drawing
End play is adjusted by adding or subtracting shims at point 10 (Section 46)

1	Flywheel	5	Felt seal	9	Oil seal	12	Crankshaft
2	Flywheel gland nut	6	Washer	10	Shims (end float setting)	13	No.1 crankshaft bearing shell
3	Needle roller bearings	7	Dowel pin	11	Crankcase	14	Bearing locating peg
4	Gearbox input shaft	8	Lockwasher				

49. Fault finding

Symptom	Reason/s	Remedy
Engine will not turn over when starter switch is operated	Flat battery Bad battery connections Bad connections at solenoid switch and/or starter motor	Check that battery is fully charged and that all connections are clean and tight.
	Starter motor jammed	Rock car back and forth with a gear engaged. If ineffective remove starter.
	Defective solenoid	Remove starter and check solenoid.
	Starter motor defective	Remove starter and overhaul.
Engine turns over normally but fails to fire and run	No spark at plugs	Check ignition system according to procedures given in Chapter 4.
	No fuel reaching engine	Check fuel system according to procedures given in Chapter 3.
	Too much fuel reaching the engine (flooding)	Slowly depress accelerator pedal to floor and keep it there while operating starter motor until engine fires. Check fuel system if necessary as described in Chapter 3.
Engine starts but runs unevenly and misfires	Ignition and/or fuel system faults	Check the ignition and fuel systems as though the engine had failed to start.
	Incorrect valve clearances	Check and reset clearances.
	Burnt out valves	Remove cylinder heads and examine and overhaul as necessary.
Lack of power	Ignition and/or fuel system faults	Check the ignition and fuel systems for correct ignition timing and carburettor settings.
	Incorrect valve clearances	Check and reset the clearances.
	Burnt out valves	Remove cylinder heads and examine and overhaul as necessary.
	Worn out piston or cylinder bores	Remove cylinder heads and examine pistons and cylinder bores. Overhaul as necessary.
Excessive oil consumption	Oil leaks from crankshaft oil seal, rocker cover gasket, oil pump, drain plug gasket, sump plug washer, oil cooler	Identify source of leak and repair as appropriate.
	Worn piston rings or cylinder bores resulting in oil being burnt by engine Smoky exhaust is an indication	Fit new rings·or rebore cylinders and fit new pistons, depending on degree of wear.
	Worn valve guides and/or defective valve stem seals	Remove cylinder heads and recondition valve stem bores and valves and seals as necessary.
Excessive mechanical noise from engine	Wrong valve to rocker clearances	Adjust valve clearances.
	Worn crankshaft bearings Worn cylinders (piston slap)	Inspect and overhaul where necessary.
Unusual vibration	Misfiring on one or more cylinders	Check ignition system.
	Loose mounting bolts	Check tightness of bolts and condition of flexible mountings.

NOTE: When investigating starting and uneven running faults do not be tempted into snap diagnosis. Start from the beginning of the check procedure and follow it through. It will take less time in the long run. Poor performance from an engine in terms of power and economy is not normally diagnosed quickly. In any event the ignition and fuel systems must be checked first before assuming any further investigation needs to be made.

Chapter 2 Cooling, heating and exhaust systems

Contents

Specifications

Air volume at 4000 rpm..	1300 — 550 litres (20 cu.ft.) per second
	1500 — 575 litres (21 cu.ft.) per second
Thermostat opens at...	65° — 70°C (149 — 158°F)

Torque wrench settings

Fan securing nut	43 lb.ft. (6.0 mkg)
Fan/generator drive pulley nut..	43 lb.ft. (6.0 mkg)

1. General description

One of the most famous and well known features of the Volkswagen engine throughout its life has been the fact that it is air-cooled. The advantages are obvious - none of the problems and cost of maintaining a water cooling system with the attendant problems of extreme temperatures. There are certain disadvantages of an air cooled system however - there is greater engine noise, more engine power used to drive the cooling fan and a less precise control of engine temperatures. Air cooled engines are not at their best in dense traffic in hot weather. Great care must also be taken to ensure that the lubrication system is not neglected as the engine oil plays a more significant part in engine cooling.

The Volkswagen system is neat and simple. A multi-bladed turbo fan is mounted on the shaft which drives the generator. It rotates in a sheet steel, semi-circular housing, drawing in air through the fan centre and directing it down to each pair of finned cylinders. The cylinders are shrouded above with carefully designed sheet steel covers. Below each pair of cylinders a contoured deflection plate is mounted centrally. Thus the air is directed over the full surface area of the cylinder cooling fins.

In order to shorten the warming up time a thermostat is mounted below the right hand pair of cylinders. This is a conventional bellows type and it operates a restriction on the through flow of air when the engine is cold. Two flaps in the fan housing are opened by the thermostat when the engine warms up, so allowing the full air flow to pass round the cylinders.

The car heating system is linked with the cooling system. In addition to the cooling air circuit there are two heat exchangers mounted one below each pair of cylinders. Basically these are sheet steel 'tanks' through which the exhaust pipe of each front cylinder passes. Air passing round the pipe inside the steel duct can be directed to the car interior. The air is directed to the heat exchangers via two hoses on the back of the fan housing.

It will be appreciated that the condition of that part of the exhaust system within the heat exchangers must always be in excellent order. Any leaks will result in exhaust fumes being forced directly into the car when the heater is in operation. Also the condition and fit of all the covers and shrouds is important. Sealing strips and grommets must all be properly positioned. If air leaks out the cooling capacity is reduced.

2. Removal of cooling and heating system components - general remarks

It is more difficult to dismantle the cooling and heating systems with the engine in the car then after the engine has been removed. Routine overhaul should coincide with engine overhaul but there may be occasions when it will be necessary to remove components from the system without disturbing the engine, for example:

a) The fan and fan housing may be removed to service a damaged fan, for generator overhaul, or to give access to the oil cooler.
b) The heat exchanger may be leaking and need renewal.

3. Fan belt - adjustment, removal and replacement

1 The Volkswagen fan belt needs more regular inspection than a water cooled engine fan belt usually gets because if it slips or breaks the consequences are more serious more quickly.
2 Adjustment takes a little more time than usual. There is no tension pulley. The pulley on the generator is split into two and the gap between the two halves governs the effective diameter. The gap is regulated by spacer rings. If the belt is too slack the gap between the two halves is decreased by removing one or more spacer rings. Spare spacers are fitted to the outside of the pulley.
3 The belt is correctly tensioned when firm thumb pressure on the

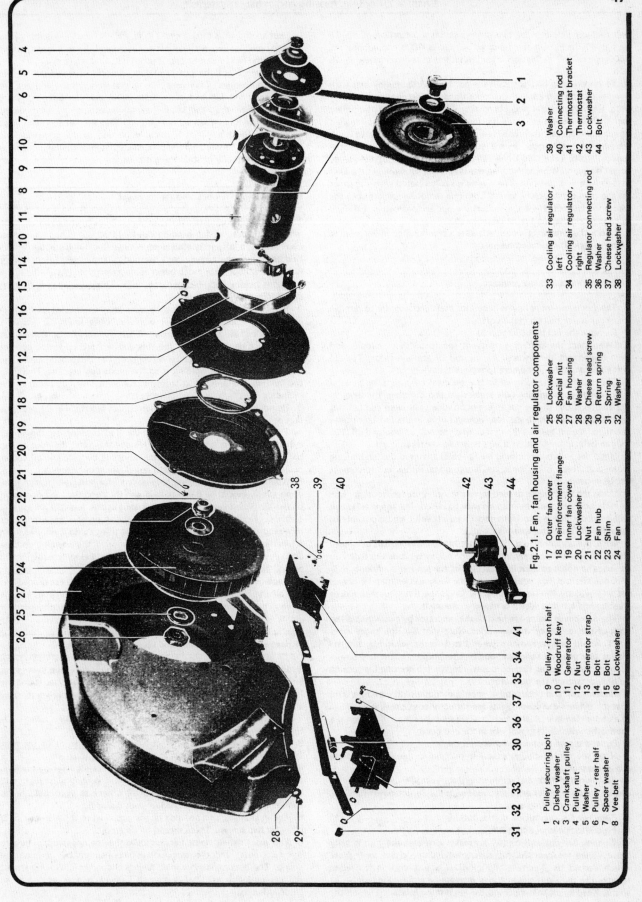

Fig.2.1. Fan, fan housing and air regulator components

1 Pulley securing bolt
2 Dished washer
3 Crankshaft pulley
4 Pulley nut
5 Washer
6 Pulley - rear half
7 Spacer washer
8 Vee belt
9 Pulley - front half
10 Woodruff key
11 Generator
12 Nut
13 Generator strap
14 Bolt
15 Bolt
16 Lockwasher
17 Outer fan cover
18 Reinforcement flange
19 Inner fan cover
20 Lockwasher
21 Nut
22 Fan hub
23 Shim
24 Fan
25 Lockwasher
26 Special nut
27 Fan housing
28 Washer
29 Cheese head screw
30 Return spring
31 Spring
32 Washer
33 Cooling air regulator, left
34 Cooling air regulator, right
35 Regulator connecting rod
36 Washer
37 Cheese head screw
38 Lockwasher
39 Washer
40 Connecting rod
41 Thermostat bracket
42 Thermostat
43 Lockwasher
44 Bolt

belt midway between the two pulleys causes a deflection of 12—18 mm (½—¾ inch). On the up-rated AB series 1300 engine and the 1500 engine this deflection is somewhat less at approximately 9—10 mm.

4 To remove the belt and split the pulley, lock the pulley first with a screwdriver in the edge of the inner flange against the top generator bolt. Remove the nut and clamp ring. The outer half of the pulley can then be separated from the inner half. To tighten the fan belt remove one spacer from between and then replace everything (with the moved spacer now on the outside of the pulley) and try the tension again. Take care when refitting the outer half of the pulley to get it square. It helps if the engine is rotated. This will get the bolt into its 'running' position. The engine is easily rotated with a spanner on the crankshaft pulley wheel. Continue removing spacers until the tension is correct. If all the spacers are out and the belt is still slack it is over-stretched and must be renewed.

5 Check the tension of a new belt after a few hundred miles running as initial stretch may need taking up.

4. Fan - removal and replacement

1 The fan is mounted on the generator shaft and in order to remove it the generator must be taken off.

2 Remove the fan belt (Section 3).

3 Disconnect the battery to prevent accidental short circuits and then disconnect the wires from the top of the generator. Tag the wires so that you know where to replace them.

4 The generator is clamped to the pedestal by means of a metal strap. Undo the clamping bolt at the right and disengage the strap. If the engine is out of the car it is a good idea to slacken the fan nut before undoing this strap. The locking notch in the fan belt pulley can then be used to hold the shaft whilst the nut is slackened off. Put the fan belt pulley back on if you have already taken it off.

5 Undo the four bolts holding the fan cover plates to the fan housing Note that there is an inner and outer plate with a reinforcement flange in between.

6 Undo the two cheese headed screws securing the fan housing - one at each side - so that the housing may be raised. The thermostat rod will need detaching also from underneath. It will then be possible to take the fan/generator assembly out.

7 With the assembly out of the car, refit the fan belt pulley and clamp the generator body in a vice. The pulley is needed so that you can use the notch to lock the shaft whilst the fan nut is undone.

8 Once the nut has been removed the lock washer may be drawn off followed by the fan. Behind the fan is the thrust washer spacer washers and fan hub which is keyed to the shaft.

9 The fan cover plates are held to the generator by two nuts on the ends of the generator through bolts. Note that the slot in the inner cover should face downwards when fitted to the generator, and the dished side goes into the fan housing. The purpose of the two covers is to provide a better suction point into the fan housing for cooling air drawn through the generator.

10 Reassembly and replacement should be done with care to ensure that the spacers and cover plates are correctly positioned.

a) Put the fan hub on the shaft making sure the spacer is also on the shaft otherwise the hub will jam in the end cover.

b) Put the spacer washer and shims on the hub.

c) Note the top of the generator in relation to the fan cover plate mounting studs.

d) Fit the outer plate and reinforcing plate in that order.

e) Put the inner cover onto the studs with the air slot downwards.

f) Tighten the securing nuts.

g) Place the fan in position on the hub.

h) Fit the lockwasher and nut.

11 Tighten the nut sufficiently to make sure that the hub is fully home. Then measure the gap between the fan and the cover plate which should be 2 mm. (0.080 ins). If any alteration is needed remove the fan from the hub and increase or reduce the number of shims. Keep spare shims behind the fan nut lockwasher. Tighten the

fan nut to the final torque of 43 lb.ft. and replace the assembly into the fan housing. Secure the generator strap and the four cover screws and spin the fan to ensure that it is not catching anywhere.

12 Replacement of the generator/fan assembly is a reversal of the removal procedure. Take care not to distort anything and get the clamp strap and fan backplate bolts all in position before any are tightened. See that the strap fits the contours of the pedestal bracket as before. When all is tightened spin the fan to ensure that nothing is touching. If it is it could be due to the generator not being set fully forward on the pedestal. Otherwise the fan housing is not seated correctly or something is bent.

5. Fan housing - removal and replacement

1 With the engine installed the engine compartment cover must be removed before the fan housing can be lifted out. The hinges must also be taken off. It is easiest to remove the lid from the hinges first and then the hinges from the body. It may seem unnecessary work but it makes for much easier replacement later. Mark the hinge positions before slackening off the bolts. This saves a lot of fiddling about later.

2 Remove the two hoses running from the fan housing to the heat exchangers. Take off the lower warm air duct under the cylinders by removing the securing screws. This will reveal the thermostat which must be detached as the link rod is attached to the control flaps in the fan housing. To disconnect the thermostat undo the hexagon headed bolt holding it to the mounting bracket. Then grip the bellows and unscrew it from the rod which runs up between the cylinders.

3 Remove the generator and fan assembly as described in the previous section.

4 There are two screws holding the fan housing to the upper cylinder covers - one at each side. Remove these and the housing can be lifted up and out. Do not force anything because the oil cooler projects up inside the housing and any strain could damage it.

5 Whenever the fan housing is removed - for whatever reason - the opportunity should be taken to examine the condition and operation of the air flaps inside. If these stick shut at any time the engine will overheat. If they are in a very poor condition and the expense of renewing them does not appeal, the best thing to do is remove them altogether. Their function is merely to shorten the warming up time and only in extremely low temperatures (well below freezing) is the engine likely to run over cold.

6 Replacement of the fan housing is a reversal of these procedures and all the joints of the ducting should fit neatly to prevent leakage of air. The air duct flaps must be reset as described in Section 8.

6. Heat exchangers - removal and replacement

1 Remove both the air hoses from the fan housing at the lower ends and take out the two screws securing the semi-circular plate round the inlet manifold adaptor pipe. Take off the air cleaner pre-heater hose at the lower end also.

2 Remove the securing screws and lift out the pulley cover plate followed by the engine rear cover plate.

3 Disconnect the warm air duct hose from the front of the heat exchanger underneath the car. It can simply be pulled off.

4 Disconnect the control wire from the operating lever by undoing the clamping screw in the toggle. This will probably be rusty and dirty so use plenty of penetrating oil otherwise you could break something which would just add to your repair list.

5 The exchanger is to one side of and attached to the warm air duct plate by two screws. These should be taken out.

6 The front exhaust pipe flange should then be released by undoing the two nuts; and the rear exhaust connection by undoing the clamp. The heat exchanger inlet duct is clipped to the main exhaust silencer unit also as this has a small heat exchanger section on it. Undo this clip.

3.4(a) Fan spacer and shims.

3.4(b) Generator the right way up.

4.10(a) Outer fan cover and stiffening ring.

4.10(b) Generator pulley split showing Spacers.

4.10(c) Replacing the generator pulley outer half

4.10(d) Fitting the fan hub to the generator shaft.

4.10(e) Inner fan cover. Note air slot (arrowed).

4.10(f) Secure the cover nuts.

4.10(g) Replace the fan.

4.10(h) Fan lockwasher and nut.

3.4(c) Tightening the fan pulley nut using a screwdriver to lock the wheel in the notch.

5.4. Lifting the fan housing off. Note thermostat rod (arrowed).

4.11. Fitting the fan assembly to the fan housing.

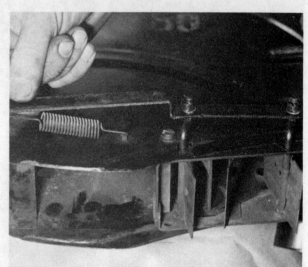

5.5. Checking the fan housing air control flaps.

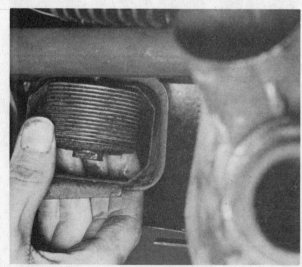

5.2. Unscrewing the thermostat bellows from the rod.

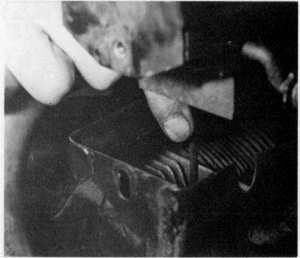

5.6. Guiding the thermostat rod between the cylinders when replacing the fan housing.

6.1. Removing the plate round pre-heater pipe.

6.9(a) Attaching lower cylinder plate to heat exchanger.

6.2(a) Removal of crankshaft pulley cover plate....

6.9(b) Heat exchanger and plate being fitted.

6.2(b) ......and rear cover plate.

7.2. Removing duct plate under right hand cylinders to get access to thermostat (engine and exhaust removed for illustrative purposes).

7 By moving the heat exchanger forward off the front exhaust studs it will then be possible to lower and remove it.

8 Before replacing a heat exchanger it should be examined carefully for signs of splits or severe corrosion or rusting. If it is damaged due to impact but otherwise sound it might be worthwhile having it straightened and/or welded. Otherwise fit a new one. Make sure also that the faces of the exhaust pipe flanges are perfectly flat. If they are distorted, steps must be taken to remedy the situation as any leak would be serious. Always fit new gaskets.

9 The replacement of the heat exchanger is a reversal of the removal procedure. Make sure that when it is offered up all the joints fit true and flush before the nuts and clamps are tightened. If the nuts and clamps have to be used to force the unit into position, rather than hold it in position, stresses will be set up and something will break sooner or later. Certainly sooner than it would normally.

7. Thermostat and controls - removal, replacement and adjustments

1 The thermostat controls flaps which restrict the air flow but do not completely obstruct it. If it should fail to operate therefore the engine will only be noticeably overheated in extreme conditions of high temperatures or hard use. The only indications of overheating are either a noticeable fall off in performance or the oil warning light indicating an exceptionally low oil pressure. It is essential to stop immediately either of these conditions appear as the engine will already have reached an undesirable state and will be seriously damaged if allowed to continue.

2 To check the operation of the flaps it is necessary to get access to the thermostat first. This is done by removing the right hand warm air duct plate under the cylinders. Remove the screws holding it to the heat exchanger and crankcase. The thermostat is accessible once the right hand lower air duct plate is removed. To adjust the flaps first remove the bolt securing the bellows to the bracket. Then make sure that the bellows is screwed fully on to the operating rod. Slacken the bolt which holds the bracket to the crankcase and then push the bellows unit upwards so that the flaps are fully open. The top of the bracket loop should now just touch the top of the bellows and the bracket bolt may be tightened. Then replace the bolt securing the bellows to the bracket (which will involve pulling the bellows down and closing the flaps if the engine is cold). If the thermostat is suspected of malfunctioning a check can be made on its length (excluding the projecting screwed bosses at each end) which should be at least 46 mm (1.8 inch) at a temperature (in water) of 65–70°C (150–158°F) or more. If you wish to set the thermostat so that the flaps are always open (i.e. if the bellows do not work and you have no immediate replacement) push the bellows and bracket up together into the 'flaps open' position and clamp the bracket at the raised position.

6 If the flaps themselves are suspected of jamming or being out of position on their spindles then the fan housing must first be taken off as described in Section 5. Both flap housings can be removed from the fan housing together once the eight securing screws are removed and the return spring unhooked. Examine the flaps and spindles for security and ability to stay in position. Once again, if there should be some doubt and the flaps are likely to jam shut they can be removed completely.

8. Heater controls

1 As previously explained the car is heated by ducting hot air from exchangers surrounding the exhaust pipes. When hot air from the exchanger is required the flap is opened so that the air pressure from the fan housing will carry it into the car. The warm air from the cylinder cooling fins has nothing to do with the heating system.

2 Should the heater efficiency drop the first thing to check is the operation of the flap control wires. These are connected to the flap operating arm on the side of the heat exchanger by means of a ferrule on the end of the wire clamped into a clevis. If the wire is broken on either side undo both. The clevis pin clamp screws are usually rusty so lubricate them well beforehand.

3 Once slackened the wire ends may be pulled out from the pins. Remove the plugs from the guide tubes. Inside the car remove the nut securing the right hand operating lever, remove the friction washers and pull the lever away. Then disconnect the hooked ends of the control wires and pull them out.

4 When fitting new cables grease them first and replace them in the reverse order of removal. Replace the sealing plugs securely in the guide tubes.

5 Having clamped the cable ends onto the flap operating levers make sure that they operate through their full range.

6 Details of the control wires and flaps for the heater outlets in the rear footwell are similar in principle to the heat exchanger flaps except that the cables are joined together where they are attached to the left hand control lever and cannot be replaced separately.

Access to the rear ends of the cables is by removing the rear seat and the vertical kick board in front of it. The cable end clamps can then be disconnected.

When renewing the twin wire assembly note that the longer of the two wires goes in the lower of the two guide tubes.

9. Exhaust system - removal, inspection and replacement

1 The Volkswagen exhaust and silencer is a complex unit made of heavy gauge material, which is expensive to replace. The silencer and tail pipe assembly is connected at five points on each side. These are (on each side):

a) to the exhaust pipe coming from the front cylinder through the heat exchanger (clamp).
b) to the exhaust port on the rear of the cylinder head (flange).
c) to the inlet manifold pre-heater pipe (flange).
d) to the heat exchanger (sleeve clip).
e) to the air inlet hose from the fan housing (clip).

The exhaust manifold has a small heat exchanger shrouding the upper pipes.

2 To remove the exhaust/silencer unit first remove the rear engine cover plate and the nuts, bolts and clamps which attach it at the ten locations. If some of the underside nuts and bolts are badly rusted buy new ones before attempting to get the old ones off. It is quite usual for them to break or need cutting. A complete set of the gaskets should also be acquired (two exhaust flange, two inlet manifold flange, two clamp rings) before disturbing the unit.

3 Once all the connections are loosened the silencer can be drawn backwards off the studs of the cylinder head rear exhaust port and lowered to the ground.

4 Depending on the reason for removal subsequent inspection and repair will have to be judged in the light of the seriousness of deterioration. The unit is made of heavier gauge material than more conventional exhaust systems. Thus small holes or cracks in the silencer may be patched and welded in the knowledge that the repair will last longer than on some other systems. This does not apply to the actual pipes leading into the silencer. If these are unserviceable repair is likely to be less successful. The flanges and connection to the other pipes must be examined for pitting, distortion or fractures. The mating faces of the flanges can be filed flat if necessary. The gaskets are thick enough to take up minor variations. Holts Flexiwrap and Holts Gun Gum exhaust repair systems can be used for effective repairs to exhaust pipes and silencer boxes, including ends and bends. Holts Flexiwrap is an MOT approved permanent exhaust repair. Holts Firegum is suitable for assembly of all exhaust system joints.

5 Before replacing the unit offer it up into position so that the line up of all the connecting points can be made without having to strain anything. If strain is necessary to make any connection then the likelihood of a fracture developing is greatly increased. It is worthwhile taking some trouble to heat and straighten any twisted parts.

6 Replacement of the system is a reversal of the removal procedure. First put new gaskets over the studs at the rear exhaust ports, offer up the unit and put the nuts on the studs enough to prevent it falling off. Then assemble the lower gasket rings and clamps loosely -

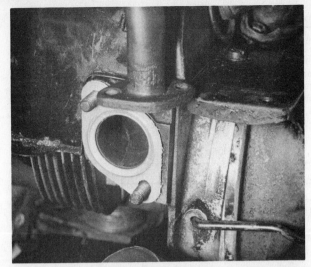

9.6(a) New exhaust gasket on No.2 exhaust port.

9.6(b) Offering the exhaust system up to the engine.

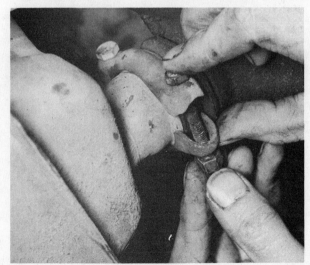

9.7. Fitting clamp joining the exhaust to the lower heat exchanger pipe.

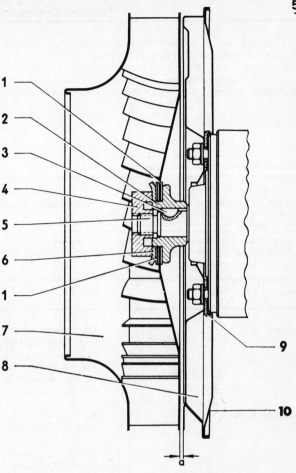

Fig.2.2. Fan assembly - cross section

1	Spacer washers	7	Fan
2	Fan hub	8	Fan cover, inner
3	Woodruff key	9	Reinforcement flange
4	Retaining nut	10	Fan cover, outer
5	Generator shaft		a= 2 mm (.080 in)
6	Lockwasher (dished)		

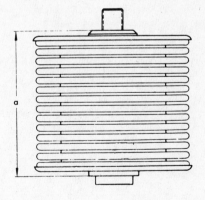

Fig.2.3. Thermostat bellows
Dimension a = 46 mm minimum at 65°–70°C (149–158°F)

but sufficiently tight to prevent them becoming dislodged. Then fit the pre-heater pipe gaskets in position and replace the bolts loosely. Finally assemble the heat exchanger connecting clips.

7 The pipe clamp and flange bolts and nuts should now be progressively tightened a little at a time until fully tight. Do not overdo the tightening on any of them. Finally tighten the heat exchanger clips. After running the engine for some miles, so that it has had the opportunity to heat up and cool down a few times, recheck the connections for tightness.

10. Fault diagnosis - cooling and heating system

It is difficult to detect heating systems faults in a rear engined air cooled car because the tell-tale head of steam is not there to show and no temperature gauges are used. The first indications over heating are a falling off in power and a flickering of the oil pressure warning light. When this occurs the car must be stopped immediately.

Over cooling is a rare experience in anything but sub-zero temperatures, even if the thermostat control was to be stuck wide open. The consequences are insignificant and need not be considered.

Possible causes of overheating and heater inefficiency are tabled below.

Symptom	Reason/s	Remedy
Overheating	Slack or broken fan belt	Renew if necessary and re-adjust tension.
	Insufficient engine oil	Top up as necessary and check for leaks.
	Engine ignition timing incorrect	Reset ignition timing.
	Thermostat and/or control flaps in fan housing stuck in closed position	Check operation and free as necessary.
	Oil cooler blocked	Remove, have tested and renew if necessary.
Heater ineffective	Air hoses from fan housing to heat exchanger insecure or damaged	Check hose and secure or renew as needed.
	Air hoses from heat exchanger to car interior insecure or damaged	Check hoses and secure or renew as needed.
	Heat exchanger flaps operating control arms and/or wires jammed, broken or disconnected	Check operation of control cables and operating arms and that arms are moving the flap spindles properly.

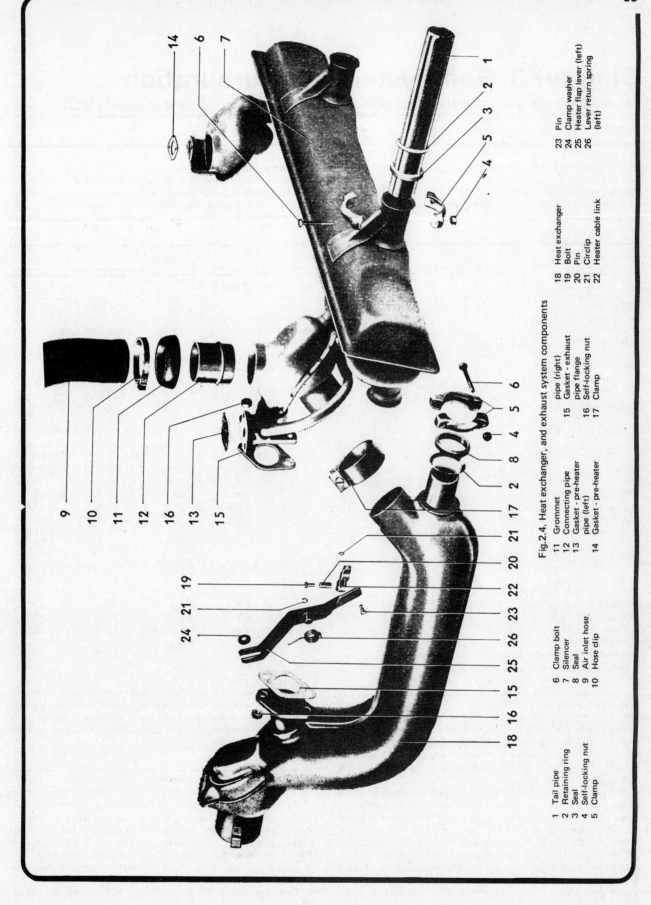

Fig.2.4. Heat exchanger, and exhaust system components

1 Tail pipe
2 Retaining ring
3 Seal
4 Self-locking nut
5 Clamp
6 Clamp bolt
7 Silencer
8 Seal
9 Air inlet hose
10 Hose clip
11 Grommet
12 Connecting pipe
13 Gasket - pre-heater pipe (left)
14 Gasket - pre-heater
15 Gasket - exhaust pipe flange
16 Self-locking nut
17 Clamp
18 Heat exchanger pipe (right)
19 Bolt
20 Pin
21 Circlip
22 Heater cable link
23 Pin
24 Clamp washer
25 Heater flap lever (left)
26 Lever return spring (left)

Chapter 3 Fuel system and carburation

For modifications, and information applicable to later models, see Supplement at end of manual

Contents

Specifications

Fuel tank capacity ... ...   8.8 Imp gal (40.0 litres)

Fuel pump

Make and type... ... ...   Pierburg mechanical VW7

Delivery rate (min) ... ...   400 cc/minute

Pressure (max) .. ..   3½ lbs/sq inch

Fuel filter L101 (1972-on)

Air filter ... ...   Champion U502 (1972 on)

Carburettor

Make (all types) ... ...   Solex

	1300		1500		August 1971
Type...	30 PICT 1	30 PICT 2	30 PICT 1	30 PICT 2	31 PICT 3
Venturi dia. mm.	24	24	24	24	25.5
Main jet...	0125	X125	0120	X120*	X130
Air correction jet	125Z	125Z	125Z	125Z	110Z
Pilot jet	55	55	55	55	g 52.5
Aux. fuel jet	–	–	–	–	42.5 (45 after Dec 71)
Aux. air drilling	–	–	–	–	130
Idling air jet drilling	–	–	–	–	100
Float needle valve. mm	1.5	1.5	1.5	1.5	1.5
Float weight. grams	5.7	8.5	5.7	8.5	8.5
Pump capacity/cc per stroke	1.3/1.6	1.3/1.6	1.3/1.6	1.3/1.6	1.45
Power fuel jet	–	–	–	–	100
Relief drilling diameter mm	–	–	–	–	1.4

* X116 on emission control models

1. General description

The Volkswagen fuel system is conventional in principle.

A fuel tank is mounted in the front luggage compartment and fuel is fed to the carburettor by a mechanically operated diaphragm pump which is driven by a pushrod actuated by a cam on the distributor drive shaft.

The carburettor is a fixed single choke downdraught type which incorporates a strangler, electrically operated, and an accelerator pump of the diaphragm type. The feed from the accelerator pump can also operate as a subsidiary fuel supply jet under certain conditions. There is a third fuel supply source in the form of an additional feed from the float chamber into the venturi. This is referred to as the 'power fuel system'. With the automatic choke a diaphragm operated pushrod overrides the choke spring slightly as soon as there is vacuum on the engine side of the throttle flap.

Another device fitted to the carburettor is an electro-megnetic cut-off valve which positively stops fuel from flowing into the inlet manifold. This is necessary because in certain high temperature conditions an over-heated engine can continue running on after the ignition is switched off.

2. Air filter - removal and servicing

1 To check the level of the oil in the filter bowl it is necessary only to undo the two clips securing the top cover and lift it off. The oil should be in line with the mark. At the same time the sludge deposits can be ascertained by dipping a suitable probe into the oil. The oil should be no less than 4–5 mm. deep above any sludge.

2 To remove the sludge the lower half of the unit should be removed from the carburettor.

3 To do this slacken the clip at the base of the cleaner and pull off

2.3(a) Remove the air cleaner clamp screw.

2.3(b) ....and stay screw on 1500 models....

2.3(c) ....and lift off the whole unit.

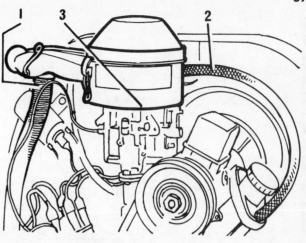

Fig.3.1. Air cleaner unit 1300

1 Pre-heater air hose   3 Retaining strap
2 Crankcase ventilator hose

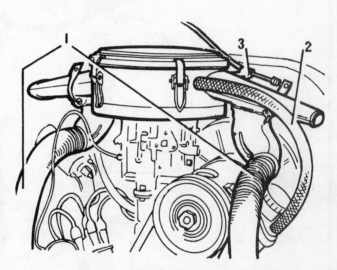

Fig.3.2. Air cleaner 1500 (later models)

1 Pre-heater hose (right side)   3 Automatic control cable
2 Crankcase ventilation hose   mounting bracket

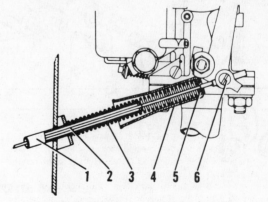

Fig.3.3. Throttle cable carburettor end
(early version)

1 Guide tube   4 Outer sleeve
2 Throttle wire   5 Retaining washer
3 Return spring   6 Clamp screw

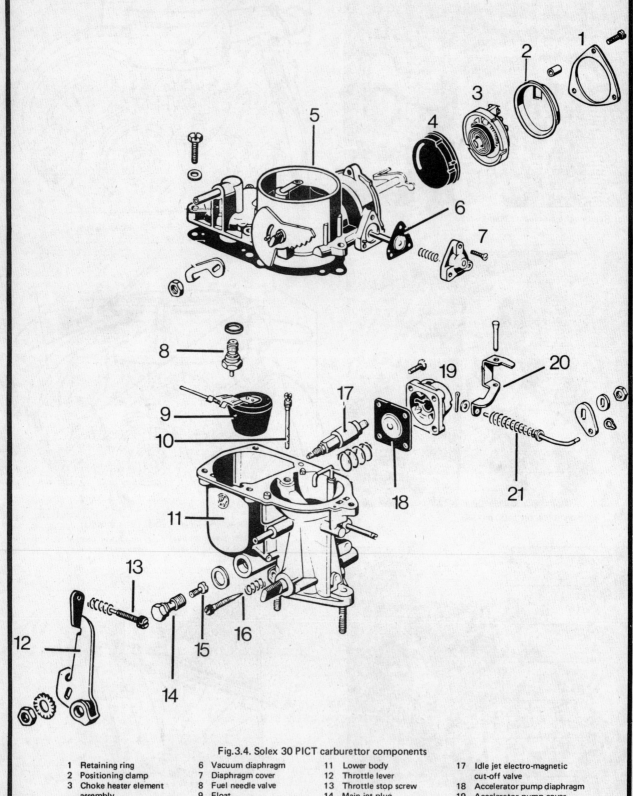

Fig.3.4. Solex 30 PICT carburettor components

1	Retaining ring	6	Vacuum diaphragm	11	Lower body	17 Idle jet electro-magnetic
2	Positioning clamp	7	Diaphragm cover	12	Throttle lever	cut-off valve
3	Choke heater element	8	Fuel needle valve	13	Throttle stop screw	18 Accelerator pump diaphragm
	assembly	9	Float	14	Main jet plug	19 Accelerator pump cover
4	Plastic housing	10	Air correction jet	15	Main jet	20 Pump cover
5	Upper body		and emulsion tube	16	Volume control screw	21 Lever spring

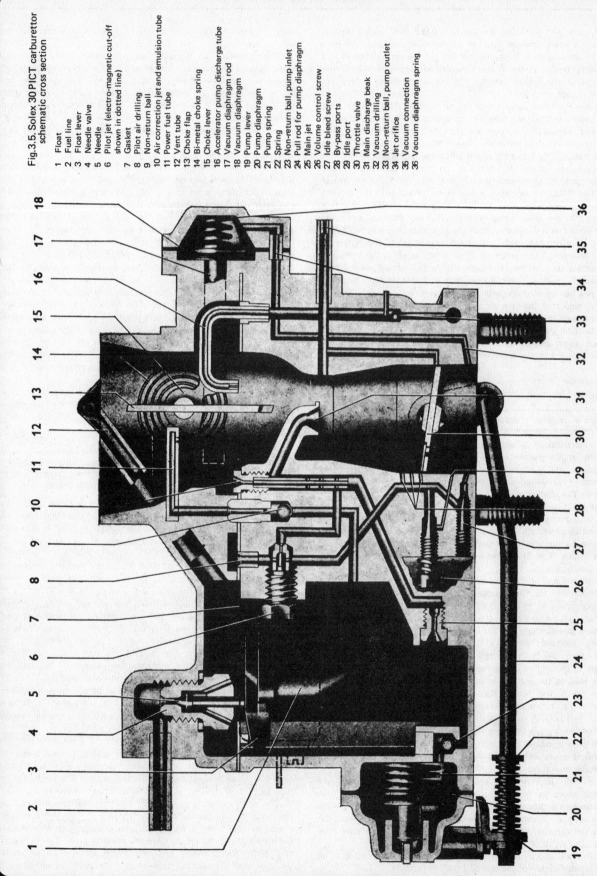

Fig.3.5. Solex 30 PICT carburettor schematic cross section

1 Float
2 Fuel line
3 Float lever
4 Needle valve
5 Needle
6 Pilot jet (electro-magnetic cut-off shown in dotted line)
7 Gasket
8 Pilot air drilling
9 Non-return ball
10 Air correction jet and emulsion tube
11 Power fuel tube
12 Vent tube
13 Choke flap
14 Bi-metal choke spring
15 Choke lever
16 Accelerator pump discharge tube
17 Vacuum diaphragm rod
18 Vacuum diaphragm
19 Pump lever
20 Pump diaphragm
21 Pump spring
22 Spring
23 Non-return ball, pump inlet
24 Pull rod for pump diaphragm
25 Main jet
26 Volume control screw
27 Idle bleed screw
28 By-pass ports
29 Idle port
30 Throttle valve
31 Main discharge beak
32 Vacuum drilling
33 Non-return ball, pump outlet
34 Jet orifice
35 Vacuum connection
36 Vacuum diaphragm spring

the air heater and crankcase breather hoses. On 1500 models there is a stay screw to be removed also. Lift off the bowl carefully otherwise you may spill oil all over the engine. Empty the contents away and thoroughly flush out the sludge deposits with paraffin. Check the condition of the gasket between the upper and lower halves and renew it if necessary.

4 Replace the lower bowl on to the carburettor. This can be done either before or after the new oil is put into it. Fit the top cover in place and reconnect the hoses and clips. It is a good idea to check also that the counter weighted flap on the air cleaner inlet tube is free to move. This flap only opens when the movement of air into the carburettor (at speed) is sufficient to swing it back thus letting cold air pass in. Otherwise the air is drawn from the pre-heater hose. The 1500 models have a double air intake into the cleaner each with a weighted flap. In 1967 however, a modification was made so that the control flap on the right hand side was controlled by and linked with the thermostatically operated air regulators inside the fan housing. The cable must be disconnected to enable the air cleaner assembly to be taken off. When refitting adjust the inner and outer cables so that the pre-heater flap lever is closed against cold air when the engine is cold. Check that it is open to cold air when the engine has warmed up - after 3—4 minutes.

5 It is important that the air cleaner assembly should be removed and replaced with care. Any excessive strain can cause it to crack at the bottom where the collar joins the carburettor. You will soon find out about this because the outside of the carburettor will get covered in oil and the level in the cleaner will eventually drop to zero.

6 Remember that in exceptionally dusty conditions the sludge build-up will be much more rapid.

3. Solex carburettor - description

The carburettor is basically a tube through which air is drawn into the engine by the action of the pistons and en route fuel is introduced into the air stream in the tube due to the fact that the air pressure is lowered when drawn through the 'tube'. A scent spray works on the same principle.

The main fuel discharge point is situated in the 'tube' - choke is the proper name for the tube to be used from now on - between two flaps which can block off the tube. One of these is the throttle flap - operated by the accelerator pedal and positioned at the engine end of the choke tube. The other is the strangler - which is operated by an automatic device.

When the engine is warm and running normally the strangler is wide open and the throttle open partially or fully - the amount of fuel/air mixture being controlled according to the required speed.

When cold the strangler is closed - partially or fully and the suction therefore draws more fuel or less air, i.e. a richer mixture to aid starting a cold engine.

At idling speeds the throttle flap is shut so that no air and fuel can get to the engine in the regular way. For this there are separate routes leading to small holes in the side of the choke tube, on the engine side of the throttle flap. These 'bleed' the requisite amounts of fuel and air to the engine for slow speeds only.

The fuel is held in a separate chamber alongside the choke tube and its level is governed by a float so that it is not too high or low. If too high it would pass into the choke tube without suction. If too low it would only be drawn in at a higher suction than required for proper operation.

The main jet, which is simply an orifice of a particular size through which the fuel passes, is designed to let so much fuel flow at particular conditions of suction (properly called depression) in the choke tube. At idling speed the depression draws fuel from orifices below the throttle which has passed through the main jet and after that a pilot jet to reduce the quantity further.

Both main and pilot jets have air bleed jets also which let in air to assist emulsification of the eventual fuel/air mixture.

On later engines a power fuel system is an additional source of fuel which improves performance at high engine speeds when the main jet cannot pass enough. It is in effect a supplementary main jet.

The strangler flap is controlled by an electrically operated bi-metal strip. This consists of a coiled bi-metal strip connected to the choke flap spindle. When the ignition is switched off the coiled metal strip is cold and the flap is shut. When the ignition is switched on current flows through the strip which heats up and uncoils - opening the choke flap after some minutes. If anything should go wrong with this electrical arrangement the flap will return to the closed position.

With the flap closed there are two features which partially open it immediately the engine starts. The flap spindle is offset so one side tends to turn around the spindle under the depression in the choke tube. Also there is a diaphragm valve connected to another rod attached to the flap spindle. Depression in the choke tube also operates this. If these devices did not exist no air at all would get through with the fuel. This would then flood the engine.

Finally there is another device - an accelerator pump. This is another diaphragm operated pump which is directly linked to the accelerator controls. When sudden acceleration is required the pump is operated and delivers neat fuel into the choke tube. This overcomes the time lag that would otherwise occur in waiting for the fuel to be drawn from the main jet. The fuel in the float chamber is regulated at the correct height by a float which operates a needle valve. When the level drops the needle is lowered away from the entry orifice and fuel under pressure from the fuel pump enters. When the level rises the flow is shut off. The pump delivery potential is always greater than the maximum requirement from the carburettor.

Another device fitted is an electro-magnetic cut-off jet. This is designed to positively stop the fuel flow when the engine is stopped. Otherwise the engine tends to run on - even with the ignition switched off - when the engine is hot.

4. Solex carburettor - removal, dismantling and replacement

Refer to Chapter 13 for Solex 31 PICT information

1 The carburettor should not be dismantled without reason. Such reasons would be for cleaning or renewal of the float and needle valve assembly and, in rare circumstances, the jets. Partial dismantling would also be necessary for checking and setting the float chamber fuel level.

2 Remove the air cleaner and then detach the accelerator cable from the throttle control lever. Undo the screw which holds the cable end to the link, withdraw the cable and remove the link so that it does not fall out and get lost. Do not disturb the spring and washer further back on the cable (on later models the spring is on the carburettor throttle lever). Pull off the wire connection clips from the automatic choke and electro-magnetic cut-off as necessary.

3 Undo the two nuts which hold the carburettor to the inlet manifold and lift the carburettor off. The exterior of the carburettor should be clinically clean before dismantling proceeds.

4 The first stage of dismantling should be to remove the screws holding the top to the base. Separate the two halves carefully and remove the paper gasket taking care to keep it from being damaged. It can be re-used.

5 To clean out the float chamber, invert the carburettor body; the float complete with pivot pin will fall out. If it needs a little help to get it out do not under any circumstances strain it in such a way that the pin or bracket are bent. When the float is removed the bowl may be flushed out and sediment removed with a small brush.

6 The needle valve is screwed into the top cover and when taking it out note the washer mounted underneath it. The simplest way to check this for leaks is to try blowing through it. It should not be possible to do so when the plunger is lightly pushed in. If in doubt, then renew the assembly, as a leaking valve will result in an over-rich mixture with consequent loss of performance and increased fuel consumption.

7 The accelerator pump diaphragm may be examined when the four

4.2. Disconnecting the throttle cable from the lever.

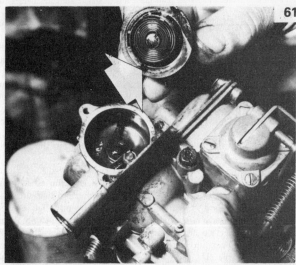

4.8(a) Automatic choke element with hook (arrowed) to engage the lever.

4.4. Separating the two halves of the carburettor.

4.8(b) Automatic choke cover indicating line up marks.

4.6. Needle valve in top cover.

4.9. Indicating the electro-magnectic cut off valve to the pilot jet.

cover securing screws and cover have been removed. Be careful not to damage the diaphragm. Renew it if there are signs of holes or cracks which may reduce its efficiency.

8 The electric automatic strangler may be removed for cleaning but do not use petrol on the cover. If any part is suspected of malfunction the whole unit must be renewed. When refitting the bi-metal spring the looped end must be positioned so that it hooks over the end of the lever. Then the cover should be turned so that the notch lines up with the notch on the carburettor. Do not overtighten the securing screws.

9 The main jet is situated behind a hexagonal headed plug in the base of the float chamber. This can of course be removed without taking the carburettor off the car. Remove the plug and then unscrew the jet from behind it with a screwdriver. The pilot jet is fixed similarly in the body alongside the accelerator pump housing. When cleaning these jets do not use anything other than air pressure. Any poking with wire could damage the fine tolerance bores and upset the fuel mixtures. The electro-magnetic pilot jet can be unscrewed from the carburettor body. If the jet is taken off the cut-off valve use two spanners. Do not clamp either the valve body or jet in a vice.

10 The air correction jet and emulsion tube is mounted vertically in the body of the carburettor by the side of the choke tube. This too may be unscrewed for cleaning. Blow through the passageway in the carburettor also when it is removed.

11 Before reassembly check that the float is undamaged and unpunctured. It can be checked by immersion in hot water.

12 The volume control screw which adjusts the amount of mixture metered for idle speeds should be removed and the tapered end examined. If it is scored, bent, or grooved it will be virtually impossible to set a smooth tickover.

13 The accelerator pump inspection tube may be inadvertently moved so check that the outlet points down in such a way that the jet of fuel cannot impinge on any part of the carburettor or open throttle on its way down to the inlet manifold.

14 If the throttle flap spindle should be very loose in its bearings in the main body of the carburettor then air may leak past and affect the air to fuel ratio of the mixture. In such cases the easiest remedy is a new carburettor. An alternative is to drill and fit bushes to suit but this needs some expertise and time.

15 Reassembly is a reversal of the dismantling procedure but the following points should be watched carefully. Do not forget the washer when replacing the needle valve. Make sure that the gasket between body and cover is correctly positioned. When refitting the accelerator pump cover, the screws should be tightened with the diaphragm centre pushed in. This means holding the operating lever out whilst the screws are tightened. Do not bend or distort the float arm when replacing it into the float chamber. When reconnecting the accelerator cable take heed of the procedure given at the end of the next section.

5. Solex carburettor - adjustments

Refer to Chapter 13 for Solex 31 PICT information

1 It must be emphasised that if the engine is running smoothly and performance and fuel consumption are satisfactory there are no adjustments that will materially improve any of these conditions beyond the manufacturers' specifications. If the engine is not performing as it should, be sure to check the ignition system before assuming that the carburettor is the cause of the trouble.

2 Assuming all components are clean and in good condition there are only two adjustments that can be made - these being the fuel level in the float chamber and the slow running speed.

3 To check the fuel level the carburettor must be fitted to the engine. The car should be standing on a level surface. Run the engine and then switch it off and remove the fuel line from the carburettor.

4 Remove the air cleaner assembly and then take out the five screws securing the upper half of the carburettor to the lower. Put a finger over the fuel inlet pipe (to prevent the little fuel in the top

cover coming out when the top is lifted) and take off the top cover and gasket.

5 The level of the fuel - with the float in position - should be 12—14 mm below the top edge of the float chamber. This can be measured by using a depth gauge or by placing a straight edge across the top of the float chamber and measuring down with a suitable rule. Do not measure too near the edge as capillary action up the side of the chamber could cause a false reading. If the level is incorrect it may be altered by fitting a washer of a different thickness under the needle valve which is screwed into the top cover. Washers are available in a range of thicknesses from ½ to 1½ mm. (it can be seen that the fuel level measurement has to be taken fairly accurately to be of any use in deciding whether alteration is necessary). If the level in the chamber needs raising a thinner washer should be fitted and vice versa. If you are tempted to try and alter the level by bending the bracket on the float - forget it. It cannot be done accurately enough to be of any use and more often than not the result of such attempts is either breakage or distortion. In the latter case the net result is a sticking float which gives you more problems than you had to start with.

6 Whilst the cover is removed it would be as well to check the condition of the needle valve as described in the previous section.

7 Reassemble the top cover with the gasket the correct way round, reconnect and clip the fuel line and replace the air cleaner. If wished the level may be checked again once any adjustment has been made but it should not be necessary provided the needle valve is in good order and the measurements were accurately taken.

8 Slow running adjustment is only carried out when the engine is warm and the strangler flap fully open.

9 With the engine adjusted on the throttle stop screw to a speed of 700—800 rpm (fast tickover) turn the volume control screw clockwise until the speed decreases. Then turn it back until even running occurs. Then continue to turn it another ¼ revolution. Note that if this adjustment is carried out before the engine is warm (and the automatic choke fully open) the throttle stop screw may still be resting on one of the steps of the cam attached to the strangler flap spindle. These steps are intended only to keep up the engine speed during the warm up period by restricting the throttle from closing fully even when the accelerator pedal may be released completely. When the volume control screw has been set the throttle stop screw may be re-adjusted to give a suitable idling speed. Do not try to set the idling speed too low - particularly if the engine is not in the first flush of youth. You will waste hours trying to achieve the impossible.

10 The setting of the accelerator cable into the throttle operating arm is important if full throttle opening is to be possible and also if excessive strain is to be avoided. Obviously one wants to have the throttle flap fully open when the accelerator pedal is fully depressed. At the same time one does not want to have the throttle fully open and up to the stop **before** the pedal has been fully depressed, otherwise the pedal pressure will stretch the cable and put considerable strain on the bracket and spindle. With the accelerator cable end in position but unclamped, move the throttle lever round to the fully open position, up to the stop. Then let it come back so that there is a gap of 1 mm between the stop and the lever. At the same time someone else should depress the accelerator pedal right to the floor. In this position the cable end may be tightened into position. Check the accelerator pedal movement to see that the gap is maintained when the pedal is pressed to the floor.

6. Fuel pump - removal and replacement

1 The fuel pump is mounted on the crankcase below the carburettor.

2 To remove the pump, first disconnect both fuel pipes. If the fuel tank is very full petrol may come out of the pipe leading from the tank, in which case it must be blocked. Chewing gum or Plasticene have been used but do not leave any behind. A better way is to find a length of flexible pipe which can be connected so that the effective end of the pipe can be raised higher in the air. Then slacken and remove the two nuts holding the pump to the crankcase and lift the

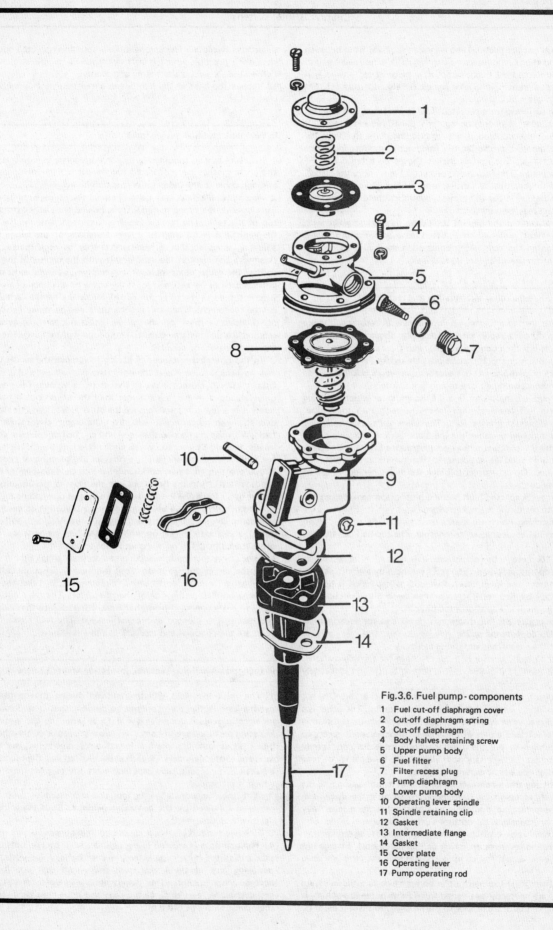

Fig.3.6. Fuel pump - components

1 Fuel cut-off diaphragm cover
2 Cut-off diaphragm spring
3 Cut-off diaphragm
4 Body halves retaining screw
5 Upper pump body
6 Fuel filter
7 Filter recess plug
8 Pump diaphragm
9 Lower pump body
10 Operating lever spindle
11 Spindle retaining clip
12 Gasket
13 Intermediate flange
14 Gasket
15 Cover plate
16 Operating lever
17 Pump operating rod

pump off. Pull out the pushrod and remove the gasket from between the pump and the plastic intermediate flange. It is not necessary to disturb the intermediate flange but stuff a piece of rag into it as if anything drops down it could be extremely difficult, if not impossible, to get it out.

3 If you are suffering from persistent fuel pump trouble of one sort or another (starvation of fuel or regularly punctured diaphragms) it is possible that the pushrod is not functioning correctly. Turn the engine until the rod protrudes the maximum amount above the intermediate flange. The normal gasket should be fitted under the intermediate flange. The rod should project 13 mm above the flange. It is possible to vary this by putting more or less gaskets under the intermediate flange. If the rod projects too much the diaphragm will be strained and may be punctured.

4 Before replacement the base of the pump should be packed with grease and a gasket, preferably new, fitted between pump and flange. Refit and tighten the nuts. After connecting the fuel lines run the engine to confirm that there are no fuel leaks.

7. Fuel pump - dismantling, examination and reassembly

1 Before dismantling a fuel pump with a view to repairing it make sure you can obtain a repair kit - that is a new diaphragm and filters and washers. If not then you are wasting your time and will be better off buying another pump. It may be possible to use a repair kit from another make of pump to cut out another diaphragm but this will be a somewhat expensive repair of a temporary nature.

2 The top part of the pump is a diaphragm valve which is spring loaded to cut off the fuel flow from the tank into the pump. Otherwise fuel would gravity feed. The valve opens as soon as the engine turns and fuel pressure lifts the diaphragm. At the side of the top section of the pump is a hexagon plug above the fuel inlet pipe. Removal of this plug gives access to the filter screen which can then be cleaned. Do not forget to block the pipe when doing this or fuel may flow out.

 If there is no suspected fault in the cut off diaphragm it need not be removed to get to the main diaphragm.

3 After scratching lining up marks unscrew the six screws which hold the two halves of the pump together. The top half can then be lifted off.

4 In order to remove the diaphragm it is first of all necessary to take out the operating lever pivot pin. This is held by a circlip at each end. First remove the small cover plate and gasket which is held to the lower body by two small screws. Then remove one circlip from the end of the pivot pin and force the pin out.

5 Press the centre of the diaphragm down and the lever can be pulled out. Do not lose the spring.

6 Draw out the diaphragm and spring assembly.

7 Inspect the diaphragm for holes or cracks in the flexible material. The material should be supple, if it is getting brittle and stiff renew the diaphragm assembly.

8 The condition of the two valves should also be checked. One is a petal valve of shim steel and this should lie quite flat. The other is a conventional disc valve which is an assembly staked into position in the top cover. Should either of these be malfunctioning it is easy to renew the petal valve but the other is slightly more difficult. It may be difficult to get the necessary parts also. If you have plenty of time to spare it might be worth waiting for spares.

9 When refitting the diaphragm make sure that the sealing ring fits snugly into its recess in the lower body. Then press the diaphragm down in the centre so that the forks of the operating lever may engage over the toggle at the bottom of the diaphragm pull rod. Still holding the diaphragm replace the pivot pin and refit the circlip.

10 The operating lever return spring can be fitted now. Engage one end on the inner lug in the pump body and snap the other end into position on the lever.

11 When refitting the top half of the pump make sure the inlet and outlet pipes are correctly positioned in relation to the lower half. If you have marked both parts prior to dismantling, this will present no

difficulty. Replace all six screws loosely and then press the operating lever to a position which is halfway through its full stroke. Then tighten the six screws alternately and evenly.

12 Repack the base of the pump with a multi-purpose grease such as Castrol LM.

8. Fuel tank and fuel gauge sender unit

1 The fuel tank is mounted in the front luggage compartment and there is a mechanically operated fuel sender which works via a float arm and cable to the indicator on the dashboard.

2 Access to the tank and gauge is from the luggage compartment First remove the lining material from behind the dashboard and on top of the tank. The fuel gauge sender unit is mounted in the top of the tank and has a snap fit cover. The back of the gauge has an adjusting screw so that if necessary it may be recalibrated. To do this move the lever at the sender unit with the cable still connected so that the gauge reads more or less empty. The lever must be kept pushed back as far as it will go. If the screw on the back of the gauge is now turned in the direction of the arrow the needle of the gauge can be set to zero. When this is done there will be about 1 gallon left on the reserve mark on the gauge. Assistance will, of course, be required to do this adjustment as someone will be needed to watch the gauge inside the car.

3 In the rare circumstances of having to remove the sender unit - a leaking float can be about the only reason - first unhook the cable from the lever. Do **not** undo all five securing screws. Take out four only. If one of these four is larger than the others put it back and screw if in a few turns and remove the other four. If you do not keep one screw in position you will drop the clamp ring into the fuel tank. With the clamp ring slack one end can be hooked over the hole in the tank itself and the whole unit lifted out. Examine the float for punctures. Replacement is a reversal of the removal procedure. If you want to fit a new cork gasket it will be necessary to remove the float arm from the body because the float is too big to pass the gasket over. Refit the long screw into a hole at one end of the clamp ring and put the whole unit back. Pick up the other screw holes in the clamp ring and tighten the unit down firmly. If you suffer from petrol smells after filling up with fuel the fuel gauge sender unit is often the culprit. The only answer is not to overfill.

4 From time to time it may become necessary to take the fuel tank from the car, if only to clean it out thoroughly. Disconnect the fuel gauge cable from the sender unit as already described and disconnect the vent hose from the side of the filler neck. The tank outlet pipe should be disconnected from the one which goes into the bodyframe and clamped or plugged to prevent leakage. The four tank retaining bolts are then undone and the tank can be lifted out.

9. Induction manifold - removal, inspection and replacement

1 The inlet manifold will be removed during the course of an overhaul or if there are reasons to suspect that it is damaged or incorrectly seated thus giving rise to air entering the system and affecting performance. It comprises two pipes jacketed together. One pipe carries out the normal function of conveying the fuel/air mixture to the cylinders via each cylinder head and the other acts as a heater. This second pipe uses heat from the exhaust manifolds to which it is clamped.

2 With the engine installed the fan/generator assembly must first be removed followed by the generator pedestal. Both these items are dealt with in Chapter 2.

3 Remove the carburettor as described in Section 4.

4 The manifold is secured to the cylinder head by two nuts on each side; and to the exhaust pipes by two small bolts on each side. Before removing any of these you must make sure that you have the necessary new gaskets. The gaskets are compressed on installation and cannot be re-used. Once the nuts and bolts have been removed, the manifold can be lifted off.

6.3. Fuel pump pushrod being replaced through new gasket on the intermediate flange.

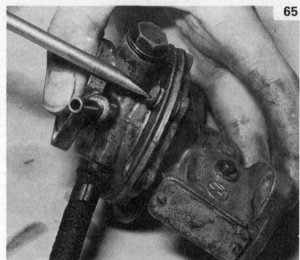

7.3(a) Undoing the main body securing screws.

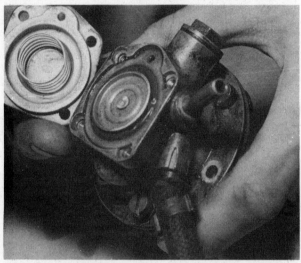

7.2(a) Fuel cut off diaphragm cover removed from top of pump.

7.3(b) View of the pump diaphragm and the inlet and outlet valves in the top half.

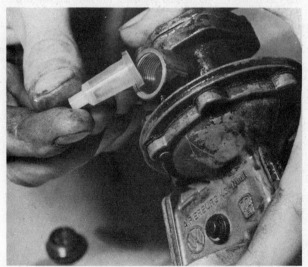

7.2(b) Fuel pump filter screen.

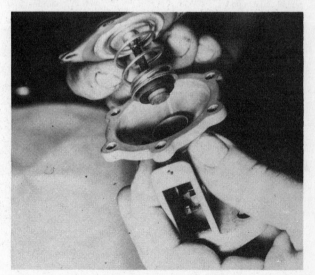

7.9(a) Fitting the diaphragm into the lower pump body.

5 Inspect the manifold and the mounting flanges for any signs of holes, cracks or distortion. It is possible to repair holes and cracks by welding or - if not very significant - with a resin filler. All the flanges should be flat on their mating faces and free from pitting. To check distortion the best way is to put the manifold in position, without gaskets, and see that all the mating faces and bolt holes match up. No stress should be necessary in order to achieve this. If necessary the pipe(s) may be heated so that they can be set correctly. Make sure any loose scale is removed from inside the pipes if this is done.

6 The pre-heater pipe ends may be carboned up and this should be cleaned away. (The reason for the small hole at one end is so that the gases flow in one direction. If both holes were the same there would be no differential, no flow and therefore no heat). Early models had the heat flow from right to left so the gasket with the small hole went on the left. This flow later changed from left to right.

7 Remove the old gaskets from the cylinder heads and manifold connections. Those in the cylinder heads will be compressed into place and will probably need digging out.

8 Take great care at all times to avoid dropping any foreign bodies into the inlet ports of the cylinder heads. It is strongly advised that a piece of cloth be stuffed in to prevent accidents of this sort because it may be impossible to retrieve them.

9 Replacement of the manifold is a straightforward reversal of the removal procedure. Always use new gaskets and be careful not to overtighten the mounting nuts and bolts. A stripped thread or broken stud can cause a lot of trouble unnecessarily.

10 In 1970 modifications were made to the cylinder head and inlet manifold. A twin branch pipe goes to each cylinder head and connections are made with flexible hoses and clips. This reduces the strains on the head mounting flanges but great care must be exercised to ensure that the hoses and clips are secure and leakproof.

10. Fault diagnosis

Unsatisfactory engine performance and excessive fuel consumption are not necessarily the fault of the fuel system or carburettor. In fact they more commonly occur as a result of ignition faults. Before acting on the fuel system it is necessary to check the ignition system first. Even though a fault may lie in the fuel system it will be difficult to trace unless the ignition is correct.

The table below therefore, assumes that the ignition system is in order.

Symptom	Reason/s	Remedy
Smell of petrol when engine is stopped	Leaking fuel lines or unions	Repair or renew as necessary.
	Leaking fuel tank	Fill fuel tank to capacity and examine carefully at seams, unions and filler pipe connections. Repair as necessary.
Smell of petrol when engine is idling	Leaking fuel line unions between pump and carburettor	Check line and unions and tighten or repair.
	Overflow of fuel from float chamber due to wrong level setting or ineffective needle valve or punctured float	Check fuel level setting and condition of float and needle valve and renew if necessary.
Excessive fuel consumption for reasons not covered by leaks or float chamber faults	Worn jets	Renew jets.
	Sticking strangler flap	Check correct movement of strangler flap.
Difficult starting, uneven running, lack of power, cutting out	One or more jets blocked or restricted	Dismantle and clean out float chamber and jets.
	Float chamber fuel level too low or needle valve sticking	Dismantle and check fuel level and needle valve.
	Fuel pump not delivering sufficient fuel	Check pump delivery and clean or repair as required.
	Intake manifold gaskets leaking, or manifold fractured	Check tightness of mounting nuts and inspect manifold.

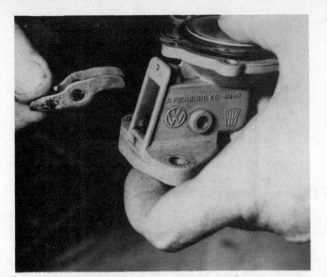

7.9(b) Putting the pump lever into position.

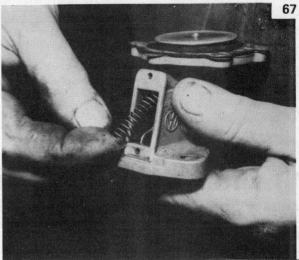

7.10. Fitting the pump lever return spring.

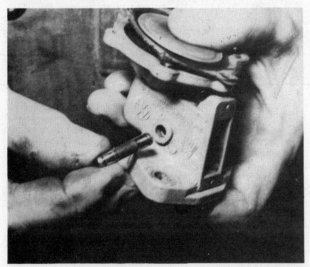

7.9(c) Fitting the pump lever pivot pin.

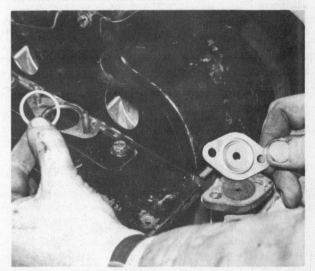

9.9(a) Placing the inlet manifold and pre-heater pipe gaskets.

9.9(b) Positioning the inlet manifold.

Chapter 4 Ignition system

For Modifications, and information applicable to later models, see Supplement at end of manual

Contents

Specifications

HT leads
    Type   ... ...   Champion CLS 4 boxed set
Spark plugs
    Type/gap   ... ...   Champion L86CC/0.8mm (0.032 in)
            or Champion L86C/0.7 mm (0.028 in)

Distributor and ignition timing
    6 volt (1300)... ... ...   ZV PAU 4R series (1965 to 1967)
    12 volt ... ...   113 905 205 series)
                  or 315 905 205 series) Bosch or VW (1968 on)
    Firing order 1 4 3 2
    Contact points gap ... ...   .4 mm (.016 ins)
    Automatic advance ... ...   Vacuum only or centrifugal and double vacuum

Coil - 6 volt ... ...   111 905 105 L
    - 12 volt ... ...   311 905 115 A

Static timing

1300 cc	Engine code F and E (low compression) to August 1970	7½° BTDC
	Engine code AB, AR from September 1970	7½° BTDC
	Engine code AC (low compression) from September 1970	5° ATDC
1500 cc	Engine code H and L (low compression) from following engine numbers:	
	H0204001 (Aug. 1966)	7½° BTDC
	H0879927 (Sept. 1967)	0° (TDC)
	HI124670 (Aug. 1969)	7½° BTDC

Timing marks

1300 cc   F range – Two marks on the crankshaft pulley, the left one when lined up with the crankshaft joint – 7° BTDC

               AB range – Up to and including October 71, one mark on the crankshaft pulley denotes either 5° ATDC or 7½° BTDC according to static timing required.
               After October 71 all pulleys are marked with one notch only denoting TDC. Advance degrees position must be calculated with a protractor.

1500 cc   Crankshaft pulleys have either 1 or 3 notches for engines with 7½° BTDC, use either the single notch or the centre notch. For engines with 0° the left notch of three indicates 0° (TDC).

General Note

    Developments and changes are continuous and with the advent of exhaust emission control systems these will intensify. When in doubt consult the VW agent.

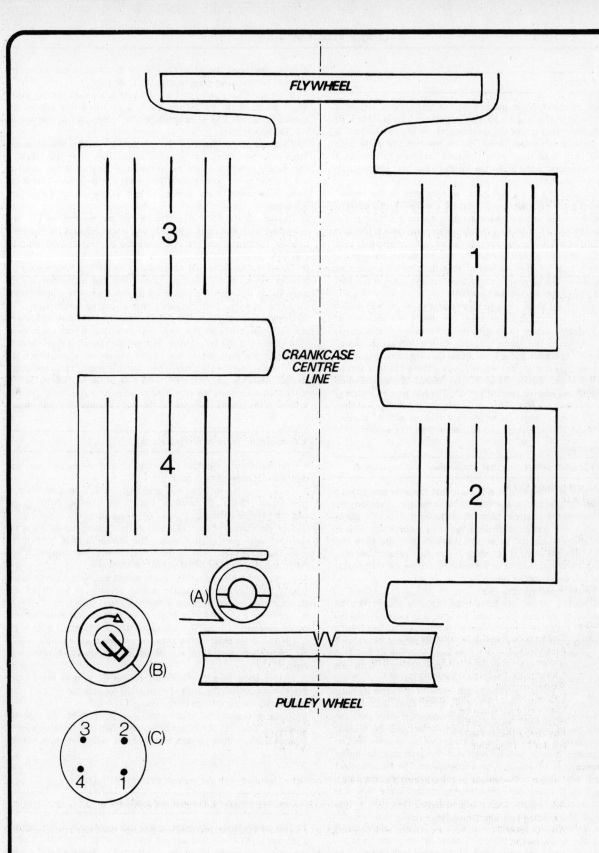

Fig.4.1. Static ignition timing diagram showing relative positions at the firing point on No.1. cylinder (See text).

A. Eccentric slot position in distributor drive shaft.
B. Rotor position relative to notch in the side of the distributor body.

1. General description

Ignition of the fuel/air mixture in the Volkswagen engine is conventional in that one spark plug per cylinder is used and the high voltage required to produce the spark across the plug electrodes is supplied from a coil (transformer) which converts the volts from the supply battery to the several thousand necessary to produce a spark that will jump a gap under the conditions of heat and pressure that obtain in the cylinder.

In order that the spark will occur at each plug in the correct order and at precisely the correct moment the low voltage current is built up (into the condenser) and abruptly discharged through the coil when the circuit is broken by the interrupter switch (contact points). This break in the low voltage circuit, and the simultaneous high voltage impulse generated from the coil, is directed through the selector switch (rotor arm) to one of four leads which connect to the spark plugs. The condenser contact points and rotor arm are all contained in and operated at the distributor.

Due to different spark timing requirements under certain engine conditions (of varying speed or load) the distributor also has an automatic advance device (advancing the spark means that it comes earlier in relation to the piston position). In the Volkswagen engine this device is operated by suction from the induction manifold. When the suction is high, for example when the throttle is almost closed at low engine speeds, the ignition is retarded. It advances when the throttle opens and reduces the suction. The low tension (battery) voltage of all cars up to late 1967 was 6 volts and the change was then made to 12 volts. It must be emphasised that no part whatsoever of either 6 and 12 volt systems can be used in the other system.

2. Contact breaker points - removal, replacement and adjustment

1 Volkswagen service agencies will insist that the only way to set a Volkswagen ignition timing correctly is by using special equipment. This will permit the points to be set not so much to a specific gap as to the cam dwell characteristics on the distributor shaft. This is doubtless correct but for those who have neither the time nor money available the alternative, which is a perfectly reasonable one, is to set the ignition according to the static timing marks, the breaker points gap and engine performance.

2 First remove the distributor cap.

3 Before starting to set the breaker points they should first be examined. Both surfaces should be smooth and clean. Neglected contacts will probably have a hole or pit in one surface and a corresponding hard peak on the other. It is impossible to set such contacts correctly so they must be renewed or cleaned up. This involves removal. If the contacts are clean continue with the adjustment procedure as described later in this section.

4 Early types of contact breaker points came in two separate parts with separate insulating washers and so forth. Even those earlier types are more often than not renewed nowadays with the one-piece assembly which comprises the fixed contact, moving breaker arm and mounting plate. This type is illustrated but in order that no mistakes occur it is as well to point out the principles to ensure correct reassembly of earlier types encountered. The fixed contact is the earth side so it is mounted and in contact with the distributor body itself via the base plate. The moving contact is the 'live' side and when assembled it must be insulated from earth. The current travels from the L.T. wire on the coil to the end of the spring arm along the spring to the contact or condenser. The end of the spring arm (and the wires connected to it) must be insulated from the distributor. Similarly the pivot point of the moving contact must be insulated. If this is borne in mind there should be no problem. When finally assembled the two contact breaker surfaces should line up.

5 To remove the points assembly first remove the securing screw which clamps the fixed point plate into position. The whole assembly may then be lifted up off the pivot post. A small screw and nut holds the spring end and the L.T. wires to the nylon insulation block and

if this is removed the wire connections can be removed. Later, the L.T. connections were simple clips (as illustrated).

6 If the points are being cleaned it is best to separate the two parts. This can be done by pulling the end of the spring out of the insulation block. The pivot insulation will come out of the hole in the fixed point plate.

7 To clean up the faces of the contacts use a very fine oil stone. Stone the two faces flat ensuring particularly that the 'peak' is completely removed. If the pit in the other contact is very deep do not try and grind it right out. The points can be adjusted once the peak is removed. Make a note to get a new set at the earliest opportunity.

8 Reassemble the two halves if separated and connect the L.T. and condenser leads and tighten the securing screw. Replace the assembly over the pivot post and put back the securing screw but do not fully tighten it down.

9 To set the gap it is first necessary to set the cam follower on the moving arm so that it rests on one of the four high points on the cam. To do this turn the engine by engaging a gear and pushing the car a little at a time until the cam follower rests on a high point.

10 Using a screwdriver in the notch, move the fixed contact plate so that a feeler blade of 0.4 mm thickness (0.016 inch) just slides lightly between the two points. Tighten the clamping screw and re-check the gap once more. Sometimes the action of tightening the screw moves the plate slightly. Then turn the engine again and check the gap when the contact is open on each of the four cams. If there is inconsistency then the cam may be worn or more likely the shaft is slack in the bushes. Try rocking the shaft sideways to check this.

3. Distributor - removal and replacement

1 The distributor should be removed only if indications are such that it needs renewal or overhaul.

2 Take off the distributor cap and pull the L.T. wire which runs to the coil off the coil terminal. Detach the pipe which fits to the vacuum advance unit.

3 The distributor is held in position by a clamp which grips the lower circular part of the body. The clamp itself is held to the crankcase by a single bolt. If the bolt is removed the distributor and clamp together may be lifted out of the crankcase.

4 It must be realised that if the bolt which secures the clamp to the distributor is slackened - and the relative positions of distributor and clamp altered - then the static ignition timing is upset.

5 The lower end of the distributor drive shaft has a driving dog with offset engagement lugs. These engage into corresponding slots in the distributor drive shaft. Being offset it ensures that the shaft cannot be inadvertently set 180° out of position when the distributor is replaced.

6 It is a good idea to renew the rubber 'O' ring in the annular exterior groove of the body if possible. This seal prevents oil from creeping up on the outside of the body.

7 Replacement of the distributor is a reversal of the removal procedure. See that the offset drive shaft dogs are correctly aligned otherwise they will not engage and the body will not go fully home.

4. Condenser - testing, removal and replacement

1 The condenser or capacitor as it is sometimes called, functions as a storage unit for the low tension current which flows into it when the points are closed. When the points open it discharges and sends a boost through the L.T. circuit to the coil. If the condenser does not function correctly the current shorts to earth across the contact points. This causes arcing and rapid deterioration of the points and also causes the spark producing properties of the coil to malfunction or cease entirely. If, therefore, persistent misfiring and/or severe burning and pitting of the contact points occurs, the condenser is

2.8(a) Fitting the fixed contact.

2.8(b) ....and screw, which is not tightened yet.

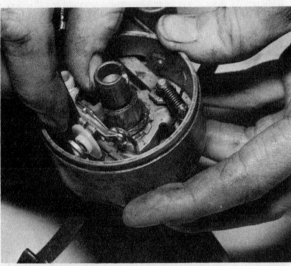

2.8(c) Positioning the sprung moving contact.

2.8(d) Connect the L.T. lead.

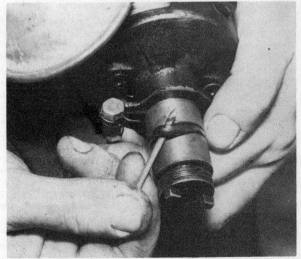

2.8(e) Setting the contact gap.

3.6. Removing the sealing ring from the distributor body.

suspect and should be tested right away.

2 To make a simple check on the condenser remove the distributor cap and turn the engine until the contact points are closed. Then switch on the ignition and push open the points with something non-metallic. If there is a considerable spark then this confirms that the condenser is faulty. Normally there should be a very mild spark - almost invisible - across the points.

3 To remove the condenser involves lifting the points out as well because the screw securing the condenser lead to the nylon terminal block is inaccessible otherwise. The condenser clamping screw may then be undone and the condenser removed. (Later types are different in detail making removal more simple).

4 Replacement is a reversal of the removal procedure.

5. Distributor - inspection, dismantling, repair and reassembly

1 Provided the component parts are kept in good order there should be little need to take the distributor apart except in cases of neglect or very high mileages. One of the indications is when the measured gap of the contact points is difficult or impossible to set accurately and consistently. This is due to wear of the shaft or shaft bushes or, more rarely, wear on the cams. When the shaft or bushes are worn the movement can be felt when sideways rocking pressure is applied to the top of the shaft.

2 In either case the only solution is to remove the distributor and renew the shaft or bushes or both. Alternatively one may find it simpler to renew the whole assembly. This might be necessary as the trend among manufacturers nowadays is generally this way. Check first that you can obtain the parts you may need.

3 Having removed the distributor, take out the contact points and condenser as described earlier.

4 The next job is to remove the driving collar from the bottom of the shaft but before doing this it is important to note which way it is fitted. See which way the driving dogs are offset in relation to the rotor arm notch in the top of the shaft. The notch and the offset of the dogs should face the same way.

5 When the relative position is noted clamp the collar in a vice and punch out the retaining pin. The collar may then be drawn off the shaft followed by the shims which control the endfloat of the shaft in the body.

6 Carefully unhook the pull rod from the vacuum unit to the contact breaker mounting plate and after removing the screws take off the vacuum unit. Then remove the mounting plate and shaft taking note of the position of the thrust washers.

7 If the shaft is obviously badly worn it must be renewed and it is most likely that the bushes will need renewal also.

8 The old bushes can be removed by driving them out with a long, flat ended punch from the inside. Take care not to damage the bore of the body. New ones can be drawn in with a long bolt and nut with a suitable flat washer at each end. New bushes should not normally need reaming but make sure that the shaft is not too tight a fit.

9 New distributor shafts when in position may need a variation in the thickness of the shims fitted between the driving dog and the body.

10 Reassembly is a reversal of the dismantling procedure. Make sure the driving dog is fitted the correct way round and when the pin is fitted peen the ends so that it cannot drop out.

6. Static ignition timing and distributor drive shaft

1 As stated in the introduction there should be little need to alter the timing except in cases of engine overhaul or distributor overhaul.

2 If the timing has to be reset from scratch the distributor should be removed first so that the distributor drive shaft position may be verified and set as required.

3 The distributor drive shaft may be removed and installed with the engine assembled and in the car provided that the distributor, fuel pump and fuel pump intermediate flange have first been removed.

(The distributor drive shaft also drives the fuel pump push rod from a face cam incorporated on the shaft). If the engine is being re-assembled after overhaul the drive shaft should be refitted after the oil pump, lower cover plate and crankshaft pulley have been refitted.

4 To withdraw the drive shaft from the crankcase first set No.1 cylinder to firing position. This is done by setting the correct mark on the pulley wheel to the crankcase joint. The offset slot in the top of the shaft should then be parallel with and towards the pulley wheel. (This, of course, assumes that the shaft is correctly engaged. If the shaft is incorrectly engaged turn the engine so that the slot is positioned the same but ignore the timing marks on the pulley wheel). This positioning is necessary so that a cut-out specially machined in the shaft lines up with the worm gear on the crankshaft. If it is not lined up the shaft will jam on the worm gear. Remove the central spring if fitted. The shaft may now be lifted up and out, rotating anticlockwise as it is lifted. The main problem is getting hold of it. If you do not have the special tool there are a variety of ways namely: jamming a piece of suitably sized wooden dowel into the centre hole, gripping the sides of the hole with a pair of long nosed expanding circlip pliers, jamming a piece of thin wooden batten into the slot.

5 When the shaft is successfully removed take out the thrust washers (one or two) from the bottom of the bore in the crankcase. This must be done carefully because if they are tipped into the timing gear chamber alongside, it may be impossible to get them out without stripping the engine.

6 To replace the distributor drive shaft, first put the thrust washers in position in the base by dropping them down over a suitable piece or rod. This will guide them where you want them to go.

7 Next turn the engine so that No.1 piston is in the correct firing position - on the compression stroke. To find the compression stroke with the distributor drive shaft removed is not easy because there are no reference points. The only sure way is to remove No.1 spark plug and turn the engine until compression is felt when the timing marks come into line. It is easy to feel the compression by placing a finger over the plug hole. If the right hand rocker cover is removed the compression stroke can also be pinpointed when both valves are closed.

8 The distributor drive shaft should now be lowered into the crankcase with the offset slot positioned slightly anticlockwise from its final correct position as detailed in paragraph 4. When it is lowered into mesh with the crankshaft worm gear it will turn slightly clockwise to the final correct position. Should you position the shaft too far anticlockwise, or not far enough, it will not go into position for the reasons given in paragraph 4. Provided, therefore, that the timing marks on the pulley are correct, and No.1 piston is on compression, it is practically impossible to fit the drive shaft incorrectly meshed.

9 With the engine and distributor drive shaft set and not moved from the position as described in the preceding paragraph the distributor may be placed in position with the shaft lined up so that the eccentric dogs engage the eccentric slots. Provided the clamp has been undisturbed no further adjustment is necessary after the clamp securing bolt has been replaced and tightened.

10 If the clamp ring has been slackened the body of the distributor should be turned so that the centre line of the rotor arm electrode matches up with the notch in the edge of the distributor body. This gives the near correct position. Final adjustment is made after the contact points have been checked and the gap set. With the crankshaft at the No.1 firing position the contact points should just be opening. To do this with precision the distributor body should be turned clockwise a fraction from the setting mark until the points are shut. The body is then turned anticlockwise until they are just open. This point is best determined electrically. Using a bulb or voltmeter make a connection from the moving contact to earth via the bulb or voltmeter. Switch on the ignition. There will be a light or reading when the points open. At this position tighten the distributor clamp bolt.

11 No two engines are exactly the same and when the car is road tested the performance may indicate that the ignition timing needs

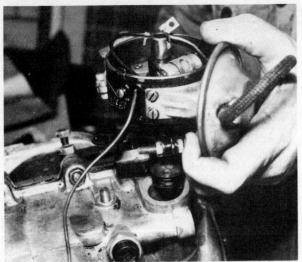

3.7(a) Placing the distributor in the crankcase.

3.7(b) Tightening the distributor securing bolt.

6.6. Lowering the distributor drive shaft thrust washer over a suitable rod.

6.7. Crankcase centre line and static timing marks on crankshaft pulley (arrowed).

6.8. Distributor drive shaft offset slot in correct position for No. 1 cylinder firing point.

minor adjustment still. Sluggish acceleration through the gears indicates that the timing may need advancing a little more (turn the distributor body anticlockwise). Conversely, 'pinking' and inflexibility at low engine revolutions would indicate that the timing is too far advanced and needs retarding a little (turn the distributor body clockwise). One word of warning - do not over-advance the timing - it can cause damage if allowed to persist. Remember the Beetle engine is not designed, in standard form, for rocket-like acceleration. It will however cruise all day flat out in top gear. Its cruising speed is maximum speed (which makes it so good for motorway work).

7. Spark plugs and H.T. leads

1   The correct functioning of the spark plugs is vital for the correct running and efficiency of the engine. It is essential that the plugs fitted are appropriate for the engine, and the suitable type is specified at the beginning of this chapter. Is this type is used and the engine is in good condition, the spark plugs should not need attention between scheduled replacement intervals. Spark plug cleaning is rarely necessary and should not be attempted unless specialised equipment is available as damage can easily be caused to the firing ends.
2   Make sure you use the correct plugs as listed in the specifications. Every type of engine has its own characteristics calling for a certain spark plug. A different type may be too 'cold' causing deposits to form on the electrodes which would normally burn off. This would result in poor sparking and eventual misfiring. Other plugs may be too 'hot'. These are much more dangerous as the electrodes would overheat and burn away and localised overheating could burn a hole in the piston.
3   Spark plugs are generally reliable and should give no trouble between service intervals of about twelve months, after which time they should be renewed. To remove the spark plugs it is best to use the special plug spanner supplied with the vehicle. This is quite conventional except that a rubber insert is fitted which grips the plug and enables easier removal through the cover plate.
4   The colour of a normally operating plug is a dirty greyish brown and any deposits on it are usually light. Whitish deposits indicate weak fuel mixtures or overheating, whereas blackish deposits indicate over-rich fuel mixture.
5   The electrodes must be in good condition, which means unburnt and comparable to the original length. The easiest way to assess deterioration is by comparison with a new plug. If there is any doubt about the condition of the spark plugs they should be renewed. The spark plugs should be adjusted with a spark plug adjusting tool and then measured with a feeler gauge to the specified gap. The correct gap is 0.7 or 0.8 mm (0.028 in or 0.032 in) depending on which of the recommended plugs are fitted.
6   When renewing the plugs make sure that the seating in the cylinder head where the plug fits is clear of grit or other things that could cause a poor seal.
7   The leads for the plug must be examined carefully along their length and at each end. The insulation should be clean, uncracked and undamaged in any other way. The metal ends should be free of corrosion. Everything should be dry. Renew any doubtful items and do not try to make do with repairs using insulating tape or such. It is not worth it.

8. Coil - testing

1   The coil serves to convert the battery current to the high voltage required to generate a spark at the spark plugs. It consists of a primary winding (low tension) and a secondary winding (high tension) which delivers the high voltage to the distributor rotor and thence to the plugs.
2   It is not normally tested separately, but during the tests applied to the whole ignition system in the course of diagnosing some fault.

The testing involves checking that current flows through the primary windings and that the secondary winding delivers a high voltage. As this is most easily done with the coil in circuit normally no separate procedure is given for a coil which is taken out of circuit.

9. Fault diagnosis

1   Failure of the engine to start easily, misfiring and poor acceleration and fuel consumption can usually be attributed to faults in the ignition system assuming, of course, that the engine is otherwise in reasonable condition. Volkswagen engines have a tendency to be fussy when starting hot. Do not attribute this to ignition until you have tried the hot start method of first pressing slowly the accelerator pedal right on the floor and holding it there before operating the starter motor. This overcomes the tendency to flood the warm engine with excess fuel.
2   The table shows the logical progression to be followed in any circumstance where the ignition is being checked for correct operation. Do not by-pass any part of this procedure unless the fault is particularly obvious and rectification solves the problem. Such obvious faults would be broken or detached wires. It is assumed that the battery is in good condition and fully charged. It is impracticable to test the circuit otherwise. It also assumes that the battery is connected properly and that the starter motor turns the engine over normally.
3   To disperse moisture, Holts Wet Start can be very effective. Holts Damp Start should be used for providing a sealing coat to exclude moisture from the ignition system, and in extreme difficulty, using Holts Cold Start will help to start a car when only a very poor spark occurs.

FAULT	CHECK
No start or starts with fuss and difficulty.	1 Remove H.T. lead from centre of distributor cap and verify that spark jumps to earth when engine is turned. If it does, the fault lies in the rotor arm, distributor cap, plug leads or plugs which should be checked in that order. 2 If no spark from coil HT lead check the LT circuit in the following order: a) Disconnect L.T. lead from terminal 15 of coil and with a bulb or voltmeter check that current is coming to the end of the lead when the ignition is switched on. If not check wiring from ignition switch. b) Remove the distributor cap. Turn the engine until the points are closed. Switch

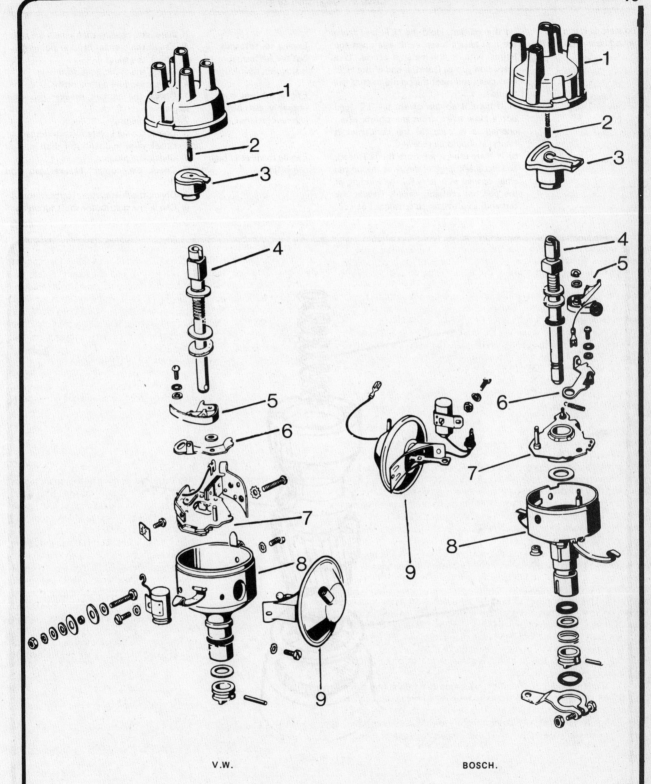

Fig.4.2. Distributor — components

1 Cap
2 Carbon brush and
   spring
3 Rotor
4 Shaft and cam
5 Moving contact
6 Fixed contact
7 Contact base
   plate
8 Distributor body
9 Vacuum advance
   unit

V.W.   BOSCH.

no start or starts
with fuss and difficulty

on the ignition. Hold the H.T. lead from the coil near a metal earth and open the points with a non-metallic article. If a spark now jumps from the end of the H.T. lead clean and reset the points to cure the trouble.

c) If there is no spark from the H.T. lead but a large spark from the points when opened as in para (b) the condenser is faulty. It should be renewed.

d) If there is no spark from the H.T. lead, and no spark large or small at the points when opened as in para (b) the winding of the coil has probably failed. Repeat the test with a voltmeter on terminal 1 of coil.

Engine starts readily
but the performance
is sluggish, no misfiring.

Engine misfires, runs
unevenly, cuts out at
low revolutions only.

Engine misfires at high
revolutions.

If there is no reading then renew the coil.
1   Check the contact breaker points gap.
2   Check the plugs.
3   Check the static ignition timing.
4   Check the fuel octane rating.
1   Check the contact breaker gap (too large).
2   Check the plugs.
3   Check the fuel system (carburettor).
4   Check wear in distributor shaft.
1   Check the plugs.
2   Check the contact breaker gap (too small).
3   Check the fuel system (carburettor).
4   Check the distributor shaft for wear.

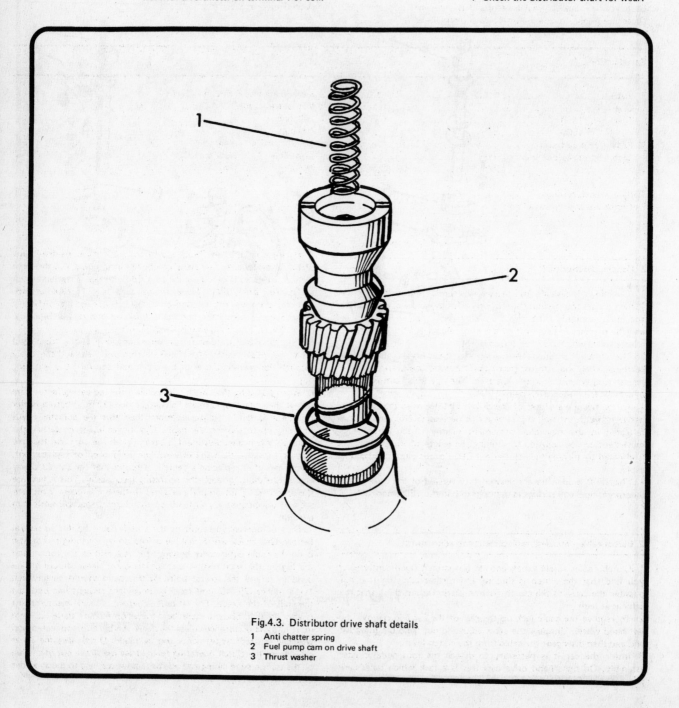

Fig.4.3. Distributor drive shaft details

1   Anti chatter spring
2   Fuel pump cam on drive shaft
3   Thrust washer

Chapter 5 Clutch

Contents

Specifications

Type...	Single plate disc Fichtel and Sachs
Operation	Mechanical - cable
Diameter - 1300	180 mm
- 1500	200 mm
Pedal free play travel	10—20 mm (.4 — .8 ins)
Clutch spring colour code - 1300	Light blue (3) Dark blue (3)
- 1500	White (6) Red (3)

Torque wrench settings

Clutch cover to flywheel bolts	18 lb.ft. (2.5 mkg)

1. General description

The clutch is a single disc design and incorporates a driven plate (which carries the friction material on each side) and a pressure plate and cover assembly. The pressure plate is tensioned by coil springs and the pressure is taken off by a central release ring linked to three release levers which pivot on the cover.

The clutch operating lever pivots in the forward end of the gearbox casing and a thrust bearing on the inner end bears on to the release ring when the arm is operated. The operating arm is moved by a cable from the clutch pedal.

As the friction surfaces of the driven plate wear so the clearance between the thrust ring and release ring decreases. This clearance is reflected in the free play movement of the clutch pedal. This movement can be adjusted by altering the length of the cable. This is effected by turning the adjuster nut fitted to the clutch end of the cable.

The 1500 models have a heavier duty version of the cover plate incorporating 9 coil springs as opposed to 6 in the 1300 model.

2. Clutch cable - removal, replacement and adjustment

1 Clutch cables rarely break and do not stretch significantly so if you find that the clutch is slipping and further adjustment is not possible the cause is the clutch friction plate. Do not think that the cable is at fault.

2 To remove the cable jack up the rear of the car and remove the left hand wheel. Unscrew the cable adjusting nut from the threaded end and then disengage the cable from the clutch lever.

3 Inside the car it is necessary to detach the foot pedal cluster assembly. On right hand drive cars this is a task which takes care and patience. For details refer to Chapter 9.

4 Having unhooked the front end of the cable it can be drawn out of the guide tube. A new cable can be fed into the tube in the same manner although it may be a bit of a fiddle to get it started as you are working partly blind. Make sure the cable is well greased and try and keep the grease off the interior trim and seats. The real difficulty comes when hooking the end on to the lever and reassembling the pedal cluster. This is covered in Chapter 9.

5 Once the cable has been connected properly at the front, and after the pedal cluster has been reassembled, replace the cable through the operating lever at the other end and refit the adjusting nut.

6 When adjusting the clutch, the pedal is the indicating factor. The top of the pedal should move forward ½ inch (12 mm) before firmer resistance is felt. If it moves more than this the adjuster needs screwing up to shorten the cable. If it moves less then slacken the adjuster. When the adjustment is taken up all the way and the free play is excessive then the driven plate is in need of replacement. Sometimes after replacing a cable it is found that the threaded rear end is too short to reach the operating lever easily. This is because the other end is not properly engaged in the hook recess. With luck a bit of waggling back and forth on the clutch pedal will settle it in position.

7 Stiff or uneven operation of the clutch could be due to several factors. One check worth making before doing anything too drastic is on the cable outer cover between the rear end of the tunnel and the lug on the transmission casing. The outer sleeve should have a bend in it and the lowest point of this bend should be between 1—1¾ inches (25—45 mm) from an imaginary straight line between the ends of the sleeve. The latitude is generous so the measurement is easy enough. Should there be a variation outside these limits (a most unusual occurrence unless the sleeve has been disconnected and wrongly refitted) adjustments can be made. Disconnect the inner cable from the clutch operating lever, draw the sleeve out of the lug on the transmission casing and add or remove washers to the shoulder of the sleeve as required.

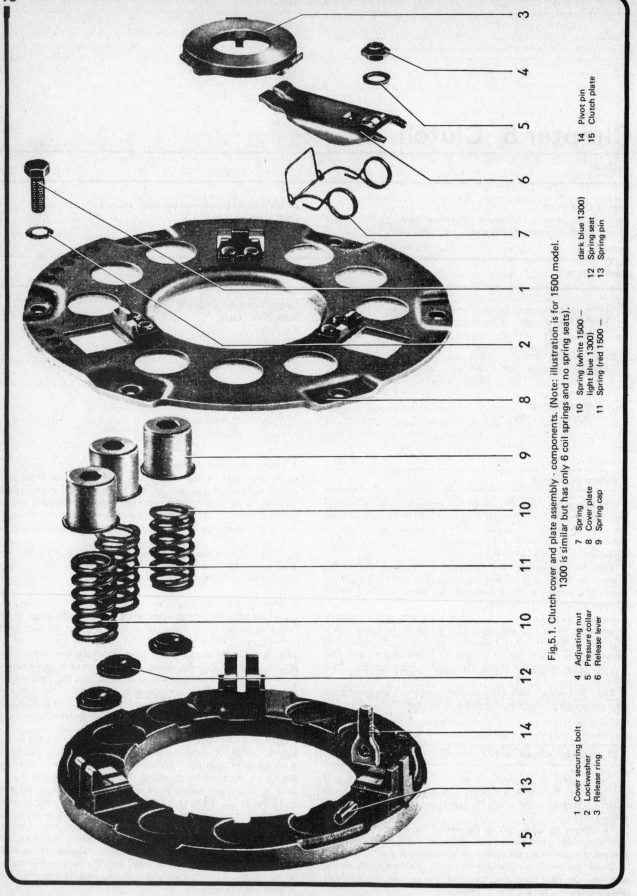

Fig.5.1. Clutch cover and plate assembly - components. (Note: illustration is for 1500 model. 1300 is similar but has only 6 coil springs and no spring seats).

1	Cover securing bolt	4	Adjusting nut	7	Spring	10	Spring (white 1500 —		dark blue 1300)	14	Pivot pin
2	Lockwasher	5	Pressure collar	8	Cover plate		light blue 1300)	12	Spring seat	15	Clutch plate
3	Release ring	6	Release lever	9	Spring cap	11	Spring (red 1500 —	13	Spring pin		

3. Clutch assembly - removal, inspection and replacement

1 Remove the engine as described in Chapter 1.
2 Mark the flywheel and clutch cover with a punch so that they may be lined up on replacement if the old cover is being fitted again.
3 Working with a diagonal rotation slacken the six mounting bolts which hold the clutch cover to the flywheel - slackening each one a little at a time until the tension on the pressure springs is completely relieved. Lift off the cover and clutch driven plate.
4 The clutch driven plate should be inspected for wear and for contamination by oil. Wear is gauged by the depth of the rivet heads below the surface of the friction material. If this is less than 0.025 inch (0.6 mm) the linings are worn enough to justify renewal.
5 Examine the friction faces of the flywheel and clutch pressure plate. These should be bright and smooth. If the linings have worn too much it is possible that the metal surfaces may have been scored by the rivet heads. Dust and grit can have the same effect. If the scoring is very severe it could mean that even with a new clutch driven plate, slip and juddering and other malfunctions will recur. Deep scoring on the flywheel face is serious because the flywheel will have to be removed and machined by a specialist, or renewed. This can be costly. The same applies to the pressure plate in the cover although this is a less costly affair. If the friction linings seem unworn yet are blackened and shiny then the cause is almost certainly due to oil. Such a condition also requires renewal of the plate. The source of oil must be traced also. It will be due to a leaking seal on the transmission input shaft (Chapter 6 gives details of renewal) or on the front of the engine crankshaft (see Chapter 1 for details or renewal).
6 If the reason for removal of the clutch has been because of slip and the slip has been allowed to go on for any length of time it is possible that the heat generated will have adversely affected the pressure springs in the cover. Some or all may have been affected with the result that the pressure is now uneven and/or insufficient to prevent slip, even with a new friction plate. It is recommended that under such circumstances a new assembly is fitted.
7 Although it is possible to dismantle the clutch cover assembly and, in theory, renew the various springs and levers the economics do not justify it. Clutch cover assemblies are available on an exchange basis. The component parts for their overhaul are held at the Central Reconditioning Depots and are not readily available at the Store Depots. It will probably be necessary to order an assembly in advance as most agencies other than the large Central Depots carry stocks only sufficient to meet their own requirements. However, it is possible to get assemblies from reputable manufacturers other than Volkswagen; Borg and Beck for instance.
8 If a new clutch cover is to be fitted make certain that the 3 clips, one at each outer end of the release levers, are prised out and discarded. No mention may be made of their presence when a new unit is acquired.
9 When replacing the clutch, hold the cover and support the friction disc on one finger through the centre. Be sure that the facing with radial lines goes towards the flywheel (greater hub projection away from flywheel). Position the cover so that the locating marks line up. If a new cover is being fitted it will be necessary to check whether there are any imbalance marks on either the flywheel or cover. On the flywheel this can be indicated by a 5 mm diameter countersunk hole or a white paint mark on the outer edge. On the clutch cover it would be indicated by a white paint mark on the outer edge. If only one (flywheel or cover) has an imbalance mark it does not matter how the cover is fitted. If both have marks make sure that they are 180º apart (i.e. on opposite sides of the circle).
10 Replace the six securing bolts and screw them up evenly just enough to grip the friction plate but not enough to prevent it being

moved. It is important to line up the central splined hub with the roller bearing in the counterbore of the flywheel locking bolt. If this is not done it will be impossible to refit the engine to the transmission. It is possible to centralise them by eye but a simple surer way is to select a suitable piece of bar or wooden dowel which will fit snugly into the flywheel nut and round which some adhesive tape can be wound to equal the diameter inside the friction plate boss. By inserting this the friction plate can be moved and centralised with sufficient accuracy.
10 Finally tighten up the six cover securing bolts evenly and diagonally a little each at a time to a final torque of 18 lb.ft.
11 Before refitting the engine after a clutch overhaul check the transmission input shaft oil seal (Chapter 6) and the clutch release operating mechanism (see Section 5).
12 Before finally offering up the engine dust the splines of the gearbox input shaft (which should, of course, be clean and in good condition) with a little graphite or molybdenum powder. Also put a little molybdenum paste (not oil or grease) on the face of the release bearing and clutch release ring.

4. Clutch release operating mechanism - inspection and repair

1 Clutch operation can be adversely affected if the release thrust ring and retaining springs are worn or damaged. Squeals, juddering, slipping or snatching could be caused partly or even wholly by this mechanism.
2 Full examination is possible only when the engine has been removed and normally it is carried out when the clutch is in need of repair. The mechanism is contained in and attached to the transmission casing. Check first that the operating lever return spring mounted on the exterior of the shaft on the left hand side is not broken. If it is it can be renewed without removing the engine; once the lever has been disconnected from the cable and taken off the cross shaft. However, the damage which failure of this spring may have caused has probably occurred already. If you are going to examine the clutch anyway it will be easier to renew the spring after the engine is removed.
3 With the engine removed examine the release bearing and the plastic face. It should spin silently and show no signs of wear or other damage. The retaining 'U' clips at each side must be a tight fit so that the bearing does not rattle about on the mounting forks.
4 Do not wash the bearing in any cleaning fluid. It is sealed and although fluid may wash some grease out you cannot get any more in. If it needs renewal pull off the clips and lift it out.
5 When replacing the thrust release bearing fit the straight ends of the 'U' clips into the holes in each end of the pivot pins on the bearing and hook the curved ends into position round the back of the operating forks.
6 Check that the cross shaft moves freely in the transmission casing. When fitting a new operating lever return spring (on the outside of the casing) it is necessary to disconnect the clutch cable and pull off the arm from the cross shaft.
7 To remove the cross shaft the clamp bolt must be completely removed as it engages in a cut-out in the cross shaft. Place the new spring over the cross shaft so that the straight end is innermost and resting on the lug. The hooked end goes in front of the lever.
8 Apply a little molybdenum paste to the face of the thrust bearing before refitting the engine.
9 Re-adjust the pedal free play once the engine is reinstalled.
10 On the latest models the clutch release bearing operates round a sleeve which is attached to the transmission casing. On these there is no thrust ring fitted in the centre of the clutch cover. The thrust bearing operates directly on to the ends of the three release levers.

3.8(a) Offering the clutch driven plate up to the flywheel.

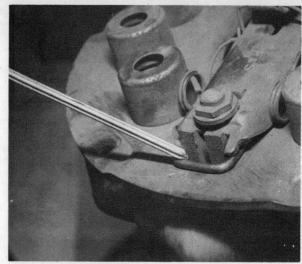

3.8(b) Remove the packing clip from each release lever on a new cover assembly.

3.8(c) Lining up the clutch cover to flywheel on marks made.

3.9. Centre the driven plate with a suitable bar.

3.10. Tightening the clutch cover bolts.

4.5. Fitting the clutch thrust release bearing. One clip is shown partially fitted.

5. Fault diagnosis and remedies

Symptom	Reason/s	Remedy
Judder when taking up drive	Loose engine/gearbox mountings or over flexible mountings	Check and tighten all mounting bolts and replace any 'soft' or broken mountings.
	Badly worn friction surfaces or friction plate contaminated with oil carbon deposit	Remove engine and replace clutch parts as required. Rectify any oil leakage points which may have caused contamination.
	Worn splines in the friction plate hub or on the gearbox input shaft	Renew friction plate and/or input shaft.
	Badly worn roller bearings in flywheel centre for input shaft spigot	Renew roller bearings in flywheel.
Clutch spin (or failure to disengage) so that gears cannot be meshed	Clutch actuating cable clearance too great	Adjust clearance.
	Clutch friction disc sticking because of rust on splines (usually apparent after standing idle for some length of time)	As temporary remedy engage top gear, apply handbrake, depress clutch and start engine. (If very badly stuck engine will not turn). When running rev up engine and slip clutch until disengagement is normally possible. Renew friction plate at earliest opportunity.
	Damaged or misaligned pressure plate assembly	Replace pressure plate assembly.
Clutch slip - (increase in engine speed does not result in increase in car speed - especially on hills)	Clutch actuating cable clearance from fork too small resulting in partially disengaged clutch at all times	Adjust clearance.
	Clutch friction surfaces worn out (beyond further adjustment of operating cable) or clutch surfaces oil soaked	Replace friction plate and remedy source of oil leakage.

4.7(a) Return spring for the clutch release lever being positioned.

4.7(b) Replacing the clutch release lever.

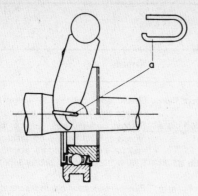

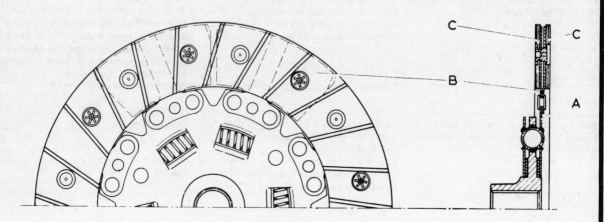

Fig.5.2. Clutch release bearing - cross section showing shape and location of retaining clip (a)

Fig.5.3. Clutch driven plate - flywheel face and cross section
A. Driven plate
B. Lining springs
C. Linings

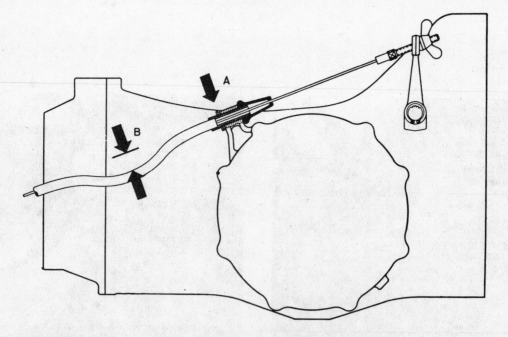

Fig.5.4. Clutch operating cable outer sleeve. Drawing showing bend measurement (B) and adjustment washer location (A).
B = 1 to 1¾ in (25 to 45 mm)

Chapter 6 Transmission and final drive (swing axle)

For modifications, and information applicable to later models, see Supplement at end of manual

Contents

Specifications

General

Final drive and gearbox main casing is a one piece tunnel type alloy casting, Type 113

Number of gears	4 forward, 1 reverse
Synchromesh	Baulk ring on all forward gears
Oil type/specification	Hypoid gear oil, viscosity SAE 80EP (Duckhams Hypoid 80)
Oil capacity of casing..	3.0 litres (5.3 pints)
Refill quantity	2.5 litres (4.4 pints)

Gear ratios

First...	3.80 : 1	
Second	2.06 : 1	
Third	1.26 : 1	(1.32 : 1 up to 1966)
Fourth	0.89 : 1	
Reverse	3.61 : 1	(3.88 : 1 up to 1967)

Final drive ratio

1300	4.375 : 1
1500	4.125 : 1

Torque wrench settings

Oil drain plugs	14 lbs.ft. (2.0 mkg)
Oil filler plug	14 lbs.ft. (2.0 mkg)
Transmission carrier to frame bolts	166 lbs.ft. (23.0 mkg)
Spring plate bolts/nuts	72 lbs.ft. (10.0 mkg)
Final drive cover nuts..	22 lbs.ft. (3.0 mkg)
Gear change cover to carrier nuts	11 lbs.ft. (1.5 mkg)
Gear carrier to housing nuts..	14 lbs.ft. (2.0 mkg)
Pinion bearing retainer screws	36 lbs.ft. (5.0 mkg)
Pinion shaft nut	43 lbs.ft. (6.0 mkg)
Input shaft nut..	43 lbs.ft. (6.0 mkg)
Reverse lever guide screw	14 lbs.ft. (2.0 mkg)
Selector fork screws	18 lbs.ft. (2.5 mkg)
Pinion shaft round nut (ball bearings)	87 lbs.ft. (12.0 mkg)
(taper roller bearing)	144 lbs.ft. (20.0 mkg)
Pinion shaft nut	43 lbs.ft. (6.0 mkg)
Input shaft nut..	43 lbs.ft. (6.0 mkg)

1. General description

The gearbox and final drive is a one piece composite assembly housed in a single 'tunnel' type magnesium alloy die casting. Unlike the more orthodox design of gearbox which has an input and output shaft aligned on the same axis with a layshaft and gears below, the VW has an input shaft and output shaft only mounted alongside each other and each carrying a synchro hub. This is because the input and output power is at the same end of each shaft. The output

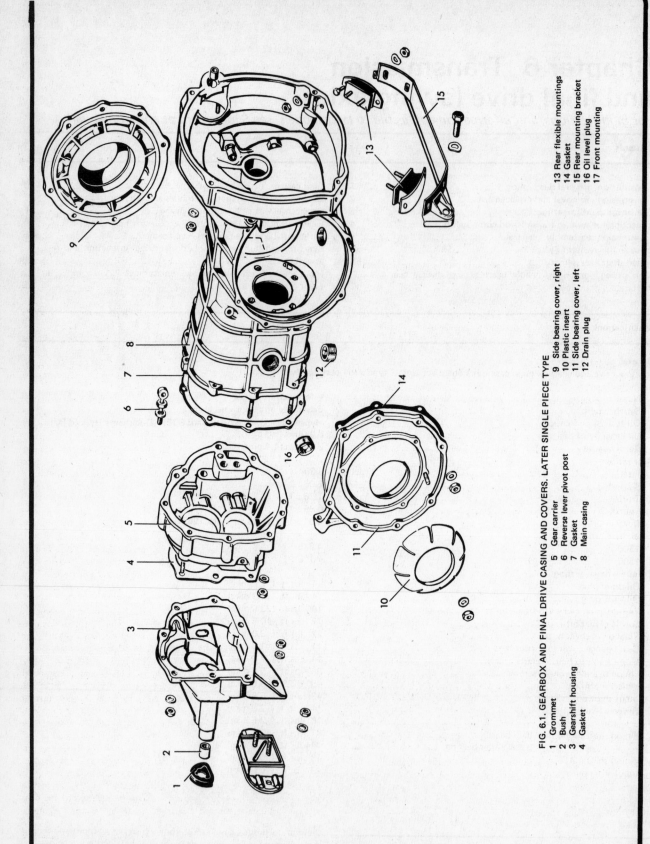

FIG. 6.1. GEARBOX AND FINAL DRIVE CASING AND COVERS. LATER SINGLE PIECE TYPE

1 Grommet
2 Bush
3 Gearshift housing
4 Gasket

5 Gear carrier
6 Reverse lever pivot post
7 Gasket
8 Main casing

9 Side bearing cover, right
10 Plastic insert
11 Side bearing cover, left
12 Drain plug

13 Rear flexible mountings
14 Gasket
15 Rear mounting bracket
16 Oil level plug
17 Front mounting

shaft in fact incorporates the pinion which meshes with the crown wheel.

Synchromesh is used for all four forward speeds.

The whole assembly is mounted in the 'Y' of the floor frame — called the frame fork for obvious reasons — ahead of the engine. The differential unit and final drive, part of the assembly as already mentioned, come between the engine and the transmission gears.

In order to dismantle the gearbox the axle shaft tubes and differential assembly must first be removed.

In view of the relative complexity of this complete unit, it is felt that a few words of warning should be given in order to let potential dismantlers fully realise what they may be letting themselves in for. First of all decide whether the fault you wish to repair is worth all the time and effort involved. Secondly, if the gearbox is in a very bad state then the cost of the component parts may well exceed the cost of a new replacement unit. Thirdly, remember that a basic knowledge of gearbox construction and function is a bare necessity before tackling this one. If you are doing one for the first time do not start on a Volkswagen!

Finally, two technical musts. You must be able to have access to the use of a press. So check this before you start. Make sure that you have made contact with an agent who is likely to be able to supply all the new gaskets and parts that may be required. It is not possible to work out exactly what may be required before you start but the minimum will be a gasket set, baulk rings and bearings so check that you can at least get these. The press is essential for dismantling the two shaft assemblies which is necessary if you want to replace the baulk rings.

If you have experience of earlier VW gearboxes there is another word of caution also. With the earlier models each gearshaft assembly was held together with a large locknut on the end of the shaft which was tightened to a specific torque. For production reasons these nuts have been replaced on later models by circlips used in conjunction with shims and special pressure washers which make assembly even more tricky even when a press is available. A selection of circlips and shims must be available. For this reason we would not recommend non-professional activity.

The detailed descriptions in this chapter are based on the earlier type of gearbox which is the basis of our experience. The differences referred to are pointed out and details can be picked up from the exploded drawings if comparison is made with drawings of the earlier gearboxes.

2. Transmission - removal and replacement

1 Remove the engine as described in Chapter 1.

2 Detach the starter motor from the transmission casing if not already done.

3 It will be necessary to undo the axle shaft outer nuts if the tube and shaft need to be separated for any reason. In any case it is a good idea to loosen these nuts in case of unforeseen circumstances so do it now while the wheels are still on and the vehicle is on the ground. You will not be able to do it when the assembly is removed from the car. The requirements for setting about slackening these very large and very tight nuts is given in Chapter 9 in connection with removal of the rear brake drums.

4 Having slackened the axle shaft nuts and wheel bolts jack up the car and remove the road wheels. Support the car on stands underneath the two rear jacking points.

5 Remove one of the front seats and the rear seat and move the other front seat fully forward.

6 Take up the floor covering and the shroud over the handbrake lever.

7 Undo the locknuts and adjusting nuts on each of the handbrake cable ends and take them off.

8 Take off the circlip in the groove at one end of the handbrake lever pivot pin and drive out the pin. Move the handbrake lever

rearwards a little and it may then be lifted out. Do not press the ratchet release button whilst doing this or the ratchet mechanism will fall out.

9 The two handbrake cables may now be drawn out from the transmission casing tubes.

10 From inside the car once more, remove the cover over the frame tunnel under the back seat. It is located by a single screw. Underneath the gear shift rod coupling will be seen and the rear square headed screw should be removed after cutting off the locking wire. If the gear lever is then moved the coupling will separate.

11 Next disconnect the rear hydraulic flexible brake hoses, one on each side where they connect at the bracket mounting on top of each axle tube. For details of this procedure refer to Chapter 9.

12 Next, if you have not already done so, clean off the area where the suspension plates are bolted to the outer ends of the axle tubes. Apply some penetrating oil now to the three nuts and bolts on each side to assist removal later (see Chapter 8 for details).

13 On the flange nearest the top nut and bolt which holds the axle to the spring plate will be seen a 'V' notch in the casting. Another notch, exactly in line with it, should be made with a chisel in the edge of the spring plate alongside. The bolt holes in the plate are slotted and it is most important that the axle tube is correctly positioned on replacement.

14 Now undo and remove the bolts which secure the lower ends of the shock absorbers.

15 The clutch cable locknut and adjusting nut should next be removed from the end of the cable.

16 Undo the nuts and bolts securing the axle tubes to the spring suspension plates. The axle tubes may then be moved out and down on each side (see Chapter 8).

17 All that now remains is to remove the two nuts and two bolts mounting the unit to the frame. First remove the two nuts at the front end which hold the casing onto the flexible mounting. Take off the washers also.

18 Next support the whole unit on a jack. A trolley jack and piece of stout board is the best way of doing this. The unit can then be lowered easily. If you do not have a trolley jack then the stout board may be supported on static jacks or bricks, whichever is most convenient and stable.

19 Having prepared the necessary support the two large bolts, one into each end of the rear frame tubes, should be removed with a socket spanner. They are not excessively tight.

20 The whole assembly can then be moved rearwards. Depending on how you have arranged and positioned your support will depend how the whole lot is balanced. Most likely it will try and drop at the front so be prepared for this. Lower it down carefully until it can be drawn out from under the rear of the car.

21 Replacement of the assembly is an exact reversal of the removal procedure. Note the following points. When the unit is in position the mounting bolts at the rear should not be tightened until the nuts securing the flexible mountings have been slackened. Then tighten the two large bolts; next the two front mounting nuts and finally the four rear mounting nuts once more. This prevents distortion stresses being set up in the flexible rubber mountings.

22 Do not forget that the line up of the notches in the axle bearing housings and spring plates is important. The hydraulic system will need bleeding after connecting the brake hoses. Reconnect the handbrake cables.

23 The correct coupling of the gear shift to the shift operating rod is essential. Make sure that the point of the locking screw engages the dimple in the shaft exactly and re-lock the screw with wire. If it is found that gear selection is not quite satisfactory on completion is in order to make minor adjustments to the position of the gear lever mounting. Details and explanations can be found in Chapter 13, Section 4.

24 Do not forget to refill the transmission with the correct quantity and grade of oil. 5¼ pints are needed. This is more easily done from above before the engine is replaced. Make sure the two drain plugs are tight and that the filler/level plug is slackened before putting the transmission back.

2.4. Stand supporting body at jacking point.

2.10(a) Undoing the gearchange rod connection locking screw.

2.10(b) The two sections of gearchange rod are separated.

2.18, Supporting the transmission on a trolley jack.

2.19. Removing the rear mounting bolts.

2.20. Work the whole assembly rearwards.

2.21. The flexible mounting bolts are tightened last after replacement.

3.11. Tapping the head of the pinion with a soft faced mallet to separate the two halves of the casing.

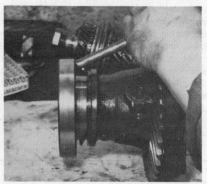
3.15. Drifting off a side bearing from the differential casing.

3.21. Pressing the bearing inner race, synchro hub and third gear from the input shaft.

3. Transmission - dismantling

1 Before proceeding according to the directions given in this Chapter read the 'General Description' section first. It is assumed that the unit has been removed from the car and the axle shafts and axle tubes removed as described in Chapter 8. Do not throw away gaskets when dismantling. They act as a guide when working out what new ones to use from the gasket set bought (see Reassembly section). Clean the casing exterior thoroughly.

2 Remove the nuts holding the gear selector lever housing and remove the housing together with the lever.

3 The main nuts on the ends of the input and output (pinion) shafts are now revealed. On later models these nuts are dispensed with and circlips are used instead. One of these circlips, on the input shaft end, must be removed before the two shafts can be drawn out of the bearings in the gear carrier. This circlip is under tension from a dished thrust washer underneath and is liable to 'fly' when released from its groove. So take care and cover the end with a cloth when releasing it. Tap back the tabs of the lockwashers which lie along a flat of each of the nuts. To prevent the shafts from rotating pull and/or push the two outer selector fork rails which protrude from the end of the casing. This will lock the two shafts by engaging two gears at once. Using a suitable socket or ring spanner the nuts can then be undone.

4 Next remove the nuts from the studs which secure the end casing (called the gear carrier) to the main casing and take off the braided electrical earth strap at the same time.

5 Turn the whole unit on its side so that the left side final drive cover is upwards. (Remember, the narrow end of the casing is the front). Then undo the nuts securing the cover to the casing.

6 With a soft-faced mallet the cover plate can now be gently tapped off from the casing. The main advice here is 'easy does it'. Do not use any force. The side bearing may or may not come off with the cover and between the bearing inner race and the differential there is a shim. If the bearing comes away with the side cover this shim(s) will be freed so collect it and tape it to the bearing to ensure it is not lost, damaged or mixed up with the shim or shims which come off in due course from the opposite side. If the bearing remains on the differential, leave it for the time being. Note the paper gasket between cover and casing.

7 Turn the casing over. With a suitable drift positioned against the inner race of the right hand bearing the whole of the differential assembly may now be tapped out. Take care to support the weight and prevent the assembly from dropping under its own weight. If it is found that it is easier to drift out the differential with the bearing left in the side cover this is in order but remember to collect up the shims which will be released between bearing and differential and tape them to the differential straight away.

8 Going back to the other side again, release the circlip which locates the splined collar/reverse gear to the input shaft. Slide it back along the shaft and slide the collar along behind it. The rear end of the shaft may now be unscrewed from the other half. Then take off the collar/gear and remove the circlip from the shaft also. The shaft may then be drawn out from the rear through the oil seal. It will be as well to replace this oil seal but if not take care not to damage it. (Note that this oil seal can be renewed with the transmission unit installed in the car. Access can be gained once the engine is removed).

9 Remove the nuts holding the right hand final drive cover and with a suitable drift gently tap it free from the inside. Note the paper gasket between cover and casing.

10 Four bolts will be seen securing the pinion shaft bearing retainer plate. Pry up the lock tabs on each bolt taking care that the tool used does not slip and come in contact with the pinion gear. Remove the bolts, still guarding against possible pinion damage.

11 The whole gearbox assembly is now ready to come out of the casing. This can be achieved by using a heavy copper faced mallet and striking the end of the pinion. Another way is to insert a scissor jack shallow enough to fit between the pinion and the casing opposite. Pad the head of the jack against the pinion and press it

out. Be sure to support the gear carrier when the gear shafts come away. As soon as it is clear, be sure to collect the shim(s) from the pinion flange.

12 The main casing has two needle roller bearings still left in it. One has the reverse gear and shaft running in it. To remove the gear first remove the circlip. The gear is a slide fit on a key and can be pulled off - levering a little with a screwdriver if necessary. The key must then be removed from the shaft and the shaft can be taken out from the front.

13 To remove the needle roller bearings of the reverse shaft, first unscrew the locating screw from the casing. This secures the spacer sleeve between the two bearings. A drift of suitable diameter can then be used to drive the two needle rollers and spacer out towards the rear of the casing.

14 Similarly, the other needle bearing outer race (no spacer) is secured by a screw in the casing. Once this is removed the needle roller bearing race may be drifted out. (This bearing is the one that supports the rear end of the forward half of the input shaft).

15 The large side bearings, which will be located in either the covers or on the differential, may remain where they are unless inspection indicates that they are worn and need renewal. They can be drifted off the differential or out of the covers. If being taken out of the covers make sure that the covers are firmly and evenly supported and drift the bearings. Do not attempt to do it the other way round or you may damage the cover and that is not the part you intend to renew.

16 So far, the dismantling process has been relatively straightforward. Now is the time to stop and reassemble if you are getting cold feet! The next step is to separate the two shafts with their clusters of gears from the gear carrier. To renew the baulk rings - which is one of the usual remedies for a less than perfect synchromesh action - this further dismantling is necessary.

17 First remove the small sliding gear and fork (reverse) from the pivot on the reverse lever.

18 Next loosen the clamping bolts which hold the two other selector forks to their respective rails. The fork for 1st and 2nd gear selection on the output (pinion) shaft can be lifted away after the rail has been drawn back sufficiently far. The other fork is shrouded by the gear carrier and is not lifted out at this stage. The rail for this one should be driven back far enough to free it from the fork. Do NOT drive the rails out of the gear carrier. If you do a lot of extra work will be caused, probably unnecessarily, because the detent balls and springs will be released.

19 The two shafts with their clusters of gears may now be removed from the carrier. It is a good plan to hold both together with a strong elastic band or a few turns of self-adhesive tape. Then, when the ends of the shaft are released, they will not fall about the place. Two pairs of hands are needed. One pair should hold the carrier - with the shafts hanging down whilst another person strikes the end of the input shaft with a soft faced mallet and supports the weight of the gear shafts as they are driven out. Do not let them drop down.

20 Once the shafts are clear of the carrier the two bearings in the carrier may be removed. The needle roller bearing is located by a screw similar to the needle roller bearings withdrawn previously. The main (input) shaft front bearing is driven out from the inside of the carrier. This particular ball bearing is flanged on the outer race and will only come out in one direction.

21 To dismantle the input shaft first take off the spacer ring, then 4th gear together with the needle bearing cage on which it runs. Remove the baulk rings. This leaves the inner race on the shaft. To get this off a press is needed and the 'V' blocks should be suitably positioned to provide support behind the 3rd gear wheel. In this way there will be no danger of damage to the shaft or gears and the synchro hub assembly will be kept together. Make sure that all parts are supported and held whilst being pressed. 3rd gear may then be taken off together with its needle roller bearing. The 3rd gear bearing inner race need not be removed nor the key which locates the synchro hub. Keep the baulk rings with their respective gear for future reference - fix them with adhesive tape to prevent muddling.

22 The output (pinion) shaft should only be dismantled to a limited

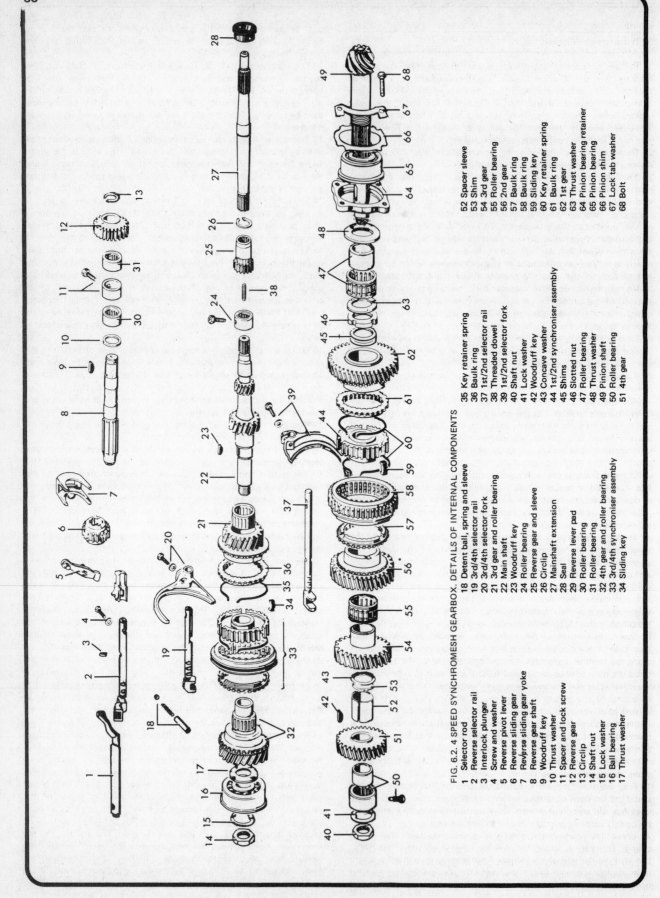

FIG. 6.2. 4 SPEED SYNCHROMESH GEARBOX. DETAILS OF INTERNAL COMPONENTS

1 Selector rod
2 Reverse selector rail
3 Interlock plunger
4 Screw and washer
5 Reverse pivot lever
6 Reverse sliding gear
7 Reverse sliding gear yoke
8 Reverse gear shaft
9 Woodruff key
10 Thrust washer
11 Spacer and lock screw
12 Reverse gear
13 Circlip
14 Shaft nut
15 Lock washer
16 Ball bearing
17 Thrust washer

18 Detent ball, spring and sleeve
19 3rd/4th selector rail
20 3rd/4th selector fork
21 3rd gear and roller bearing
22 Main shaft
23 Woodruff key
24 Roller bearing
25 Reverse gear and sleeve
26 Circlip
27 Mainshaft extension
28 Seal
29 Reverse lever pad
30 Roller bearing
31 Roller bearing
32 4th gear and roller bearing
33 3rd/4th synchroniser assembly
34 Sliding key

35 Key retainer spring
36 Baulk ring
37 1st/2nd selector rail
38 Threaded dowel
39 1st/2nd selector fork
40 Shaft nut
41 Lock washer
42 Woodruff key
43 Concave washer
44 1st/2nd synchroniser assembly
45 Shims
46 Slotted nut
47 Roller bearing
48 Thrust washer
49 Pinion shaft
50 Roller bearing
51 4th gear

52 Spacer sleeve
53 Shim
54 3rd gear
55 Roller bearing
56 2nd gear
57 Baulk ring
58 Baulk ring
59 Sliding key
60 Key retainer spring
61 Baulk ring
62 1st gear
63 Thrust washer
64 Pinion bearing retainer
65 Pinion bearing
66 Pinion shim
67 Lock tab washer
68 Bolt

extent - which is sufficient to remove the gears, synchro hub and baulk rings. The pinion double taper roller bearing which is held by the notched locking nut should be left intact as this requires the use of more special tools to which we do not feel most owners will have ready access. The services of a press will be required in order to carry out the partial dismantling necessary to remove the baulk rings. Repeated striking on the threaded end of the shaft - even with a soft headed mallet - can distort the threads and if this were severe the shaft could be ruined. Any conventional press with V-blocks will suit. 4th gear together with the inner race of the needle bearing which is still on the shaft, can be pressed off. Behind 4th gear is a spacer and then, in order follows a shim, concave washer, 3rd gear, needle roller bearing and 2nd gear and the 1st and 2nd gear synchro hub. The baulk rings are then able to be renewed if required. On later models which have no nuts on the ends of the two shafts there is a circlip which must first be removed. Then the 4th gear wheel and the inner race may be pressed off. Behind the gear there is a spring spacer and another circlip which must be removed before 3rd gear can be drawn off.

23 The synchro hub assemblies should be handled with care so as to prevent them coming apart inadvertently. It is important that if the centre hub and outer sleeve are separated that they be refitted in the same relative position. Some hubs have marks etched on each part to aid reassembly so before anything else examine them on both sides for such marks. If none can be found make some of your own with a small dab of paint to ensure reassembly in the same position. To dismantle the hubs first lift out the spring retaining clip on each side. Then carefully slide the sleeve from the hub taking care not to drop and lose the three sliding keys.

24 Do not remove the selector fork rails from the gear carrier casing unless inspection indicates that there is something wrong with the detent balls and springs.

4. Inspection for wear in transmission components

1 As mentioned in the introduction to this Chapter the degree of wear in the components will to a large extent dictate the economics of repair or replacement with a new unit. If the crown wheel and pinion is obviously badly worn, resulting in noise and significant backlash, then it is possible that this may be repaired alone for approximately half the cost of a new unit provided that is the only major complaint. Such work is not within the competence of the average owner and this manual does not cover it as the author did not do the job. The gearbox used for the illustrations in this Chapter was fitted with new ball bearings, baulk rings and synchro hub keys and retaining clips. Apart from the press all dismantling and reassembly was carried out with normal hand tools.

2 Having been able to obtain the use of a simple mechanical press it is possible to remove all baulk rings for examination. The grooved taper face of the ring provides the braking action on the mating face of the gear wheel cone and if the ridges are worn the braking or synchro action will be less effective. The only way to determine the condition effectively is by comparison with new parts. As the parts are relatively cheap it is considered foolish not to renew them all anyway once the gearbox is dismantled. As a guide, when a baulk ring is fitted over its cone on the gear wheel there should be a minimum gap of 0.6 mm (0.024 inch) between the baulk ring and the gear teeth. The normal gap is 1.1 mm (0.043 inch) so it is obvious that if the gap is near the lowest limit new rings should be fitted. When obtaining new baulk rings make sure that you get the parts store to identify and mark each one according to its appropriate gear. Modifications have taken place over the years and although the new ones will still fit and work they are not necessarily identical to the ones you take out. So if you muddle them up you could get problems. They are also not all the same in the set - some have wider cut-outs for example. So mark the new ones you get carefully.

3 Two types of bearings are fitted - ball and needle roller. As a rule needle roller bearings wear very little, not being subject to end thrust of any sort. Check them in position and if there are signs of

roughness then they should be renewed. The ball bearings are the two large side bearings and the special flanged bearing which carries the forward end of the input shaft. If any of these bearings should feel the slightest bit rough or show any sign of drag or slackness when revolved then it should be renewed. The double taper roller bearing should be similarly checked. If there is any sign of roughness or endfloat then this is a task for a specialist. If this bearing is needing renewal the condition of the pinion gear and crownwheel must be very carefully examined. Once these need renewal then the setting of the whole box is altered and clearances and shims have to be re-calculated and changed.

4 The teeth of all gears should be examined for signs of pitted mating surfaces, chips or scoring. It must be appreciated that if one gear is damaged then its mate on the other shaft will probably be as bad and that one way or another a new shaft could be required.

5 The synchro hubs should be assembled for checking. It is important that there is no rock or backlash on the splines between the inner hub and outer sleeve. When the baulk rings are being renewed it is good policy to renew the three sliding keys and their locating spring rings as well. The keys fit into the cut-outs in the baulk rings and are subject to wear and the springs weaken with time.

6 One of the most critical parts of the Volkswagen gearbox is the operation of the selector forks. The two forks run in grooves in the outer sleeves of the synchro hubs and if the clearance of the forks in the grooves is excessive then there is a likelihood of certain gears jumping out. The clearance of the fork in the groove should not exceed 0.3 mm (0.012 inch). Clearance in excess of the maximum could be due to wear on the fork or in the groove or both. It is best therefore first of all to take the forks along to the spares supplier and ask him to compare their thickness with new ones. If the difference in thickness is not enough to compensate for the excess gap between fork and hub groove then the hub assembly will need replacement as well. This is an expensive item but as the gap is somewhat critical there is no alternative. Much depends on the total degree of wear.

7 The selector rails on which the forks are mounted need not be removed from the casing. A certain force is needed in order that they overcome the pressure of the spring loaded ball in the groove. This can be measured with a spring balance hooked on to the end of each selector fork. If the required pull is significantly outside the range of 15—20 kgs (33—44 lbs) then it is advisable to check the detent springs and balls. To do this push the selector rods right out of the casing. This will release the ball and spring but to get the springs out it is necessary to prise out the plastic plugs from the drillings opposite. Before doing this make sure you obtain some new plugs to drive in when reassembling. Check the spring free length which should be 25 mm (1 inch). If less than 22 mm they should be changed. The balls should be free from pitting and grooves and the selector rods themselves should not be a sloppy fit in the bores. The detent grooves in the rails should not be worn. When the rails are removed do not lose the interlock plungers which fit between the selector rod grooves.

9 Examine all parts of the casing for signs of cracks or damage, particularly near the bearing housings and on the mating surfaces where the gear carrier and side bearing plates join.

10 It should not normally be necessary to completely wash all the gearbox components in fluid. Wipe components on clean cloth for examination. In this way the likelihood of dry spots during the first moments of use after reassembly are minimised. The casing itself should be thoroughly washed out with paraffin. Do not leave the needle roller bearings in position when doing this.

5. Transmission reassembly - general

Spend time in preparing plenty of clean, clear space and if your work bench is rough cover it with hardboard or paper for a good non-gritty surface. Do not start until you have all the necessary parts

4.6. Using a feeler blade to check the clearance between fork and groove in the 3rd/4th gear hub.

5A.1(a) Fitting the needle roller to the input shaft.

5A.1(b) Fitting 3rd gear and synchro ring on to the needle rollers.

5A.2(a) Fitting 3rd/4th synchro hub.

5A.2(b) Lining up the keyway for 3rd/4th hub.

5A.2(c) Driving 3rd/4th hub onto the shaft.

5A.3(a) Driving the inner race for 4th gear needle bearings on to the shaft.

5A.3(b) Fit 4th gear needle bearings.

5A.3(c) Replace 4th gear and synchro ring.

5A.4(a) Fit the thrust washer.

5A.4(b) Input shaft assembly complete.

and gaskets assembled and make sure that all the ones you have obtained are going to fit. Gasket sets often contain items covering a variety of models so you will not need them all - this is why it helps to keep the old gaskets you take off until the job is eventually finished.

5A. Input shaft - reassembly

1 First reassemble the input shaft, beginning by putting the needle roller cage for 3rd gear in position on the shaft. Then put third gear with its matching synchro ring onto the roller bearings with the cone towards the front end of the shaft.

2 The 3rd/4th gear synchro hub assembly goes on next. This has to line up with the key in the shaft. Once the keyway in the centre part of the hub is lined up with the key in the shaft the hub can be driven on using a suitable piece of tube and heavy hammer. There are three very important points to note when doing this. Make sure that the hub is on the right way round - some later models have a groove in the outer sleeve 1 mm deep and this must be towards the front end of the shaft. If there is no indication then you may put the hub on either way round. Secondly, make sure that you only drive the centre part of the hub. Otherwise it will come apart and have to be reassembled. Thirdly, the slots in the baulk ring must be lined up with the keys in the hub. This is best done by someone holding the baulk ring in position with the keys whilst the hub is driven on the final amount. Be careful not to trap any fingers!

3 Next the inner race for the 4th gear needle roller bearing has to be driven on to the shaft in the same manner that the hub was driven on before it. Drive it right down to the hub. Then replace the needle roller cage followed by the baulk ring and 4th gear. The baulk ring also has three cut-outs which engage with the sliding keys in the hub.

4 Finally, place the thrust washer on the end of the shaft with the V cuts (if any) facing the front end of the shaft. Put the whole assembly on one side with the locknut and lockwasher loosely fitted. If a circlip is used this is best fitted now.

5B. Pinion shaft - reassembly

1 As pointed out earlier, the pinion shaft has been dismantled only as far as the pinion bearing which has been left in position. If this bearing has been renewed then the gearbox and final drive will need resetting and this is a skilled job requiring special equipment and a selection of special shims to hand from which the necessary requirements are available.

2 The first 'loose' item therefore which goes behind the pinion bearing locking ring is the shim or shims which control 1st gear end float. This endfloat is measured after the 1st gear and hub are installed. The gap is that between the thrust washer (already locked in position behind the 1st gear needle bearing) and the face of the gear. If the gap should be outside the limits of 0.10—0.25 mm (0.004—0.010 inch) then different shims will be required to correct this. The shims in effect determine the position of the inner sleeve of the 1st/2nd gear synchro hub in relation to the captive thrust washer. 1st gear endfloat is controlled between the thrust washer and centre hub face.

3 Next put the bearing retainer over the shaft and up to the pinion bearing with the smooth, machined face towards the pinion gear at the end of the shaft.

4 Now put 1st gear (the largest one with helically cut teeth) in position on the needle roller bearings with the cone face of the synchro pointing away from the pinion gear.

5 Select the 1st gear baulk ring and place it over 1st gear and then replace the 1st and 2nd gear hub over the splines on the shaft with the selector fork groove of the outer sleeve facing towards the front end of the shaft. Make sure that the three cut-outs in the synchro ring engage with the sliding keys in the hub before pushing the hub fully home. Remember that the baulk rings for 1st and 2nd gears are slightly different. That for 1st gear has narrower cut-outs

than those in the 2nd gear ring.

6 Now check the 1st gear endfloat as mentioned in paragraph 2.

7 Put the 2nd gear baulk ring in position in the hub so that the slots engage with the sliding keys.

8 Replace 2nd gear with the cone towards the hub.

9 Third gear, which has a large bearing boss integral with it, should now be replaced with the needle roller bearing which fits together with 3rd gear, inside 2nd gear.

10 The dished washer is now put over the shaft with the raised inner circumference towards the end of the shaft. After this goes the shim. If the only renovations to the pinion shaft have been new baulk rings, then one may assume that the existing washer and shim can be fitted as before. If, however, the synchro hub or any gears have been renewed then it is most likely that the shim thickness will need alteration. The dished washer is designed to exert a pressure of approximately 100 kg (220 lbs) on to 3rd gear and the hub to eliminate sloppiness along the shaft. The critical distance is that between the face of 3rd gear and the shoulder on the shaft up to which 4th gear will be fitted. This length of shaft has a spacer collar which bears on the concave washer (and shim) when 4th gear is finally installed. Obviously a thicker shim will increase the pressure and vice versa. If, therefore, it is necessary to recalculate the shim requirement an accurate measuring device is necessary. The dished washer is given a spring travel of 0.17 mm in order to exert its pressure and is also a constant thickness of 1.04 mm. Thus the length of the distance collar plus the total concave washer dimensions (1.23 mm) should equal the shaft distance from 3rd gear face to 4th gear shoulder. The appropriate shims are selected to make this distance up.

11 On later gearboxes a selective circlip is fitted where the concave washer would go and the end play of 3rd gear measured with a blade between the gear and circlip. This should be 0.10 and 0.25 mm (0.004—0.010 inch).

12 Install the shim after the dished washer and then put the spacer sleeve on top of that (later models have a spring spacer after the circlip).

13 4th gear is now ready to go on. Although it could be pressed off it cannot be pressed on as it is virtually impossible to line it up to the keyway as once started it cannot be re-aligned. It must therefore be heated to at least 90°C (194°F) in order that it may expand enough to slide easily down the shaft and over the key. This heating is best done in a bath of oil. A blow torch can be used provided a careful watch is kept to prevent overheating. 4th gear must only go on one way and that is with the wider protruding face of its hub towards the spacer collar. Put the hot gear on to the shaft and make sure it is fully home to the shoulder on the shaft.

14 Last of all, the inner race for the needle roller bearing is pressed or driven on to the shaft. On later models the gear is pressed on against the spring spacer and a circlip is installed afterwards. It is necessary to force the circlip down against the concave washer in order to bed it into its groove. If the proper press and jig are not readily available, select a piece of tubing that will fit round the shaft and which can be used to drive the circlip against the spring pressure. While this is being done the whole assembly should be wrapped in cloth and gripped firmly on the bench by someone else. Then the inner race for the needle bearing is pressed on. The pinion shaft is now assembled and should be put on one side.

5C. Main casing - installing needle bearings and reverse gearshaft

1 Two sets of needle roller bearings are fitted at the rear end of the main casing. One set comprises two roller cages and a spacer between and in this the reverse drive shaft runs. Drive one cage into the casing with a socket on an extension or suitable drift so that it is flush with one end of the bore. The metal face of the needle cage end should face inwards. The spacer should then be inserted with its slot so lined up that it will engage with the locking bolt which is screwed in through the side of the casing. Put the locking bolt in position and then drive the other needle roller bearing into the other end of the

5B.1. Pinion (output) shaft with bearing and 1st gear needle rollers assembled.

5B.2. 1st gear shim.

5B.3(a) Pinion shaft bearing retainer goes next.

5B.3(b) ... with the machined face towards the pinion.

5B.4. Replace 1st gear wheel.

5B.5. Fit the 1st gear baulk ring (arrowed) followed by 1st/2nd synchro hub.

5B.6. Checking 1st gear endfloat.

5B.7. Fitting 2nd gear baulk ring into the hub.

5B.8. Replacing 2nd gear.

5B.9. Replacing 3rd gear with its boss and needle roller bearing.

5B.10. Fit the dished washer after 3rd gear.

5B.12(a) Fit the shim(s) on the distance washer.

5B.12(b) Replace the spacer sleeve.

5B.13. Replacing the (hot) 4th gear.

5B.14. Drift on the inner race for the needle bearing.

5C.1(a) Needle bearings and spacer for reverse drive shaft.

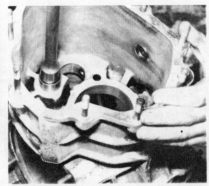
5C.1(b) Fitting reverse drive shaft bearings and spacer into the casing.

5C.1(c) Replacing the locking bolt.

5C.2. The single needle roller (arrowed) is fitted for the input shaft front section.

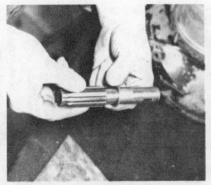
5C.3(a) Putting the spacer on the reverse gear shaft.

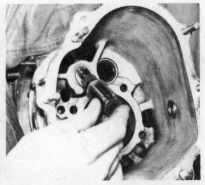
5C.3(b) Placing reverse gear shaft in the casing.

5C.3(c) Fitting the key.

5C.3(d) Fit the gear onto the shaft over the key.

5D.1(a) Fitting the roller bearing for the pinion shaft into the gear carrier casing.

5D.1(b) ... tapping it home, ...

5D.1(c) ... and fitting the securing screw.

5D.2. Fit the ball bearing with the flange into the gear carrier casing.

5E.2. Tape the two shafts together and position 3rd/4th selector fork.

5E.3(a) ... and then offer them all up to the gear carrier casing.

5E.3(b) Note the selector rail (arrowed) drawn back to let the fork be fitted.

5E.4. Tapping the shafts into the casing.

5E.6(a) Fit new lock washers (or dished washers when circlips are used).

5E.6(b) ... and the shaft nuts (or circlips) as appropriate.

5E.7. Tighten nuts to the correct torque.

5E.10. Tightening the clamp screw on 1st/2nd gear selector fork.

5E.11(a) Position reverse sliding gear and yoke.

bore.

2 The other bearing supports the rear end of the input shaft front half. Fit the single needle roller cage into the larger bore so that the circular recess in the outer race will line up with the lock screw hole in the casing. Tap it into position and replace and tighten the lock screw.

3 The reverse gear shaft may now be fitted. First slide the spacer ring over the shaft so that it abuts the splined section. Then pass the shaft through the needle bearings from the front of the casing. Fit the key into the keyway, tilting the outer end down a fraction to aid fitting the gear. Support the front end of the shaft and push the gear on engaging the key. The projecting side of the gear hub should face outwards. Finally, fit the circlip into the groove making quite sure that it is fully seated all round.

5D. Gear carrier - fitting bearings

1 The needle roller bearing for the forward end of the pinion shaft should be lined up so that the hole for the locking screw corresponds with the recess in the bearing. Tap it into position and fit the locking screw.

2 The special ball bearing with the flange outer race should then be driven into position from the outside of the carrier casing.

5E. Gear carrier - refitting shafts and selector forks

1 It is assumed that the selector rails are in order (see Section 4, paragraph 7) and the forks are a correct fit in the hub sleeve grooves (Section 4, paragraph 6).

2 The first task is to fit the two shafts into the gear carrier. First of all place the two assemblies together and hold them with strong elastic bands or adhesive tape.

3 When the two shafts are finally in position in the carrier the selector fork for 3rd/4th gear is shrouded so this must be put in position on the synchro hub and kept there whilst both shafts are being pushed home. For the same reason the fork rail must be pulled back so that as the fork is carried in it can be fitted on to the rail. It will be appreciated that there are several things to keep in line therefore and more than one pair of hands is almost essential.

4 With the selector fork for 3rd/4th speeds in position in its groove - with the clamp lug facing outwards from the casing - offer up the two shafts together into their bearing locations. The main resistance will be from the ball bearing and this will tend to come out of the carrier as the shaft is tapped in. Put something behind the bearing therefore to support it.

5 As the two shafts progressively go into the casing line up the selector fork with its appropriate rail so that eventually that is being pushed on as well. It is important to ensure that the fork does not jam. Also once the fork is on the rail the rail may be moved back in line with the others.

6 Once both shafts are fully home in the carrier bearings, the shaft nuts have to be replaced and tightened. Fit new lock washers (from the gasket set) and make sure that the tags engage in the grooves in the shaft. Put the nuts on finger tight. In order to hold the whole assembly whilst the nuts are tightened it is simplest to replace it temporarily over the studs of the main casing.

7 Stand the main casing on end and carefully place the gear carrier assembly in it so that the studs are engaged sufficiently for the unit to be held firm. Then tighten both of the nuts to a torque of 87 ft.lb. 12 mkg) and slacken them off. Retighten to 43 ft.lbs. (6 mkg). Do not bend up the lock washers on to the nuts just yet in case some disaster necessitates them being undone again. On later models that have circlip fixings instead of nuts a dished washer and circlip are fitted to the input shaft. As the washer has to be compressed in order to fit the circlip into its groove a press and suitable tubular tool are needed in order to do this successfully.

8 Once the nuts have been tightened the gear carrier should be removed from the casing in preparation for setting the selector forks.

9 The selector forks setting is critical. If the wear between the fork and groove is outside the limit the possibility of a gear not being fully engaged and jumping out is increased. If you can get the unit set up in a Volkswagen agent's jig you would be well advised to do so. Otherwise, lay the assembly on the bench and fit the selector fork for 1st/2nd gears into its groove and mount it on the selector rail.

10 Set all three selector rails in the neutral position, which is when the cut-outs in their ends all line up, and set the synchro hub outer sleeves also in neutral with the forks in position. Then tighten the fork clamp bolts sufficiently to prevent them slipping. Now push each selector in turn so that each gear is fully engaged. The outer sleeve of the appropriate synchro hub must move fully over the dogs of the baulk ring and gear in question. In each gear selected the fork must not bind in the groove. If difficulty is experienced in engaging a gear slacken the fork clamp nut and get the synchro hub sleeve fully into mesh and then retighten the fork clamp in position. Then move the selector back to neutral and into the opposite gear position. In all three positions there must be no semblance of pressure in either direction from the fork on to the groove in which it runs. Do not forget also that the synchro hub and 2nd and 3rd gears on the pinion shaft are pre-loaded with the dished washer and will be stiff to rotate. This may cause something of a struggle in order to line up the dogs when engaging 2nd gear. Once both forks have been correctly set the clamp bolts may be tightened to a torque of 18 ft.lbs. (2.5 mkg).

11 No mention has been made yet of the reverse selector rod and relay lever. This would not have been dismantled from the gear carrier except in rare circumstances because it is the least likely to suffer from wear. The small sliding gear and yoke (which will have come off the lug from the relay lever during dismantling of the unit) may now be repositioned on it. To check that the setting is correct first engage second gear. The reverse sliding gear should be held square and in this position should be midway between the straight cut teeth on the synchro hub sleeve and the helical teeth of 2nd gear on the input shaft. Then move out of 2nd gear and shift into reverse and check that the reverse gears mesh completely. Adjustment can be made if necessary on the block which is clamped to the selector rail. It is most unlikely that the relay lever pivot post in incorrect but as a check the distance from the centre of the eye to the face of the gear carrier should be 38.6 mm (+ or − 0.4 mm).

5F. Gear carrier - assembly to main casing

1 The main casing should be ready with bearings and reverse gear shaft installed.

2 In order to assist lining up the bolt holes in the pinion bearing flange (which is impossible to move when fully in position) two studs about three inches long are fitted into the flange. These will act as leaders in to the holes in the casing and automatically line up the flange. If you have no metal studs with suitable threads (or bolts with the heads cut off) find two pieces of wooden dowel rod a suitable size which can be screwed into the flange. Make sure they will not splinter or break.

3 Fit the pinion setting shims in position on the face of the flange. The two guide studs will help to locate them. If the flange has small 'pips' cast into the edge line up the shim accordingly and note that they should line up with the corresponding points in the casing. Put a dab of grease on the shim to prevent it falling off later.

4 Place a new gasket over the studs on the casing, having made sure that no traces of old gasket are left and that the two mating surfaces are quite clean and smooth.

5 Make sure that the reverse sliding gear is not forgotten. It can be prevented from dropping out if reverse gear is engaged.

6 It is best to fit the gear carrier to the casing with the casing standing upright. There are three points to watch.

a) See that the pinion shim stays put.

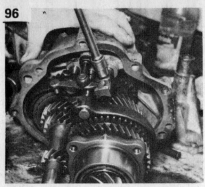

5E.11(b) ... and clamp the reverse selector block to the rail.

5F.2. Pinion bearing flange fitted with leader studs.

5F.3. Positioning the pinion bearing flange shim.

5F.4. Fit a new gasket.

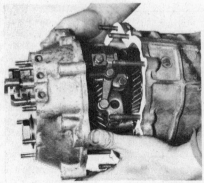

5F.6. Place the gear carrier assembly into the casing.

5F.7(a) Tighten the pinion bearing flange bolts.

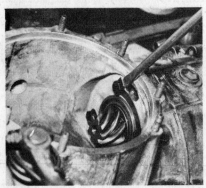

5F.7(b) ... and bend up the lock plate tabs.

5F.8. Tighten the carrier nuts.

5F.9. ... and if all is well lock up the shaft nuts.

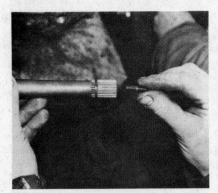

5F.10. Fit the stud into the end of the front section of the input shaft.

5F.11. After the input shaft has been positioned put the circlip over the splines.

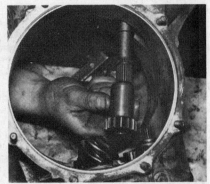

5F.12(a) ... and slide on the splined muff and gear.

b) Guide the temporary studs into the bolt holes in the casing so that the flange lines up properly.

c) See that the splined reverse gear shaft lines up with and goes into the sliding reverse gear.

Provided the foregoing points are watched carefully the whole unit will drop into place quite easily and a few final taps with a soft mallet will butt the mating faces together. If for any reason something 'solid' is encountered while replacing the assembly stop and look. Do not force anything. Remember the three points mentioned and take care with the lining up.

7 As soon as the gear carrier is in position turn the casing on its side and remove the two guide studs from the pinion bearing flange. Using the new lock plates (included in the gasket set) replace the four pinion flange bolts and tighten them diagonally and evenly to 36 ft.lbs. (5 mkg). The bolt head nearest the splined end of the pinion shaft should be arranged so that a flat on the head faces the shaft. This prevents any possibility of the reverse gear sleeve fouling the bolt head. Do not exceed the specified torque to do this. Back the bolt off if necessary and retighten to a slightly lower torque. Take care to avoid slipping and damaging the pinion in any way when tightening up. Bend up the lock plate tabs.

8 Replace the carrier nuts, noting that one carries the earth strap, and tighten them all evenly to a torque of 14 ft.lbs. (2 mkg).

9 Provided all is well and the shafts revolve freely the lock washers for the two shaft nuts may now be turned up against a flat on the nuts.

10 The front section of the input shaft is now ready for installation. Oil the land in the centre which will run in the oil seal and see that the small link stud is screwed into the end of the shaft. Then carefully insert the shaft through the oil seal from the rear of the main casing.

11 Once through, fit the circlip - preferably a new one - over the splines and past the groove onto the smooth part of the shaft.

12 Put the reverse gear/splined sleeve onto the shaft, plain end first. Then screw the shaft stud into the end of the protruding input shaft. Screw it in as far as it will go and then come back one spline in order to let the splined collar engage both halves of the shaft. Do not under any circumstances engage the sleeve with the ends of the shafts butted tight together. Move the sleeve forward so that the gears engage and then move the circlip back along the shaft so that it engages fully into the groove.

5G. Gear shift housing - reassembly

1 Clean up the mating surfaces on the end of the gear carrier and shift housing and place a new gasket in position over the studs in the gear carrier.

2 See that the gearbox is in neutral by checking that the cut-outs in the ends of the three selector rods are line up.

3 The gear change lever in the housing should be an easy slide fit in the housing. If it is sloppy in any way it could cause jamming or other problems of changing gear.

4 Fit the housing over the studs, at the same time fiddling the lever so that the end locates in the cut-outs of the ends of the three selector rails.

5 Replace the nuts and tighten to 11 ft.lbs. (1.5 mkg).

5H. Differential and side bearings - replacement

1 Ensure that all parts are scrupulously clean and that the shims and spacers are correct for each side of the differential casing. Remember that the shims fitted serve two functions - one is to put a pre-load on the side bearings and the other is to position the crownwheel correctly in relation to the pinion.

2 It may be argued that if new bearings are fitted then the shim requirements should be recalculated. In practice this is not necessary provided that the same crownwheel and pinion are being refitted and that no previous shim alteration has taken place in an abortive

attempt to improve some earlier malfunction.

3 When fitting new bearings, support the side cover evenly and securely and arrange the bearing so that the closed side of the ball race faces the outside of the casing on assembly. The bore in the side cover must be scrupulously clean and free of any snags or burrs.

4 The new bearing can be tapped into place using a heavy mallet and a suitable article to apply the load evenly across it. Make sure that it does not tilt, particularly at the start. If it does, bring it out and start again.

5 The right hand side bearing and cover is installed first. Make sure both mating faces are perfectly clean and fit a new gasket over the studs of the casing. No sealing compound is necessary. Place the cover in position (it will only fit one way) and tighten the nuts evenly to 22 ft.lbs. of torque (3 mkg).

6 The differential assembly goes in next. With everything perfectly clean the shims may be held in position with a dab of grease. If for some reason there has been a mix up with the shims and you do not know which should go on each side, you are in trouble because you will be unable to set the pinion/crownwheel backlash correctly. In such cases you should take the whole assembly to a Volkswagen specialist and ask him to reset it. With the proper gear it will not take too long. Do not guess!

7 If you know exactly what shims came off each side make sure they are arranged so that the thicker spacer ring is fitted first, with the chamfered side inwards and the shims after that (so that they go between the ring and the bearing).

8 With the spacer and shims in place put the differential into the casing carefully and tap it in so that the shoulder abuts fully against the inner race of the bearing in the cover already fitted.

9 Make sure the remaining shims are properly located on the crownwheel end of the differential and then fit the left hand final drive cover into position using a new gasket as for the other one. As this cover has to fit over the differential it will be necessary to tap it down into position fully before the nuts can be replaced. It is important to note that the cover retaining nuts must not be used to pull the cover and bearing down. This could easily crack or break it. Tighten the nuts finally to the same torque as the other cover.

10 The transmission case is now completely reassembled and ready to receive the axle shafts and tubes.

6. Synchromesh hub assemblies - dismantling, inspection and reassembly

1 Unless the transmission is the victim of neglect or misuse, or has covered very high mileages, the synchro hub assemblies do not normally need replacement. If they do they must be renewed as a complete assembly. It is not practical to fit an inner hub or outer sleeve alone - even if you could buy one.

2 When synchro baulk rings are being renewed it is advisable to fit new blocker bars (sliding keys) and retaining springs in the hubs as this will ensure that full advantage is taken of the new, unworn cut-outs in the rings.

3 Whether or not a synchro hub is dismantled intentionally or accidentally there are some basic essentials to remember:

a) The splines of the inner hub and outer sleeve are matched - either by selection on assembly or by wear patterns during use. Those matched on assembly have etched lines on the inner hub and outer sleeve so that they can be easily re-aligned. For those with no marks, a paint dab should be made to ensure correct reassembly. If the hub falls apart unintentionally and there are no marks made then you will have to accept the fact that it may wear more quickly (relatively speaking) in the future. But do not have a heart attack if this happens - it will still work for a long time to come.

b) Fit the retaining spring clips so that the ends fit behind but not into the keys; and that the clips overlap on each side, i.e. do not have more than two clip ends over one key (see Fig.6.3).

4 When examining for wear there are two important features to

98

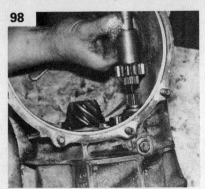

5F.12(b) Screw the input shaft halves together.

5F.12(c) Slide the gear muff forward into engagement and fit the circlip.

5G.1. Fit a new gasket for the gear shift housing.

5G.4. Put the housing on to the casing and engage the lever into the selector rail cut-outs (arrowed).

5H.4. Fitting a new bearing into the side cover.

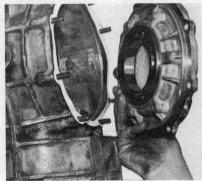

5H.5. Fit the right hand cover to the casing.

5H.6. Fit the differential shims on the right hand side.

5H.8. Put the differential into the casing.

5H.9. Replace the left hand cover on the casing.

6.3(b) Fitting a synchro hub sliding key retainer clip.

7.3. Removing input shaft oil seal (shaft removed in this photo).

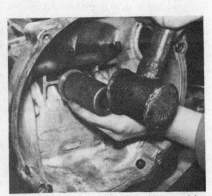

7.5. Driving new input shaft seal into position.

look at:

a) The fit of the splines. With the keys removed, the inner and outer sections of the hub should slide easily with minimum backlash or axial rock. The degree of permissible wear is difficult to describe in absolute terms. No movement at all is exceptional yet excessive 'slop' would affect operation and cause jumping out of gear. Ask someone with experience for advice.

b) Selector fork grooves and selector forks should not exceed the maximum permissible clearance of 0.3 mm (0.012 inch). The wear can be on either the fork or groove so it is best to try a new fork in the existing hub first to see if the gap is reduced adequately. If not, then a new hub assembly is needed. Too much slack between fork and groove induces jumping out of gear. Where a hub also carries gear teeth on the outer sleeve these should, of course, be in good condition - that is unbroken and not pitted or scored.

7. Input shaft oil seal - removal and replacement

1 It is possible that clutch contamination may be caused by failure of the oil seal that goes round the input shaft in the transmission casing. During the course of transmission overhaul it would be automatically renewed but it is possible to fit a new one with the transmission installed. The engine must be removed first.

2 With the engine removed detach the clutch release bearing from the operating forks.

3 The seal surrounds the input shaft where it goes through the casing. It can be dug out with a sharp pointed instrument provided care is taken to avoid damaging the surrounding part of the transmission casing.

4 A new seal should be treated with sealing compound on the outside rim (taking care to prevent the compound getting anywhere else on the seal) and then placed in position with the inner lip of the seal facing into the transmission. Be careful not to damage the lip when passing it over the splines of the shaft and make sure it does not turn back when it reaches the part of the shaft on which it bears.

5 It should be driven into position squarely and a piece of tube is ideal for this put round the shaft. If the seal should tip in the early stages of being driven in take it out and start again. Otherwise it may be badly distorted and its life will be shortened considerably.

6 The seal should be driven in until the outer shoulder abuts the casing.

8. Fault diagnosis

It is sometimes difficult to decide whether it is worthwhile removing and dismantling the gearbox for a fault which may be nothing more than a minor irritant. Gearboxes which howl, or where the synchromesh can be 'beaten' by a quick gear change, may continue to perform for a long time in this stage. A worn gearbox usually needs a complete rebuild to eliminate noise because the various gears, if re-aligned on new bearings, will continue to howl when different wearing surfaces are presented to each other.

The decision to overhaul therefore, must be considered with regard to time and money available, relative to the degree of noise or malfunction that the driver has to suffer.

Symptom	Reason/s	Remedy
Ineffective synchromesh	Worn baulk rings or synchro hubs	Dismantle and renew.
Jumps out of one or more gears (on drive or over-run)	Weak detent springs or worn selector forks or worn gears	Dismantle and renew.
Noisy, rough, whining and vibration	Worn bearings and/or laygear thrust washers (initially) resulting in extended wear generally due to play and backlash	Dismantle and renew.
Noisy and difficult engagement of gear	Clutch fault	Examine clutch operation.

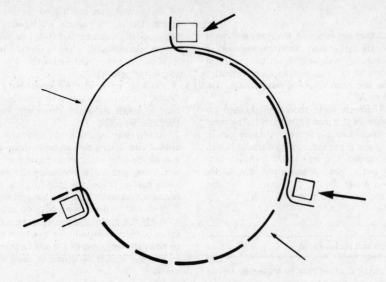

Fig.6.3. Synchroniser hubs - arrangement of retainer clips for sliding keys

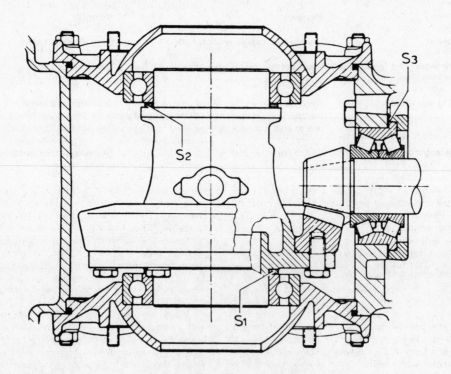

Fig.6.4. Differential assembly — cross section
S1 and S2 - Differential casing shims. S3 Pinion shim

Chapter 7 Automatic stick shift transmission

For modifications, and information applicable to later models, see Supplement at end of manual

Contents

Specifications

Gear ratios

Low	2.06 : 1
Medium	1.26 : 1
High	.89 : 1
Reverse	3.07 : 1

Stall speed	2000 − 2250 rpm
Final drive ratio	4.375 : 1
Torque multiplication	2.1 (maximum)
Maximum torque at 2000 rpm - 1300	64.4 lbs.ft. (8.9 mkg)
— 1500	73.8 lbs.ft. (10.2 mkg)
Converter oil type	Dexron type ATF (Duckhams D-Matic)
Converter oil capacity (dry)...	3.6 litres (7½ pints)
Transmission/final drive oil capacity (dry)	3.0 litres (6¼ pints)
Converter oil pressure at 4000 rpm (80°C)	38−52 p.s.i. (2.7−3.7 kg/cm^2)

Torque wrench settings

Torque converter drive plate gland nut	282 lbs.ft. (39 mkg)

1. General description

Later models (1968 on) of the 1300 and 1500 Beetle were offered with the optional extra of a semi-automatic transmission. Where such units are fitted the rear axle is of the double jointed drive shaft type. This latter is inherently a much more stable arrangement than the conventional swing axle. Many feel that the advantage of the optional extra lies more in the modified rear suspension than the automatic transmission!

The system works as follows:

A 3 speed gearbox of conventional design, a clutch of conventional design and a torque converter are all married together. Gears are changed by a conventional gear lever. The gear lever, however, is connected to the clutch in such a way that as soon as the lever is moved longitudinally (i.e. in a gear selection direction) the clutch disengages.

The torque converter operates to transmit power when the engine is turning above idling speed and so therefore acts as a moving off clutch. It also acts as a form of 'slip' between engine and gear — In other words when engine load is higher — such as when moving from rest or uphill — the engine speed can increase to impart more power even though the vehicle remains in the same gear at the same speed. This enables the gearbox to manage with only 3 forward gears. These are the same as 2nd, 3rd and top of a conventional 4 speed manual gearbox.

If the torque converter is called upon to 'slip' too much — for example when driving up a long hill in top gear, the oil will overheat. When this happens a temperature sensitive warning light on the dashboard lights up and indicates that a lower gear should be selected. Lowest gear is adequate for all normal conditions and no warning light for the low range is installed.

The operation of the clutch is pneumatic via a control valve and servo. Vacuum is drawn from the engine intake manifold and there is also a vacuum tank. The control valve is fitted on the left side of the engine compartment and the vacuum tank under the left rear wing. The vacuum control valve is actuated by a solenoid switch and this in turn is actuated by a special switch incorporated in the gear lever base. As soon as the gear lever is moved forward or backwards the switch contacts close, and the solenoid operates. In addition there is a second switch. This acts as a starter inhibitor which avoids the engine being started with a gear engaged. It also prevents the clutch from engaging again during the brief period of lateral movement of the lever from one range to another through neutral.

The control valve also incorporates a device to regulate the speed with which the clutch engages. In accelerating circumstances (throttle open) the operation of the servo is quicker than would be possible with a foot pedal change. In decelerating conditions — (throttle closed) the control valve controls the servo to operate less quickly. This enables the clutch to re-engage smoothly and without snatch.

Oil for the torque converter is circulated by a pump from the converter and through a reservoir tank which is mounted under the right rear mudguard. The pump is fitted on the end of the engine oil pump shaft. This oil circulation serves to cool the oil as well as maintain a constant pressure, (by means of a restriction in the return line). A relief valve is incorporated in the pump to limit maximum pressure.

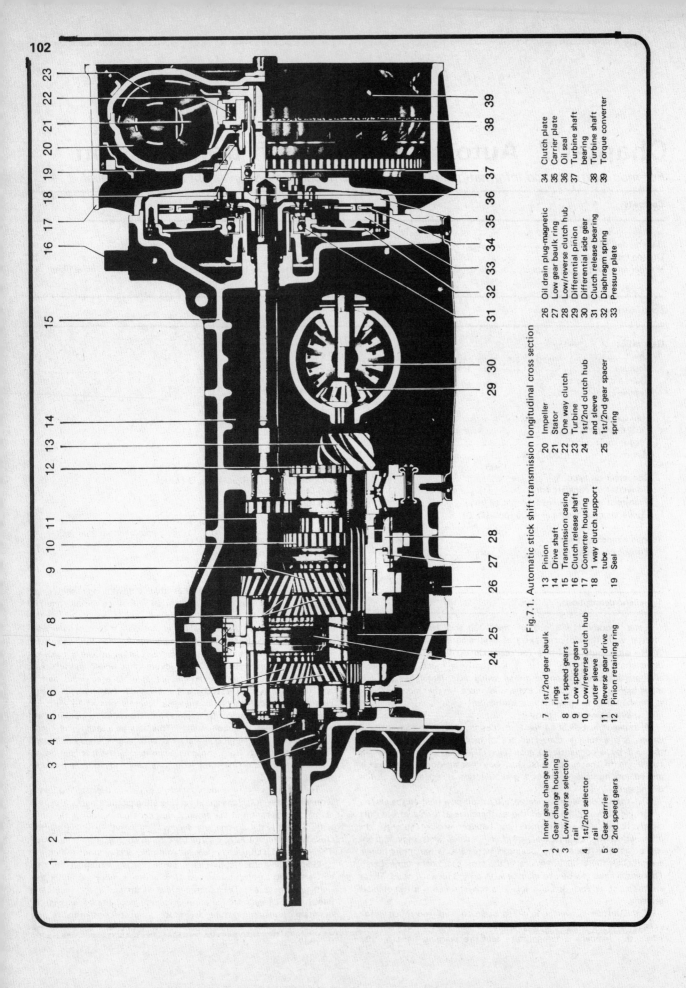

Fig.7.1. Automatic stick shift transmission longitudinal cross section

1 Inner gear change lever
2 Gear change housing
3 Low/reverse selector rail
4 1st/2nd selector rail
5 Gear carrier
6 2nd speed gears
7 1st/2nd gear baulk rings
8 1st speed gears
9 Low speed gears
10 Low/reverse clutch hub outer sleeve
11 Reverse gear drive
12 Pinion retaining ring
13 Pinion
14 Drive shaft
15 Transmission casing
16 Clutch release shaft
17 Converter housing
18 1 way clutch support tube
19 Seal
20 Impeller
21 Stator
22 One way clutch
23 Turbine
24 1st/2nd clutch hub and sleeve
25 1st/2nd gear spacer spring
26 Oil drain plug-magnetic
27 Low gear baulk ring
28 Low/reverse clutch hub
29 Differential pinion
30 Differential side gear
31 Clutch release bearing
32 Diaphragm spring
33 Pressure plate
34 Clutch plate
35 Carrier plate
36 Oil seal
37 Turbine shaft bearing
38 Turbine shaft
39 Torque converter

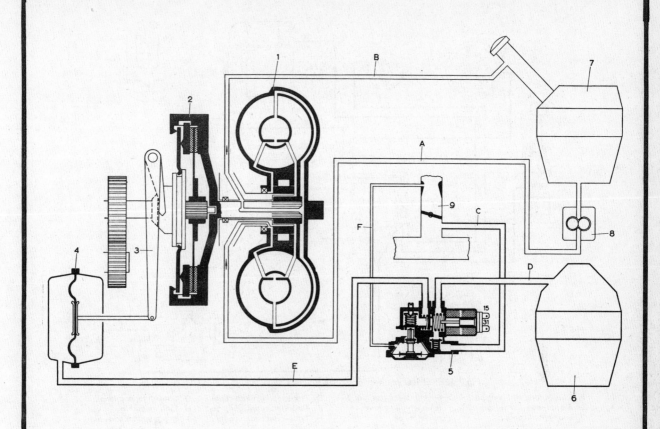

Fig.7.2. Schematic layout of torque converter and auto stick shift clutch operating systems

1	Torque converter	6	Vacuum tank
2	Clutch	7	Converter oil tank
3	Clutch operating lever	8	Converter oil pump
4	Clutch servo	9	Carburettor venturi
5	Servo control valve	A	Oil pressure line

B Oil return line
C Vacuum line. Inlet manifold to control valve
D Vacuum line. Tank to control valve
E Vacuum line servo to control valve
F Vacuum line. Control/reduction valve to venturi

Fig.7.3. Vacuum servo control valve mounted in engine compartment

Arrow indicates the clutch engagement time regulating screw. Note perforated plate of air-filter unit behind.

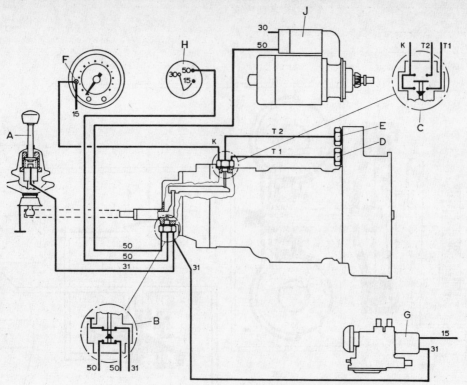

Fig.7.4. Electrical connections for auto-stick shift (early versions)

A Change lever and contacts
B Starter inhibitor switch and neutral contact
C Selector switch for 1 or 2 range temperature of converter oil
D Temperature switch-range 2
E Temperature switch-range 1
F Temperature warning light
G Control valve solenoid
H Ignition switch
J Starter motor solenoid

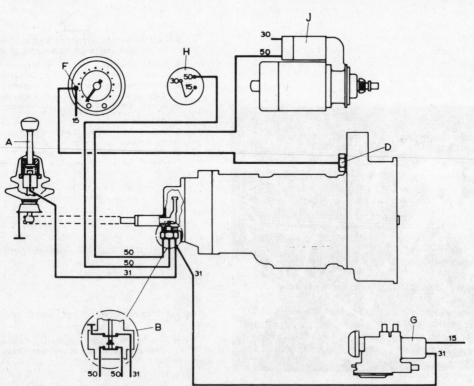

Fig.7.5. Electrical connections for auto-stick shift (later versions)

A Shift lever and contact
B Starter inhibitor switch and neutral contact
D Temperature switch (140–150°C)
F Warning lamp
G Control valve
H Ignition switch
J Starter motor solenoid

2. Driving technique

1 The gear change lever looks and functions like a conventional floor change except that there are only 4 positions - 3 forward and 1 reverse. In order that the 'automatic' conventions are impressed on the driver the three forward speeds are referred to as 'L', 1 and 2, (even though they are 1st, 2nd and 3rd!). The change is through the conventional H pattern.

2 The engine can be started only in the neutral position. When the engine is cold (and the automatic choke in operation) the idling speed is higher than when warm so before engaging a gear apply brakes, otherwise the car will creep forward.

3 For normal driving it is necessary to use only the top two gears (1 and 2). This is because the torque converter applies the engine power over a wider range.

4 To engage a gear whilst stationary move the lever into position 1. As soon as the lever starts to move, the clutch will automatically disengage. It is important that the engine speed is not above idling. Let go of the gear lever and depress the accelerator. The torque converter will take up the drive and the car will move off. Speed range 0—55 mph.

5 If starting on a steep slope or where tight manoeuvring is involved select 'L' for forward movement. Speed range 0—30 mph approximately.

6 Once the car is under way the gear change lever can be moved when required into the most suitable driving range.

7 If excessive load is placed on the torque converter in 1 and 2 ranges the oil temperature warning light will come on indicating the need to drop to a lower gear.

8 It is not necessary to disengage from the selected gear for temporary stops in traffic, but the brakes must be applied to prevent 'creep'.

9 When the car is parked the handbrake must be fully on. There is no transmission brake by selecting a gear because the torque converter effectively disconnects the transmission from the engine.

10 The vehicle can be tow started if the 'L' range is selected and a speed of more than 15 mph is attained. If less than that the torque converter will not 'bite'.

11 The car may be towed in case of breakdown or accident with the gear change lever in neutral.

3. Maintenance and adjustments

1 The automatic transmission fluid (ATF) level in the tank should be checked at 1,000 mile or one month intervals. At the same time the converter, tank and all connecting hoses should be examined for signs of leakage.

If the ATF level drops, yet there is no sign of external leakage, check the engine oil level. If this has risen it indicates that there is probably a leak from ATF pump to engine oil pump. This must be attended to immediately otherwise both engine and converter could be ruined.

2 Every 6,000 miles check the oil level in the final drive and gearbox.

3 Every 12,000 miles change the gearbox/final drive lubricant and clean the magnetic drain plugs.

4 Check shift clutch adjustment should be checked every 6,000 miles. Indications of malfunction are slip or noisy engagement of reverse - assuming of course that the torque converter is operating correctly and engine revolutions are not too high at the time of gear engagement.

The clutch clearance can be checked by pulling the vacuum hose off the servo unit and then measuring the distance between the bottom of the adjuster sleeve and the upper edge of the servo mounting bracket (Fig.7.6).

If this measurement is more than 4 mm, the clutch needs adjustment.

To adjust the clutch, first slacken the adjuster sleeve locknut just enough to enable the adjuster to be turned. Then turn the adjuster away from the locknut until there is a gap of 6.5 mm between the two. Then move the locknut back to the end of the adjuster sleeve and tighten it once more.

If, as a result of adjustment the operating lever is found to be touching the clutch housing then it indicates that the clutch plate is worn out.

5 The control valve air filter will need cleaning at intervals depending on the condition in which the car is operating. 3,000 miles is a suitable interval for normal conditions.

The filter is a mushroom shaped unit fitted to the side of the control valve, (Fig.7.3). Simply unscrew it with a spanner on the hexagon shank of the mounting stud. Thoroughly flush it in petrol and if possible blow it dry completely with compressed air. It is important to avoid the possibility of any cleaning fluid being drawn into the system after it is refitted. Do not oil the filter.

6 Shift clutch engagement may need adjustment. As described earlier, the control valve governs the speed of clutch engagement. When changing to a higher gear it tends to be quick and slower from high to low. This prevents any undue snatch. To check the clutch try changing from 2 to 1 at about 45 mph without depressing the accelerator pedal. There should be a delay of about 1 second before the drive is fully taken up. If there is any snatch then it indicates that adjustment may be necessary - all other things being equal.

To adjust the speed of clutch engagement remove the cap from the top of the control valve to expose the head of the adjusting screw (Fig.7.3). To decrease the speed of engagement turn the screw ¼—½ turn clockwise. To increase engagement speed turn it ¼—½ turn anticlockwise.

7 After some time it may be necessary to clean, adjust or renew the switch contacts inside the gear lever which operates the shift clutch. Raise the rubber boot round the base of the lever and slacken the locknut at the bottom of the sleeve (Fig.7.7). Then screw the shift sleeve right off to expose the contacts when the top section of the lever comes off.

To set the contacts the sleeve must be screwed down until they just touch and then unscrewed ½ turn which gives a gap of 0.25—0.4 mm (0.010—0.016 inch). It is important that after this setting is made the longated hole in the sleeve runs fore and aft. It is the slight movement of the lever in this slot which pushes the contacts together prior to shifting the gear. If the slot does not lie fore and aft within the setting limits then undo the other locknut on the threaded sleeve. The whole unit can then be turned into position.

4. Engine and transmission - removal and replacement

Due to the more complex nature of the automatic transmission it is not considered within the competence of the average owner to overhaul or repair it himself.

Removal and replacement of the assembly may be carried out. The principles of removal are the same as for a conventional model.

The following additional points should be noted as well.

1 It will be necessary to detach the torque converter oil lines. The pressure line from the pump should be raised so that oil does not run out.

2 If is necessary to detach the torque converter from the engine flex plate. If the engine is rotated each of the four screws will appear through a hole in the transmission casing. When they have been removed the engine can be separated from the transmission in the usual way.

3 When the transmission unit is being taken off, first devise a way of keeping the torque converter from falling out of the housing, a simple metal strap fixed to two of the mounting studs will do this.

4 Detach the inner ends of the double jointed axle shafts. (See Chapter 6 for details). Cover the inner joints with plastic sheeting to keep dirt out and hang them up to the underframe with wire.

5 Disconnect the oil hose banjo unions where they join the transmission casing, pull off the two wires to the temperature switches

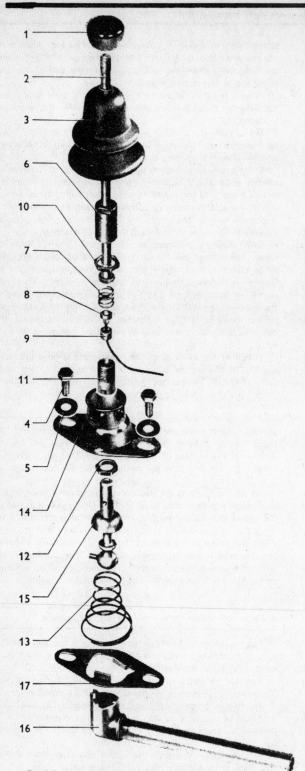

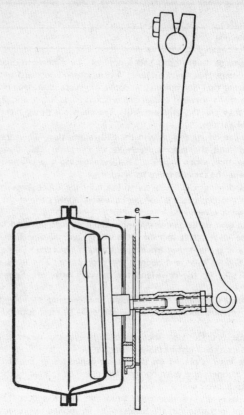

Fig.7.6. Clutch/servo adjustment
Dimension 'e' is 4 mm maximum.

Fig.7.7. Automatic stick shift - change lever assembly - exploded view

1	Grip	10	Locknut
2	Upper lever	11	Threaded sleeve
3	Boot	12	Lower locknut
4	Mounting bolt	13	Spring
5	Spring washer	14	Mounting plate
6	Shift sleeve	15	Lower lever
7	Spring	16	Change rod
8	Contact	17	Reverse stop plate
9	Insulating sleeve		

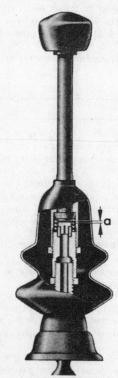

Fig.7.7a. Gearchange lever switch contact adjustment; (a) = 0.25 to 0.4 mm

and unclip and pull off the hose from the servo unit.

6 Pull the three pin plugs from the temperature selector switch on the transmission case, and also the starter inhibitor switch on the gear change housing at the front of the transmission casing.

7 Replacement is a reversal of this procedure. When restarting the engine it is important to check that the converter oil is flowing back to the tank. If not after 2 or 3 minutes then there is probably an air lock in the system. Slacken the banjo joints on the transmission to bleed air out whilst the engine is running at idling speed.

5. Torque converter - stall speed test

1 The torque converter stall speed is that speed beyond which the engine will not turn when drive is engaged and the brakes are fully on. To carry it out it is necessary to be able to know the engine rpm. This involves temporary connection of an electric tachometer.

2 It is important that the engine be in proper tune for this test and thus developing its rated power output. The converter oil level must be correct.

3 With the engine warmed up and running, range 2 selected, and all brakes firmly on, increase engine speed to maximum possible and note the revolutions per minute. This must be done quickly and not continue longer than the time taken to read the instruments. Otherwise the converter oil will overheat seriously. If the stall speed exceeds

Specification 1900—2100 rpm (or 2100—2300 from Chassis No. 1112504386) it is indicative of a slipping gear change clutch. If it does not reach stall speed revolutions then the power output of the engine is down.

6. Engine differences

a) Oil pump

The engine oil pump is elaborated to incorporate the converter fluid pump as well. Modifications to the crankshaft pulley wheel position allow the extra length to be accommodated.

The two pumps are separated by a plate and oil seals for the common lower gear spindle are incorporated in the plate. The same 4 studs provide the mounting for both pumps.

It is important, when checking both engine and torque converter oils to ensure that a drop in the level of either does not correspond with an increase in the level of the other. Such a condition could indicate faulty seals within the pump. Damage will occur if the two oils mix.

b) Torque converter drive plate

In place of the flywheel a drive plate is fitted to the crankshaft by a gland nut. This nut is tightened further than that for a flywheel. The torque setting is 282 lb/ft. A special tool locked into the holes in the plate is normally needed to tighten the nut satisfactorily. Makeshift methods are likely to distort the plate which is then rendered unserviceable.

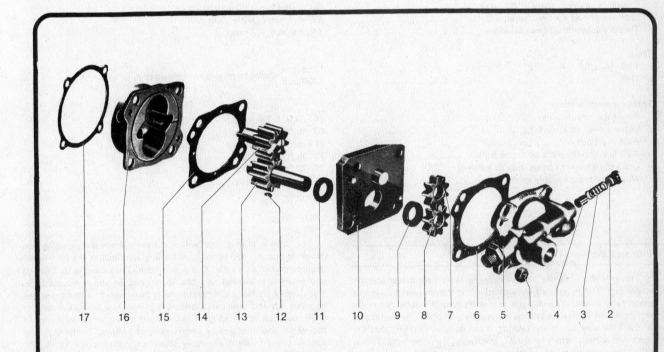

Fig.7.8. Torque converter oil pump

1	Sealing nut	6	Gasket	10	Dividing plate
2	Plug	7	Converter oil pump - upper gear	11	Plate oil seal
3	Spring	8	Converter oil pump - lower gear	12	Woodruff key
4	Piston	9	Plate oil seal	13	Engine oil pump - lower gear and shaft
5	Converter oil pump housing			14	Engine oil pump -

	upper gear and shaft
15	Gasket
16	Engine oil pump housing
17	Housing gasket

Chapter 8 Rear axle shafts

Contents

Specifications

Axle shaft

Maximum run-out between centres	.5 mm (.20 ins)

Axle shaft/side gear clearances (swing axles)

Clearance across spade end in gear	.03 — .1 mm (.001 — .004 in)
Clearance between spade end fulcrum plates..	.03 — .244 mm (.00 — .010 in)
Side gear thrust washer clearance	.05 — .2 mm (.002 — .008 in)
Thrust washer thicknesses available	3.9, 4.0, 4.1, 4.2 mm

Track

1300 (Aug 66 — Aug 67)..	1358 mm
1500...	1350 mm (refer to page 5 for complete details)

Torque wrench settings

Axle tube retainer nuts	14 lb.ft. (2.0 mkg)
Bearing retainer screws	43 lb.ft. (6.0 mkg)
Axle shaft nut	217 lb.ft. (30.0 mkg)
Axle tube/spring plate bolts and nuts...	72 lb.ft. (10.0 mkg)
Drive shaft socket screws (double jointed)	25 lb.ft. (3.5 mkg)
Wheel shaft nut (double jointed axle)...	253 lb.ft. (35.0 mkg)

1. General description

The axle shafts to the Volkswagen rear wheels are independently suspended. The inner ends are located in the transmission casing in a spade type universal joint. Each axle shaft runs in a tube, the outer end of which is attached to the rear suspension plate. The outer end of the tube also carries the bearing. It can be seen therefore that the shaft and wheel form a rigid unit, pivoted at the inner end. This is called the swinging axle type of drive.

The axle tubes are oil filled from the transmission casing and this provides lubrication for the outer wheel bearing. Oil is retained at the outer end by a conventional seal on the shaft and at the inner end by a heavy duty flexible boot which shrouds the axle tube retainer plate. The lateral location of each axle is all carried at the inner end by the axle tube retainer plate. It can be seen that the shaft outer bearing and tube are all locked together so that the side thrust is therefore carried by the inner pivoting end of the tube. The spade end of the axle shaft in fact floats in the side gear. The side gear lateral location is by a thrust ring and circlip.

The outer bearing and oil seal are secured by a bearing cover plate on the tube and the drum and wheel secured to the axle by a single nut.

The double jointed rear axle is different from the swinging arm design in that an additional semi-trailing arm locates the rear wheel in place of the axle tube. This arm is bushed in rubber at its forward end where it is pivoted to a bracket welded on the rear cross tube. The drive shaft has a universal joint at both ends to allow the wheel to move up and down in a different plane As a result the camber angle variation is not so great throughout the up and down range of the wheel and this greatly improves road holding. In the U.K. the double jointed axle is normally found only on models fitted with stick shift automatic transmission.

2. Oil seals and bearings (swing axle) - removal and replacement

1 To renew an oil seal or bearing requires the rear axle shaft nut to be undone so before jacking the car up remove the hub caps and take out the split pin from the castellated nut on the shaft. Using a 36 mm socket spanner and a proper long handle attachment slacken the nut. It is advisable to have the handbrake on also. If the wheel still turns then some additional weight will be needed in the back of the car to prevent the wheel slipping on the ground. Slacken the road wheel bolts at the same time.

2 Jack up the car, remove the road wheel and take off the hub nut.

3 Slacken off the brake shoe adjusters as far as they will go (see Chapter 9 for details).

4 It should now be possible to draw the brake drum off the splined end of the drive shaft. If any difficulty is experienced it should be tapped with a soft mallet progressively round the edges. If this does not seem to work bolt the wheel back onto the drum again and see whether the additional grip provided enables you to pull the drum off with it. If the drum should be really tight and unmovable then it will be necessary to obtain a puller which will hook into the holes in the drum and bear on to the outer end of the axle shaft. Do not strike the drum hard around the edges or you will probably crack it.

5 Once the drum is removed the heads of four bolts which hold the bearing cover to the axle tube are revealed. This cover houses the oil seal. The brake backplate is also held by the four bolts and although the illustrations show the brake shoes removed the whole plate assembly may be moved off the axle and hung on one side without disconnecting either the hydraulic fluid pipes or handbrake cable. The bearing cover is removed so that the 'O' ring round the bearing may be renewed at the same time as the main seal. This 'O' ring should be taken off now and if only the seal renewal is being done then adopt the method described later in this section.

6 To remove the bearing take off the shim next. The easiest way to remove the bearing is with a fine pronged puller which engages in between the steel balls of the bearing itself; but this is a special tool which may be difficult to obtain. It is possible to drive the shaft inwards just far enough to enable the bearing and shaft together to be pulled out of the housing just enough to get levers behind the bearing; and so remove it with a more conventional puller. There is sufficient clearance at the inner end of the shaft to permit this, but great care must be taken not to overdo it or damage will be caused to the differential pinion gears. Make sure to protect the splined and threaded end of the shaft by replacing the nut and using a block of wood as further protection. Use a heavy hammer and after each blow check by pulling the shaft outwards how far the bearing has moved in relation to it. Once there is a gap sufficient to get a lever in, stop striking the shaft. A third alternative is to lock a self-grip wrench on to the lip of the outer bearing race and then use the nose of the wrench jaws to lever against to ease the bearing out. Two wrenches - one at each side - are best for this method and the jaw teeth must be in good condition. Once the bearing is clear of the housing it is a reasonably straightforward operation to get it right off.

7 Behind the bearing is another spacer but this need not be disturbed. If it comes out make sure it goes back the same way — with the bevelled edge inwards.

8 To replace the bearing put it over the shaft with the covered side of the ball race if any, facing outwards. It can then be 'drifted' right into the housing.

9 Next fit the large 'O' ring from the seal kit round the outside of the bearing and up to the axle tube flange.

10 Fit the shim over the shaft followed by the smaller rubber 'O' ring.

11 Next drive out the old seal from inside the bearing cover using a suitable punch. Take care not to damage the inner surface of the flange. The new seal may then be driven into the cover with the lip of the seal facing inwards. If, when you drove out the old seal a washer (oil slinger) came out from behind it make sure that the hole which is in one edge of the bearing cover is clear and that the washer goes into the cover before the seal - which can only be fitted from the inside. Tap the seal in with a soft faced mallet or block of wood until the outer face is flush with the cover.

12 Next replace the brake backplate onto the axle tube flange (with the hydraulic cylinder uppermost). The outer spacer collar should be lubricated on its outer face and put onto the shaft.

13 Place the bearing cover in position. The cover has either a raised lug or a hole in one edge. In either case the lug or the oil drain hole goes on the bottom edge but the cover with the oil hole has a paper washer between it and the backplate. If you obtained the correct seal kit for your chassis number the paper washer will be included.

14 Replace the four cover bolts and tighten them evenly to a torque of 43 ft/lbs (6 mkg).

15 Replace the brake drum and refit the nut. Replace the road wheel and tighten the axle shaft nut as described in Chapter 9, Section 4 (see Fig. 8.6).

3. Oil seals and bearings (double joint axle) - removal and replacement

1 To renew or repack the rear wheel bearings with grease it is first necessary to remove the diagonal suspension arm from the vehicle as described in Chapter 11, Section 10.

2 With the arm clamped in the vice by the spring plate bracket remove the slotted nut (already slackened before the arm was removed) and brake drum.

3 Remove the four screws holding the bearing cover to the arm and then take off the cover, 'O' ring, outer spacer and back plate.

4 Using a soft faced mallet knock the wheel shaft out and remove the inner spacer.

5 Using a tyre lever take out the inner oil seal.

6 Remove the circlip behind the oil seal and then knock out the ball bearing from the other side using a suitable drift.

7 Remove the spacer sleeve and the inner race of the roller bearing. Drift out the outer race of the roller bearing from the arm.

8 Begin reassembly by first driving in the ball race. Then refit the circlip and oil seal with the lip facing inwards.

9 Pack 60 grams of suitable grease into the hub centre working some of it into the ball bearing and onto the lip of the seal. Put the inner spacer inside the oil seal so that the chamfered edge will marry up with the radius on the shaft flange. Then press or drive the wheel shaft through the ball bearing until the flange just touches the inner race.

10 Fit the spacer sleeve over the wheel shaft, grease the outer race of the roller bearing and drive it into position in the housing.

11 The inner race has to be fitted over the shaft next and this is best done by using the outer spacer and a suitable length of tube. The large shaft nut can then be used to force it in. Remove the spacer.

12 If necessary fit a new seal into the bearing cover and fill the double lip of the cover with grease.

13 Fit a new 'O' ring round the bearing and install the backplate and bearing cover. Replace the bolts and tighten them to 43 lb/ft. Refit the outer spacer brake drum and hub and replace the slotted shaft nut which will be finally tightened after the arm has been replaced and the wheel fitted.

4. Axle shafts and tubes (swing axle) - removal and replacement

1 The need to renew an axle shaft is rare and can only be caused by breakage or damage to the splined and threaded outer end. If it is suspected of being badly worn on the inner spade end a check can be made but it is most unusual for such wear to take place separately from any other general wear in the transmission or final drive. Volkswagen do not recommend the removal of axle shafts unless the whole of the transmission assembly has first been removed from the vehicle. This is because in order to assess the correct clearance of the axle tube at the inner end it is considered necessary to be able to swing the tube around freely - without the restriction which results from it being in position on the car. Nevertheless it can be done; although the placing of the necessary gaskets and the constant guard against dirt contaminating the differential make it something of a struggle. It is reasonable to say that if you have no other reason to remove engine and transmission it would be a lot of effort just to remove an axle shaft.

2 To remove an axle shaft first remove the wheel, brake drum, brake backplate assembly and bearing as described in the previous section. Do not forget to drain out the oil first.

3 Thoroughly clean the whole area surrounding the axle tube retainer plate on the transmission casing. Clean also the axle tube

2.6. Pulling the bearing off.

2.7. Fitting the inner spacer.

2.8. Putting the bearing on the shaft.

2.9. Fitting the large 'O' ring.

2.10(a) Fit the shim washer....

2.10(b) ....followed by the small 'O' ring.

2.11. Fit a new seal in the bearing cover.

2.12(a) Fit the brake backplate.

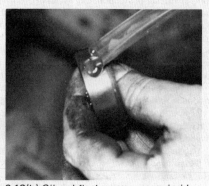

2.12(b) Oil and fit the outer spacer inside the seal....

2.13 .... and refit the bearing cover.

4.5. Marking the rear suspension plate before moving the axle tube.

4.11. Using circlip pliers on the circlip holding the side gear in position.

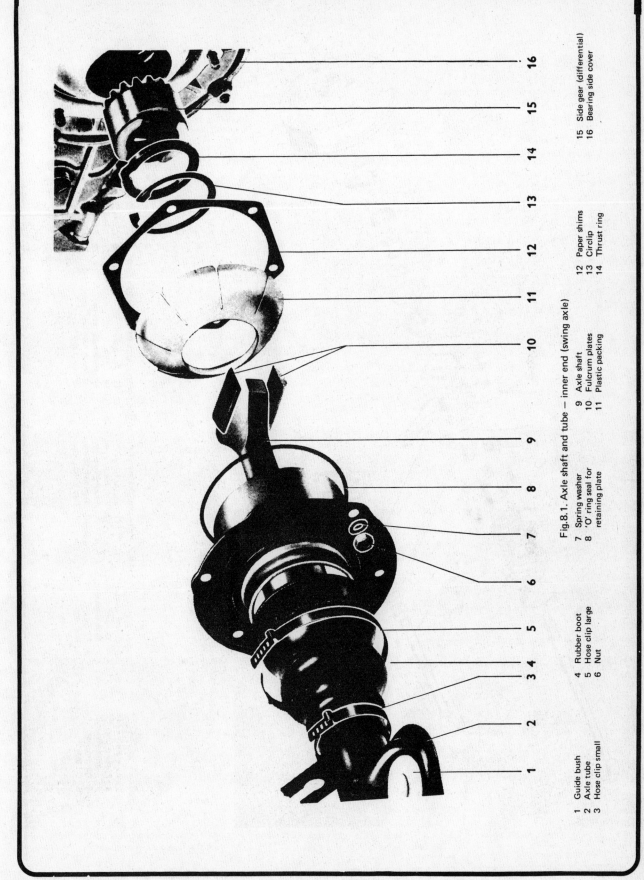

Fig.8.1. Axle shaft and tube — inner end (swing axle)

1 Guide bush	4 Rubber boot	7 Spring washer	9 Axle shaft	12 Paper shims	15 Side gear (differential)
2 Axle tube	5 Hose clip large	8 'O' ring seal for	10 Fulcrum plates	13 Circlip	16 Bearing side cover
3 Hose clip small	6 Nut	retaining plate	11 Plastic packing	14 Thrust ring	

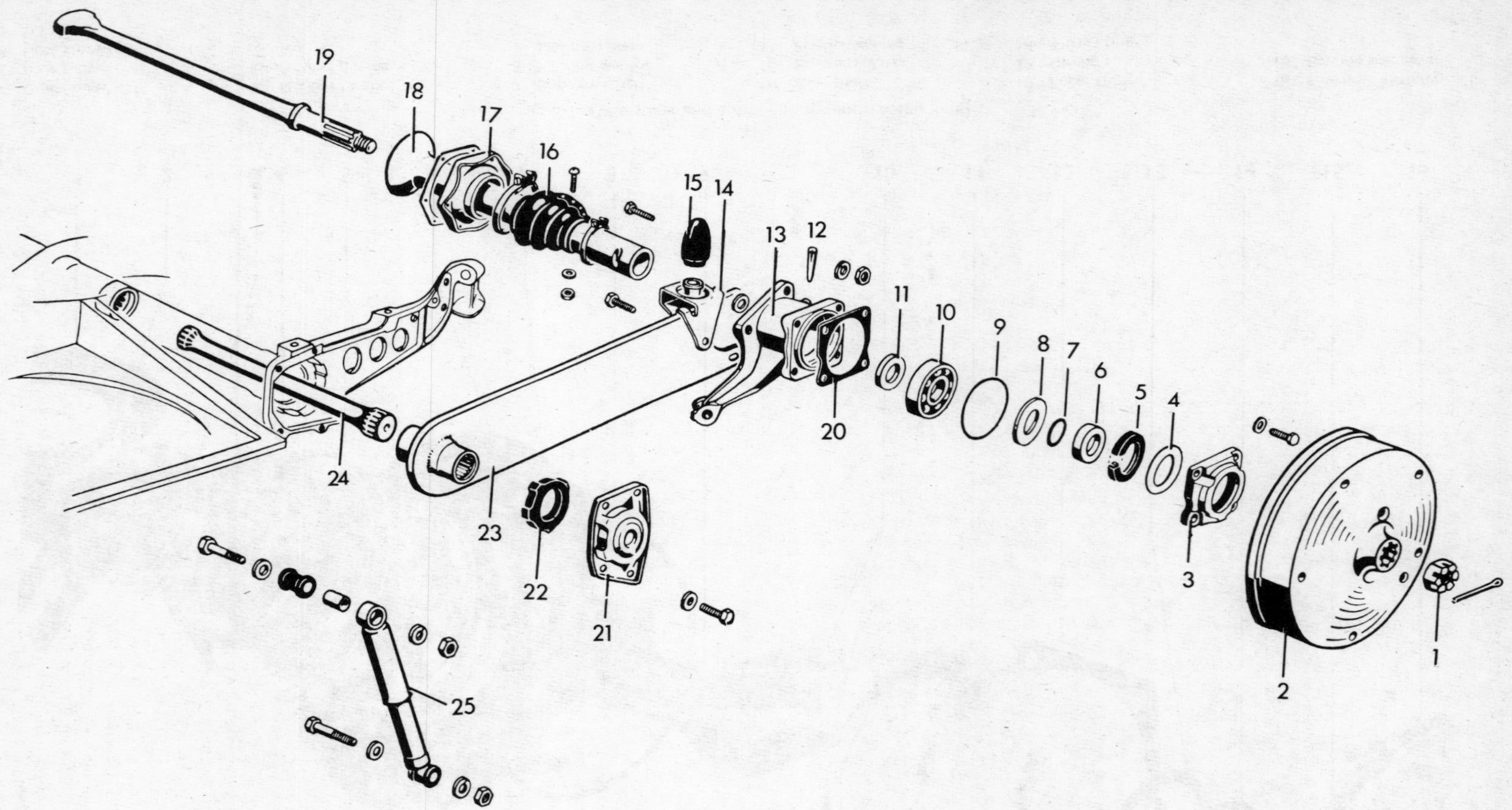

Fig.8.2. Rear axle shaft and suspension components (swing axle)

1	Axle shaft nut	6	Spacer (outer)	
2	Brake drum	7	'O' ring	
3	Bearing retainer	8	Shim washer	
4	Oil thrower	9	'O' ring	
5	Oil seal	10	Bearing	

11	Spacer (inner)	15	Bump stop	20	Gasket
12	Pin (locating bearing housing to tube)	16	Gaiter	21	Retainer plate
13	Bearing housing	17	Axle tube retainer	22	Support bush
14	Bump stop bracket	18	Axle tube	23	Spring plate
		19	Axle shaft	24	Torsion bar
				25	Damper

itself for a distance of about six inches back from the end of the large oil retainer boot. Then slacken both boot retainer clips and draw the boot off the retainer plate and leave it a little way down the tube. This is done so that it does not get abnormally stretched and possibly ruptured during subsequent operations.

4 The next task is to detach the outer end of the axle tube which is secured to the suspension arm plate by three nuts and bolts. Clean up the bolts thoroughly and apply penetrating oil.

5 The position of the outer end of the axle tube in relation to the suspension plate can vary and it is most important that a mark is made to ensure correct re-alignment. A notch exists in the top edge of the axle tube flange so with a cold chisel make another notch exactly in line with it in the edge of the suspension plate. Be accurate.

6 Remove the bolt securing the lower end of the telescopic damper and then put a suitable support under the end of the axle and remove the three nuts and bolts. They are big, tight and probably rusty so make sure you have two spanners of the correct size available — socket or ring. It is quite likely that the spring washers for the nuts will break when the nut is undone so make a note to get some more. They are important. Note also that the front bolt of the three also secures the bump stop buffer bracket. As a result it is slightly larger than the other two.

7 With the bolts removed the axle tube outer end may be moved to the rear, clear of the suspension plate. If you have been reading this in connection with the removal of the transmission unit (Chapter 6) this is as far as you need go here now. Go back to Chapter 6 until you have removed the transmission from the car. Then come back here!

8 Moving to the inner end of the axle tube, next remove the six nuts securing the axle tube retainer plate (do not confuse these with the eight nuts surrounding them).

9 The retainer plate may now be pulled off the studs and the axle tube, together with the plate, taken right off the axle shaft. Carefully remove, intact if possible, the gaskets between the retainer plate and the transmission housing.

10 Fitted over the convex face of the axle tube location on the transmission casing is a plastic hemispherical packing piece. Carefully take this off.

11 Inside the transmission housing it will be possible to see the two eyes of a large circlip which needs contracting in order to be released. Do this with a pair of circlip pliers. The circlip and thrust ring behind it will now come out. The axle shaft, fulcrum plates and side gear can all be withdrawn also.

12 Replacement of the axle shaft and axle tube is a reversal of the removal procedure but there are one or two points which must be carefully considered.

13 When refitting the thrust ring for the side gear note the protrusion in the outer edge which engages a groove in the casing to prevent it rotating.

14 If the transmission has been completely dismantled and both axle tubes have been removed you must make sure you get them back on the correct side as they are handed. With the notch in the bearing housing upwards the shock absorber mounting lug faces forward and down.

15 It will be appreciated that the domed end of the axle tube pivots on the mating face of the transmission. The plastic packing piece in between acts as a bearing surface. The two are held together by the retainer plate. The thickness of the gaskets behind the retainer plate determines the amount of pressure it applies. Too few gaskets and it will be so tight it will move only with difficulty. Too many and it will be slack and result in endfloat of the whole axle assembly. Provided there was no evidence of excessive endfloat on dismantling and that the plastic packing piece is in good condition there is no reason why the same gaskets should not be refitted. The theoretical clearance is between 0.00—0.2 mm (0.00—0.008 inch) but as there is no satisfactory way of measuring this the only practical way is by moving the axle tube in all directions as far as possible. Friction should be felt but there should be no jamming or sticking at any point.

16 If the gaskets have been damaged carefully separate them to see how many there are. Each is identified by having one or two holes punched in it indicating that it is either 0.1 or 0.2 mm (0.004 or 0.008 inch) thick. Make up a pack the same thickness and then add or subtract as required.

17 There is an additional rubber 'O' ring which fits in the recess in the bearing cover inside the gaskets. This should always be renewed on reassembly. Do not fit it until the gasket thicknesses have been worked out. Then fit it after the gaskets so that their edges do not get caught up on it causing possible distortion.

18 If you have some molybdenum disulphide paste available (any moly additive will be better than nothing) smear the mating faces of the axle tube and packing to aid lubrication particularly in the early stages of re-use. In any case lubricate them well with transmission oil. Tighten the retainer plate securing nuts evenly to 14 lb/ft. (2.0 mkg).

19 When reconnecting the outer end of the axle tube to the suspension plate make sure that the two marks made before removal line up exactly. Do not forget to re-fix the bump stop bracket to the front bolt. Incidentally, the bolts should be fitted with their heads inwards (to the centre of the car).

20 Do not try and replace the rubber boot until the axle tube has been re-installed. It is much easier (and less likely to cause strain) to fit when the axle is as near horizontal as possible. Make sure that the parts are perfectly clean and that the clips are serviceable and not overtightened.

21 Refill the transmission case with oil.

5. Axle shafts and tubes (swing axle) - examination for wear

1 Under normal circumstances the wear on the inner spade ends of the axle shaft will be negligible and in any case should not be greater or less than the wear that will occur in the transmission unit generally.

2 To check the wear, place the end of the shaft in the side gear. First measure the gap across the end with a feeler. If it exceeds 0.20 mm (0.008 inch) then a new shaft, new gear or both will be needed to reduce it.

3 Next fit the fulcrum plates into the side gear and refit the shaft. Then measure the clearance between shaft and fulcrum plate. It should not exceed 0.25 mm (0.010 inch). It is possible to obtain oversize fulcrum plates in order to rectify any excessive clearance here. Renewal plates have grooves cut in their flat faces so you will be able to tell if this has already been done.

4 If examination shows that the gear/shaft clearances warrant buying new parts it should be remembered that the gear and shaft are grouped by size tolerance. These tolerances are colour coded and the shaft has a paint band round it. The gear has a matching colour in a recess. The specifications section gives the details.

5 Axle shafts should, of course, be straight and with the shaft held between centres the run-out at the bearing seat should not exceed 0.05 mm (0.002 inch). As this is not the sort of measurement that can be made accurately without precision holding and measuring equipment you should not need to worry about checking it unless you have specific reason for thinking the shaft is bent. Shafts can be straightened - cold only - so it is best to get this done at a Volkswagen agency.

6 The splines and thread on the end of the shaft should not deteriorate unless you have had the misfortune to have the shaft nut come loose for some rare reason. The best way to test the thread is with the full torque of 217 lb/ft when the nut is re-tightened. If nothing gives then you can assume that it will serve. If the thread strips - on either nut or shaft - then you will probably need a new shaft as well as nut.

7 Axle tubes should not deteriorate. Examine the concave bearing surface at the inner end and check that the plastic packing is not breaking up. The bearing housings have been known to get damaged

4.12. Putting the axle shaft and side gear into position.

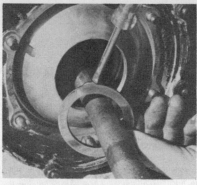

4.13(a) Replacing the thrust ring ....

4.13(b) .... and circlip.

4.14. L.H. axle tube end showing notch and damper mounting lug facing forward.

4.15. Positioning the plastic packing piece.

4.16(a) Selecting gaskets.

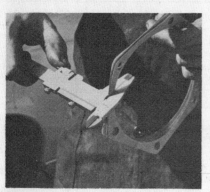

4.16(b) Checking the thickness of the gasket pack.

4.17. Gaskets in position.

4.18(a) Replacing the axle tube.

4.18(b) .... and tightening the axle tube retainer nuts.

4.19. Lining up the marks in the axle tube flange and spring plate. The front securing bolt (arrowed) also carries the bump stop bracket.

5.2. Measuring the shaft to side gear clearance across the spade end.

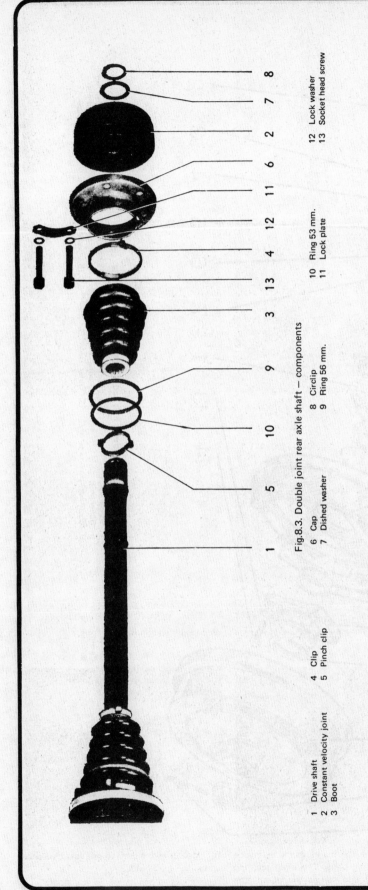

Fig.8.3. Double joint rear axle shaft — components

1 Drive shaft	4 Clip	8 Circlip	12 Lock washer
2 Constant velocity joint	5 Pinch clip	9 Ring 56 mm.	13 Socket head screw
3 Boot	6 Cap	10 Ring 53 mm.	
	7 Dished washer	11 Lock plate	

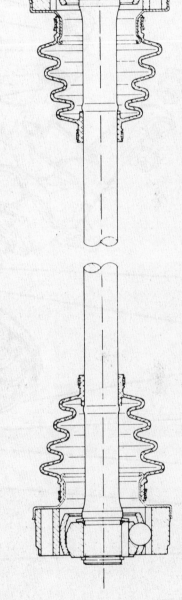

Fig.8.4. Double joint rear axle shaft and joints. Cross section.

116

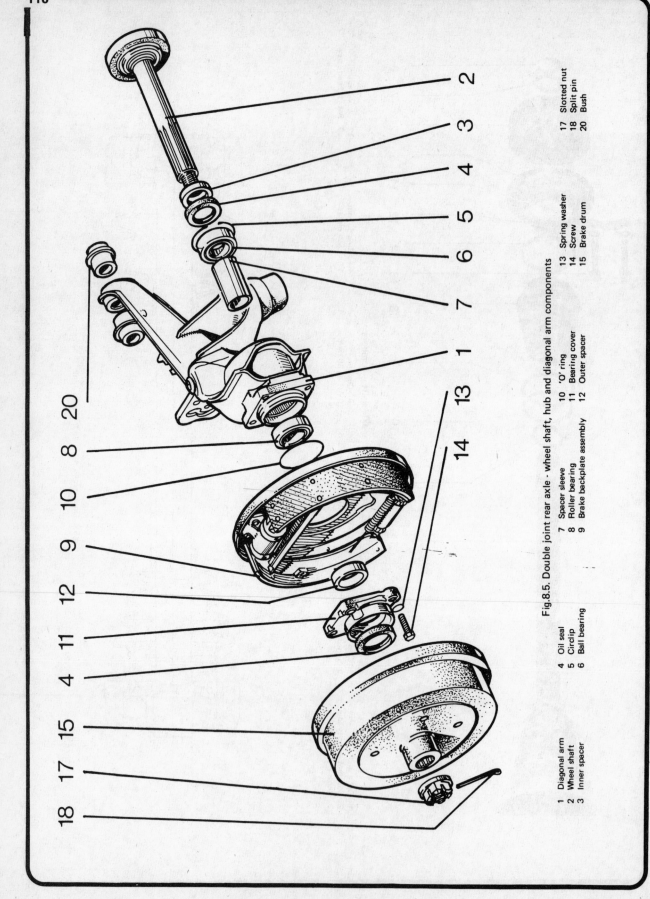

Fig.8.5. Double joint rear axle - wheel shaft, hub and diagonal arm components

1	Diagonal arm	4	Oil seal	7	Spacer sleeve	10	'O' ring	13	Spring washer	17	Slotted nut

1 Diagonal arm
2 Wheel shaft
3 Inner spacer

4 Oil seal
5 Circlip
6 Ball bearing

7 Spacer sleeve
8 Roller bearing
9 Brake backplate assembly

10 'O' ring
11 Bearing cover
12 Outer spacer

13 Spring washer
14 Screw
15 Brake drum

17 Slotted nut
18 Split pin
20 Bush

in cases of extreme bearing wear or seizure with the result that a new bearing does not fit tightly. In such cases a new housing can be fitted to the tube but once again you are advised to have this done by a Volkswagen agent.

6. Axle tubes - oil seal gaiter renewal

1 If an axle tube oil seal gaiter leaks oil, action must be taken without delay. Replacements are split so that they can be fitted without having to dismantle everything.

2 Drain off at least 2—3 pints of the transmission oil unless you have lost so much that it will not run out when the gaiter is removed.

3 Undo the clips and cut the old gaiter off. The new split gaiter will be supplied complete with screws and clips.

4 Thoroughly clean the retainer plate and axle tube where the gaiter fits. Then coat the joining edges of the new gaiter with sealing compound and place it in position round the tube so that the joint faces towards the rear of the car. Do not put sealing compound on the ends where the circular clips go.

5 Put the small screws into position with a washer under the head and fit the nuts with a washer also. Tighten them all up evenly but do not overtighten. If the washers appear to be squeezing into the rubber the bolts are too tight.

6 Put the two clips in position and tighten them but not so much that they squeeze and distort the gaiter.

7. Double joint axle shafts - removal and replacement

1 Models with automatic stick-shift were fitted with double jointed drive shafts. These are immediately recognisable from the fact that there are two rubber boots on each shaft and there is no tube.

2 To remove the drive shafts undo the 6 socket head screws at each end and the shaft may be taken off.

3 When replacing a shaft make sure that the flange mating faces are perfectly clean. Install the lock plates correctly — one to each pair of screws, and use new lock washers.

4 Tighten the screws to 25 lbs/ft.

8. Double joint axle shafts - renewal of constant velocity joints

1 If the constant velocity joints are to be renewed, first remove the axle shaft and then loosen the boot clips and slide the boots out of the way. Then drift off the protection cap over the joint. When this is done the joint will shed all the balls if the outer ring is tilted out of line too far.

2 Remove the circlip and dished washer from the end of the shaft. The shaft may then be pressed out or the joint carefully drifted off. Take off the dished washer behind it.

3 New joints are fitted with the unstepped side of the joint outer cage towards the boot. Put the dished washer on the shaft first and press or drive the joint on until the circlip can be refitted in the groove.

4 Joints should be packed with 60 grams of molybdenum grease Put two thirds into the joint from the shaft side before refitting the protective cap and the other third from the opposite side.

5 Keep all jointing faces of the joint, flanges, boot and protective cap clear of grease.

6 Tap the cap back into position over the joint and refit the rubber boot and clips. Squeeze the boot to help force the grease into the joint.

5.3(a) Putting the fulcrum plates into the side gear.

5.3(b) Measuring the clearance between the spade and fulcrum plates.

6.4(a) Preparing gaiter joint faces with sealing compound.

6.4(b) Putting the gaiter round the axle tube.

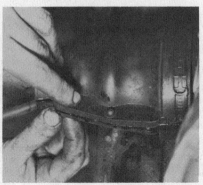

6.4(c) Fit the retaining screws.

6.4(d) .... and the clips.

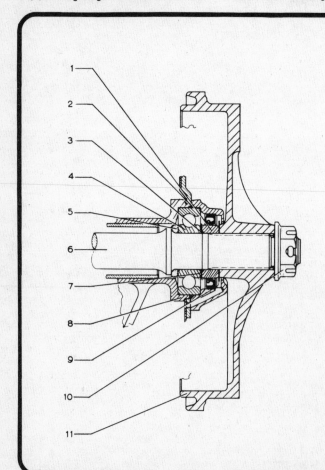

Fig.8.6. Cross section drawing of rear bearing and hub assembly (see Section 2)

1 Outer spacer
2 Large 'O' ring seal
3 Small 'O' ring seal
4 Bearing
5 Inner spacer
6 Axle shaft
7 Thrust washer
8 Bearing housing
9 Oil deflector disc
10 Shaft nut
11 Brake drum

Chapter 9 Braking system

Contents

Specifications

Type...	Drums with hydraulically operated shoes. The 1500 has disc brakes at the front. Handbrake operates two independent cables, one to each rear wheel.
Brake fluid type	Hydraulic fluid to SAE J1703 or DOT 3 (Duckhams Universal Brake and Clutch Fluid)

Brake drums
Internal diameter	230.1 mm (max. 231.5)

Brake shoes
Lining width	40 mm
Lining thickness (new)	3.8 – 4.00 mm
(oversize)	4.3 – 4.5 mm
Surface area (total)	
(equal on all 4 wheels)	716 cm^2

Discs
Diameter..	277 mm
Thickness	9.5 mm (minimum 8.5 mm)
Runout limit	.2 mm

Calipers
Piston diameter	40 mm
Friction pad thickness	10 mm
Minimum pad thickness	2 mm
Total friction area 4 pads	72 cm^2

Master cylinder
Bore	17.46 mm
Stroke	33 mm

Tandem master cylinder
Bore	19.05 mm
Stroke (front circuit)...	15.5 mm (discs 14 mm)
(rear circuit)	12.5 mm (with disc 14 mm)

Wheel cylinders
Bore (front)..	22.2 mm
(rear)	17.46 mm

Handbrake cable lubricant ... ... Multi-purpose lithium based grease (Duckhams LB 10)

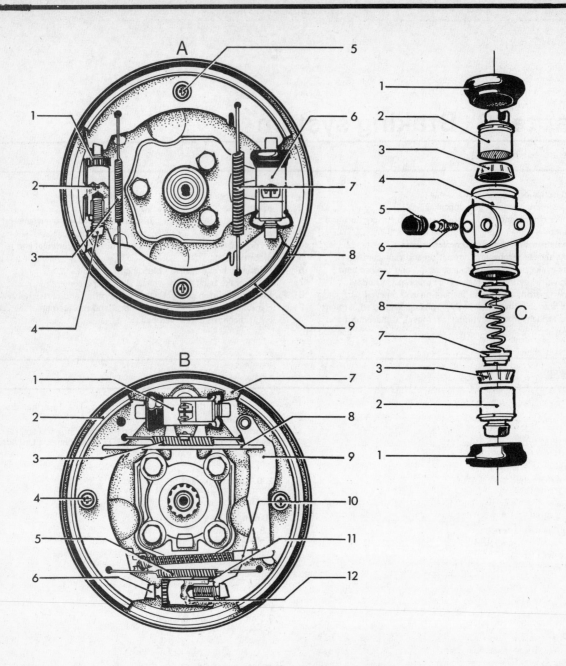

Fig 9.1A FRONT BRAKE ASSEMBLY - COMPONENTS

1	Adjusting wheel	3	Front retractor spring	5	Steady pin spring and cup retainer	7	Rear retractor spring
2	Anchor piece	4	Adjusting screw	6	Hydraulic cylinder	8	Back plate
						9	Brake shoe and lining

Fig. 9.1B REAR BRAKE ASSEMBLY - COMPONENTS

1	Hydraulic cylinder	4	Steady pin, spring and cup retainer	7	Back plate	10	Handbrake cable
2	Brake shoe and lining	5	Lower retractor spring	8	Connecting plate	11	Adjusting wheel
3	Upper retractor spring	6	Adjusting screw	9	Handbrake connecting lever	12	Anchor piece

Fig. 9.1C HYDRAULIC WHEEL CYLINDER

1	Dust boot	3	Seal	5	Dust cap	7	Seal expander
2	Piston	4	Cylinder	6	Bleed nipple	8	Expander spring

Torque wrench settings

Master cylinder to frame bolts	18	lb.ft. (2.5 mkg)
Backplate to steering knuckle screws	36	lb.ft. (5.0 mkg)
Brake hose and pipe unions...	11-15	lb.ft. (1.5-2 mkg)
Stop light switch	14	lb.ft. (2.0 mkg)
Caliper to steering knuckle bolt M10	36	lb.ft. (5.0 mkg)
Cylinder to rear wheel backplate	14-22	lb.ft. (2-3 mkg)
Axle shaft nut (securing rear brake drum)	253	lb.ft. (35 mkg)
Caliper halves securing screws	15	lb.ft. (2.2 mkg)

1. General description

On the 1300 models drum brakes are fitted to all four wheels. The operation of the brake shoes is by hydraulic pressure. Each pair of brake shoes is operated by a single cylinder which contains two opposed pistons, one operating each shoe in the drum. This means that there is one leading shoe only in each drum. Each shoe may be adjusted nearer to the drum by a screw type tappet and notched wheel mounted on each hydraulic piston.

A master hydraulic cylinder is operated by the foot pedal and generates the pressure which passes to the four wheel cylinders. The pipe lines are rigid metal except where they link from body to moving assemblies, for example from the front axle tube to the wheel cylinder direct and from the body to each of the rear axle tubes. From 1967 onwards the master cylinder is the tandem type which maintains the hydraulic pressure to either the front or rear wheels should the others fail.

The handbrake operates on the rear wheels only and the leverage from the handle is transmitted by two cables running in tubes inside the floor frame tube.

Hydraulic fluid level is maintained in the master cylinder by a reservoir located in the front luggage compartment behind the spare wheel.

On 1500 models the front brakes are discs and calipers, the rear brakes and handbrake being similar to the 1300.

The system operates when pressure on the foot pedal moves a piston in the master cylinder (in effect a pump). This pressurizes the hydraulic fluid in the pipe lines and forces the pistons outwards in the wheel cylinders. These in turn press the shoes against the drums. When pressure is relieved the shoes are drawn off the drums by retractor springs. The friction pads of the disc brakes are forced against the disc by hydraulic pistons also. When the pressure is relieved the piston seals flex sufficiently to permit the piston to retract fractionally. No springs are necessary.

The master cylinder piston is fitted with a spring loaded check valve which maintains a slight residual pressure in the fluid lines but not enough to actually move pads or shoes. This ensures instantaneous movement when the brake pedal is applied.

2. Brake adjustment (including handbrake)

1 It is possible to adjust the brakes without removing the wheels. Remove the wheel caps and jack up each wheel in turn.
2 For the front wheels the two adjuster wheels are positioned at centre front as you face the wheel. If the wheel is revolved they can be seen through the hole in the drum. For the rear wheels the two adjusters are at the bottom of the drum.
3 Each adjuster should be moved in the appropriate direction (see Fig.9.2) with a screwdriver engaged in the notch until it can be

moved no further and the wheel is locked. Then back off the adjuster one or two notches until the wheel revolves freely.
4 If any shoe(s) needs considerable adjustment (because they have been allowed to go unadjusted too long) then they will have to 'bed in' again to a different radius and this will call for further adjustment after a short interval. This is why regular brake adjustment is necessary to ensure top braking efficiency at all times. The linings will also last longer as it will ensure that the whole surface area is used evenly all the time.
5 When adjusting the rear brakes remember that when turning the wheels the drag of the transmission will be felt. Do not confuse this with binding brake shoes.
6 Having completed adjusting one wheel it is good practice to operate the brake pedal once or twice and then adjust again. Sometimes the shoes can move fractionally off-centre during adjustment. The extra time required is well worth the trouble.
7 If a shoe still rubs against the drum a little even after being backed off more than 3 notches, leave it (provided it is only superficial). However, if the binding is quite severe then it is possible that the lining is very unevenly worn. In such instances remove the drum and have a look.
8 Once the rear brake shoes have been adjusted to the drums the handbrake may be checked. If both back wheels can be jacked off the ground together it will save some time. Pump the footbrake two or three times (to centralise the shoes) and apply the handbrake two notches. Pull back the rubber shroud at the base of the lever and slacken the locknut on the threaded end of each cable. Then tighten each cable with the adjusting nut (holding the cable with a screwdriver in the slotted end) until an equal amount of drag can be felt on each rear wheel when it is turned. Pull the handbrake on four notches. At this it should not be possible to turn the wheels. Make sure any further adjustment is kept even between the two rear wheels.

3. Front brake drums and brake shoes - removal, inspection and replacement

1 The front brake drums form part of the wheel hub casting so they have to be taken off the stub axle. This involves releasing the front wheel bearings, details of which are given in Chapter 11. Before pulling the drum off it is a good idea to back the shoe adjusters off as far as they will go.
2 In the centre of each shoe a retaining pin, held in position by a spring loaded, slotted cup washer, must first be removed. This can be done with a pair of pliers, turning the washer so that the slot aligns with the head of the pin. Washer, spring and pin can then be removed.
3 Unhook the retractor spring which connects the two shoes nearest to the notched adjuster wheels. The end of one shoe can then be lifted out of the adjuster. Both shoes can then be disengaged quite

LEFT FRONT

LEFT REAR

RIGHT REAR Fig.9.2. Brake shoes — Adjustment to drums *RIGHT FRONT*

Arrows indicate direction of turning to move shoes to drums

2.3. Adjusting a brake shoe. The adjuster can be seen through the hole in the drum.

3.3. Removing the small retractor spring.

3.4(a) Fitting a new lining to a shoe.

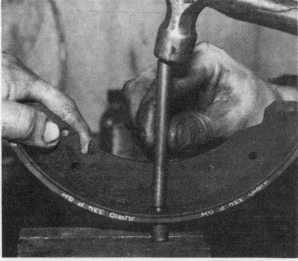

3.4(b) Riveting a new lining - working from the centre outwards.

easily from the hydraulic wheel cylinder. Immediately tie a piece of string around the wheel cylinder to prevent the pistons popping out. Do not apply pressure to the brake pedal either. If the pistons come out it will be necessary to bleed the hydraulic system.

4 The shoe lining surface should be not less than 0.5 mm (0.020 inch) above the rivet heads. Anything less and new linings should be fitted. If the linings have been contaminated with oil they will not work efficiently again and should be renewed. Great care should be exercised when handling brake shoes as oily or greasy hands can contaminate them significantly. The material is extremely absorbent. It is important to isolate the cause of contamination. If not the wheel cylinder, the only other source can be from grease flung out from the wheel bearing. Make sure the bearing grease seal is intact, renew it if necessary (see Chapter 11, Section 3, which deals with front wheel bearings). Volkswagen supply linings and rivets to fit the original shoes. If you should contemplate renewing the linings yourself it is essential to have the proper punch tools for fixing the rivets. If you do not have these the simplest thing is to ask the supplier to fix them. Provided you have cut off the old linings and rivets it takes about two minutes per lining to fix the new ones, if you have the correct tools. One of the punches is clamped in the vice and the new lining, shoe and rivet head held over it whilst the end is belled over with the other special punch. Riveting should start from the centre and work outwards diagonally. Alternatively, other sources of supply may provide exchange shoes complete with linings fitted. Whatever you do it is important that the linings are all of the same make and type. It is best to fit a complete new set and make a proper job of it, or you will have uneven braking and trouble on wet road surfaces. Never try to renew the lining on one wheel only, always in pairs, and best in complete sets. Note also that the front brake shoes may be wider than the rear ones and are not interchangeable.

5 Examine the friction surfaces of the brake drums. If they are in good condition they should be bright, shiny and perfectly smooth. If they show signs of deep scoring (due to over-worn brake linings) then they will need renewal. It may be possible to have them machined out on a lathe but if this is done it will be essential to fit oversize brake linings accordingly. This work should be carried out by a Volkswagen agent or an acknowledged brake specialist. It is a waste of time fitting new linings to work in scored drums (except when the scoring is only very light).

6 Before replacing the shoes the backplate should be thoroughly brushed off and the two adjusters removed and cleaned so that they can be freely turned. The threads may be treated with a very light touch of high melting point grease. Replace the adjusters; if the bottom one tends to fall out leave it until the shoes are refitted. Both adjusters should be screwed right in to the notched wheels.

7 Examine the hydraulic cylinder. The rubber boots should be intact and there should be no sign of fluid leakage. If there is then the cylinders must be overhauled (see Section 7).

8 Assemble the two shoes together with the heavier of the two retractor springs engaged in the two holes nearest the cut-out slots on the inner radius of the shoe. These shoe ends should then be put into place in the slots in the ends of the pistons. Next fit the other ends of the shoes into the adjusters (replace the bottom one now) so that they fit properly in the adjuster slots. Then hook the other retractor spring into the holes in the shoes.

9 Reassemble the steady pins, springs and washers, turning the washers 90° across the pin heads to secure them. If you have dismantled all the brakes together note that the steady pins may be different lengths (front wheels 40 mm) so do not get them mixed up. This is when the front linings are wider than the rear - wider linings - longer pins.

10 Centralise the shoes (otherwise you may have difficulty replacing the drum) and then refit the drum and wheel bearing, adjusting the bearings as described in Chapter 11. If the wheel cylinders have been overhauled bleed the hydraulic system (Section 14).

11 Adjust the shoes to the drums as described in the previous section. If new linings have been fitted further adjustment may be needed after a few hundred miles.

4. Rear brake drums - removal and replacement

1 Removal of the rear brake drums is a considerable task. It necessitates having a suitable socket (36 mm) and handle available to undo the axle shaft nut which is tightened to a torque of 30 mkg (217 lb/ft), (253 lb/ft on models with double joint rear axles). The drums are splined to the shafts, and if these are a very tight fit a special puller may be required to get them off the axle shaft. Fit new split pins of the correct size when replacing the axle shaft nut. Under no circumstances should any attempt be made to remove the nuts with anything other than a proper socket spanner otherwise damage will be done. The car must be standing firm on the ground when the nuts are being loosened initially.

2 Remove the hub cap and extract the split pin from the end of the axle shaft. Put the handbrake on and place the socket and handle on the nut. You will probably need a piece of pipe to give you 4–5 feet of leverage (single handed).

3 If the handbrake does not hold the wheels then adjust it until it does. Alternatively, chock the wheels and put some people or weight in the back seat to hold the wheels from turning. Once the nut is slackened enough to move normally do the same for the other brake drum.

4 Slacken off the wheel bolts and then jack the car up and remove the wheel.

5 Remove the nut from the axle shaft.

6 Release the handbrake and back off the brake shoe adjusters as far as they will go. If you are fortunate, careful tapping around the edge of the drum with a soft faced mallet (a heavy one) or block of wood and hammer, will move the drum off the splines of the shaft. If the drum does not come off by this method then you will have to use a wheel puller, taking care not to distort the drum. Once removed, examine the drum for signs of scoring on the friction surfaces (see details as for front drums).

7 Before replacing the brake drum it is as well to check the efficiency of the axle shaft oil seals. If these are leaking and causing contamination of the brake linings then replacement is relatively simple now that the drum has been removed. For details see Chapter 8.

8 Centralise the brake shoes and see that the adjusters are fully backed off. Thoroughly clean the splines of both shaft and drum and smear them with a little grease or one of the proprietary anti-seize compounds if you have some.

9 Fit the drum on the splines and push it fully home and then refit the axle shaft nut as far as possible without excess force.

10 Replace the wheels and bolts and lower the car to the ground.

11 It is possible that you do not have a torque wrench so to tighten the nut first fit the socket with a standard handle, say 12–18 inches long, and tighten as far as you possibly can. It is unlikely that you will be capable of overtightening the nut with a regular handle. Then look carefully at the shaft and the split pin hole that you are going to need to use will almost certainly be showing - albeit not yet quite lined up. If no hole shows yet, put a piece of pipe extension onto your handle and move the nut a fraction more at a time until one does appear. Then continue turning the nut carefully until the pin hole lines up with a slot in the nut. This should be the correct tightness. Appreciate that the amount of turn needed to increase the torque from say, 150 lb/ft to the required 217 lb/ft may be less than 30° (or a twelfth of a revolution). If you are using a torque wrench the same principle applies. Look for the hole once you have reached somewhere between 150–200 ft/lbs. You do not want to go past it. Provided the nut was correctly tightened and pinned before you took it off it must go back to the same position. If it does not then the threads must have been damaged. Take it off, sort out the thread damage, and try again.

12 The importance of correct tightening of the axle shaft nut cannot be over-emphasised. It locates the axle shaft and bearing as well as the brake drum and any mistake could result in serious (and expensive) faults developing.

3.6. Replacing the adjuster.

3.8(a) Positioning the shoe into the wheel cylinder.

3.8(b) ....and adjuster notch at the other end.

3.10(a) Brake shoe assembly completed on left front wheel.

3.10(b) Fitting the front brake drum.

4.11(a) Tightening the rear axle nut with a torque wrench.

5. Rear brake shoes - removal, examination and replacement

1 Remove the rear brake drum.

2 Remove the steady pins, springs and washers in the same fashion as for the front brake shoes.

3 Unhook the lower of the two retractor springs and then unhook the handbrake cable from the operating lever.

4 Disengage the ends of the two shoes from the adjusters and the two shoes together with the handbrake lever and plate may be lifted out.

5 Linings should be renewed if the surface is worn to within 0.4 mm (0.020 inch) or less of the rivet heads at any point. Also, if there is any indication of oil contamination the linings must be renewed. Details for relining may be found in the section dealing with front brakes.

6 If the shoes are to be changed remember to remove the handbrake operating lever by pulling off the clip which fixes it to the shoe.

7 When reassembling the two shoes prior to refitting, the spreader plate should engage in the two slots and the shoe with the lever attached goes to the rear with the lever notch facing the rear.

8 Make sure that the adjuster wheels are free-moving and fully backed off before locating the ends of the shoes in the slots.

9 It must be emphasised that any leaks, either from the bearing or the hydraulic cylinder, should be dealt with to prevent both further contamination or failure of the hydraulic system.

6. Front disc brake pads - removal, inspection and replacement

1 Remove the front wheel.

2 There are two visual examinations to be made before dismantling anything. These are the thickness of the friction pad and the gap between the pad and disc.

3 Pad friction material thickness must not be less than 2 mm otherwise the pads should be renewed.

4 The residual clearance should not be more than 0.2 mm (0.008 inch) between disc and pad. This can be measured with a feeler gauge.

5 If the gap is greater it is probably due to a sticking piston. A simple remedy is given later on in this section.

6 If the pads are to be used again mark where they came from beforehand so they may be put back in the same position. Then drive out the retaining pins from the outside with a long nosed punch. Lift off the spring retainer plate.

7 Before removing the old pads it is best to force them away from the disc carefully, with a suitable flat metal lever. This will push the pistons back. Before doing this it will be necessary to remove some hydraulic fluid from the reservoir to prevent it overflowing when the pistons are pushed back. Do this with a suitable suction device such as an empty flexible plastic bottle.

8 Once the pistons are pushed back remove the pads and piston retaining plate. Note that there is a cutaway portion on one side of the piston. Provided the piston is not rotated after the retaining plate is taken out there should be no cause for difficulty on replacement of the plate. For details of the correct position of the piston cut-out refer to Section 8.

9 Blow out the aperture in the caliper and examine the seal which should show no signs of cracking or brittleness. If it does it should be renewed. (See Section 8).

10 Clean off the piston retaining plate and replace it together with the new friction pads. New pad retaining spring plates are normally provided with the pads and these should be used. Note that later versions have a wider section on one side and this should face downwards. When replacing the retaining pins (from the inside) do not use a punch smaller in diameter than the pin. Preferably, use no punch at all otherwise there is a possibility of shearing the shoulder off against the split clamping bush.

11 Pump the brake pedal to bring the pads up to the disc and check the level of hydraulic fluid in the reservoir.

12 If the clearance between the disc and pad is too great after brake operation then this is an indication that the inner piston rubber seal is sticking somewhat and distorting more than normally. This retracts the piston more than usual when the pressure is taken off. Movement of the piston can usually cure this. Remove a brake pad and put in a block of wood no less than 6 mm thick. Pump the brakes to force the piston further out and then force it back again. Do this a few times and the problem should disappear. If not it will be necessary to check the piston seals and caliper cylinders thoroughly as described in Section 8.

7. Hydraulic wheel cylinders - renewal of seals and cylinders

1 If the wheel cylinders show signs of leakage, or of pistons being seized up, then it will be necessary to dismantle them and fit new seals. The procedures for front and rear cylinders are the same although the bores of the cylinders are different requiring different diameter seals.

2 Remove the brake drum and the brake shoes and seal the cap of the fluid reservoir with a piece of plastic film to minimise loss of fluid from the system when the cylinder is dismantled.

3 Pull off the rubber boots from the ends of the cylinder, bringing the pistons and slotted ends with them. Behind the pistons are the seal cups and in the centre there is a spring with two 'cup expanders' which fit inside each seal and as their name implies force the seals outward into the cylinder bore under the pressure of the spring.

4 With the cylinder clear examine the bore surfaces for signs of ridging or scoring. Any residue stuck in the bore should be cleaned out with brake fluid or meths - if very stubborn a gentle rub with some No.400 wet and dry paper will clean it up. Any noticeable scores or ridges indicate that a new cylinder should be fitted. No attempt should be made to smooth them out as this will be unsuccessful.

5 To remove the cylinder undo the brake pipe union from behind the backplate. Cover the end of the pipe with the dust cap from the bleed nipple pro tem. Undo the two securing screws from the backplate and the cylinder may be lifted out. If a new cylinder is fitted the diameter of the bore must be exactly the same as the diameter of the one being replaced, otherwise the balance of the brakes will be upset.

6 With the cylinder perfectly clean lubricate the bore with brake fluid and insert the spring complete with seal cup expanders at each end.

7 Lubricate the new seals with fluid and put one in at each end of the cylinder with the lip facing inwards. Take great care not to turn the lip back whilst doing this.

8 Put a piston into the bore of the cylinder behind each seal and then fit the rubber boot over the cylinder and piston so that it engages in the grooves.

9 Absolute cleanliness of hands and parts is essential during reassembly.

10 If a new wheel cylinder is being fitted reconnect the brake pipe union taking care not to cross the thread, kink the pipe or overtighten the union.

8. Disc caliper pistons and seals - inspection and renewals

1 Before assuming that anything is wrong which requires removal of the caliper pistons make sure that the checks in connection with renewal of the friction pads as described in Section 6 have been carried out.

2 Discs may deteriorate, if left unused, due to corrosion. If this happens it is best to let a VW agency repolish them with special blocks which can be inserted in place of the friction pads. Discs which are badly scored or distorted must be renewed. It is possible to have them re-machined but the economics of this against fitting new parts should be examined.

The run-out of the disc can be checked only with a dial gauge micrometer, With the bearing properly adjusted the run-out should

4.11(b) Using a suitable extension to line up the pin hole if necessary.

4.11(c) Fit the new split pin.

5.7(a) Fitting the top ends of the rear brake shoes into the piston grooves.

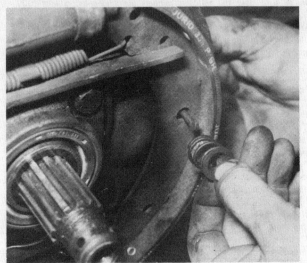

5.7(b) Fitting the steady pins and washer.

5.7(c) Replacing the rear shoes retractor spring.

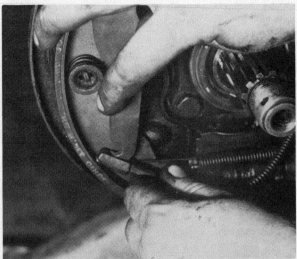

5.7(d) Hooking the handbrake cable onto the lever.

6.8. Removing a disc pad.

6.10. Refitting the pad retaining pin.

7.8. Refitting a piston assembly to a wheel cylinder.

8.3. Removing the disc caliper securing bolts.

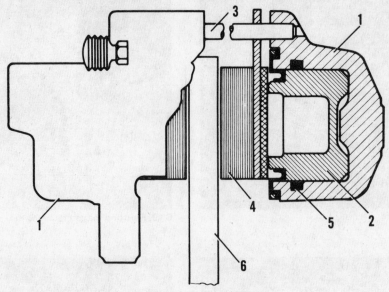

Fig.9.3. Disc brakes - cross section

1	Caliper	3	Friction pads retaining	4	Friction pad	6 Disc
2	Piston		pin	5	Fluid seal	

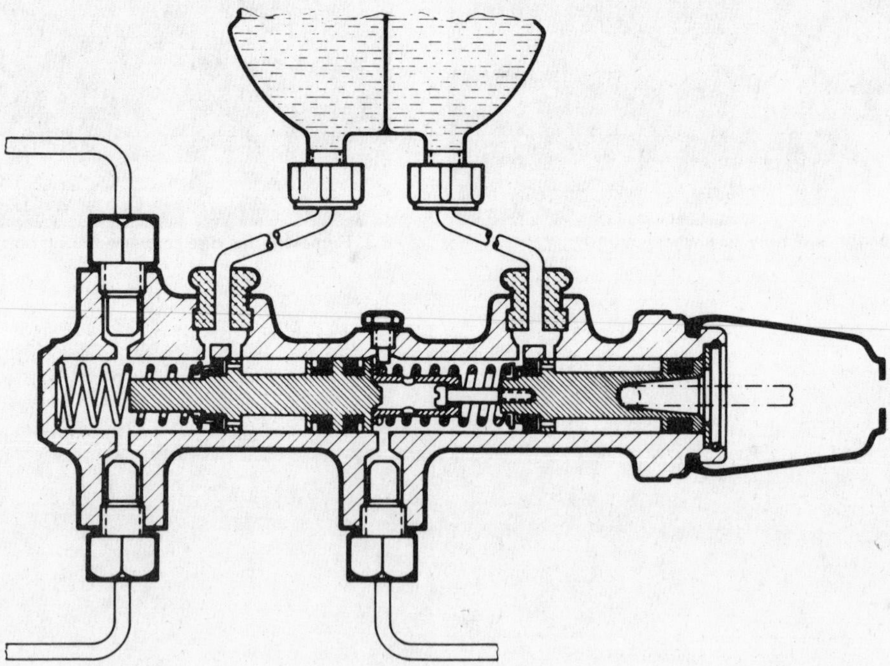

Fig.9.4. Tandem master cylinder for dual circuit braking systems - cross section of
assembly at rest. (See Section 12)

The two front pipes go to each front wheel cylinder and the third to the rear. Each of the three outlet pipe unions
incorporates a residual pressure valve.

not exceed 0.2 mm (0.008 inch).

3 To renew a disc or repair piston seals, the caliper assembly must first be removed. It is held by two bolts from the back of the steering knuckle. (If the disc only is to be removed it is not necessary to disconnect the hydraulic fluid hose. The whole assembly should be tied up onto the bodywork to prevent any strain on the hose). If the pistons are to be removed from the caliper thought must first be given as to how pressure can be applied to force them out. Only one piston can be worked on at a time as the other piston must be installed and clamped in position so as to maintain pressure to force the other out. Pressure can be applied from a foot pump if you rig up a spare hydraulic pipe union and short length of pipe to which the pump connector will fit. One piston will have to be clamped in such a way that there will still be room enough for the other to come right out. Here again a tong-like clamp may have to be made up from some 1½ x 1/8 inch flat steel bar if you are unable to obtain a suitable tool.

4 Mount the caliper assembly in the vice padding the jaws suitably so that the flange of the caliper will not be scored or marked. The friction pads and retaining plates should be removed (see Section 6).

5 Prise out the spring ring from the outer seal using a screwdriver. Then, with a blunt plastic or wooden tool prise out the seal itself. Do not use sharp tools for fear of scoring the piston or cylinder.

6 Using a clamp to hold one piston force the other out under pressure as described in paragraph 3. To prevent damage in case the piston should come out with force put some cloth in the caliper to prevent it striking the piston and clamp opposite.

7 With the piston out the rubber sealing ring can be taken out of its groove in the cylinder; once again use only a blunt article to get it out.

8 With methylated spirit or hydraulic fluid, clean the piston and cylinder thoroughly. If there are any signs of severe scoring or pitting then renewal will be necessary. With the cylinder this involves renewing the whole caliper unit.

9 When renewing seals the spring ring and piston retaining plate must also be renewed. The VW service kit includes all the items needed. Use them. Before reassembly it is advantageous to coat the piston and new rubber seal with VW cylinder paste specially formulated for this job. Otherwise make sure they are thoroughly lubricated with clean hydraulic fluid. On no account use anything else.

10 Fit the rubber seal in the cylinder groove and then fit the piston into the seal. Great care must be taken to avoid misaligning the seal when doing this and the piston must be kept square while it is pushed in. The cut-out portion of the piston should lie at an angle of 20° from a line across the disc diameter facing in to the centre of the disc and against the direction of forward disc rotation.

11 Fit the new outer seal and spring ring.

12 Repeat the process for the other piston.

13 Refit the caliper to the knuckle, tightening the securing bolts to 29 lb/ft. Replace the piston retainer plates and pads as described in Section 6.

14 The disc itself may be removed after the caliper is taken off.

15 Remove the hub cap — (on the left wheel, this involves removing the 'C' washer securing the speedo cable). Undo the bearing nut (or nuts) and pull off the disc which is an integral part of the wheel hub.

16 Replace the disc in the reverse order and re-adjust the wheel bearing as detailed in Chapter 11.

17 Refit the caliper to the knuckle and tighten the two retaining bolts to the correct torque of 36 lb/ft (5.0 mkg)

18 It is rare that the caliper housing has to be split and this should not be done unless it is obviously leaking. Renewal of the interior 'O' rings on the fluid channels may then be needed. Undo the four socket head screws to separate the two halves. Remove the two 'O' rings and fit new ones. Re-align the two halves and replace the screws. Tighten them from the centre outwards in sequence to 7 lb/ft (1 mkg) and then again in sequence to a final torque of 15 lb/ft.

19 When the caliper is replaced reconnect the hydraulic fluid hose

and bleed the system as described in Section 14.

9. Hydraulic master cylinder - removal, replacement and ajustment

1 Provided the slave cylinders and fluid lines are all in good condition and there is no air in the system then any softness or sponginess in the system will probably be due to worn seals in the master cylinder. As these are internal there will be no visible leak to indicate this.

2 To remove the cylinder assembly first jack up the car and remove the right hand front wheel (R.H. drive) or left as the case may be. The cylinder is bolted to the bulkhead alongside the floor tunnel.

3 Have a suitable receptacle handy to collect the contents of the fluid reservoir - if possible siphon the contents out of the reservoir itself. Otherwise pull the pipe and plug from the top of the cylinder body and drain it into the receptacle there. Keep fluid away from paintwork.

4 Unscrew the three rigid pipe unions from the body of the cylinder. It is not necessary to undo the brake light switch. Just disconnect the wires.

5 The two screws in the bulkhead behind the brake pedal should now be removed to release the assembly. Take care not to drop the washers or spacers off the screws into the space below or you may have a difficult job retrieving them.

6 Replacement is a reversal of the removal procedure. Make sure that the spacers are correctly refitted. As soon as the unions have all been reconnected and the system replenished with fluid and bled, see that the unions are all perfectly leakproof.

7 It is important that the pushrod which operates the plunger from the brake pedal is correctly set. In the rest position, the ball end of the pushrod should have a 1 mm clearance before it contacts the bottom of the recess in the piston. If this clearance is absent (and the piston cannot return fully) the operation of the system is seriously affected. To adjust the length of the rod slacken the locknut and screw the rod in or out as required. This adjustment will also be affected if the pedal cluster mounting plate is moved.

10. Hydraulic tandem master cylinder - removal, replacement and adjustment

1 The tandem master cylinder comprises a single cylinder in which there are two pistons one behind the other. Each circuit is supplied independently with fluid. If the pressure in one circuit should fail the other is not affected.

2 The cylinder is mounted in exactly the same way as the single piston version and apart from the fact that the inlet port elbows, outlet pipes and brake light switch leads are duplicated removal procedure is the same. The replacement procedure is the same in reverse.

3 Adjustment of the pushrod must be so that there is a clearance of 1 mm between the end of the pushrod and the piston recess. It is also important that the pedal stop is set far enough back so that if one brake circuit fails the pedal can move far enough to operate the other circuit before it comes up against the panel.

11. Hydraulic master cylinder - dismantling, overhaul and reassembly

1 Obtain a complete repair kit which contains all the necessary seals all of which must be used.

2 Thoroughly clean the exterior before beginning dismantling.

3 Unclip the circlip from inside the cylinder bore and remove the various parts in order. Pull out the reservoir pipe sealing plug.

4 Examine the inside of the cylinder bore for any sign of scoring or pitting. Unless it is perfectly smooth the body should be renewed.

5 Thoroughly clean all parts. Pull off the seal from the groove in the piston.

6 Before reassembly lubricate all parts with clean brake fluid.

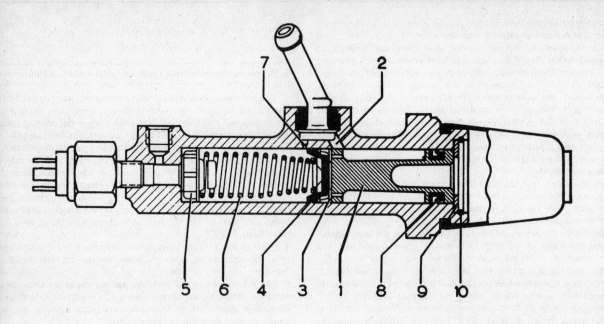

Fig.9.5. Brake master cylinder - cross section

1 Piston	3 Piston washer	6 Residual pressure valve spring	8 Secondary cup seal
2 Intake port (fluid from reservoir)	4 Primary cup seal	7 Compensating port (excess fluid back to reservoir)	9 Stop plate
	5 Check valve		10 Circlip

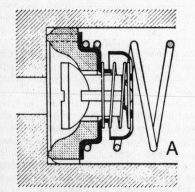
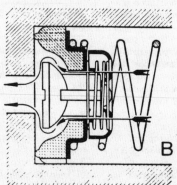
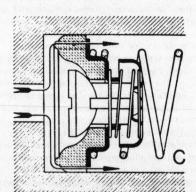

Fig.9.6. Brake master cylinder - function of residual pressure valve(s).

A At rest. Main valve seated on end of cylinder under main spring pressure and inner valve seated in centre of main seal under secondary spring pressure.

B Braking. Secondary valve opens under pressure of fluid which passes into system.

C Brakes released. Main valve opens under fluid back pressure until main spring overcomes pressure - keeping some pressure in system. Secondary valve stays seated.

7 Assemble the wide end of the spring to the boss on the check valve and place both in position in the cylinder.

8 Place the new primary cup seal into the cylinder, concave side inwards and take great care to ensure that the lips of the seal edges do not turn back in the process. Put the piston washer in immediately behind it.

9 Take the piston and fit the new secondary seal into the groove at the rear end. This seal must be fitted so that the tapered lip faces into the cylinder when the piston is replaced. Make sure it is squarely seated in position.

10 Put the piston into the cylinder (the recessed end faces outwards) and when the seal goes in once again make quite sure that the lip does not turn back.

11 Fit the stop plate followed by the circlip which must snap securely into the annular groove in the cylinder.

12 Make sure that the rubber plug washer and elbow are intact and ready for connection to the reservoir feed pipe on installation. The rubber boot is fitted over the cylinder (or pushrod) before the cylinder is replaced.

12. Hydraulic tandem master cylinder - dismantling, overhaul and reassembly

1 Thoroughly clean the exterior of the unit before starting to dismantle. Then remove the piston stop screw located between the two fluid inlet ports. (Figs 9.4 and 9.9).

2 Remove the boot from the rear of the cylinder and take out the internal circlip.

3 The two pistons and all their component parts may then be drawn out. Do this carefully, taking note of the order and position in which they come out.

4 Renewal of seals is carried out in the same fashion as for a conventional unit. The front brake piston is fitted with three seals all the same size and shape. The front two face forward and the third to the rear. The secondary piston has two seals, both facing forwards. The front seal is the same as those on the primary piston but the rear one is the odd one out so do not confuse it with the others.

5 When reassembling the pistons into the cylinder first place the cup washer, primary cup, support washer, spring plate and spring, in that order over the nose of the primary piston (to which the new secondary cup and rear seal should have been already fitted). Hold the cylinder vertical with the open end downwards and feed the whole assortment back in so that the loose items do not fall off the piston.

6 The secondary piston primary cup is held in location by a support washer and spring plate also. These in turn are held firm by the stop sleeve and stroke limiting screw. By undoing the stroke limiting screw inside the stop sleeve all these component parts may be released. The new seal is then easily place in position.

7 When replacing the secondary piston it should be pushed far enough forward to enable the stop screw to be put in so that it fits behind the rear end of the primary piston. This is most important. It must not be fitted so that it engages the recessed part in the shank of the primary piston.

8 Refit the stop ring, circlip and rubber boot over the end of the cylinder.

9 Some cylinders incorporate a pressure differential warning system. This consists of a single piston held centrally in balance by the equal pressure of the two circuits. To remove the piston with its equilibrium springs the switch must first be screwed out of the body. Then the end plug can be removed and the internal components taken out.

13. Hydraulic fluid lines and hoses - examination, removal and replacement

1 Regular examination of the pipes which carry the pressurised fluid from the master cylinder to the four wheel cylinders is very important. Any sudden leak due to fracture or corrosion will result in total loss of pressure and the brakes will be inoperative except for the handbrake which is inadequate for driving purposes.

2 Trace the routes of all the rigid pipes and wash or brush away accumulated dirt. If the pipes are obviously covered with some sort of underseal compound do not disturb it. Examine for signs of kinks or dents which could have been caused by flying stones. Any instances of this mean that the pipe section should be renewed but before actually taking it out read the rest of this section. Any unprotected sections of pipe which show signs of corrosion or pitting on the outer surfaces must also be considered for renewal.

3 Flexible hoses, running to each of the front wheels and from the underbody to each rear axle tube, should show no signs of external signs of chafing or cracking. Move them about and see if surface cracks appear. Also if they feel stiff and inflexible or are twisted they are nearing the end of their useful life. If in any doubt renew the hoses.

4 Before attempting to remove any pipe for renewal it is important to be sure that you have a replacement source of supply within reach if you do not wish to be kept off the road for too long. Pipes are often damaged on removal. If a Volkswagen agency is near, you may be reasonably sure that the correct pipes and unions are available. If not, check first that your local garage has the necessary equipment for making up the pipes and has the correct metric thread pipe unions available. The same goes for flexible hoses.

5 Where the couplings from rigid to flexible pipes are made there are support brackets and the flexible pipe is held in place by a 'U' clip which engages in a groove in the union. The male union screws into it. Before getting the spanners on, soak the unions in penetrating fluid as there is always some rust or corrosion binding the threads. Whilst this is soaking in, place a piece of plastic film under the fluid reservoir cap to minimise loss of fluid from the disconnected pipes. Hold the hexagon on the flexible pipe coupling whilst the union on the rigid pipe is undone. Then pull out the clip to release both pipes from the bracket. For flexible hose removal this procedure will be needed at both ends. For a rigid pipe the other end will only involve unscrewing the union from a cylinder or connector. When you are renewing a flexible hose, take care not to damage the unions of the pipes that connect into it. If a union is particularly stubborn be prepared to renew the rigid pipe as well. This is quite often the case if you are forced to use open ended spanners. It may be worth spending a little money on a special pipe union spanner which is like a ring spanner with a piece cut out to enable it to go round the tube.

6 If you are having the new pipe made up take the old one along to check that the unions and pipe flaring at the ends are identical.

7 Replacement of the hoses or pipes is a reversal of the removal procedure. Precautions and care are needed to make sure that the unions are correctly lined up to prevent cross threading. This may mean bending the pipe a little where a rigid pipe goes into a fixture. Such bending must not, under any circumstances, be too acute, otherwise the pipe will kink and weaken.

8 When fitting flexible hoses take care not to twist them. This can happen when the unions are finally tightened unless a spanner is used to hold the end of the flexible hose and prevent twisting.

9 After removal or slackening of a brake pipe union the hydraulic system must be bled.

14. Hydraulic brake system - bleeding

1 The purpose of the process known as bleeding the brakes is to remove air bubbles from the hydraulic system. Air is compressible - hydraulic fluid is not. Bleeding should be necessary only after work on the hydraulic system has allowed air into the system. If it is found necessary to bleed brakes frequently then there is something wrong and the whole system should be checked through to find where the air is getting into the system. Cars left unused for a long time may also require brake bleeding before full efficiency is restored.

2 Normally, if work has been carried out at the extremities of the system - e.g. at wheel cylinders or adjacent pipes, then it should only

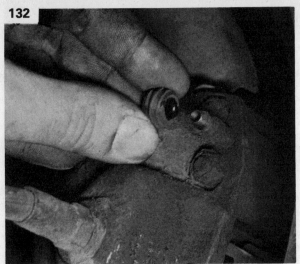

14.4. Pulling the protective cap off a disc caliper bleed nipple.

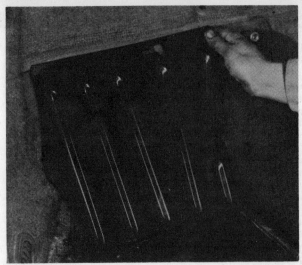

16.2. Removing the toe panel.

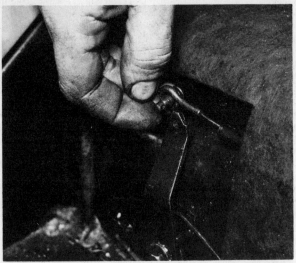

16.4(a) Disconnecting the accelerator cable.

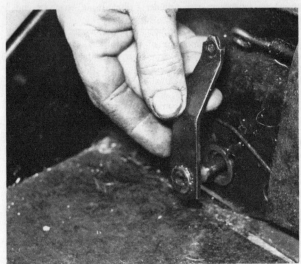

16.4(b) Removing the accelerator rod lever.

16.5(a) Remove brake master cylinder pushrod by disconnecting the circlip on the clevis pin.

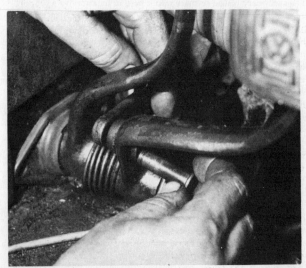

16.5(b) ....and pulling out the clevis pin.

be necessary to bleed that particular section. Work on the master cylinder however would call for all four wheels to be bled.

3 Before starting, make sure you have an adequate supply of the proper fluid, a clean receptacle and a tube which will fit over the bleed nipple securely and which is conveniently long enough. A useful device is the tube which is fitted with a non-return valve. This avoids the necessity of keeping the other end of the tube submerged in liquid whilst bleeding is in progress.

4 Clean off the bleed nipple (or pull off the protective cap). Put about 1 inch depth of fluid in the receptacle (a salad cream jar is ideal and needs less fluid!). Connect the pipe to the nipple and put the other end in the jar and undo the nipple about half a turn - no more is necessary.

5 A second person is needed to operate the brake pedal at your instruction. The pedal should be depressed smartly one full stroke to the floor and allowed to return slowly. This should be repeated until no more bubbles emerge from the tube in the jar. Smart operation of the pedal ensures that the air is forced along the pipe rather than by-passed. Keep a watch on the level of fluid in the reservoir. If it gets too low it will let air into the master cylinder and then you will have to bleed all four wheels.

6 Once all the air is expelled, the best moment to tighten the bleed nipple is during the return stroke of the pedal.

7 Repeat the procedure for each wheel as necessary. Do not put fluid bled out of the system back in. Always use fresh.

8 It is considered by many a good idea to completely replenish the brake fluid, by bleeding, at regular intervals. Such intervals would be two years or 30,000 miles, whichever came first. Renewal of the slave cylinder seals (at least) at the same time would be well worth the small cost and time involved.

15. Drum brake backplates - removal and replacement

1 If it is necessary to remove the brake backplates for any reason, which would be rare, then the brake drums and shoes must first be taken off. This procedure is described in Sections 3, 4 and 5 of this Chapter. To remove the front brake backplates all that is then required is to remove the four securing screws.

2 The rear brake backplate is clamped behind the bearing housing cover. Care must be taken when removing the cover to avoid any damage to the seals and gasket.

3 Renew the 'O' rings and gaskets if possible. Details of these can be ascertained from the relevant section in Chapter 8.

16. Brake and clutch pedal cluster - dismantling and reassembly

1 The brake and clutch pedals are mounted on a common shaft which in turn is supported by two brackets. One of these brackets (on R.H. drive cars) is fitted to the right of the brake pedal and is held to the floor by two bolts. The other is bolted to the left hand side of the floor tunnel. The shaft is hollow allowing the accelerator rod to pass through it. At the left hand end of the pivot shaft a bracket links to the accelerator cable. The clutch cable hooks onto a lug which is part of the pedal inside the tunnel. This section explains how to deal with matters connected with all three items on the cluster.

2 Remove the carpet from the left hand toe panel and pull out the panel.

3 Remove the two bolts holding the cover on the side of the tunnel. These two screws hold the bracket supporting the left end of the cross shaft as well so some movement will be noticed.

4 If only the accelerator cable is being renewed the split pin can be removed from the clevis pin, the cable eye released and the cable drawn out. If the cross shaft is being taken out then remove the lever from the accelerator rod by taking off the circlip.

5 At the other end of the shaft remove the clevis pin securing the brake master cylinder pushrod to the pedal. It is held in position by

a circlip.

6 Then remove the large circlip on the end of the main cross shaft next to the mounting bracket. The two mounting bracket bolts can then be undone. When these bolts are being undone take precautions to ensure that the clutch pedal remains in an upright position - it does not matter about the brake pedal which can fall back to the floor. This will ensure that the clutch cable does not get unhooked inside the tunnel. There is a separate plate also behind the pedals which has upturned lugs acting as pedal stops. Do not disturb this although it will need adjustment on reassembly.

7 Unclip the accelerator rod from the back of the accelerator pedal, remove the link and draw the brake pedal and accelerator rod out of the tube together with the brake pedal return spring. Note the position of the intermediate washers.

8 If you wish to draw out the clutch pedal and cable detach the other end of the cable from the clutch operating lever on the transmission casing.

9 Now draw out the clutch pedal and shaft together, keeping the pedal as upright as possible so that the cable may be drawn out with it.

10 A new clutch cable must be fed into the tube through the aperture in the tunnel. All that is needed is patience to guide the end into the tube.

11 Reassembly is a reversal of the dismantling procedure. The setting of the pedal stop plate requires some care, bearing in mind that the clutch pedal free play adjustment is affected and also the setting of the master cylinder pushrod. When replacing the clutch pedal the end of the cable has to be hooked on first and then the pedal manoeuvred into position without letting the end of the cable come loose or get snagged on the hook in the wrong position. It is best to get a second person to hold the other end of the cable and keep tension on it whilst the pedal is being positioned. If the cable appears to be too short after positioning, it is probably because the hook has slewed round. Waggle the pedal back and forth a few times - still with the other end of the cable being held, and it will probably straighten out. If it does not go back to square one.

12 Before finally tightening the mounting bracket bolts check that at the end of the return movement the rubber faces of both pedals are vertical. If they are not the stop plate has slotted holes to allow their adjustment to the vertical.

13 Finally check the master cylinder pushrod clearance (as described in Section 9 of this Chapter) and then check and if necessary, adjust the free play of the clutch pedal (as described in Chapter 5).

17. Handbrake cables and lever - removal and replacement

1 Slacken off the locknuts at the lever end of both handbrake cables and remove them together with the adjusting nuts.

2 Remove the rear brake drums and unhook the cable from the operating lever on the shoe.

3 Undo the bolt which holds the outer sleeve clip to the brake backplate where the cable passes through. Disengage the clip from behind the washer and spring on the cable and draw the cable out from the backplate. Then pull the cables out of the tube from the other direction.

4 Before fitting a new cable make sure that at the brake end the spring and washer are properly fitted between the eye of the cable and the outer sleeve.

5 It is necessary to remove the handbrake lever before the threaded ends of the cable can be reconnected to it. Remove one of the circlips from the end of the lever pivot pin and withdraw the pin. Keep the hands well clear of the ratchet button and then move the whole lever assembly forward so that it disengages from the floor plate. If the ratchet button is inadvertently pressed the ratchet will fall down. It must be put back before replacing the lever.

6 Put the cable through the backplate and then work the sleeve clamp through the hole in the backplate so that the spring and washer are on the inside of the slotted bracket of the clamp. Replace the bolt into the back of the backplate and tighten it. Then hook the

16.6. Remove the mounting bracket.

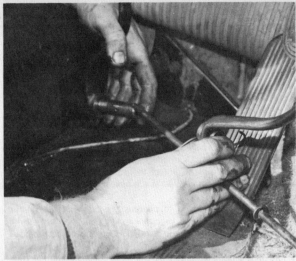

16.7. Remove the brake pedal and accelerator rod.

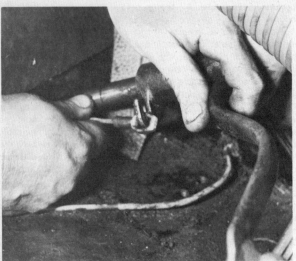

16.8. Unhooking the clutch cable.

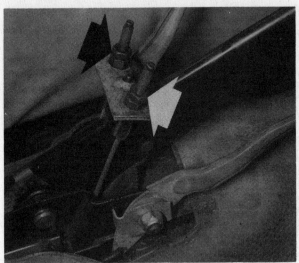

17.1. Handbrake lever showing cable adjuster nuts and locknuts (arrowed).

17.5(a) Removing the handbrake lever pivot pin.

17.5(b) Lifting out the lever to engage the cable ends.

cable onto the lever.

7 Feed the threaded end of the cable into the tubes in the frame fork and finally see that the outer sleeve fits into position in the end of the tube. The threaded ends should appear inside the car under the handbrake lever mounting position. It may be necessary to hook them up with a piece of wire.

8 Making sure that they are not crossed, insert the cables into the two eyes in the base of the lever and then put the lever in position checking that the rear section engages properly in the floor section. Once again be careful not to press the ratchet release button. Replace the pivot pin and circlip and screw on the adjuster and locknuts.

9 Adjust the handbrake as described in Section 3.

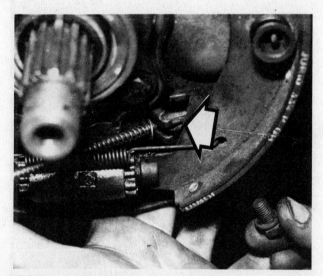

17.6. Slotted cable clamp (arrowed) with the spring and washer on the cable behind the slot.

17.7. Feeding a handbrake cable into the guide tube at the rear end of the floor tunnel.

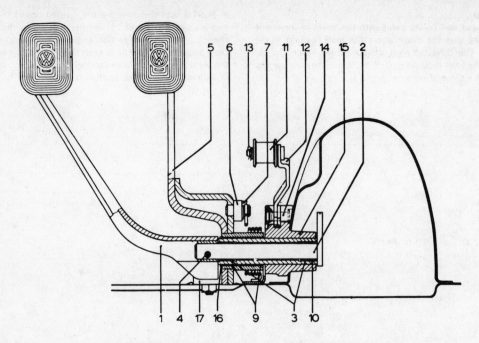

Fig.9.7. Brake and clutch pedal cluster LHD - cross section view

1 Clutch pedal	5 Brake pedal	10 Mounting tube	14 Accelerator pedal lever pin
2 Pedal shaft	6 Master cylinder pushrod	11 Accelerator pedal roller	15 Mounting bracket
3 Bush	7 Pushrod lock plate	12 Accelerator connecting lever	16 Circlip
4 Locating pin	9 Bush	13 Clip	17 Stop plate

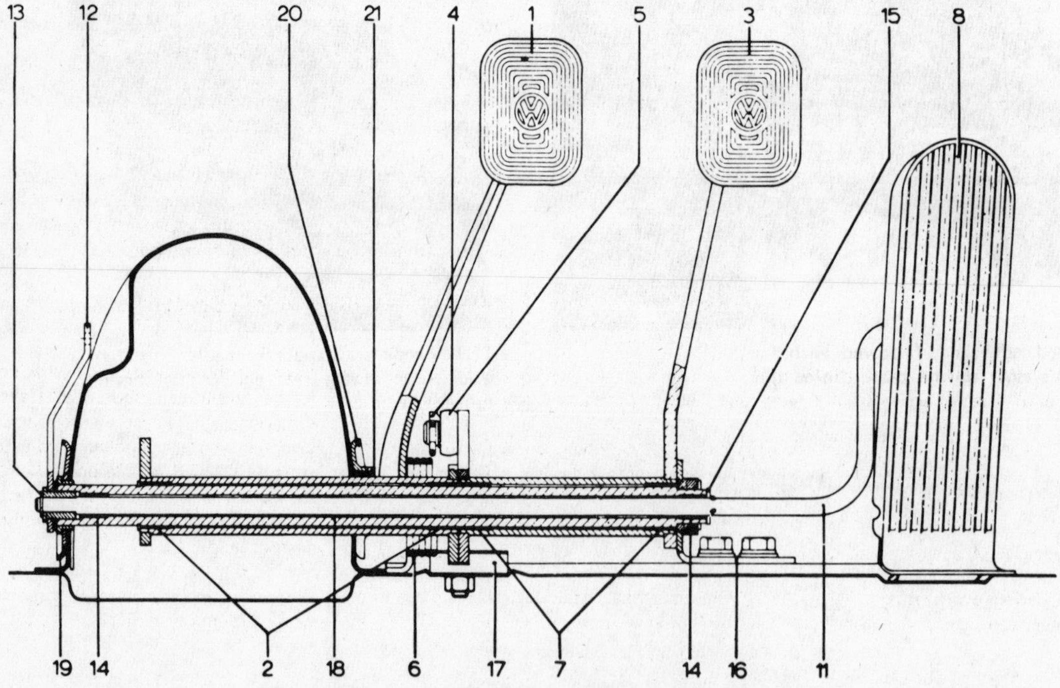

Fig.9.8. Brake and clutch pedal cluster RHD - cross section view

1 Clutch pedal	6 Brake pedal return	12 Accelerator connecting lever	17 Stop plate
2 Bush	spring	13 Circlip	18 Cross shaft
3 Brake pedal	7 Bush	14 Bush	19 Mounting bracket
4 Pushrod lock plate	8 Accelerator pedal	15 Washer	20 Cover plate
5 Master cylinder pushrod	11 Accelerator pedal shaft	16 Mounting bracket	21 Cover plate guide

18. Fault diagnosis and remedies

Before diagnosing faults in the brake system check that any irregularities are not caused by:

1 Uneven and incorrect tyre pressures
2 Incorrect 'mix' of radial and cross-ply tyres
3 Wear in the steering mechanism
4 Defects in the suspension and dampers
5 Misalignment of the bodyframe

Symptom	Reason/s	Remedy
Pedal travels a long way before the brakes operate	Brake shoes set too far from the drums	Adjust the brake shoes to the drums. (This applies equally where disc brakes are fitted but only the rear drums need adjustment).
Stopping ability poor, even though pedal pressure is firm	Linings and/or drums badly worn or scored	Dismantle, inspect and renew as required.
	One or more wheel hydraulic cylinders seized, resulting in some brake shoes not pressing against the drums (or pads against discs)	Dismantle and inspect wheel cylinders. Renew as necessary
	Brake linings contaminated with oil	Renew linings and repair source of oil contamination.
	Wrong type of linings fitted	Verify type of material which is correct for the car and fit it.
	Brake shoes wrongly assembled	Check for correct assembly.
Car veers to one side when the brakes are applied	Brake linings on one side are contaminated with oil	Renew linings and stop oil leak.
	Hydraulic wheel cylinder(s) on one side partially or fully seized	Inspect wheel cylinders for correct operation and renew as necessary.
	A mixture of lining materials fitted between sides	Standardise on types of linings fitted.
	Unequal wear between sides caused by partially seized wheel cylinders	Check wheel cylinders and renew linings and drums as required.
Pedal feels spongy when the brakes are applied	Air is present in the hydraulic system	Bleed the hydraulic system and check for any signs of leakage.
Pedal feels springy when the brakes are applied	Brake linings not bedded into the drums (after fitting new ones)	Allow time for new linings to bed in after which it will certainly be necessary to adjust the shoes to the drums as pedal travel will have increased.
	Master cylinder or brake backplate mounting bolts loose	Retighten mounting bolts.
	Severe wear in brake drums causing distortion when brakes are applied	Renew drums and linings.
Pedal travels right down with little or no resistance and brakes are virtually non-operative	Leak in hydraulic system resulting in lack of pressure for operating wheel cylinders	Examine the whole of the hydraulic system and locate and repair source of leaks. Test after repairing each and every leak source.
	If no signs of leakage are apparent the master cylinder internal seals are failing to sustain pressure	Overhaul master cylinder. If indications are that seals have failed for reasons other than wear all the wheel cylinder seals should be checked also and the system completely replenished with the correct fluid.
Binding, juddering, overheating	One or a combination of causes given in the foregoing sections	Complete and systematic inspection of the whole braking system.

138

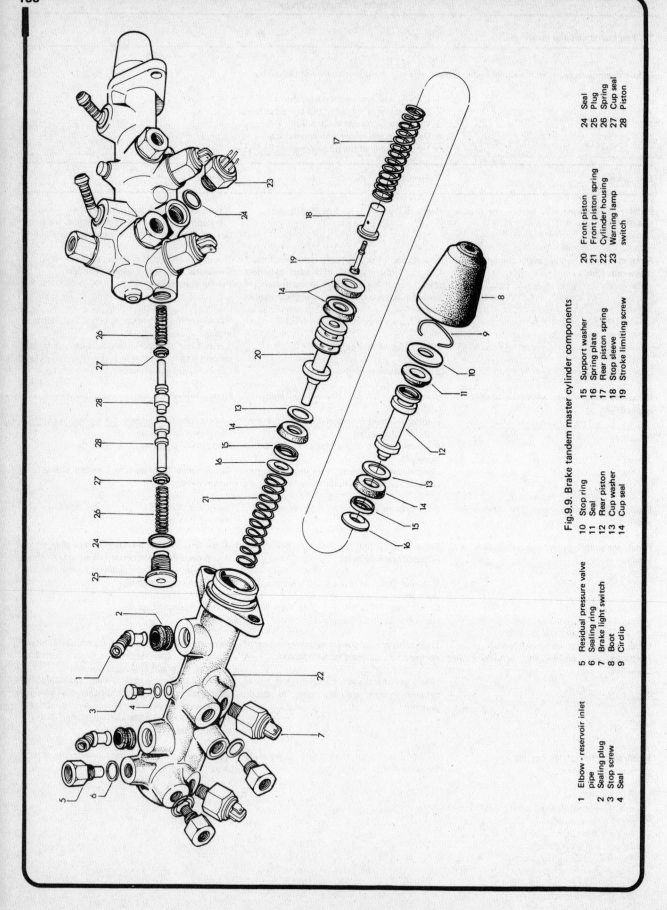

Fig.9.9. Brake tandem master cylinder components

1 Elbow - reservoir inlet pipe
2 Sealing plug
3 Stop screw
4 Seal
5 Residual pressure valve
6 Sealing ring
7 Brake light switch
8 Boot
9 Circlip
10 Stop ring
11 Seal
12 Rear piston
13 Cup washer
14 Cup seal
15 Support washer
16 Spring plate
17 Rear piston spring
18 Stop sleeve
19 Stroke limiting screw
20 Front piston
21 Front piston spring
22 Cylinder housing
23 Warning lamp switch
24 Seal
25 Plug
26 Spring
27 Cup seal
28 Piston

Chapter 10 Electrical system

For modifications, and information applicable to later models, see Supplement at end of manual

Contents

Specifications

Battery

Type...	6 volt (1965 to 1967) or 12 volt (1968 on)
Capacity..	66 amp/hours or 36 amp/hours
Earth..	Negative

Generator

Type...	Bosch or VW D.C. dynamo (for alternator see Chapter 13)

	12 volt	6 volt
Maximum current...	30 amps	45 amps
Mean regulating voltage	14 volts	7 volts
Nominal output speed	2000 rpm	2700 rpm
Cut in speed..	1450 rpm	1600 rpm
Commutator minimum diameter	32.8 mm	
Segment insulation undercut	.5 mm	
Brush length	Must be greater than length of holder	
Pulley ratio - crankshaft/generator - 1300	1 : 1.8	
- 1500	1 : 1.9	

Regulator

Type...	Bosch or VW - matched to generator

Starter motor

Type...	Bosch or VW - pre-engaged
Nominal power	6 volt .5 hp 12 volt .7 hp

Lamps (wattage indicated is for 6v or 12 volts as required)

Headlamp bulb..	45/40w
Parking lamp bulb..	4w
Stop/tail lamp bulb	21/5w
Turn indicator lamp bulbs	21w
Rear number plate bulb	10w festoon
Interior light bulbs	10w festoon
Warning lamp bulbs	1.2w and 2w

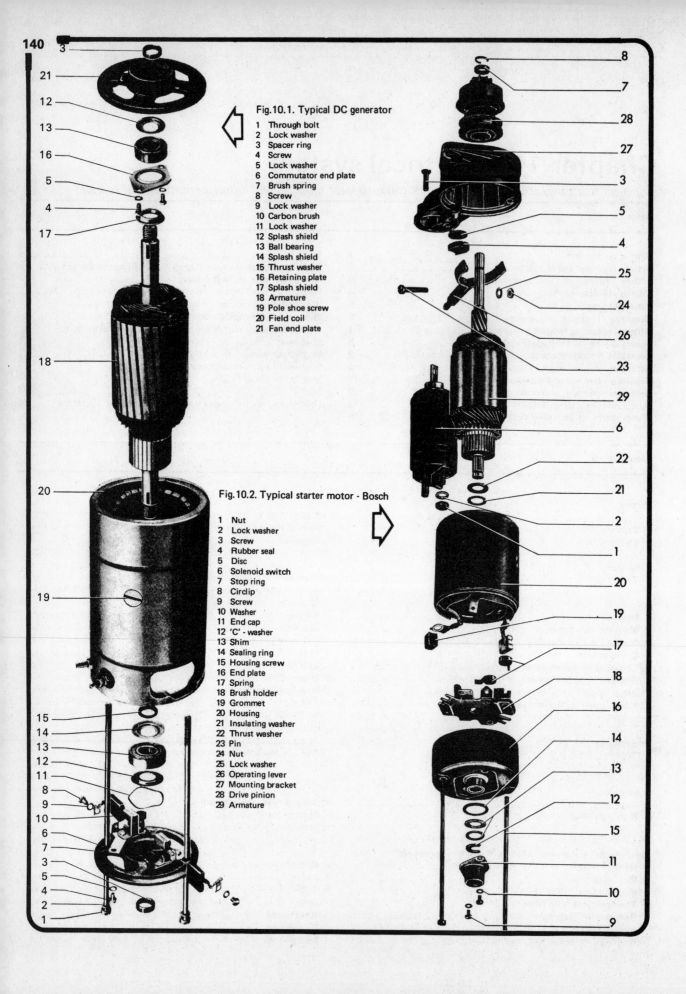

140

Fig.10.1. Typical DC generator

1 Through bolt
2 Lock washer
3 Spacer ring
4 Screw
5 Lock washer
6 Commutator end plate
7 Brush spring
8 Screw
9 Lock washer
10 Carbon brush
11 Lock washer
12 Splash shield
13 Ball bearing
14 Splash shield
15 Thrust washer
16 Retaining plate
17 Splash shield
18 Armature
19 Pole shoe screw
20 Field coil
21 Fan end plate

Fig.10.2. Typical starter motor - Bosch

1 Nut
2 Lock washer
3 Screw
4 Rubber seal
5 Disc
6 Solenoid switch
7 Stop ring
8 Circlip
9 Screw
10 Washer
11 End cap
12 'C' - washer
13 Shim
14 Sealing ring
15 Housing screw
16 End plate
17 Spring
18 Brush holder
19 Grommet
20 Housing
21 Insulating washer
22 Thrust washer
23 Pin
24 Nut
25 Lock washer
26 Operating lever
27 Mounting bracket
28 Drive pinion
29 Armature

Fuses ... ...

10. For all circuits except starter mounted on the lower part of the left hand instrument panel insert.

The circuit/fuse numbers indicated vary from year to year and country to country.

Some, but not all alternatives are given.

No.1 fuse is at the left.

1 Horn, flashers, stop lights, fuel gauge, dual circuit warning light, automatic stick shift switch, heated rear window.
2 Windscreen wipers, stop lights.
3 Main headlamp beam (left) and warning light.
4 Main headlamp beam (right).
5 Dipped headlamp beam (left).
6 Dipped headlamp beam (right).
7 Side lights, front and rear (right or left). Number plate light.
8 Side lights, front and rear (right or left). Number plate light.
9 Radio, interior light, headlamp flasher, hazard warning light.
10 Interior light, headlamp flasher, radio.

Wiper blades

Type... ... ... ,.. ...   Champion C-2901 (1968 on)

Torque wrench settings
General pulley nut ... ...   43 lb.ft. (6.0 mkg)
Fan nut ... ...   45 lb.ft. (6.1 mkg)

1. General description

The system is 6 or 12 volt (depending upon date of production) comprising:
A battery with negative earth mounted in a carrier under the rear seat.

A D.C. generator mounted on a pedestal above the engine driven by a belt from the crankshaft pulley. The generator armature shaft also carries the cooling fan at the opposite end.

A voltage regulator and cut-out unit mounted on the generator (or under the back seat in later versions).

A starter motor of the pre-engaged type (one which meshes with the flywheel ring gear before the power is switched to the motor).
The battery provides the necessary power storage source for operating the starter and providing the current to operate the lights, accessories and ignition circuit. It is kept in a state of full charge by the generator. The regulator controls the generator output. This control automatically adjusts according to the state of charge of the battery, the electrical load demanded and engine revolutions in such a way that the generator is never overloaded and the battery never over or undercharged. It must be appreciated that indiscriminate additions of electrical accessories can upset this balance.
The starter motor is mounted on the transmission casing. Drive pinion engagement and switching is effected by a solenoid. The pinion is engaged by the solenoid before the same solenoid switches current to the starter motor itself. The pinion is driven through a one-way roller clutch to obviate any damage from over-run.
With the 6 volt system the current loadings are double those of 12 volt systems and the cables are consequently heavier.

2. Battery - removal and replacement

1 The battery is fixed under the rear seat which must first be lifted up and out. A metal strap and clip hold a cover over the battery and to release the clip the panel on the front edge of the seat must be removed.
2 Take care when removing both strap and cover as it is easy to cause an accidental short circuit with them.
3 Unclamp the battery terminals (earth [or negative] terminal first) and lift the battery out vertically to prevent electrolyte spillage.
4 When replacing the battery see that both terminals and terminal

clamps are clean and free from corrosion or deposits of any sort. Smear them with petroleum jelly (not grease) before connection. See also that the insulation on the inside of the cover is intact before replacing it. Never replace the rear seat without the battery cover in position. The springs of the seat can short circuit the terminals and start a fire.

3. Battery - maintenance and inspection

1 Normal weekly battery maintenance consists of checking the electrolyte level of each cell to ensure that the separators are covered by ¼ inch of electrolyte. If the level has fallen, top up the battery using distilled water only. Do not overfill. If a battery is overfilled or any electrolyte spilled, immediately wipe away the excess as electrolyte attacks and corrodes any metal it comes into contact with very rapidly.
2 As well as keeping the terminals clean and covered with petroleum jelly, the top of the battery, and especially the top of the cells, should be kept clean and dry. This helps prevent corrosion and ensures that the battery does not become partially discharged by leakage through dampness and dirt.
3 Once every three months, remove the battery and inspect the battery tray and battery leads for corrosion (white fluffy deposits on the metal which are brittle to touch). If any corrosion is found, clean off the deposits with ammonia and paint over the clean metal with an anti-rust/anti-acid paint.
4 At the same time inspect the battery case for cracks. If a crack is found, a new battery is the only answer. Cracks are frequently caused in the top of the battery cases by pouring in distilled water in the middle of winter after instead of BEFORE a run. This gives the water no chance to mix with the electrolyte and so the former freezes and splits the battery case.
5 If topping up the battery becomes excessive and the case has been inspected for cracks that could cause leakage, but none are found, the battery is being over-charged and the regulator will have to be checked.
6 With the battery on the bench at the three monthly interval check, measure its specific gravity with a hydrometer to determine the state of charge and condition of the electrolyte. There should be very little variation between the different cells and if a variation in excess of 0.025 is present it will be due to either:

a) Loss of electrolyte from the battery at some time caused by

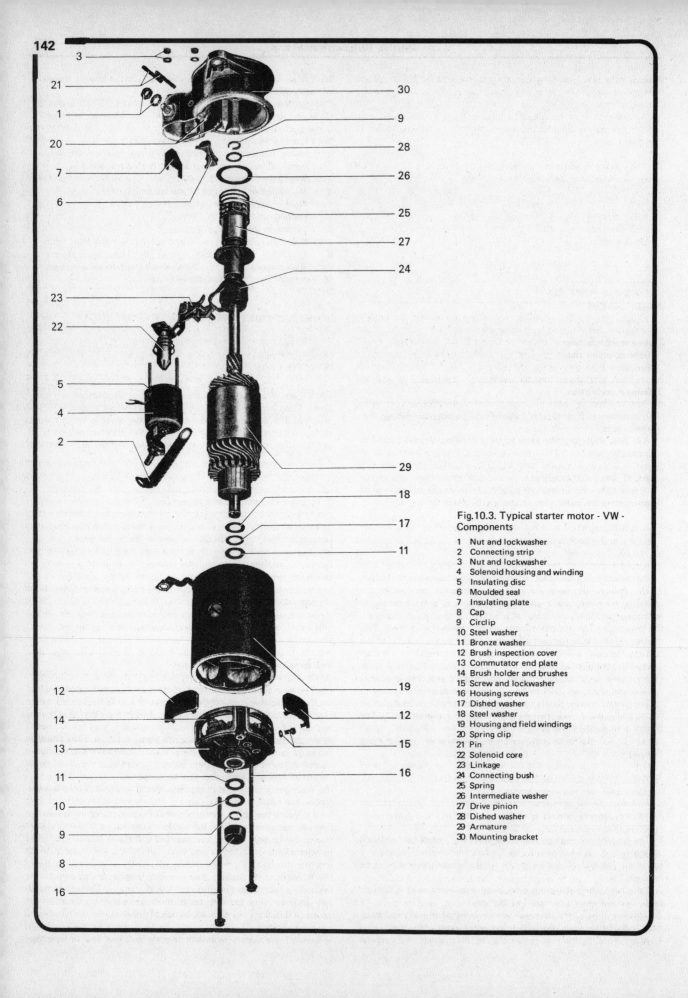

Fig.10.3. Typical starter motor - VW -
Components

1   Nut and lockwasher
2   Connecting strip
3   Nut and lockwasher
4   Solenoid housing and winding
5   Insulating disc
6   Moulded seal
7   Insulating plate
8   Cap
9   Circlip
10 Steel washer
11 Bronze washer
12 Brush inspection cover
13 Commutator end plate
14 Brush holder and brushes
15 Screw and lockwasher
16 Housing screws
17 Dished washer
18 Steel washer
19 Housing and field windings
20 Spring clip
21 Pin
22 Solenoid core
23 Linkage
24 Connecting bush
25 Spring
26 Intermediate washer
27 Drive pinion
28 Dished washer
29 Armature
30 Mounting bracket

spillage or a leak, resulting in a drop in the specific gravity of the electrolyte when the deficiency was replaced with distilled water instead of fresh electrolyte.
b) An internal short circuit caused by buckling of the plates or a similar malady pointing to the likelihood of total battery failure in the near future.

7 The correct readings for the electrolyte specific gravity at various states of charge and conditions are:

	Temperate	Tropical
Fully charged	1.285	1.23
Half charged	1.20	1.14
Discharged	1.12	1.08

4. Electrolyte replenishment

1 If the battery is in a fully charged state and one of the cells maintains a specific gravity reading which is 0.025 or more lower than the others, and a check of each cell has been made with a voltage meter to check for short circuits (a four to seven second test should give a steady reading of between 1.2 to 1.8 volts), then it is likely that electrolyte has been lost from the cell with the low reading at some time.
2 Top the cell up with a solution of 1 part sulphuric acid to 2.5 parts of water. If the cell is already fully topped up draw some electrolyte out of it with a pipette.
3 When mixing the sulphuric acid and water NEVER ADD WATER TO SULPHURIC ACID — always pour the acid slowly onto the water in a glass container. IF WATER IS ADDED TO SULPHURIC ACID IT WILL EXPLODE.
4 Continue to top up the cell with the freshly made electrolyte and then recharge the battery and check the hydrometer readings.

5. Battery - charging

1 In winter time when heavy demand is placed upon the battery, such as when starting from cold, and much electrical equipment is continually in use, it is a good idea occasionally to have the battery fully charged from an external source at the rate of 3.5 to 4 amps.
2 Continue to charge the battery at this rate until no further rise in specific gravity is noted over a four hour period.
3 Alternatively, a trickle charger, charging at the rate of 1.5 amps, can be safely used overnight.
4 Specially rapid 'boost' charges which are claimed to restore the power of the battery in 1 to 2 hours are most dangerous as they can cause serious damage to the battery plates through over-heating.
5 While charging the battery note that the temperature of the electrolyte should never exceed 100°F.
6 Make sure that your charging set and battery are set to the same voltage.

6. Generator - routine maintenance

1 The main requirement is maintaining the fan belt at the proper tension as described in Chapter 2.
2 Both armature shaft bearings are sealed and additional lubrication is not possible as a frequent routine.
3 Keep an eye on the condition of the commutator and carbon brushes. These can be seen through the aperture in the casing. The brushes should protrude from the upper ends of their holders. If they do not then they are getting short and need renewal. The commutator should not show serious signs of discolouration and there should be no indication of a channel worn where the brushes track.

7. Generator - testing in position - general

1 If the ignition warning light does not go out when the engine is running at a fast tickover or only goes out at high revolutions it is usually due to a fault in either the generator or regulator. If checked and dealt with quickly it is often possible to avoid expensive repairs.
2 First examine the generator brushes and the surface of the commutator. If the brushes are worn or commutator dirty it is possible to deal with them without removing the generator from the car. Section 12 explains how to remove the brushes and clean the commutator.
3 In order to carry out even the simplest check a voltmeter is required.

8. Generator - no load voltage check

1 Disconnect the wires from terminal 51 (B+) on the regulator and make sure the ends cannot touch any nearby part and short to earth.
2 Connect the positive lead from the voltmeter to terminal 51 (B+) on the regulator and the negative lead to earth.
3 Start the engine and increase speed slowly to a fast tickover. The voltmeter should rise to a reading of 7–8 volts on a 6 volt system, 13–14 volts on a 12 volt system, and stay there. If there is no reading the fault is most likely in the generator. If the reading is incorrect then the regulator is most probably at fault. Nevertheless, both could be faulty in either case.

9. Generator - voltage check without regulator connected

1 This check will tell you if the generator is at fault and must be done quickly or you could damage an otherwise sound generator.
2 Disconnect both cables from terminals 51 and 61 on the regulator and then connect terminal DF (F) on the generator to earth with a piece of wire. It will be necessary to undo the two regulator mounting screws in order to get to this terminal and the D+ terminal.
3 Connect the voltmeter + terminal to the D+ terminal on the generator and the voltmeter negative terminal to earth.
4 Start the engine. At a fast tickover - say 1500 generator rpm the voltage should be approximately 6 or 12 volts according to the system. At twice this speed the voltage should increase to 18 or 36 volts. Check quickly and switch off within a few seconds. If the voltage is nil or low then the generator is faulty.

10. Generator - current output check

1 The two previous tests have confirmed the presence or lack of voltage. This does not confirm the presence or lack of amps which are needed to charge the battery (even though the warning light may go out). For the current output check you will need an ammeter - with a range of 50 amps negative and positive. (If you have fitted an ammeter as an extra into the charging circuit already, this, of course, performs the function of this test and in fact tells you at all times whether the generator is doing its job properly.
2 Disconnect the battery negative (earth) terminal. There are two cables on terminal 51 (B+) on the regulator. Detach the one that comes from the starter motor terminal (leaving the other in position which leads on to the fuse block). Then connect the ammeter between the end of this disconnected cable and terminal 51 (B+) on the regulator in such a way that none of the connections touch earth.
3 Reconnect the battery and start the engine. Switch on all the lights. At low speed the ammeter should show a discharge although at very low idling speed it should move to zero when the regulator cut-out functions. At high engine speed the ammeter should show a positive reading. If the lights are switched off this reading should increase for a short time and then settle back to a 1–3 amp positive

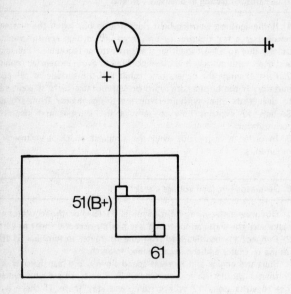

1 Voltmeter for no load voltage
   test

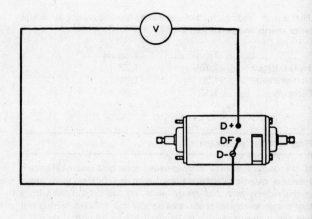

2 Voltmeter for generator
   voltage test

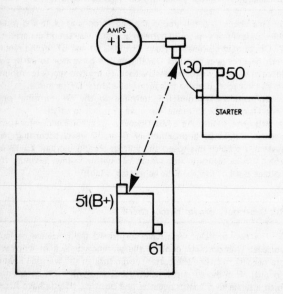

3 Ammeter for current
   output test

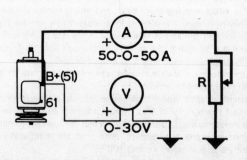

4 Voltmeter, ammeter and
   variable resistance for full
   regulator output test

Fig.10.4. Generator and current regulator test connections. (Sections 8—10)

reading. The actual charge rate depends on the state of the battery.

4 If no positive ammeter reading can be obtained then the regulator is defective.

5 To check the current regulator independently, a voltmeter, a 50 amp ammeter and a variable resistance are required. However, if you have already established that the regulator is faulty there is no point in going any further. Regulators cannot be repaired - they must be renewed as a unit. The connections necessary for regulator checking are shown in Fig.10.4. for academic interest.

11. Regulator - removal and replacement

1 First disconnect the battery. Disconnect the cables from terminal 51 (B+) and 61. Undo the two screws which hold the regulator to the generator, lift it up and then disconnect the two wires from terminals + (D+) and F (DF) on the regulator. On later models the regulator is held by two screws to the body panel under the rear seat on the left. The connections are the same.

2 Replacement is a reversal of this procedure. Note that the thicker of the two wires from the generator is the one that connects to terminal.+ (D+). It is most important to get these connections correct. Otherwise the generator and regulator could be ruined in the first few seconds of operation.

12. Generator - removal, dismantling and replacement

1 The generator is removed in the manner described for the fan in Chapter 2. Before deciding to take it out completely make sure that the renewal of the brushes and cleaning the commutator are not the sole things to be done because these can be dealt with without removing the generator.

2 If the brushes need renewing, hook up the ends of the springs which press them into the holders and then pull the brushes out. Then undo the screw which connects the leads.

3 Whilst the brushes are removed the commutator can be cleaned with a piece of clean cloth soaked in petrol. If the commutator is very scored, changing the carbon brushes may improve things temporarily but the improvement in generator output is likely to be small and short lived.

4 When fitting new brushes make sure that they are of the correct type and fit snugly in the holders and slide freely. Brushes which are too loose will clatter about and soon wear out. Those which are tight will probably stick and eventually lose contact with the commutator as they wear away.

5 If any of the brush retaining springs are broken or the commutator is scored the generator must be removed for the repairs to be made.

6 To dismantle the generator is not a procedure we recommend, principally because there is very little the normal do-it-yourself man can do to repair it anyway. If the bearings have failed (a very rare occurrence) then the armature will need reconditioning. Skimming the commutator must be done in a lathe. Should the insulation of the armature or field coils have broken down then they will need renewal.

7 Having removed the generator and taken off the fan, therefore, we recommend it be replaced with an exchange unit or overhauled by a specialist firm dealing with auto electrics. Make sure when taking it to the repair firm that the regulator goes with it as their tests after rebuild will cover the complete unit.

8 Replacement of the generator is described in Chapter 2. Check that the spacer collar behind the fan hub is in position, otherwise the shaft will bind solid when the fan nut is tightened.

13. Starter motor - testing, removal and replacement

1 On the Volkswagen the starter is an inaccessible article and short of checking that the mounting bolts are tight and the electrical connections properly made to the solenoid, there is nothing else to be done except take it out if it malfunctions. If the starter

fails to kick at all ascertain that current is being fed from the starter switch to the solenoid. This can be done by connecting a suitably long lead to the two terminals on the solenoid in turn, and connecting the other end via a voltmeter or bulb to earth. When connected to the smaller terminal (the lead from the ignition switch), there should be an indication on the bulb or voltmeter when the starter switch is operated. If there is not then check the other end of the wire at the starter switch terminal in the same way. If there is no voltage then the fault is not with the starter. Then connect the lead to the larger terminal on the solenoid. If there is no voltage when the starter switch is operated the solenoid is defective. If there is voltage and the starter does not turn the starter is defective.

2 Disconnect the battery and pull off the right heater hose. The starter motor is secured by two bolts, the top one also being the upper right engine mounting bolt. To get this undone a spanner must be put on the nut in front of the fan housing in the space between it and the bodywork. With luck the nut will turn without the bolt moving. If the bolt turns then another spanner (a socket with long extension) must be put on the bolt head from underneath the car.

3 From underneath the car, pull off the small lead at the connection and then undo the nut securing the large cable. All this must be done mainly by feel. Do not confuse the two large terminal nuts on the solenoid. The lower one connects the strap between solenoid and starter.

4 Remove the lower bolt and the starter can be lifted out.

5 Replacement is a reversal of the removal procedure. Before fitting, grease the end of the pinion shaft. It runs in a plain bush in the engine crankcase casting.

14. Starter motor - dismantling and reassembly

1 The first stage of dismantling is to remove the end cover plate to get access to the brushes. If these do not protrude above the tops of thier holders renewal is necessary, which calls for further dismantling.

2 Undo the nut connecting the strap between the solenoid and the starter and undo the two screws holding the solenoid casing to the end frame.

3 The solenoid plunger can now be unhooked from the operating lever inside the end frame.

4 If the solenoid only is faulty this is as far as it is necessary to go. A new solenoid unit can be fitted now.

5 Undo the two hook studs or bolts which clamp the end frame to the main casing of the starter.

6 Hook up the springs holding the carbon brushes in the holders and push them to one side so that the pressure is relieved.

7 Undo the nut on the end of the shaft and take off the three washers behind it noting their order of assembly. The end frame and armature shaft can now be pulled out. Do not lose the washers on the end of the shaft next to the commutator. If the commutator is badly scored it will need renovation in the same manner as for the generator.

8 To remove the end frame from the drive end of the shaft first push back the stop ring with a suitable tube so that the jump ring underneath can be released from its groove. The end cover assembly complete with pinion may then be drawn off.

9 To renew the brushes, two may be detached by simply removing the screws whilst the other two need to be cut off and new ones soldered to the braided leads. Leave sufficient length to solder the new ones onto easily.

10 The pinion drive should turn one-way only inside the clutch easily. If it does not the whole unit needs renewing. The pinion teeth should not be badly worn or chipped. The yoke of the pinion operating lever should be a good fit in the groove of the pinion sleeve.

11 Reassembly is a reversal of the dismantling procedure. Thoroughly grease the moving parts of the pinion operating lever first.

12 The carbon brushes should all be held up in their holders and this can be achieved if the springs are jammed against the sides of the brushes. The armature has three washers on the end and these must be fitted so that the curved spring washer goes on first, the steel

11.1. Regulator mounted under the rear seat at the left.

14.1. Removing starter motor end cover.

14.2(a) Undo the connecting strap nut.

14.2(b) Remove solenoid casing screws.

14.3. Take out the solenoid.

14.6. Hooking up the carbon brush springs and arranging the end to hold the brush up away from the commutator (arrowed).

washer next with the lug towards the spring washer, followed by the fibre bearing washer.

13 If either of the bearing bushes for each end of the shaft are a very slack fit then they should be driven out and new ones fitted. Use a shouldered mandrel and soak them in oil well in advance.

14 When the pinion stop ring is refitted stake it into position over the jump ring after the latter has been fitted in its groove.

15 Fit the fibre washer, steel washer and nut on the end of the shaft.

16 Lift up the brush springs and reposition them over their respective brushes.

17 When refitting the solenoid ensure the plunger hooked end is securely placed over the operating lever.

18 The screw heads and joint faces of the commutator end cover, the solenoid and end frame should all be treated with sealing compound to keep water out. Use the Volkswagen product specially prepared for this if possible. It is important that it is not applied too thickly, otherwise clearance distances may be upset. If, after reassembly, the endfloat of the shaft exceeds 0.012 inch it should be reduced by adding shim washers behind the lockwasher on the commutator end of the armature shaft.

19 Because the pinion end bearing (bush) is located in the engine crankcase casting, it is not possible to rotate the starter under load or at speed when not fitted to the engine. The customary bench tests are therefore not applicable to this starter.

15. Fuses

1 The fuses are located under the dash panel. The wire connections to the fuse block however, are to be found in the other side by removing the fibre cover panel inside the front luggage compartment. Their function is as detailed in the specification. If any fuse should blow it is normally due to a short circuit in the circuit concerned. With the aid of the wiring diagram, therefore, first check visually at all the points in the circuit where such a fault is most likely to occur. The most likely places are where wires pass through individual holes into lamp units or through holes in the bodywork where grommets have been disturbed. In the ignition circuit check the connections at the coil and choke. Remove the fibre cover from behind the dash panel in the front luggage compartment and see if there are any broken or loose wires. Feel switches to see if they are hot, which they should not be.

2 If no obvious solutions occur disconnect all items on the particular circuit (e.g. the parking light bulbs on the left if that is the circuit concerned). Fit another fuse of the proper rating. Then reconnect one item at a time, switching on each time until the fuse blows again. This will isolate the faulty part of the circuit and a closer examination can be made in that area. If you choose to fit a fuse of a much higher rating to try and overcome persistent blowing, the least that can happen is that the wiring will burn out somewhere. The worst result could be a fire.

16. Direction indicators - fault tracing and rectification

1 One of the most usual causes of failure is due simply to bad connections to earth. This can occur at the bulb holders (usual) or the terminal connections. If, therefore, the flashers can be heard but do not light - or only operate slowly - check all the bulbs, holders and screws for signs of whitish corrosion deposits (which may have been caused by seepage of water past the lamp housing seals). Check also the appropriate fuse.

2 First check that the flasher relay itself is not faulty. The simplest way to do this is by substitution with a new one. The relay is located behind the dash panel and access is from inside the luggage compartment.

4 Finally, the fault may be in the indicator switch. Before going to the trouble of taking this off, which involves removal of the steering wheel (see Chapter 11), a check can be made at the flasher relay terminals. (This of course assumes that the flasher relay is in working order). The feed wire to the switch from the flasher relay is that leading from terminal 'S'. If this is disconnected and another temporary feed wire connected then it can be used to bridge out the switch. It merely needs connection to the feed wire to one of the flasher bulbs. When the ignition is switched on the flasher should operate both the bulbs of the side linked in. If they still do not work then there is more than just the switch at fault.

17. Windscreen wipers - fault finding

1 If the wipers do not work when they are switched on, first check the fuse. If this is sound then there is either an open circuit in the wiring or switch, the wiper motor is faulty, or the pivot spindles or linkages may be binding.

2 If the wipers work intermittently then suspect a short circuit in the motor or a poor contact to earth. The earth is connected at the main mounting screw. Alternatively, the armature shaft endfloat adjustment may be too tight or the wiper linkage may be binding.

3 Should the wipers not stop when they are turned off there must be a short circuit in the switch or wiring.

18. Windscreen wiper motor - removal and replacement

1 Disconnect the battery earth lead.

2 Slacken the clamping screw on the wiper arm brackets and pull the arms off the spindles.

3 Remove the hexagon nut, washers and seals from around the spindles.

4 Remove the glove box if necessary and the fresh air vent.

5 Disconnect the cables from the motor.

6 Undo the screw which holds the motor and frame to the strip steel mounting bracket. The motor and the linkage can then be removed together.

7 To detach the motor from the linkage first remove the lockwasher and spring washer from the motor shaft and detach the connecting rod. Then undo the motor shaft clamp nut and the single screw holding the motor to the frame and take the motor away from the frame.

8 Replacement of the motor and wiper mechanism is a reversal of the removal procedure. Ensure the replacement of the spring washer between the motor shaft and frame and the coil spring between the connecting rod and frame. When refitting the unit to the car make sure the spindles are at right angles to the windscreen. The mounting hole in the frame is slotted to permit adjustment. The earthing strip contact at the mounting screw should be clean.

9 The sealing washers around the spindles must be correctly positioned and care taken not to overtighten the clamping screw - the correct torque being 2–3 lb/ft. (30–40 cmkg).

19. Windscreen wiper motor - dismantling and reassembly

1 Other than for renewal of the carbon brushes, dismantling for further repair is not economical.

2 To renew the carbon brushes the wiper motor and frame assembly must be removed from the car as described in the previous sections and the motor separated from the frame.

3 Remove the armature end cover by undoing the screw or clip.

4 The brush holders are held in tension against the commutator by a common spring. Unhook this and swing the holders outwards. The

14.8(a) Remove the stop ring and jump ring.

14.8(b) Withdrawing the end frame together with the pinion assembly.

14.14. Staking the pinion stop ring over the jump ring.

14.18. Washers at commutator end of the shaft to regulate endfloat.

15. Fuses mounted under the facia panel to the right of the steering column.

old brushes can be removed with a pair of fine nosed pliers. The new ones should be a tight fit in the holders and should seat squarely onto the commutator when the holder is moved back into position.

5 On motors fitted with a self-parking device check that the points gap is 0.8 mm (0.031 inch) and that the points are clean.

20. Windscreen wiper spindle bearings - renewal

1 One of the causes of jamming could be due to wear in the spindle bearings and these can be renewed after the assembly has been removed from the car.

2 Having disconnected the driving link and connecting rod by means of removing the spring clips and washer, take off the seal and washer and undo the locknut securing the bearings to the frame.

3 Replace any of the smaller nylon bushes that may be worn also.

4 When reassembling see that the hollow sides of the pressed steel links face towards the frame.

21. Windscreen wiper switch and washer pump - removal and replacement

1 The combined wiper switch and washer pump can be easily removed after first disconnecting the battery earth cable and unscrewing the knob from the switch.

2 Then, from behind the panel (in the front luggage compartment), pull off the wires and washer pipes. Unscrew the retaining ring and take off the switch.

22. Windscreen washer - fault finding

1 Early models had a single mechanical pump which was incorporated in the wiper switch body. When pulled out and released water drawn from the reservoir (behind the spare wheel) and sprayed onto the screen through two fine jets mounted on the front compartment lid. Later models have a valve incorporated in the switch and the water reservoir tank is pressurised so that water is automatically forced along the pipes when the valve is opened.

2 If no water issues from the jets first check that all pipes are connected and intact and that the reservoir is pressurised where applicable.

3 Then check that the nozzles of the jets are clear. Use a piece of fine wire to poke them out if necessary.

4 If it becomes obvious that the pump/valve is not working, then it must be renewed.

23. Instrument panel, speedometer and warning lights

1 Access to all instruments on the panel is from behind, after the front luggage compartment lid has been raised, and the fibre backing panel taken off.

2 The ignition, main beam and oil warning lamp bulbs are contained in snap fit holders in the speedometer head and can be renewed and changed simply by pulling out the holders.

3 The speedometer cable can be detached from the head by unscrewing the knurled retaining collar. The other end is driven by the bearing dust cover on the front left wheel and this can be released after removing the hub cap and taking the clip off the end of the cable. The cable may be drawn out.

4 The speedometer head is released once the two retaining screws are slackened. If turned anticlockwise the mounting lugs will disengage and the whole head can be lifted out. Make sure that the warning lamps, panel lamp and earth lead have been disconnected also.

24. Stop lamps - fault finding

1 The stop lamps are operated by a hydraulic switch mounted on the end of the brake master cylinder (see Chapter 9).

2 If, after checking that the bulbs, fuse and connections are in order, the brake lights still do not work (with the ignition switched on) pull off the two leads from the hydraulic switch and touch them together. If the stop lamps now light the switch is at fault and should be renewed. The brakes must be bled afterwards (see Chapter 9).

3 If the stop lights still do not work when bridging the terminals of the switch then the fault lies in the wiring circuit. First check that voltage is coming to the switch terminal and carry on from there, tracing back to the connections with the aid of the wiring diagram.

25. Horn

1 The single horn is mounted behind the left front wing (behind a small oval grille. It has a 16 amp fuse).

2 If the horn should fail to work after checking the fuse check that the horn ring is operating the contact in the centre of the steering wheel. This can be seen after the steering wheel hub has been levered out. The three screws will release the ring. The lead from the switch runs down the steering column to the coupling on early models, and a slide contact takes the circuit to the horn. Later on a contact spring was fitted in the turn signal switch to carry the horn earth wire. It must be remembered that when the ignition is switched on the current flows first to the horn and the circuit is made when the horn ring switch is earthed.

3 The terminals on the horn itself should be perfectly clean and the insulation in good condition.

4 If the horn has to be removed check it once again with an independent supply before condemning it. There is a central adjusting nut in the back of the horn which may possibly give advantageous results if rotated in one direction or the other. It is not normally adjustable and if wrongly set can damage an otherwise good horn. It is important to emphasise therefore that any 'fiddling' with this is a positively last resort, having checked the complete circuit first.

5 The horn is removed by undoing the mounting bolt which secures it to the bracket.

6 When refitting the horn it is important to make sure that it does not contact the surrounding bodywork in any way. If it does it will not function properly.

26. Headlamps, side lamps and stop lamps - bulbs and adjustment

1 Arrangement and fixings have varied somewhat over the years but the principles are much the same. Rear lamp bulbs are accessible after removing the lenses. These are held by two screws on the outside. The same goes for the front direction indicator lamps mounted on the wings. With the lenses removed the bulbs can be extracted by pressing them in firmly and turning them anticlockwise and releasing. The twin filament stop/tail light bulb only fits one way and for this reason the bayonet pins are offset. Check the offset when replacing them. On 1968 models and later, a reversing light is incorporated in the same housing on some models.

2 Headlamp units also incorporate the front parking light which is a separate bulb set into the reflector casing. On some models fitted with sealed beam units the parking light bulb holder is mounted in the lower part of the main casing instead.

3 To remove the headlamp unit from the car, unscrew the lowest screw which secures the rim. Lift up the lower edge of the rim to unhook the top edge and then pull the whole lot out.

4 To remove the bulb undo the bulb holder from the back of the reflector by turning it anticlockwise and then pull the bulb and connection apart.

5 When fitting the new bulb avoid handling the glass with

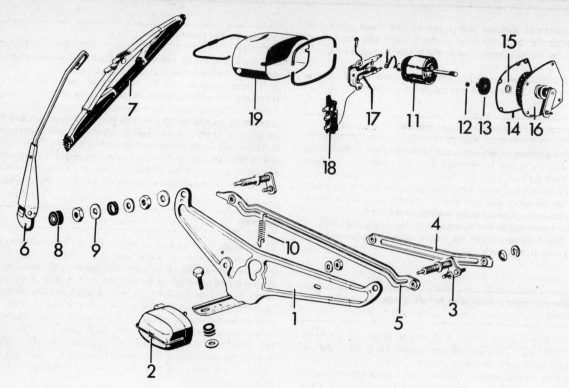

Fig.10.5. Wiper mechanism components

1	Frame	6	Arm assy.	11	Armature	16	Cover with gear and
2	Motor	7	Blade assy.	12	Thrust washer		crank
3	Shaft with crank (left)	8	Cover piece	13	Gear	17	Carbon brush yoke
4	Connecting link	9	Washer	14	Cover gasket	18	Contact breakers
5	Connecting rod	10	Retaining spring	15	Thrust washer	19	Motor cover, gasket and clip

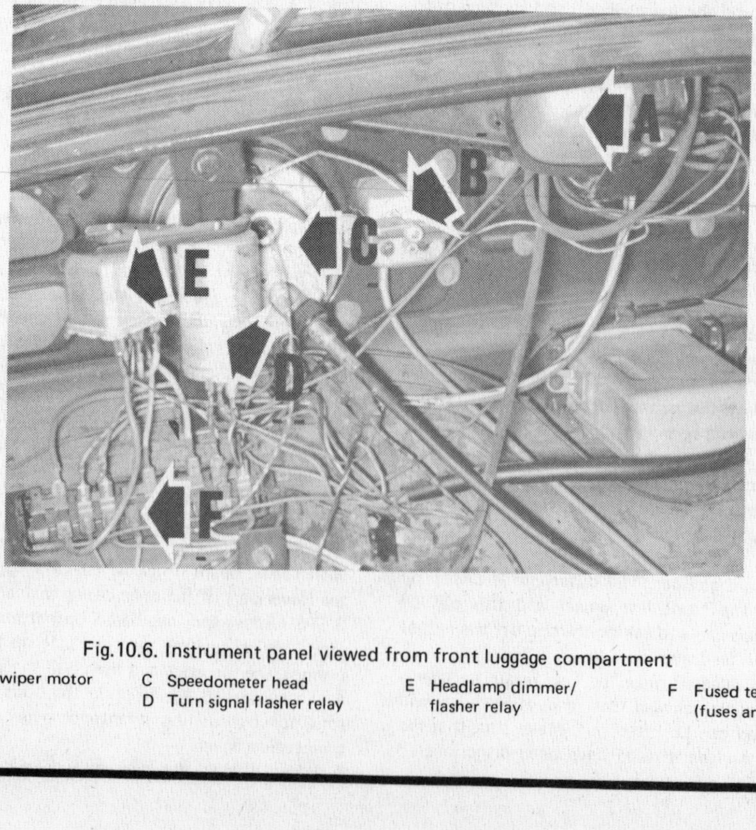

Fig.10.6. Instrument panel viewed from front luggage compartment

A	Windscreen wiper motor	C	Speedometer head	E	Headlamp dimmer/	F	Fused terminal block
B	Fuel gauge	D	Turn signal flasher relay		flasher relay		(fuses are the other side)

fingers which will leave a deposit which can eventually cause discolouration. Fit the bulb and connector together and then fit the holder into the reflector so that the lugs and notches line up.

6 Should the headlamp lens need renewal proceed as described in paragraphs 3 and 4 and pull out the parking lamp bulb holder as well.

7 It will then be necessary to remove the adjusting screws; so if these are very rusty, clean them properly first.

8 The reflector is held into the rim with long curved wire springs and these must be held at one end whilst the other is carefully released. They are strong and could 'fly'; prevent accidents by taking precautions.

9 When fitting a new glass the same type must be used and the sealing ring should be in perfect condition. Make sure the glass is fitted the correct way up.

10 Replace the spring clips and put the adjusting screws back.

11 On sealed beam lamps the bulb and reflector are a single unit and can be identified by the absence of a bulb holder. The wire connection fits straight onto the three terminals at the back of the unit. This item is removed and replaced in the same way that would be used for releasing the reflector and glass on a conventional model.

12 Headlamp alignment is a task which can only be done properly with optical alignment equipment. However, a rough setting can be made until the time when the beams can be properly set. Regulations vary between countries and dimensions given here apply to right hand drive vehicles in the United Kingdom.

13 The car should be standing on level ground with the tyre pressures correct and the equivalent of a 70 kg (154 lbs) passenger in the back seat. For headlamps fitted with replaceable headlamp bulbs the car should face a vertical wall 5 metres (16½ feet) away. It is important that the centre line of the car be exactly at right angles to the wall. Measure the height of the lamp centres above the ground and make a horizontal line on the wall at a height 5 cms (2 inches) less. Then mark the centre line of the car on the wall. This is best done by sighting. Measure the distance between the headlamps and mark two points on the horizontal line equal to this distance. The points should be equidistant from the car centre line. These are the reference points and with the headlamps dipped the angle point between the dark/light zones should coincide for each lamp. Cover the lamp not being adjusted. The adjusting screws are in the lamp rim and the upper one does the vertical adjustment. For sealed beam lamps follow the same procedure with the car 25 feet from the wall. Aim the light intensive areas so that the top edge coincides with the lamp centre line height and the right hand edge is 5 cms (2 inches) to the left of the vertical centres. The two sketches indicate the requirements. (Fig.10.8 and 10.9).

14 Holts Amber Lamp is useful for temporarily changing the headlight colour to conform with the normal usage on Continental Europe.

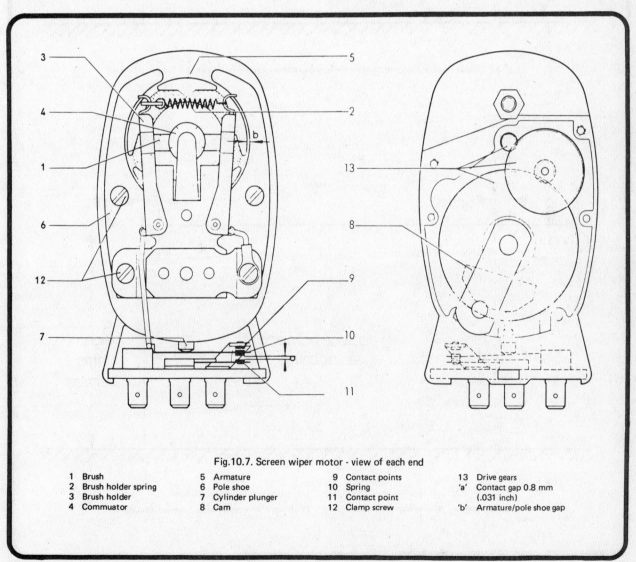

Fig.10.7. Screen wiper motor - view of each end

1	Brush	5	Armature	9	Contact points	13	Drive gears
2	Brush holder spring	6	Pole shoe	10	Spring	'a'	Contact gap 0.8 mm
3	Brush holder	7	Cylinder plunger	11	Contact point		(.031 inch)
4	Commuator	8	Cam	12	Clamp screw	'b'	Armature/pole shoe gap

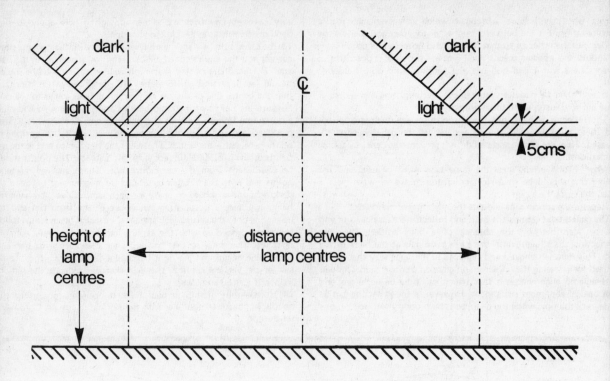

Fig.10.8. Diagram showing alignment requirements of headlamp main beams (replaceable headlamp bulbs)

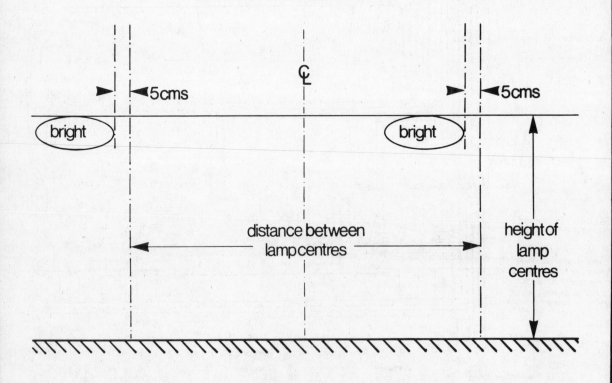

Fig.10.9. Diagram showing alignment requirements of headlamp main beams (sealed beam headlamps)

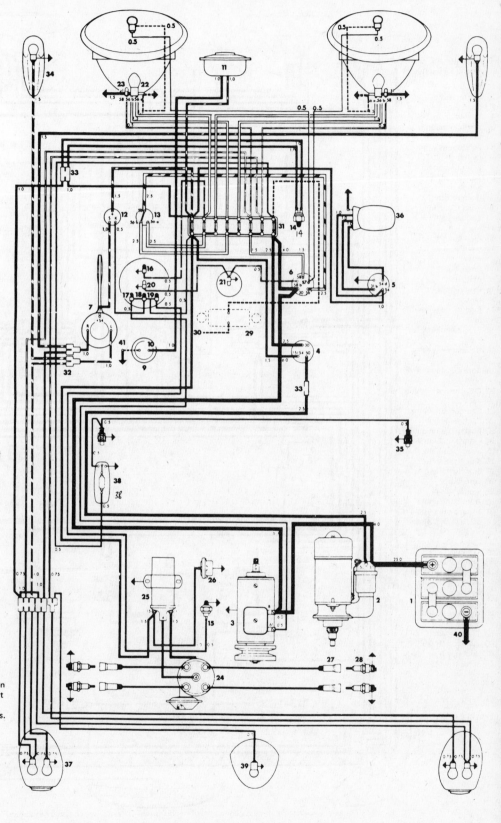

Typical wiring
diagram (6 volt)

1 Battery
2 Starter
3 Generator
4 Ignition/starter
   switch
5 Windscreen wiper
   switch
6 Light switch
7 Direction indicator
   dip switch
8 Emergency light
   switch
9 Horn ring
10 Steering column
   connector
11 Horn
12 Flasher relay
13 Dip relay
14 Stop light switch
15 Oil pressure switch
16 Main beam indicator
   light
17 Generator/fan
   warning light
18 Flasher indicator
   light
19 Oil pressure warning
   light
20 Panel light
21 Fuel gauge light
22 Headlamps
23 Side lights
24 Distributor
25 Coil
26 Electric choke
27 Spark plug connections
28 Spark plugs
29 Radio
30 Aerial
31 Fuse box
32 Cable adaptor
33 Cable connections
34 Flasher lights
35 Courtesy light
   switches
36 Windscreen wiper
   motor
37 Stop, turn and tail
   lights
38 Interior light
39 Number plate light
40 Battery earth
   connection
41 Steering column to
   earth connection

   Special Note
Small figures alongside
cables refer to cross-section
area (and therefore current
carrying capability) mea-
sured in square millimetres.

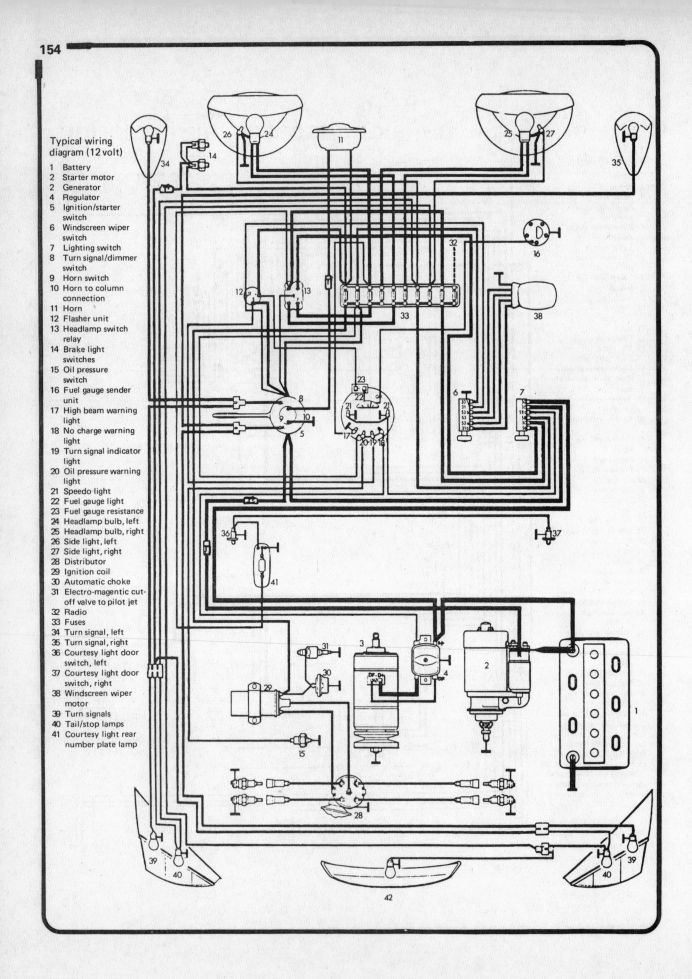

Typical wiring
diagram (12 volt)

1 Battery
2 Starter motor
2 Generator
4 Regulator
5 Ignition/starter
   switch
6 Windscreen wiper
   switch
7 Lighting switch
8 Turn signal/dimmer
   switch
9 Horn switch
10 Horn to column
   connection
11 Horn
12 Flasher unit
13 Headlamp switch
   relay
14 Brake light
   switches
15 Oil pressure
   switch
16 Fuel gauge sender
   unit
17 High beam warning
   light
18 No charge warning
   light
19 Turn signal indicator
   light
20 Oil pressure warning
   light
21 Speedo light
22 Fuel gauge light
23 Fuel gauge resistance
24 Headlamp bulb, left
25 Headlamp bulb, right
26 Side light, left
27 Side light, right
28 Distributor
29 Ignition coil
30 Automatic choke
31 Electro-magentic cut-
   off valve to pilot jet
32 Radio
33 Fuses
34 Turn signal, left
35 Turn signal, right
36 Courtesy light door
   switch, left
37 Courtesy light door
   switch, right
38 Windscreen wiper
   motor
39 Turn signals
40 Tail/stop lamps
41 Courtesy light rear
   number plate lamp

Chapter 11 Suspension, dampers and steering

For modifications, and information applicable to later models, see Supplement at end of manual

Contents

Specifications

Lubrication

Front axle torsion arm bushes, steering and suspension
balljoints — where applicable, and front wheel bearings ... ...   Multi-purpose lithium based grease (Duckhams LB 10)

Front suspension

Type... ... ...   Independent, twin transverse laminated leaf torsion bars, each with a trailing arm to the steering knuckle

Torsion bars

Number of leaves	10
Length	954 mm
Fitting angle (top)..	44° (± 30')
(bottom)	35° 30' (± 30')

Steering knuckles

Upper ball joint maximum vertical play	2.00 mm
Lower ball joint maximum vertical play	1.00 mm

Rear suspension

Type... ... ...   Independent. Single transverse solid torsion bar divided in the centre. Trailing spring plate from outer ends of torsion bar to outer ends of swing axle tube.
(For double joint axle suspension see Chapter 7).

Torsion bars

	Length (each side)	Diameter	Spring plate angle
Without equaliser bar...	552 mm	22 mm	17° 30' (+ 50') 18° 30' (wide track)
With equaliser bar...	552 mm	21 mm	20° (+ 50')

Steering

Type... ... ...   Worm and roller

Geometry:

Front wheel toe-in	0° 30' positive ± 0° 15'
Front wheel camber (wheels in straight-ahead position)	0° 30' positive ± 0° 20'
Maximum camber difference between sides	0° 30'
Front wheel toe-out angle difference (side-to-side) at 20° lock:	
LHD models to left	− 1° 20'
to right	− 2° 10' ± 0° 30'
RHD models to left	− 2° 15' ± 0° 30'
to right	− 1° 35' ± 0° 30'
Castor angle	3° 20' positive ± 1°
Maximum castor difference between sides...	1°

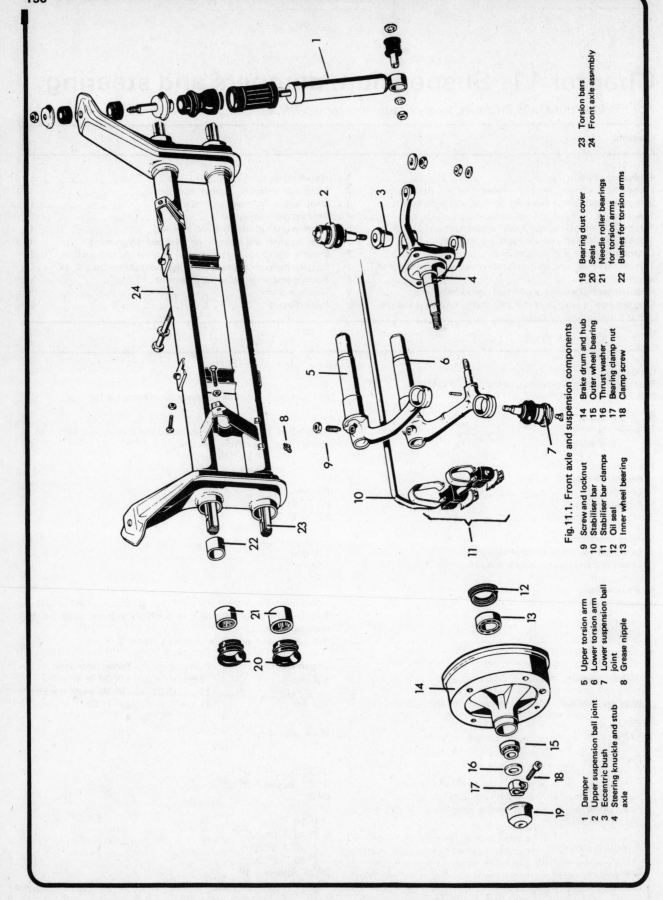

Fig.11.1. Front axle and suspension components

1	Damper	5	Upper torsion arm	9	Screw and locknut	14	Brake drum and hub	19	Bearing dust cover
2	Upper suspension ball joint	6	Lower torsion arm	10	Stabiliser bar	15	Outer wheel bearing	20	Seals
3	Eccentric bush	7	Lower suspension ball joint	11	Stabiliser bar clamps	16	Thrust washer	21	Needle roller bearings for torsion arms
4	Steering knuckle and stub axle	8	Grease nipple	12	Oil seal	17	Bearing clamp nut	22	Bushes for torsion arms
				13	Inner wheel bearing	18	Clamp screw	23	Torsion bars
								24	Front axle assembly

Swing axle rear wheel camber (Chassis 116,000,001-1,021,298).. ...　　2° 30'
Swing axle rear wheel camber (Chassis 117,000,001 on) ... ...　　1°
Double joint rear axle wheel camber ... ...　　1° 20' negative
Rear wheel toe out (swing axle).. ... ...　　5'
　　　　　　(double joint axle) ... ...　　0°

Dampers ... ...　　Telescopic double acting hydraulic front and rear

Wheels
　Type... ... ...　　Steel disc 5 bolt fixing up to 1968 and 4 bolt fixing thereafter
　Rim ... ...　　4J x 15

Tyres.. ... ...　　5.60 − 15 PR, crossply, fitted to 1968
　　　　　　　　　　　　　　　　　　　　　　　　155 SR 15, radial ply, fitted 1968 on

Pressures

	1300		1500	
	Normal	Laden	Normal	Laden
Front (crossply)	16 psi	18 psi	16 psi	18 psi
Rear (crossply)..	27 psi	27 psi	27 psi	
Front (radials)		18 psi		
Rear (radials)		27 psi		

Torque wrench settings
Front axle
Damper bolt on side plate ... ...　　24 lb.ft.　　(3.4 mkg)
Damper nut on side plate.. ... ...　　14 lb.ft.　　(2.0 mkg)
Damper nut on lower torsion arm ... ...　　24 lb.ft.　　(3.4 mkg)
Steering ball joint to knuckle ... ...　　38 lb.ft.　　(6.0 mkg)
Tie rod ball joints to drop arm and knuckle - M10 ... ...　　18 lb.ft.　　(2.5 mkg)
　　　　　　　　　　　　　　- M12 ... ...　　22 lb.ft.　　(3.0 mkg)
Wheel bearing inner nut ... ...　　29 lb.ft.　　(4.0 mkg) *
Wheel bearing locknut ... ...　　50 lb.ft.　　(7.0 mkg) *
Wheel bearing clamp nut socket screw.. ... ...　　9 lb.ft. max　(1.3 mkg)
Steering damper nut on tie rod... ... ...　　18 lb.ft.　　(2.5 mkg)
Steering damper screw on axle tube ... ...　　31 lb.ft.　　(4.4 mkg)
Torsion bar set screw and lock nut.. ... ...　　33 lb.ft.　　(4.5 mkg)

Rear axle (swing arm)
Spring plate nuts and bolts ... ...　　72 lb.ft.　　(10.0 mkg)
*　See text for procedure

Steering
Steering gear to front axle ... ...　　20 lb.ft.　　(2.7 mkg)
Worm spindle to steering coupling .. ..　　16 lb.ft.　　(2.2 mkg)
Drop arm to roller shaft ... ...　　51 lb.ft.　　(7.0 mkg)
Steering wheel to column ... ...　　36 lb.ft.　　(5.0 mkg)
Roadwheel bolts　　... ... ...　　94 lb.ft.　　(12.8 mkg)

1. General description

The Volkswagen Beetle suspension has always been noted for its strength which is due largely to the use of torsion bars as the method of springing. At the front, two torsion bars - made of leaves clamped together - are mounted across the car, one directly above the other. Each runs in a tube and in the centre it is clamped to the tube. The outer ends fit into the tubular ends of the torsion arms (which support the wheels). These tubular ends of the torsion arms themselves fit inside the axle tubes and pivot on needle roller bearings and plain bushes. The rearward facing torsion arms, two on each side support the steering knuckles on ball joints.

A single telescopic hydraulic damper is attached to the lower torsion arm on each side and to a body bracket. An anti-roll bar connects the lower torsion arms on each side also.

The rear axle is in effect incorporated with the gearbox. The axle shafts and their tubes pivot at their inner ends. Two separate torsion bars are used for the rear suspension, so although they are in effect like a single bar clamped in the centre running across the car each half can be removed separately. A centrally mounted splined boss supports the inner ends of each torsion bar and the outer end is splined to the front end of the spring plate. The spring plate trails rearward and the rear end is attached to the outer end of the axle tube. A single double acting hydraulic damper is attached to a bracket which is part of the end of the axle tube.

Steering is by a worm and roller type gear.

From the drop arm a single track rod runs directly to the steering knuckle of each front wheel. A hydraulic piston type damper mounted transversely is fitted to absorb transmitted road shock.

2. Front wheel bearings - removal, replacement and adjustment

1 The front wheel hubs each run on two taper roller bearings. Adjustment is effected by a clamp nut which is locked into position by a socket head cap screw incorporated into it.
2 The left hand front hub has a left hand thread. The axle is hollow to permit the speedometer drive cable to go through it. This cable is driven by a square hole in the bearing dust cover. Jack up the wheel and remove the securing bolts and wheel.
3 To remove the bearing dust cover, first take out the split pin or

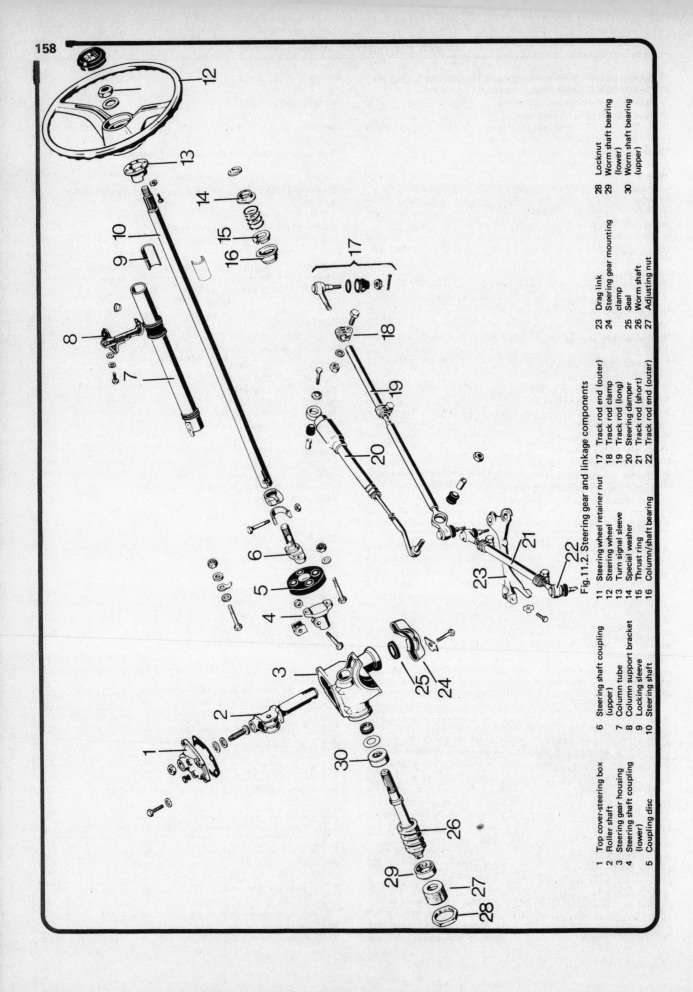

Fig.11.2. Steering gear and linkage components

1	Top cover-steering box	11	Steering wheel retainer nut	23 Drag link
2	Roller shaft	12	Steering wheel	24 Steering gear mounting
3	Steering gear housing	13	Turn signal sleeve	clamp
4	Steering shaft coupling	14	Special washer	25 Seal
	(lower)	15	Thrust ring	26 Worm shaft
5	Coupling disc	16	Column/shaft bearing	27 Adjusting nut
6	Steering shaft coupling	17	Track rod end (outer)	28 Locknut
	(upper)	18	Track rod clamp	29 Worm shaft bearing
7	Column tube	19	Track rod (long)	(lower)
8	Column support bracket	20	Steering damper	30 Worm shaft bearing
9	Locking sleeve	21	Track rod (short)	(upper)
10	Steering shaft	22	Track rod end (outer)	

circlip securing the speedometer cable and tap the dust cover from side to side until it comes free.

4 Undo the socket head cap screw and undo the wheel bearing clamp nut.

5 If the thrust washer is now taken off, the complete drum may be removed. There will be the outer races of each bearing left in the hub and the inner race of the inner bearing left on the axle. These should be drifted out of the hub from the inside, if the bearings are to be renewed. If the same bearings are being replaced, they may be left in position and merely flushed out. The race on the shaft should be drifted off also. Note that if the races are renewed then the oil seal on the inner part of the hub will be driven out at the same time as the race. This must be renewed as well.

6 It is possible that the bearing race is a loose fit on the shaft. If this is so, which would tend to let it turn, a few centre punch marks around the axle where it fits will give it some grip once again when fitted.

7 Refitting of new bearings means that the outer races will first have to be driven into the hub and the new oil seal fitted on the inside. Coat the bearings and the space between them in the hub with liberal quantities of grease and place the hub back on the shaft. Fit the outer bearing followed by the thrust washer and screw on the clamp nut.

8 To adjust the bearing endfloat correctly the nut should be tightened up firmly to make sure the bearings are properly located, spinning the wheel at the same time to ensure the bearings are not overtightened. Then the nut should be backed off until the axial play is between 0.03—0.12 mm (0.001—0.005 inch) at the spindle. This seems quite a lot and can result in some quite noticeable rock at the outer rim of the wheel. It is nevertheless correct although the axial play should be kept to the lower limit where possible, when correct tighten the socket screw.

9 Replace the hub cover and re-secure the speedometer drive cable where appropriate. Replace the wheel and lower to the ground.

3. Suspension ball joints - removal, inspection and replacement

1 With the exception of the correct setting of the camber adjusting bush on the upper joint pin there are no adjustments which can be made. When the joints are worn beyond specification limits they must be renewed. The lower joint has a removable plug. When removed, a grease nipple can be fitted to add more grease if the joint should squeak. Regular greasing is not necessary.

2 To check the vertical play first turn the front wheels to one side and find a jack that will fit under the lower torsion arm at the ball joint end. If ground clearance is too little jack the car up and rest the wheel on a block. If the jack under the torsion arm is now raised any play in the joint should be apparent. It is difficult to measure accurately unless you have a caliper gauge which can be placed across the head of the joint pin and the bottom of the torsion arm.

3 The upper joint is a little more difficult but in general practice if the lower joint is within tolerance limits the upper one will be also. If the lower one is not then it is easier to check the top one when the steering knuckle has been removed. In any case the joints should normally be renewed in pairs on each side.

4 In order to renew the ball joints they have first to be removed from the knuckle by unscrewing the taper pin nuts and pressing them out of the knuckle eyes with a claw clamp. To do this, first remove the hub and brake backplate assemblies as described in Chapter 9, and disconnect the upper damper mounting. It must be emphasised here that these ball joint pins are usually a very tight taper fit. If you do not have a proper clamp you might succeed by striking the side of the eye with a hammer to spring it loose. If this does not succeed do not risk bending anything by excessive use of striking force. Also the two torsion arms will have a tendency to force the two joints towards each other so before they can be taken out of the knuckle the two torsion arms must be spread apart. One way to do this is by using a scissor jack between them.

5 Finally the ball joints have to be pressed out of the torsion arms

and to do this the torsion arms must be removed from the torsion bars. The renewal of the torsion arms is explained in the next section.

6 With the torsion arms removed we strongly recommend that you take them to the Volkswagen agent when the new parts are to be ordered and get him to fit them. Without the proper press tools it is easy to make a real nonsense of this job. If they are not properly fitted the whole safety and steering properties of the car are in jeopardy.

7 With new ball joints fitted the torsion arms are replaced and the knuckle refitted in the reverse order of removal. The top ball joint is fitted with an eccentric bush which controls the camber angle setting. This bush has a positioning notch in the edge which should be set to face directly forward. The nuts (new ones always) should be tightened to the specified torque.

4. Torsion arms - removal and replacement

1 If indications show that a torsion arm is distorted or worn then it must be renewed.

2 First remove the wheel hub assembly. If a lower torsion arm is being removed the stabiliser bar must also be taken off (see Section 6).

3 Loosen the locknuts on the ends of the torsion arm securing pins and then screw the pins right out. The torsion arm can then be pulled out of the axle tube. The torsion arm tube is positioned in two bearings - an inner bush and outer needle roller. If either of these is seriously worn causing radial movement of the torsion arm they should be renewed by a specialist with the correct tools. If you have already carried the dismantling of the front axle a considerable way it may be simplest to disconnect the brakes and steering gear as well and detach the whole assembly from the car. This can be done by removing the four securing screws from the centre section (see Section 11 for complete procedure).

4 Replacement is a reversal of the removal procedure.

5. Torsion bars (front) - removal and replacement

1 One would normally only need to remove a torsion bar if it broke and this is a rare occurrence.

2 First remove the hub and steering knuckle and torsion arm from one end of the torsion bar concerned. Then detach the steering knuckle from the torsion arm on the opposite side but do not remove the other arm from the torsion bar.

3 In the centre of the torsion bar tube slacken the locating pin locknut and remove the pin. The bar and the attached torsion arm may then be drawn out.

4 The torsion bar is composed of a number of leaves and this number varies between models and over the years. Make sure that any replacement is of the correct type.

5 When refitting a torsion bar make sure first it is liberally coated with grease and position it so that the recesses for the locating pins will line up. Fix the centre pin and locknut and then reassemble the torsion arm and steering assemblies in the reverse order of dismantling.

6. Stabiliser bar - removal and replacement

1 The stabiliser bar is fixed to the lower torsion arms on each side of the car and is clamped in position. The bar is held by special clamps secured by sliding clips. Lift up the lugs on the ends of the clips and slide them off the ends of the clamps which go round metal securing plates.

2 When refitting the clamps and clips note that the tapered slot end goes towards the wheel and that the lugs which bend down on the clips point towards the centre of the car when being installed.

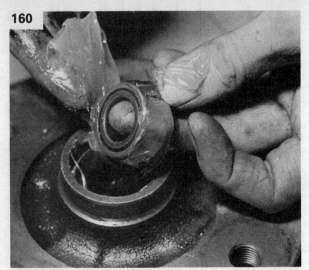

2.7(a) Packing the bearing with grease.

2.7(b) Replacing the hub (incorporating the brake disc) to the stub axle.

2.7(c) Fitting the thrust washer.

2.7(d) Replacing the clamp nut.

2.7(e) Tightening the socket screw after the bearing float has been adjusted.

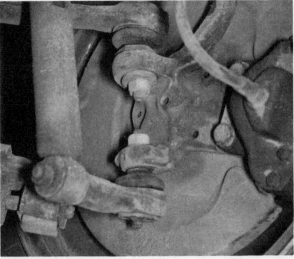

3.1(a) Right hand suspension ball joints.

7. Dampers - removal and replacement

1 Rear dampers are simply removed by undoing the nut and bolt which secures them at top and bottom.

2 Front dampers can be a little more difficult due to the upper mounting which is through a horizontal plate. The buffer stud at the top is also detachable from the main piston rod of the damper.

3 Jack up the car and remove the wheel.

4 The steering tie rod on the same side should also be detached from the steering knuckle or it will be severely strained by the downward force exerted by the torsion bars when the damper is released.

5 The top hexagon nut of the damper should now be undone. If the whole rod turns, the flats on the buffer stud must be held with thin open ended spanner. If difficulty is experienced the alternative is to unscrew the piston rod from the buffer stud now. This will make it easier to detach the damper from the bracket.

6 Remove the nut securing the lower end to the torsion arm and take the damper off.

7 If the upper mounting buffers and damper rings are damaged they should be renewed. The stud can be unscrewed from the piston rod to release the buffer.

8 The lower bush is a tight press fit. If this needs renewal use the new one and a piece of tube to press out the old one between the jaws of a vice.

9 When refitting the damper make sure that the buffer stud is screwed back tightly on to the piston rod and that the damper rings are fitted one each side of the mounting plate with the shoulders against the plate.

8. Torsion bars (rear) and spring plates - removal, replacement and setting

1 Figure 8.2 in Chapter 8 is relevant to this section. Before any work can be carried out on the rear torsion bars and spring plates it is necessary to detach the rear axle tubes from the ends of the spring plates. To do this it will be first necessary to support the car firmly on axle stands under the rear jacking points and remove the wheels. The handbrake cables should be slackened off at the hand lever and the spring plate marked so that it can be lined up with the axle tube on replacement. Details of the foregoing are given in the sections dealing with transmission removal and axle shaft and tube removal. The damper should be disconnected at the lower mounting. The three large mounting bolts securing the axle tube flange to the plate must then be undone and the axle tube drawn back.

2 The spring plate butts up against a lug in the frame casting along its lower edge and to relieve residual tension in the torsion bar it must be sprung out so that it rides over the lug. This can be done quite easily with a tyre lever.

3 At this stage the setting of the suspension can be checked. The angle of the plate in this unstressed position should be somewhere between 17° and 20° (see Specifications for differences) from the horizontal line of the car. For this measurement therefore a spirit level and protractor are needed. The horizontal line of the car is taken from the bottom of the door opening in the body shell. Using a level and protractor work out how far this now deviates from the true horizontal.

4 Measure the angle of the spring plate from the true horizontal in the same way, eliminating any play there may be by lifting the plate while the measurement is taken.

5 Depending on which way the body deviates, the angle is added or subtracted to the plate angle to give the differences between the two. Reference to Fig.11.3 will illustrate the examples given below.

Body deviation angle	4°
Plate deviation angle	20°
Plate/body angle (AA)	16°
Plate body angle (BB)	24°

If the correct plate/body angle is 17° 30' then in situation AA the plate angle needs increasing by 1° 30'. In BB it needs decreasing by 6° 30'.

6 The torsion bars are splined at each end. The inner end anchors to a splined bracket fixed in the centre of the cross tube. The outer end is splined to the spring plate. The inner end has forty splines (9° per spline) and the outer has forty-four splines (8° 10' per spline) affording an alteration possibility in graduations of 50' (9°–8° 10'). In example AA, if the inner end of the torsion bar is rotated anticlockwise two splines (18°) and the spring plate rotated clockwise on the outer end by two splines (16° 20') the net increase in the angle will be 18°–16° 20' = 1° 40' which is as near as one can get. In example BB the inner end is rotated clockwise eight splines (72°) and the plate on the outer end rotated anticlockwise eight splines (65° 20'). The net decrease in the angle is thus 6° 40'.

7 To withdraw the torsion bar sufficiently to rotate the splines for adjustment first remove the four screws which secure the cover clamping the rubber cushion mounting. The spring plate can now be pulled off the torsion bar and at the same time the inner end of the bar may be drawn out of the centre splined location. (Note that if one wishes to take the torsion bar right out then about five or six of the screws which hold the forward edge of the rear mudguard to the body must be removed. The mudguard can then be pulled out of the way. Torsion bars are not interchangeable side for side).

8 Having reset the torsion bar so that the plate angle is correct make sure that the rubber outer mounting bush is in good condition. Renew it if in doubt. Cover it with flake graphite (to prevent squeaking) and make sure it is installed the proper way up. (The top edge is marked 'Oben'). Before the cover is reinstalled over the rubber bush it will be necessary to raise the plate above the stop lug on the frame casting. If this is not done now the pre-loading of the rubber bushing will be all wrong when the cover is put back. It will also be very nearly impossible to move the plate. To lift the plate put a jack under the end. If it looks as though the car is going to lift before the plate is up in position get some people to sit in the back seat for a minute or two. With the plate held in position replace the cover plate and setscrews.

9 It may be difficult to get the four plate securing screws to pick up their threads on replacement - particularly with a new bush. In such instances two longer screws will have to be obtained and used diagonally so that the plate may be drawn down enough to refit the shorter screws. (The short screws must be used finally otherwise the cover plate will not pull down far enough to stress the rubber bush properly).

10 With the cover tightened down the rear axle tube may be reassembled to the spring plate.

11 The angle adjustment of the spring plates must be the same on both sides of the car.

12 If the spring plates have been renewed or any other work has been carried out on the rear suspension which could affect the alignment then it is important that the camber and toe-out settings (yes — toe-out on the rear wheels!) be checked with optical alignment equipment. It would also be timely to mention here that if the rear suspension spring plate settings are purposely altered to give an increased or reduced ground clearance then the effects on handling under certain circumstances are, to say the least, unusual. Tyre wear is also greatly increased if the rear wheel alignment is incorrect.

9. Equalizer spring (rear) - removal and replacement

1 Some later models are fitted with an additional suspension feature consisting of a lateral torsion bar (parallel to the normal one) which goes under the bottom of the luggage space behind the rear seat. It is attached at each end by a rubber bushed bracket to the body panel behind the rear wheel. It is connected to the axle tubes by levers and operating rods angled in opposite directions at each side. The effect is to progressively assist the main torsion bar under load but not to have any effect on body roll characteristics.

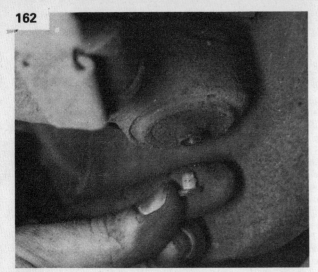

3.1(b) Plug removed from lower ball joint.

3.7. Eccentric bush for upper ball joint has a notch facing directly forward.

8.7(a) Rear suspension spring plate showing cover and rubber buffer removed.

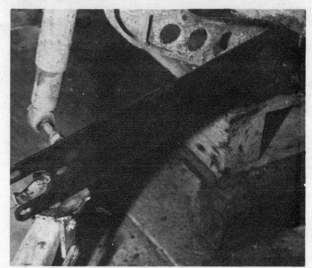

8.7(b) Rear suspension spring plate lowered.

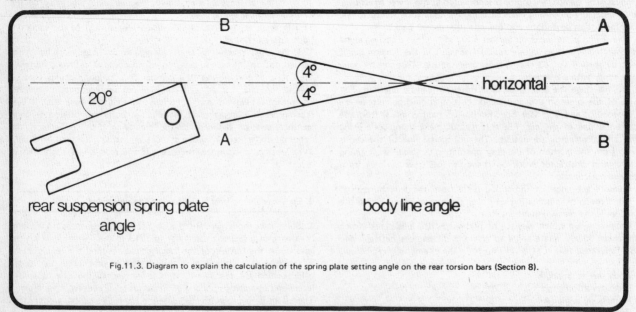

rear suspension spring plate angle

body line angle

Fig.11.3. Diagram to explain the calculation of the spring plate setting angle on the rear torsion bars (Section 8).

2 To remove the spring and its components take off the rear wheels and remove the nuts at each end of the operating rods and take out the rods and associated buffers.

3 Undo the nuts holding the supports and rubber bushes at each end of the torsion bar.

4 Remove the lever from the left hand side of the torsion bar by undoing the locknut and unscrewing the setscrew far enough to release the lever from the bar. The spring and the right hand lever can then be withdrawn together.

5 The operating rods run in guides bolted to the axle tube flange and the bushes in these may be worn. They can be prised out with a screwdriver.

6 When reinstalling remember that the right lever should point downward towards the front and the left lever downwards to the rear. The left lever is marked 'L'. Also do not overlook the hard rubber washer which goes on the torsion bar outside the levers before the inner support plates are fitted.

7 The longer of the two operating rods is fitted on the right side and the rubber clamping rings should go one each side of the lever. Fit the rods to the levers first and then put them into the guides and fit the guides to the axle tubes. This makes sure that the clamping rings are properly seated on the levers.

10. Diagonal arm (double joint rear axle shaft) - removal and replacement

1 Fig. 8.5. in Chapter 8 is relevant to this section. Before removal of the diagonal arm can take place the axle shafts must be removed as described in Chapter 8, and the wheel and brake drum and brake backplate detached as described in Chapter 9.

2 The outer end of the diagonal arm is attached to the spring plate by 5 nuts and bolts. Before slackening these carefully mark the relative positions of the spring plate and arm with accurate chisel notches at top and bottom. Then undo the nuts and bolts.

3 The inner end of the arm pivots on a bonded rubber bush. The pivot pin takes the form of a socket head screw which can be undone with a hexagon key and removed.

4 Any further work to be done on the bearings and seals is described in Chapter 8.

5 When reinstalling the diagonal arm the socket head screw should be peened with the bracket collar into one of its grooves with a blunt chisel to lock it. The outer flange and spring plate must be lined up on the marks and the nuts and bolts tightened to 87 lb/ft. (12 mkg).

6 Refit the brakes and axle shafts as described in the appropriate chapters. If a new diagonal arm is fitted it is important to have the rear suspension alignment checked and reset on specialised VW equipment.

11. Front axle assembly - removal complete

In certain circumstances, such as damage, which has caused the axle tubes to be bent or where the complete assembly is in need of thorough overhaul and checking, it may be advantageous to remove it as an assembly and dismantle it afterwards. The sequence of necessary operations to achieve this is given below and the details of these procedures can be found in the Chapters which cover them.

1 Detach the flexible fuel hose under the fuel tank and plug or clip it.

2 Remove the fuel tank.

3 Detach the horn cable from the steering column and uncouple the flange of the steering column where it joins the steering box.

4 Unclip the split pin or circlip from the end of the speedometer cable in the left front wheel bearing dust cap. Pull the cable out.

5 Undo the hydraulic brake fluid lines at the unions where the brackets on the axle tube are fitted.

6 Undo the steering damper mounting bolt at the axle end and then undo the two track rod ends on the long track rod. Take off the track rod and damper together.

7 Remove the two body securing screws on the upper side of the top axle tube.

8 Support the axle securely and remove the four setscrews holding the assembly to the frame head.

9 The complete unit can now be lowered and taken out.

12. Steering gear - removal and replacement

1 The steering gear is mounted on the upper axle tube and held by a clamp. It is connected to the steering column by a flanged coupling.

2 The simplest way to disconnect the gear from the track rods is to pull the drop arm off the shaft with the tie-rods still attached. This can be done after undoing the drop arm clamping screw and turning the wheels to a position where the arm can be drawn away.

3 Moving to the coupling flange undo the clip holding the horn wire and then remove the two nuts and bolts from the flange.

4 Before undoing the two bolts which clamp the steering box to the upper axle tube it is important to make sure that you know the correct position to refit it. There is a cut-out in the clamp plate which locates over a welded stud on the tube.

5 Once the correct repositioning of the steering box is assured undo the clamp bolts and take it off.

6 When replacing the clamp make sure that the clamp is fitted the correct way round. There will be two numbers on it, 13 and 14, next to the two cut-outs. No.13 is the one for Beetles and the arrow should point forward with the cut-out on the left.

7 Always use new lock plates on the clamp bolts and bend the tabs down over the hexagon flats. It is also recommended that new self locking nuts are used for the column coupling flange.

8 The steering geometry should be checked for alignment after replacing the steering gear.

13. Steering gear - adjustments

1 If play in the steering can be positively traced to the steering gear rather than wear in the track rod ends or suspension linkage it is possible to make certain adjustments (with the steering gear fitted in the car) to improve the situation. Play occurs at two main points - in the worm shaft bearings and between the worm and roller. A third point - the axial play of the roller can also cause sloppiness but rectification of this requires dismantling of the steering gear.

2 To check the worm axial play (i.e. in the bearings) first set the wheels straight ahead and move the steering wheel from side to side until resistance is felt. The circumferential movement of the wheel should not exceed 25 mm total across this central position. If it does, begin the adjustment check by getting hold of the steering column at the coupling (with the wheels now lifted from the ground) and turning it from side to side. Any endfloat in the shaft will be visible.

3 To adjust the play turn the steering to either side on full lock. Then loosen the large locknut on the adjuster plug at the lower end of the steering box and with a suitable box spanner turn the adjuster until no more end play can be discerned in the worm shaft. Hold the adjuster and tighten the locknut. Turn the steering from lock to lock. There should be no tight spots whatsoever.

4 If the original overall steering play (as measured at the steering wheel) is still not eliminated, go to the next step which is adjustment of the play between the worm and roller. With the front wheels still off the ground set the steering to the straight ahead position.

5 Turn the steering wheel 90° only to left or right.

6 Loosen the roller shaft adjuster locknut which can be reached through the hole in the floor pan. Turn the adjuster anticlockwise about one turn. Then turn it clockwise until the roller can be felt just to make contact with the worm. Do not overtighten.

7 Hold the screw and tighten the locknut.

8 Lower the vehicle to the ground and with the steering wheel set in turn at the 90° position both left and right, check that the circumference backlash does not exceed 25 mm at each position. If it does repeat the adjustment on the affected side only.

13.1. Access to the steering gear can be made through an aperture at the right of the front luggage compartment behind the spare wheel.

16.2. Inner track rod ends (arrowed). (Note horn wire connection to steering shaft coupling).

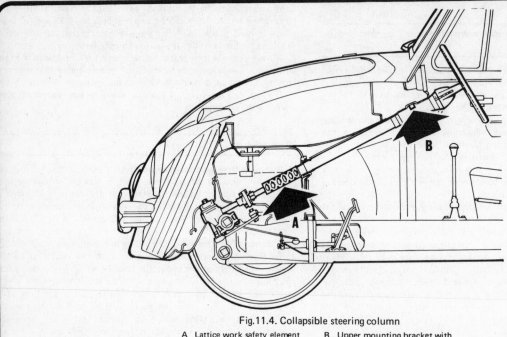

Fig.11.4. Collapsible steering column

A Lattice work safety element   B Upper mounting bracket with
                                          shear type fittings

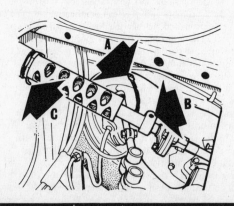

Fig.11.5. Collapsible steering column. Detail of column
            mounting (tank removed)

A Horn cable connection
B Column clamp screw
C Column tube support ring

9 Before a conclusive road test can be made the toe-in adjustment must be checked. Then go on the road and check that the steering still has its self centring action. If it does not then the roller shaft adjustment must be slackened off, otherwise damage can occur to either the worm or roller.

10 If neither of the foregoing adjustments rectifies the play in the steering gear then the third involves dismantling the assembly to check the axial play on the roller itself. If this is excessive the whole unit needs renewal or reconditioning.

14. Steering gear - dismantling and overhaul

1 The decision to dismantle and rebuild a steering gear assembly will depend to a large extent on the availability of parts. It is inevitable that if adjustments fail to rectify play adequately then most of the interior components will need renewal. The steering gear with its hour glass worm and roller is subject to some very critical settings and requires shims and setting jigs which only a Volkswagen agency is likely to have. We do not therefore recommend that the do-it-yourself owner attempts this job. The time and cost expended to do the job properly cannot justify any saving over the purchase of a replacement unit.

15. Steering wheel and column - removal and replacement

1 The steering wheel is fixed to the column on a splined boss. Before starting to take it off detach the battery earth lead to prevent accidental short circuits. Carefully prise away the cover in the centre of the wheel and then disconnect the wire from the horn switch underneath. Remove the nut and spring washer in the centre of the wheel and pull off the wheel together with the horn ring.
2 If it is wished to remove the column (shaft) it is not necessary to take the wheel off at this stage although it is easier to slacken the nut now. If the car is fitted with a steering lock, however, the wheel must be taken off. Then the indicator switch must be taken off as well.
3 Next go to the coupling at the bottom end of the shaft and disconnect the horn cable connection there.
4 Still at the coupling remove the single screw which clamps the shaft into the upper coupling half.
5 The column may now be drawn out of the tube with or without the steering wheel as appropriate. Where there is a steering lock fitted take care not to damage the bearing in the process.
6 The bearing is now accessible in the tube and can be renewed if necessary. On models with a steering lock it will come out with the column. The bearing inner support ring and thrust spring are held to the top of the column by a circlip. The brass washer with the cut-out for the indicator cancellation is also held there. Renew the support ring if badly worn.
7 On models with steering locks fit the ball bearing to the column first.
8 Fit the bearing support ring, spring, brass washer and circlip.
9 Put the bearing in position in the tube for non-lock columns then replace the column shaft. The bearing on the column will have to be driven into the tube on the locked steering models.
10 Turn the brass washer on the column so that the cut-out portion faces exactly to the right with the wheels in the straight ahead position.
11 Replace the steering wheel with the spokes horizontal and with the tongue of the cancelling ring in the centre of the washer cut-out. Replace the spring washer and nut and secure the wheel by tightening the nut (36 lb/ft).
12 Move the steering wheel and column in or out so that the gap between the lower edge of the wheel hub and the indicator switch sleeve is between 1 and 2 mm (0.040–0.080 inch).
13 Using a new lock plate the screw clamping the bottom end of the column into the upper part of the mounting flange may now be tightened. Check finally that the wheels, steering wheel and indicator

cancellation are all centred correctly.
14 Later models are fitted with safety steering columns. Incorporated into the steering shaft is a lattice work section which will telescope under impact. In addition the upper column mounting bracket is held together with special plastic rivets which will shear off under impact allowing the wheel and column to move forward.

The procedure for removal of the column is similar in principle to the earlier types but the fuel tank will have to be removed as well, in order to get at the column tube support ring at the upper end of the lattice work section (Fig.11.4 and 5). This also provides upper access to the coupling clamp.
15 The support ring is horseshoe shaped and held in position by two tags which can be bent up. Then take it off. Disconnect the clamp bolt on the upper half of the coupling and draw the column shaft out as one would with the earlier types.

16. Steering track rods and joints - removal and replacement

1 From the drop arm (or steering arm) on the steering gear the movement is transmitted to each wheel by a track rod. The inner and outer ends each have a swivel ball joint which allows the variety of angles to be adopted by the wheels during movement of steering and suspension. If the track rods are bent, or of the incorrect length, or if the swivel joints are worn, the wheels will take up an incorrect position of alignment or, in the case of worn joints, be able to move independently of the steering gear. Both these conditions result in inaccurate steering and control.
2 Each ball joint is attached to the steering knuckle at the outer end, or drop arm at the inner end by a tapered pin through a tapered hole and secured by a hexagon nut. The joints are screwed on to the tie-rods with a left and right hand thread on each rod.
3 Jack up the car and remove the wheel(s). Remove the split pin from the castellated nut and remove the nut. The joint pin may be a very tight fit. If you have no proper extractor hold a hammer to one side of the eye and strike opposite with another. This normally succeeds.
4 One track rod has the steering damper fitted into it so this must be detached from it if the whole rod is to be removed. If only the outer ball joints are being renewed it is, of course, unnecessary to detach the joints from the drop arm.
5 The ball joints are screwed into the rod and held by one of two methods - both of which may be used on the same vehicle. The ends of the tie-rods are split and these are clamped to the threaded end of the ball joint. The difference is in the method of clamping. One uses a simple U clamp and pinch bolt. The other method uses a sleeve with a tapered inner face and a hexagon outer face. This taper is forced up to the matching tapered end of the tie-rod by a second hexagon nut. Between the two there is a double tab washer. Whichever type is used slacken it off but before screwing out the joint take careful note of its position (by counting the number of visible threads). This will help to ensure that the toe-in setting is disturbed as little as possible when it is replaced.
6 When obtaining a new joint make quite sure that the correct handed thread is obtained.
7 Screw the new track rod end on to the rod but do not lock it tight yet.
8 If the steering damper has been detached at one end take the opportunity to check it as described in the next section.
9 If a track rod is bent it must be replaced with a new one. Attempts to straighten track rods can only weaken the metal and may result in fracture with disastrous results on the road. If the rubber bush for the steering damper in the long rod is in poor condition take the opportunity to renew it.
10 It is most important that the rubber seals on the track rod joints are intact and capable of retaining grease. On early models fitted with grease nipples this problem is not so critical because grease may be added easily. On later sealed joints any grease which escapes or which is contaminated needs special attention. It is possible to fit new seals and have them repacked but more often than not it is too

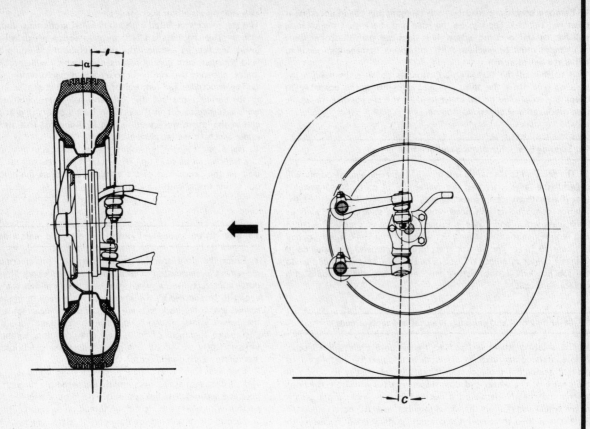

Fig.11.6. Diagram illustrating camber and king pin inclination
Angle 'A' = camber, Angle 'B' = kin pin inclination

Fig.11.7. Diagram illustrating caster angle. Angle 'C' = caster angle.

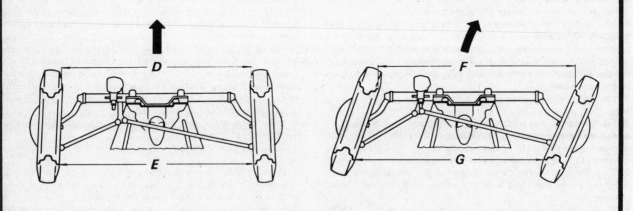

Fig.11.8. Diagram illustrating toe-in. 'D' is smaller than 'E'.

Fig. 11.9. Diagram illustrating toe-out (on turns). 'F' is greater than 'G'.

late by the time the fault is seen in which case the joint must be renewed.

11 When the track rods are fitted with the ends replace the taper pins into their respective eyes and refit and tighten the hexagon nuts to the correct torque (see specifications - depending on type of thread fitted). Replace the split pins after lining up the holes.

12 It is important to see that both ball joints are correctly aligned on the rod so push both of them either fully forward or backwards. Then tighten the nut or pinch bolt and bend over the lock tabs.

13 It is important to have the wheel alignment checked properly at the earliest opportunity.

17. Steering damper - removal, checking and replacement

1 The steering damper is a double acting piston which serves to smooth out vibration and shocks through the steering. One end is attached to a bracket on the top axle tube in a rubber bush. The other is fitted similarly to the longer of the two track rods.

2 If the bushes are worn allowing play the damper and tie-rod should be removed and new bushes fitted. New bushes comprise a rubber buffer with a steel central sleeve. They can be cut or driven out and new ones pressed in between the jaws of a vice.

3 Remove the two securing bolts which will necessitate jacking up the car and removing the front wheels.

4 To test the action of the damper push and pull the piston throughout its full travel. There should be no roughness or variations in resistance anywhere along the travel of the piston. If there is it should be renewed. Note that the damper is different between vehicles with right and left hand drive.

5 Replace the damper (with the piston end inwards) by fitting the securing bolts and nuts and tightening them to the specified torques.

18. Steering geometry and wheel alignment

1 The correct alignment of the front wheels does not normally alter and the need for checking and re-aligning only normally occurs after certain conditions, namely:

a) Renewal of track rod joints
b) Damage to front suspension or steering linkage

Theoretically, if worn ball joints, wheel bearings and so on, are all renewed the steering geometry will automatically be correct. This, of course, presumes that no adjustment has been made in a misguided attempt to compensate for wear. If adjustments have been made then, of course, when the various parts are renewed the steering will have to be re-aligned.

2 The only adjustments which can be made to the geometry (except of course outside the standard specifications) are on the track rods for toe-in and on the eccentric bush of the upper suspension ball joint for king pin inclination. Alteration of the king pin inclination automatically alters the camber angle because the relationship

between these two is fixed in the design of the king pin carrier/steering knuckle assembly. The term 'king pin inclination' is the same as 'steering pivot angle'. The former expression dates from the time when front wheels pivoted on spindles rather than ball joints.

3 Adjustments of steering geometry should never be made in a haphazard manner. In order to check all the angles correctly proper equipment is needed. Furthermore it is quite pointless trying to re-align the steering if one or more of the components is worn. A reputable garage would not normally undertake to re-adjust steering which had significant wear - although they may be prepared to inform you of the state of the alignment.

19. Wheels and tyres

1 To provide equal, and obtain maximum wear from all the tyres, they should be rotated on the car at intervals of 6,000 miles to the following pattern:—

Crossply
Spare to offside rear,
Offside rear to nearside front;
Nearside front to nearside rear;
Nearside rear to offside front;
Offside front to spare.

Radial
Front to rear) on same side of car only,
Rear to front)   not side to side.

Wheels should be re-balanced when this is done. However, some owners baulk at the prospect of having to buy five new tyres all at once and tend to let two run on and replace a pair only. The new pair should always be fitted to the front wheels, as these are the most important from the safety aspect of steering and braking.

2 Never mix tyres of a radial and crossply construction on the same car, as the basic design differences can cause unusual and, in certain conditions, very dangerous handling and braking characteristics. If an emergency should force the use of two different types, make sure the radials are on the rear wheels and drive particularly carefully. If three of the five wheels are fitted with radial tyres then make sure that no more than two radials are in use on the car (and those at the rear). Rationalise the tyres at the earliest possible opportunity.

3 Wheels are normally not subject to servicing problems, but when tyres are renewed or changed the wheels should be balanced to reduce vibration and wear. If a wheel is suspected of damage - caused by hitting a kerb or pot hole which could distort it out of true, change it and have it checked for balance and true running at the earliest opportunity.

4 When fitting wheels do not overtighten the nuts. The maximum possible manual torque applied by the manufacturers wheel brace is adequate. It also prevents excessive struggle when the same wheel brace has to be used in emergency to remove the wheels. Overtightening may also distort the stud holes in the wheel causing it to run off centre and off balance.

20. Fault diagnosis

Before diagnosing faults in the mechanics of the suspension and steering itself, check that any irregularities are not caused by:—

1 Binding brakes
2 Incorrect 'mix' of radial and cross-ply tyres
3 Incorrect tyre pressures
4 Misalignment of the bodyframe or rear axle tubes

Symptom	Reason/s	Remedy
Steering wheel can be moved considerably before any sign of movement of the wheels is apparent	Wear in the steering linkage, gear and column coupling	Check movement in all joints, and steering gear and overhaul and renew as required.
Vehicle difficult to steer in a consistent straight line - wandering	As above	As above.
	Wheel alignment incorrect (indicated by excessive or uneven tyre wear)	Check wheel alignment.
	Front wheel hub bearings loose or worn	Adjust or renew as necessary.
	Worn suspension ball joints	Renew as necessary.
Steering stiff and heavy	Incorrect wheel alignment (indicated by excessive or uneven tyre wear)	Check wheel alignment.
	Excessive wear or seizure in one or more of the joints in the steering linkage	Repair as necessary.
	Excessive wear in the steering gear unit	Adjust if possible, or renew.
Wheel wobble and vibration	Road wheels out of balance	Balance wheels.
	Road wheels buckled	Check for damage.
	Wheel alignment incorrect	Check wheel alignment.
	Wear in the steering linkage or suspension	Check and renew as necessary.
Excessive pitching and rolling on corners and during braking	Defective dampers and/or broken torsion bar	Check and renew as necessary.

Chapter 12 Bodywork and underframe

Contents

1. General description

The bodywork of the Volkswagen is noted for its simplicity, rigidity and corrosion free properties.

It consists basically of a flat floor pan stiffened down the centre with a fabricated sheet steel tube. At the front is a 'frame head' to which the front axle assembly is bolted and at the rear a 'frame fork' into which the engine/transmission assembly is bolted. Just forward of the frame fork a lateral tube is welded to which the rear suspension spring plate supports are fitted at the outer ends. The frame tunnel is closed in underneath and carries inside it the necessary guide tubes for brake cables, heater cables, clutch cable, accelerator cable and gearchange connecting rods.

The bodywork is a unit fabricated from steel panels welded together with the exception of sill panels, wings, doors and engine and luggage compartment lids. The unit is bolted to the floor frame. The doors, wings, lids and sill panels are bolted to the body and are readily detachable.

The whole frame body assembly is remarkable for its lack of 'nooks and crannies' where water/dirt can collect and is noteable for being almost airtight (it is virtually impossible to slam the doors shut with the windows closed due to the air pressure build up inside).

2. Maintenance – bodywork and underframe

1   The general condition of a vehicle's bodywork is the one thing that significantly affects its value. Maintenance is easy but needs to be regular. Neglect, particularly after minor damage, can lead quickly to further deterioration and costly repair bills. It is important also to keep watch on those parts of the vehicle not immediately visible, for instance the underside, inside all the wheel arches and the lower part of the engine compartment.

2   The basic maintenance routine for the bodywork is washing – preferably with a lot of water, from a hose. This will remove all the loose solids which may have stuck to the vehicle. It is important to flush these off in such a way as to prevent grit from scratching the finish. The wheel arches and underframe need washing in the same way to remove any accumulated mud which will retain moisture and tend to encourage rust. Paradoxically enough, the best time to clean the underframe and wheel arches is in wet weather when the mud is thoroughly wet and soft. In very wet weather the underframe is usually

cleaned of large accumulations automatically and this is a good time for inspection.

3 Periodically, except on vehicles with a wax-based underbody protective coating, it is a good idea to have the whole of the underframe of the vehicle steam cleaned, engine compartment included, so that a thorough inspection can be carried out to see what minor repairs and renovations are necessary. Steam cleaning is available at many garages and is necessary for removal of the accumulation of oily grime which sometimes is allowed to become thick in certain areas. If steam cleaning facilities are not available, there are one or two excellent grease solvents available such as Holts Engine Cleaner or Holts Foambrite which can be brush applied. The dirt can then be simply hosed off. Note that these methods should not be used on vehicles with wax-based underbody protective coating or the coating will be removed. Such vehicles should be inspected annually, preferably just prior to winter, when the underbody should be washed down and any damage to the wax coating repaired using Holts Undershield. Ideally, a completely fresh coat should be applied. It would also be worth considering the use of such wax-based protection for injection into door panels, sills, box sections, etc, as an additional safeguard against rust damage where such protection is not provided by the vehicle manufacturer.

4 After washing paintwork, wipe off with a chamois leather to give an unspotted clear finish. A coat of clear protective wax polish, like the many excellent Turtle Wax polishes, will give added protection against chemical pollutants in the air. If the paintwork sheen has dulled or oxidised, use a cleaner/polisher combination such as Turtle Extra to restore the brilliance of the shine. This requires a little effort, but such dulling is usually caused because regular washing has been neglected. Care needs to be taken with metallic paintwork, as special non-abrasive cleaner/polisher is required to avoid damage to the finish. Always check that the door and ventilator opening drain holes and pipes are completely clear so that water can be drained out. Bright work should be treated in the same way as paint work. Windscreens and windows can be kept clear of the smeary film which often appears, by the use of a proprietary glass cleaner like Holts Mixra. Never use any form of wax or other body or chromium polish on glass.

3. Maintenance – upholstery and floor coverings

Mats and carpets should be brushed or vacuum cleaned regularly to keep them free of grit. If they are badly stained remove them from the vehicle for scrubbing or sponging and make quite sure they are dry before refitting. Seats and interior trim panels can be kept clean by wiping with a damp cloth and Turtle Wax Carisma. If they do become stained (which can be more apparent on light coloured upholstery) use a little liquid detergent and a soft nail brush to scour the grime out of the grain of the material. Do not forget to keep the headlining clean in the same way as the upholstery. When using liquid cleaners inside the vehicle do not over-wet the surfaces being cleaned. Excessive damp could get into the seams and padded interior causing stains, offensive odours or even rot. If the inside of the vehicle gets wet accidentally it is worthwhile taking some trouble to dry it out properly, particularly where carpets are involved. *Do not leave oil or electric heaters inside the vehicle for this purpose.*

Repair of rust holes or gashes in bodywork

Remove all paint from the affected area and from an inch or so of the surrounding 'sound' bodywork, using an abrasive pad or a wire brush on a power drill. If these are not available a few sheets of abrasive paper will do the job just as effectively. With the paint removed you will be able to gauge the severity of the corrosion and therefore decide whether to renew the whole panel (if this is possible) or to repair the affected area. New body panels are not as expensive as most people think and it is often quicker and more satisfactory to fit a new panel than to attempt to repair large areas of corrosion.

Remove all fittings from the affected area except those which will act as a guide to the original shape of the damaged bodywork (eg headlamp shells etc). Then, using tin snips or a hacksaw blade, remove all loose metal and any other metal badly affected by corrosion. Hammer the edges of the hole inwards in order to create a slight depression for the filler paste.

Wire brush the affected area to remove the powdery rust from the surface of the remaining metal. Paint the affected area with rust inhibiting paint like Turtle Wax Rust Master; if the back of the rusted

area is accessible treat this also.

Before filling can take place it will be necessary to block the hole in some way. This can be achieved by the use of aluminium or plastic mesh, or aluminium tape.

Aluminium or plastic mesh or glass fibre matting, such as the Holts Body + Plus Glass Fibre Matting, is probably the best material to use for a large hole. Cut a piece to the approximate size and shape of the hole to be filled, then position it in the hole so that its edges are below the level of the surrounding bodywork. It can be retained in position by several blobs of filler paste around its periphery.

Aluminium tape should be used for small or very narrow holes. Pull a piece off the roll and trim it to the approximate size and shape required, then pull off the backing paper (if used) and stick the tape over the hole; it can be overlapped if the thickness of one piece is insufficient. Burnish down the edges of the tape with the handle of a screwdriver or similar, to ensure that the tape is securely attached to the metal underneath.

Bodywork repairs – filling and re-spraying

Before using this Section, see the Sections on dent, deep scratch, rust holes and gash repairs.

Many types of bodyfiller are available, but generally speaking those proprietary kits which contain a tin of filler paste and a tube of resin hardener are best for this type of repair, like Holts Body + Plus or Holts No Mix which can be used directly from the tube. A wide, flexible plastic or nylon applicator will be found invaluable for imparting a smooth and well contoured finish to the surface of the filler.

Mix up a little filler on a clean piece of card or board – measure the hardener carefully (follow the maker's instructions on the pack) otherwise the filler will set too rapidly or too slowly. Alternatively, Holts No Mix can be used straight from the tube without mixing, but daylight is required to cure it. Using the applicator apply the filler paste to the prepared area; draw the applicator across the surface of the filler to achieve the correct contour and to level the filler surface. As soon as a contour that approximates to the correct one is achieved, stop working the paste – if you carry on too long the paste will become sticky and begin to 'pick up' on the applicator. Continue to add thin layers of filler paste at twenty-minute intervals until the level of the filler is just proud of the surrounding bodywork.

Once the filler has hardened, excess can be removed using a metal plane or file. From then on, progressively finer grades of abrasive paper should be used, starting with a 40 grade production paper and finishing with 400 grade wet-and-dry paper. Always wrap the abrasive paper around a flat rubber, cork, or wooden block – otherwise the surface of the filler will not be completely flat. During the smoothing of the filler surface the wet-and-dry paper should be periodically rinsed in water. This will ensure that a very smooth finish is imparted to the filler at the final stage.

At this stage the 'dent' should be surrounded by a ring of bare metal, which in turn should be encircled by the finely 'feathered' edge of the good paintwork. Rinse the repair area with clean water, until all of the dust produced by the rubbing-down operation has gone.

Spray the whole repair area with a light coat of primer, either Holts Body + Plus Grey or Red Oxide Primer – this will show up any imperfections in the surface of the filler. Repair these imperfections with fresh filler paste or bodystopper, and once more smooth the surface with abrasive paper. If bodystopper is used, it can be mixed with cellulose thinners to form a really thin paste which is ideal for filling small holes. Repeat this spray and repair procedure until you are satisfied that the surface of the filler, and the feathered edge of the paintwork are perfect. Clean the repair area with clean water and allow to dry fully.

The repair area is now ready for final spraying. Paint spraying must be carried out in a warm, dry, windless and dust free atmosphere. This condition can be created artificially if you have access to a large indoor working area, but if you are forced to work in the open, you will have to pick your day very carefully. If you are working indoors, dousing the floor in the work area with water will help to settle the dust which would otherwise be in the atmosphere. If the repair area is confined to one body panel, mask off the surrounding panels; this will help to minimise the effects of a slight mis-match in paint colours. Bodywork fittings (eg chrome strips, door handles etc) will also need to be masked off. Use genuine masking tape and several thicknesses of newspaper for the masking operations.

Before commencing to spray, agitate the aerosol can thoroughly, then spray a test area (an old tin, or similar) until the technique is mastered. Cover the repair area with a thick coat of primer; the thickness should be built up using several thin layers of paint rather than one thick one. Using 400 grade wet-and-dry paper, rub down the surface of the primer until it is really smooth. While doing this, the work area should be thoroughly doused with water, and the wet-and-dry paper periodically rinsed in water. Allow to dry before spraying on more paint.

Spray on the top coat using Holts Dupli-Color Autospray, again building up the thickness by using several thin layers of paint. Start spraying in the centre of the repair area and then work outwards, with a side-to-side motion, until the whole repair area and about 2 inches of the surrounding original paintwork is covered. Remove all masking material 10 to 15 minutes after spraying on the final coat of paint.

Allow the new paint at least two weeks to harden, then, using a paintwork renovator or a very fine cutting paste such as Turtle Wax New Color Back or Holts Body + Plus Rubbing Compound, blend the edges of the paint into the existing paintwork. Finally, apply wax polish.

4. Minor body repairs

Note: *For more detailed information about bodywork repair, the Haynes Publishing Group publish a book by Lindsay Porter called The Car Bodywork Repair Manual. This incorporates information on such aspects as rust treatment, painting and glass fibre repairs, as well as details on more ambitious repairs involving welding and panel beating.*

Repair of minor scratches in bodywork

If the scratch is very superficial, and does not penetrate to the metal of the bodywork, repair is very simple. Lightly rub the area of the scratch with a paintwork renovator like Turtle Wax New Color Back, or a very fine cutting paste like Holts Body + Plus Rubbing Compound, to remove loose paint from the scratch and to clear the surrounding bodywork of wax polish. Rinse the area with clean water.

Apply touch-up paint, such as Holts Dupli-Color Color Touch or a paint film like Holts Autofilm, to the scratch using a fine paint brush; continue to apply fine layers of paint until the surface of the paint in the scratch is level with the surrounding paintwork. Allow the new paint at least two weeks to harden: then blend it into the surrounding paintwork by rubbing the scratch area with a paintwork renovator or a very fine cutting paste, such as Holts Body + Plus Rubbing Compound or Turtle Wax New Color Back. Finally, apply wax polish from one of the Turtle Wax range of wax polishes.

Where the scratch has penetrated right through to the metal of the bodywork, causing the metal to rust, a different repair technique is required. Remove any loose rust from the bottom of the scratch with a penknife, then apply rust inhibiting paint, such as Turtle Wax Rust Master, to prevent the formation of rust in the future. Using a rubber or nylon applicator fill the scratch with bodystopper paste like Holts Body + Plus Knifing Putty. If required, this paste can be mixed with cellulose thinners, such as Holts Body + Plus Cellulose Thinners, to provide a very thin paste which is ideal for filling narrow scratches. Before the stopper-paste in the scratch hardens, wrap a piece of smooth cotton rag around the top of a finger. Dip the finger in cellulose thinners, such as Holts Body + Plus Cellulose Thinners, and then quickly sweep it across the surface of the stopper-paste in the scratch; this will ensure that the surface of the stopper-paste is slightly hollowed. The scratch can now be painted over as described earlier in this Section.

Repair of dents in bodywork

When deep denting of the vehicle's bodywork has taken place, the first task is to pull the dent out, until the affected bodywork almost attains its original shape. There is little point in trying to restore the original shape completely, as the metal in the damaged area will have stretched on impact and cannot be reshaped fully to its original contour. It is better to bring the level of the dent up to a point which is about ⅛ in (3 mm) below the level of the surrounding bodywork. In cases where the dent is very shallow anyway, it is not worth trying to pull it out at all. If the underside of the dent is accessible, it can be hammered out gently from behind, using a mallet with a wooden or plastic head. Whilst doing this, hold a suitable block of wood firmly against the outside of the panel to absorb the impact from the hammer blows and thus prevent a large area of the bodywork from being 'belled-out'.

Should the dent be in a section of the bodywork which has a double skin or some other factor making it inaccessible from behind, a different technique is called for. Drill several small holes through the metal inside the area – particularly in the deeper section. Then screw long self-tapping screws into the holes just sufficiently for them to gain a good purchase in the metal. Now the dent can be pulled out by pulling on the protruding heads of the screws with a pair of pliers.

The next stage of the repair is the removal of the paint from the damaged area, and from an inch or so of the surrounding 'sound' bodywork. This is accomplished most easily by using a wire brush or abrasive pad on a power drill, although it can be done just as effectively by hand using sheets of abrasive paper. To complete the preparation for filling, score the surface of the bare metal with a screwdriver or the tang of a file, or alternatively, drill small holes in the affected area. This will provide a really good 'key' for the filler paste.

To complete the repair see the Section on filling and re-spraying.

5. Major body repairs

1 Volkswagen owners are fortunate in that what would be relatively severe damage in some cars is not so for them. This is where wings or sills are badly damaged beyond economical repair. Being bolted on they can be removed and a new unit fitted by the owner (see subsequent sections).

2 Where serious damage has occurred or large areas need renewal due to neglect it means certainly that completely new sections or panels will need welding in and this is best left to professionals. If the damage is due to impact it will also be necessary completely to check the alignment of the body structure. In such instances the services of a Volkswagen agent with specialist checking jigs are essential. If a body is left misaligned it is first of all dangerous as the car will not handle properly - and secondly, uneven stresses will be imposed on the steering, engine and transmission, causing abnormal wear or complete failure. Tyre wear will also be excessive.

6. Front wings - removal and replacement

1 Jack up the car and remove the headlamp and direction indicator lamp housing.

2 Pull the wires and grommets out of the holes where they pass through the wing.

3 Remove the nut and bolt holding the wing to the sill panel and subsequently the nine bolts holding the wing to the bodywork. It is more than likely that these bolts are difficult to move. If this is so clean the heads and surrounds thoroughly and use plenty of penetrating fluid to ease the threads. If resort to cutting is necessary - with either saw or chisel - take care not to damage or bend the bodywork. One of the safest ways if you have a power drill and stone is to grind the heads off stubborn bolts.

4 When clear lift off the wing and beading strip.

5 It is a good idea to fit a new beading strip when putting the wing back. If the wing is a new one do any necessary paint spraying before fitting.

6 Use new bolts and treat them with grease or some anti-seize compound before fitting. There should be a new rubber washer on the bolt between wing and sill panel.

7 The headlamp must be re-aligned after replacement. Make sure all the wires and grommets are properly replaced to avoid chafing or strain which could lead to failure.

7. Rear wings - removal and replacement

1 The principle of removing and replacing the rear wing is exactly the same as that for the front wing as described in the previous section except that the rear bumper and bumper brackets should be removed first. Do not forget to remove the bolt securing the wing to the sill panel.

2 On replacement fit new beading and rubber washer between wing and sill as required.

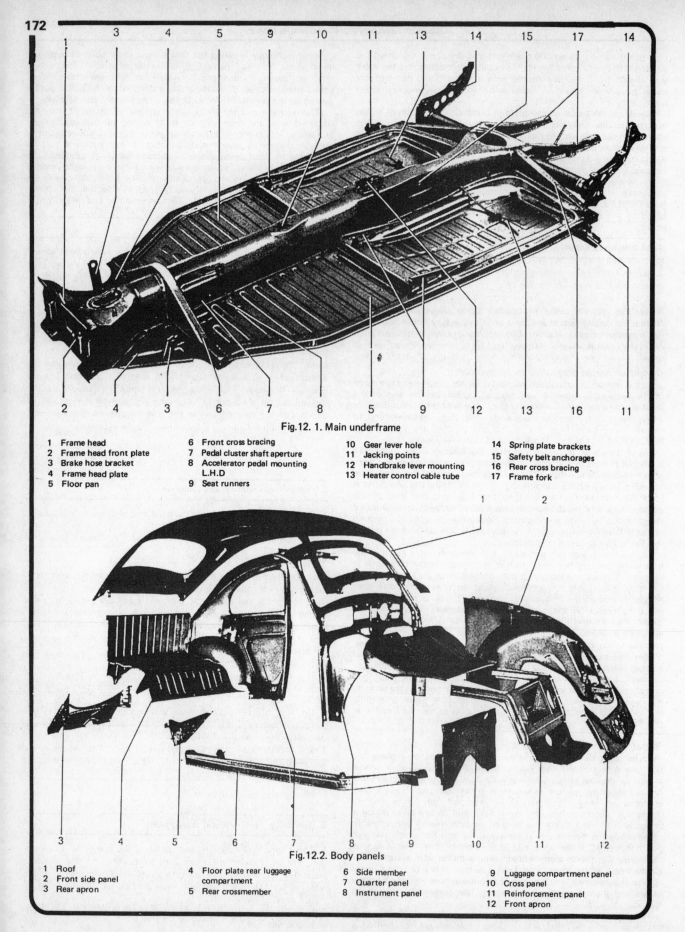

Fig.12. 1. Main underframe

1	Frame head	6	Front cross bracing	10	Gear lever hole	14	Spring plate brackets
2	Frame head front plate	7	Pedal cluster shaft aperture	11	Jacking points	15	Safety belt anchorages
3	Brake hose bracket	8	Accelerator pedal mounting	12	Handbrake lever mounting	16	Rear cross bracing
4	Frame head plate		L.H.D	13	Heater control cable tube	17	Frame fork
5	Floor pan	9	Seat runners				

Fig.12.2. Body panels

1	Roof	4	Floor plate rear luggage	6	Side member	9	Luggage compartment panel
2	Front side panel		compartment	7	Quarter panel	10	Cross panel
3	Rear apron	5	Rear crossmember	8	Instrument panel	11	Reinforcement panel
						12	Front apron

8. Sill panels - removal and replacement

1 The sill panel is bolted to the body and to the wings at the front and rear. Once all the bolts have been removed - bearing in mind the precautions for stubborn bolts as mentioned in the section on front wing removal - the sill can be lifted off.

2 When fitting a new sill panel make sure the washers fit correctly over the slots and when tightening the bolts tighten up the ones to the bodywork before the ones to the wings.

9. Front bumper - removal and replacement

1 The bumper can be removed together with the brackets or otherwise as wished. The bumper can be detached from the brackets by undoing the two screws holding it to each bracket. To remove the brackets unship the spare wheel from its well and undo the two screws holding the brackets in place.

2 When replacing a bumper assemble the bumper to the brackets (loosely at first) and then bolt the brackets in position. If the bumper is not level or the gaps at each end between the bumper and wing are uneven then the brackets must be bent (if the bumper is new).

3 Make sure the bracket rubber seals are in good condition if you wish to prevent the spare wheel and well getting wet and rusty.

10. Rear bumper - removal and replacement

The rear bumper is mounted in exactly the same way as the front one and should be removed and refitted in the same manner.

11. Windscreen and fixed glass - removal and replacement

1 Make sure you know what kind of glass is fitted. Toughened safety glass will stand a certain amount of impact blows without breaking but any other kind will crack at least and only carefully applied sustained pressure may be used with safety.

2 After taking off the windscreen wiper arms, loosen the rubber sealing strip on the inside of the car where it fits over the edge of the window frame. Use a piece of wood for this. Anything sharp may rip the rubber weatherstrip. The screen can be pushed out, weatherstrip attached, if pressure is applied at the top corners. Two people are needed on this to prevent the glass falling out. Push evenly and protect your hands to avoid accidents. Remove the finisher strip from the weatherstrip.

3 When fitting a screen first make sure that the window frame edges are even and smooth. Examine the edges of the screen to see that it is ground smooth and no chips or cracks are visible. Any such cracks could be the source of a much bigger one. The rubber weatherstrip should be perfectly clean. No traces of sealing compound should remain on rubber, glass or metal. If the sealing strip is old, brittle or hard, it is advisable to fit a new one even though they are not cheap.

4 Fit the weatherstrip to the screen first so that the joint comes midway along the top edge.

5 Next fit the decorative moulding into the weatherstrip. This is done by first feeding fine cord into the slot (use a piece of thin tubing as a guide and time saver) and leave the ends overlapping sufficiently to grip later. The two halves of the moulding are then put in place and the cord drawn out so that the edge of the strip locks them into place.

6 Apply suitable sealing compound to the weatherstrip where it will seat onto the metal window frame and also onto the outside faces of the frame at the lower corners.

7 Fit a piece of really strong thin cord into the frame channel of the weatherstrip as already described and then offer up the screen to the aperture. A second person is essential for this.

8 When you are sure that the screen is centrally positioned, pull the cord out so that the lip of the weatherstrip is drawn over the inner edge of the frame flange. One of the most frequent difficulties in this job is that the cord breaks. This is often because of sharp or uneven edges on the frame flange so a little extra time in preparation will pay off.

12. Doors - removal and replacement

1 The door hinges are welded to the door and fixed to the car by four countersunk crosshead screws. Two of the screws are concealed under rubber plugs in the body.

2 If the same door is being put back the simplest way to take it off is to drive out the hinge pins with a punch but you will have to remove the sill panel to get at the bottom one. If this is done no re-alignment problems will occur.

3 To slacken the hinge screws an impact screwdriver is essential. Similarly for tightening them properly on replacement.

4 When hanging a new door (or re-aligning one which is out of position) insert all hinge screws loosely and then tighten just one in each hinge sufficiently to hold the door whilst it is set centrally and flush in the opening. It makes things easier if you remove the latch striker plate whilst this is being done.

13. Door rattles - tracing and rectification

Door rattles are due either to loose hinges, worn or maladjusted catches, or loose components inside the door. Loose hinges can be detected by opening the door and trying to lift it. Any play will be felt. Worn or badly adjusted catches can be found by pushing and pulling on the outside handle when the door is closed. Once again any play will be felt. To check the window mechanism open the door and shake it with the window first open and then closed. Rattles will normally be heard.

14. Door trim panels - removal and replacement

1 First remove the window winder and door handles by pressing the escutcheons against the panel so that the locating pins can be punched out. On later models the winder handle has a plastic cover which should be prized off at the spindle end. A crosshead screw is then accessible and should be removed. On these later models the recessed finger plate behind the inner door handle lever can be prized out also with a screwdriver. The crosshead screw behind it can then be removed to release the assembly. Then use a piece of flat metal strip to put round the edge of the panel and pull out the retaining clips. Take care not to tear the clips off the trim panel itself. On the passenger side it will be necessary to lift the panel a little to disengage the arm rest inner support from the door panel.

2 Replacement is a reversal of the removal procedure.

15. Window lifter mechanism - removal and replacement

1 Remove the door trim panel.

2 Disconnect the door check strap by taking out the link pin.

3 Take out the four screws holding the window lifter channel and push the window up and jam it. There is also a vertical stay on the panel which must be removed.

4 Remove the five screws holding the window lifter to the door panel and another screw which holds the dividing strip between quarterlight and window. Pull the lifter mechanism out from the bottom of the door.

5 Replacement is a reversal of this procedure. Check the operation of the mechanism before replacing the trim panel.

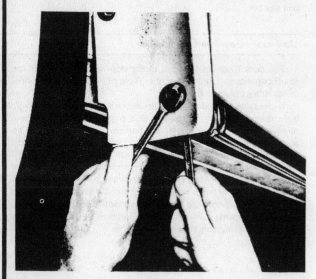

Fig.12.3. Undoing bolt connecting front wing to door sill panel.

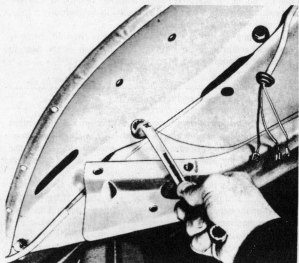

Fig.12.4. Removing rear wing panel bolts.

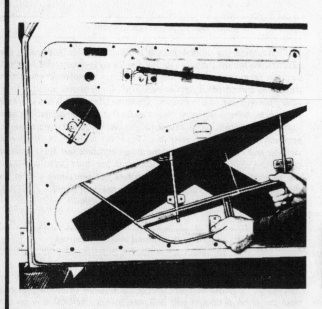

Fig.12.5. Removing door window lifter mechanism.

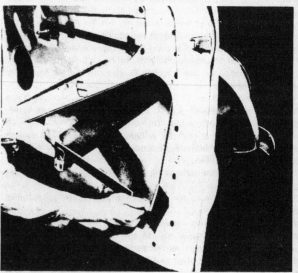

Fig.12.6. Removing door window glass.

16. Door window glass - removal and replacement

1 Remove the door trim and lifter mechanism.
2 Take out the wedges used to jam the glass in position when the lifter was taken out and then lower and tilt the glass so that it comes out of the bottom of the door. Replacement is a reversal of the procedure.
3 If new glass is being fitted into the existing channel the rear end of the channel must be positioned 80 mm from the rear corner of the glass.

17. Quarterlight - removal and replacement

1 Remove the door trim, lifter mechanism and main window glass.
2 Undo the crosshead screw securing the top of the quarterlight frame to the door frame and the whole assembly can be lifted out.
3 Replacement is a reversal of this procedure.

18. Door latch mechanism - removal and replacement

1 Remove the door trim.
2 Take out the two bolts holding the remote control handle shaft to the door frame and disconnect the link arm.
3 Remove the three crosshead screws holding the latch to the door and then push it inside the door and down - manoeuvring the link arm sufficiently to enable it to come clear so that it can be disconnected.
4 Replacement is a reversal of the removal procedure.

19. Door latch striker plates - adjustment and renewal

1 Rattles in doors are usually due to an incorrect striker plate position or the wedge being out of adjustment.
2 First check that the door fits the aperture properly by seeing that the gaps are more or less equal all round and that it fits flush with the side panel of the bodywork. There should be no rubbing and all the weatherstrip should show signs of equal compression.
3 Then make sure that the latch on the door is working properly. The top and bottom surfaces of the latch housing must be flat and the openings in it should not be worn. When the latch button is operated the bolt should retract fully.
4 If there are signs of wear on the lower surface and notches of the striker plate then it should be renewed. Similarly the plastic wedge should be renewed if worn.
5 Slacken all the striker plate mounting screws and tighten them just enough to prevent the plate from moving easily.
6 Loosen the locknut on the wedge adjusting rod and turn the screw until the stop comes against the housing. This gives the wedge maximum free movement.
7 To adjust the plate laterally first close the door gently and push or pull it until the door lines up with the body. To adjust the striker plate vertically it is best to pull back the weatherstrip so that the latch housing can be seen when the door is nearly shut. The bottom of the latch should ride on the plate and rise about 2 mm when the door is fully closed. To judge this, see that the gap between the latch and striker plate is less at the bottom than at the top. These adjustments, if done properly, take quite a time so a certain amount of patience is necessary.
8 Finally the wedge must be set. Its job is to keep the door held tight when shut. When the door closes the wedge is pushed in and its inward movement is stopped by the shoulder on the screwed pin. If this shoulder is too far out the wedge will butt against it before the door is fully closed and it will require excessive force or be impossible to close the door. If the shoulder is too far the other way the door will rattle. Consequently the adjusting screw should be turned until a little drag is felt when operating the latch and

opening the door. When the wedge is set satisfactorily, tighten the locknut on the screw.
9 The fitting of a new striker plate assembly merely requires that the mounting screws are completely removed. They lock into a movable keep plate in the body pillar.
10 Later models have a different type of latch and striker plate. The general arrangements are almost.   the same but the wedge is no longer adjustable. To correct the symptoms of a loose or tight latch the striker plate screws should be slackened and the top of the striker plate tilted in out out as appropriate.
11 If adjustment still fails to prevent any looseness when the door is shut then it is in order to put some packing between the wedge and the bracket, to which it is held by two screws.

20. Engine compartment cover - removal and replacement

1 The lid is held by two conventional hinges and is kept open by a strong spring.
2 Mark the position of the hinge and brackets as clearly as possible and slacken off all the hinge and bracket bolts. Remove the spring by squeezing the two 'L' shaped ends out of their holes. If you have doubts about the spring flying off and causing an accident leave it where it is and undo the bolts, using the cover to hold and eventually ease the spring tension.
3 If the cover is being removed in order to remove the engine fan housing the hinge brackets will need taking off as well.
4 When replacing the cover the spring can be fitted after the lid has been attached provided you are able to get sufficient leverage on to it. If not, replace the brackets and then hook the spring into position and use the cover once again to take up the tension whilst the hinge bolts are replaced.
5 Do not first attach the hinge brackets to the cover. It is much easier to fit the brackets to the body and then fit the cover to the brackets.
6 It is important to position the lid so that when closed it is central in the aperture. For this reason the bracket holes are slotted to allow adjustment.

21. Luggage compartment cover - removal and replacement

1 Mark the position of the hinge plates on the cover and then slacken all the upper hinge mounting bolts and remove one from each side.
2 Support the cover and remove the bolt securing the top end of the telescopic prop.
3 Remove the other hinge bolts with assistance from another person and lift the cover off.
4 Replacement is a reversal of the removal procedure. Fit all the hinge bolts loosely to start with so that the cover can be positioned correctly in the slotted holes.

22. Engine compartment cover latch - adjustment

1 Before adjusting the latch the cover must be correctly set on its hinges so that it fits centrally in the aperture. If the cover is distorted or out of position no adjustment of the latch can rectify it.
2 The adjustment is confined to the striker plate fitted to the body. The hook on the latch should centralise in the notch and the plate should be raised or lowered to ensure adequate engagement. Slacken the two striker plate mounting screws and move the plate as required.

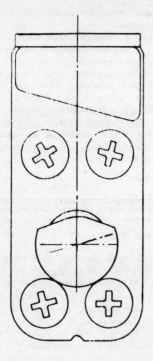

Fig. 12.7. Latch striker plate - later type. The top of the plate can be moved in or out.

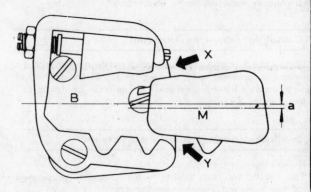

Fig. 12.8. Striker plate and latch gaps (early type). X is greater than Y and latch rise on engagement, 'a' = 2 mm.

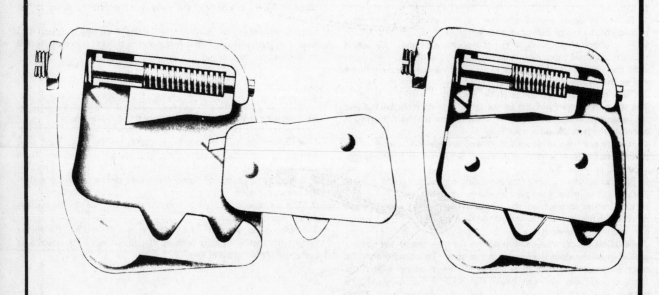

Fig. 12.9. Early type latch and striker plate - entering and locked.

23 Luggage compartment cover latch and release cable - adjustment

1 Before any adjustment is made see that the cover fits centrally over the aperture. If it has been buckled the latch can be adjusted only a limited amount to compensate for it.
2 To centralise the lock bolt (on the cover) to the aperture in the latch, the latch must be removed after first slackening the latch securing screws. To adjust the engagement of the lock bolt into the latch plate the lock bolt can be lengthened or shortened in its

mounting. The bolt should engage when firm pressure is applied to the bottom of the cover. If the cover needs slamming the bolt should be screwed out a little. If the cover rattles, move the bolt in.
3 The latch has a fail safe arrangement in the design so that if the cable breaks the latch will release rather than lock the cover.
4 To gain access to the cable end the latch mounting screws should be removed and the cover plate eased down from the lower half. The clamping screw is undone and the cable drawn out of the bracket. It can then be drawn out from inside the car.
5 When fitting a new cable into the bracket push the bracket back against the spring tension before tightening the screw.

Fig. 12.10. Inner latch lever screw (arrowed) under the finger plate.

Fig. 12.11. Window winder handle retaining screw

Chapter 13 Supplement:
revisions and modifications to later models

Contents

1 Introduction

This Supplement has been added to provide information on modifications to specifications and servicing and repair pro-cedures, particularly those applicable to the later models manu-factured before production ceased.

The information contained in Chapters 1 to 12 still applies unless superseded by information contained in this Supplement. Therefore, always use this Chapter in conjunction with the rest of the book.

2 Specifications

Engine (1300cc)
Code
To August 1970 ... ...   F
September 1970 to 1973 ... ...   AB
1973 to 1975 ... ...   AR

Specification differences for AR engine
Compression ratio ... ...   7.5 : 1
Power output... ... ...   44 bhp at 4100 rpm
Torque ... ...   65 lbf ft at 3000 rpm
Octane requirement ... ...   91 RON

Engines designed for operation on low grade fuel
Code:
   To August 1970 ... ...   E
   September 1970 to 1974 ... ...   AC
Compression ratio ... ...   6.6 : 1
Power output (E) ... ...   37 bhp at 4000 rpm
Power output (AC) ... ...   40 bhp at 4000 rpm
Torque (E) ... ...   64 lbf ft at 2000 rpm
Torque (AC) ... ...   59 lbf ft at 3000 rpm
Octane requirement (E)... ... ...   81 RON
Octane requirement (AC) ... ...   83 RON

Engine (1500cc)
Code (standard) ... ...   H

Code (for operation on low grade fuel)...   L

Compression ratio ... ...   6.6 : 1

Power output ... ...   40 bhp at 4000 rpm

Torque ... ...   69 lbf ft at 2000 rpm

Octane requirement ... ...   83 RON

Fuel system
Carburettor (1300cc engine)
Type ... ...   Solex 31-PICT-4
Application ... ...   Engine code AR from August 1973
Calibration (mm):
   Venturi 25.5
   Main jet X130
   Air correction jet 110Z
   Pilot jet 52.5
   Pilot air jet   100
   Auxiliary fuel jet   45
   Auxiliary air jet   150
   Enrichment jet ... ...   2 x 100 without ball
   Fuel volume per stroke of accelerator pump ... ...   1.15 to 1.45 cc (above 20°C) 1.80 to 2.20 cc (below 20°C)
   Fuel inlet needle valve washer thickness 1.5
Octane requirement ... ...   91 RON
Idle speed (manual) ... ...   750 to 900 rpm
Idle speed (automatic) ... ...   850 to 1000 rpm
CO level ... ...   2 to 4%

Ignition system
Dwell angle (all engines) ... ...   44 to 50°

3 Fuel system

Fuel pump
1 The fuel pump fitted to later models is of the semi-sealed type. This means that if more than routine filter cleaning is needed then a new pump complete will be required.
2 Some versions of this pump incorporate a cut-off valve, and as both versions of the pump appear the same externally then the type with the cut-off valve can only be identified by the number PE20000 stamped on it.

Air cleaner
3 On later models, a disposable paper element type air cleaner was fitted.
4 The air cleaner casing should be opened and the filter element renewed every 18 000 miles (30 000 km), or more frequently in dusty terrain.
5 This type of air cleaner can be fitted in place of the earlier oil bath type, but it will mean fitting a new oil breather/filler/hose arrangement.

Solex 31-PICT-4 carburettor - thermostat valve
6 This unit is fitted to later models (see Specifications at the beginning of this Supplement) and incorporates a thermostat ball valve to control the volume of fuel injected by the accelerator pump depending upon the engine temperature. Performance during the warm-up period is improved by this device.

Solex 31-PICT-4 carburettor - overhaul and adjustment
7 The carburettor fitted to later models may be dismantled and reassembled in a similar way to that described for earlier versions in Chapter 3, but the modified design, particularly of the idling circuit components, should be noted from the exploded drawing.
8 The method of adjusting the idle speed is by means of a volume control screw. The mixture control screw and the throttle speed screw should not normally require touching, and in fact have sealing caps fitted to them. However, after overhaul it may be necessary to remove the caps and adjust in the following way.

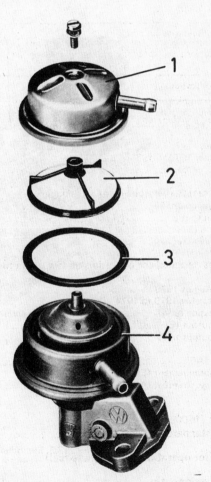

Fig. 13.1. Semi-sealed type of fuel pump (Sec 3)

| 1 | Cover | 3 | Gasket |
| 2 | Filter | 4 | Body |

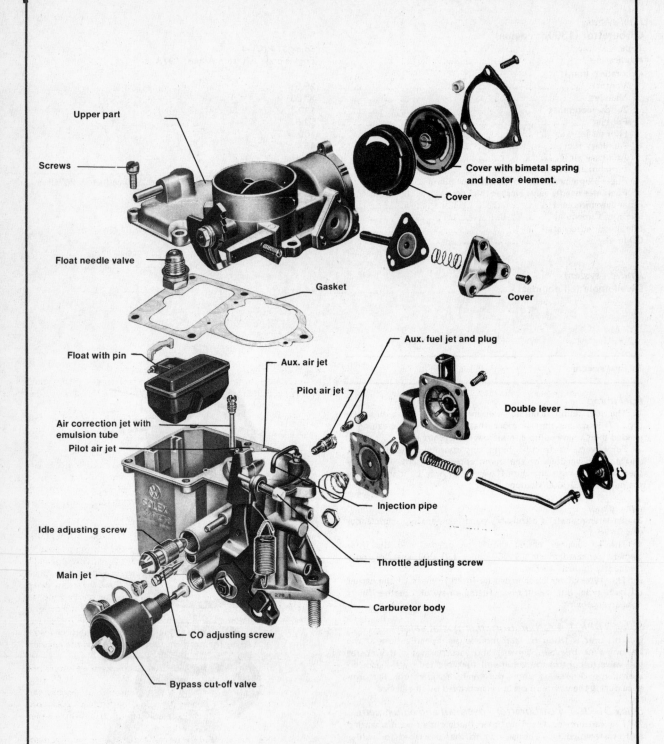

Upper part

Screws

Cover with bimetal spring and heater element.

Cover

Float needle valve

Gasket

Cover

Float with pin

Aux. fuel jet and plug

Aux. air jet

Pilot air jet

Double lever

Air correction jet with emulsion tube

Pilot air jet

Injection pipe

Idle adjusting screw

Throttle adjusting screw

Main jet

Carburetor body

CO adjusting screw

Bypass cut-off valve

Fig. 13.2. Exploded view of Solex 31-PICT-4 carburettor (Sec 3)

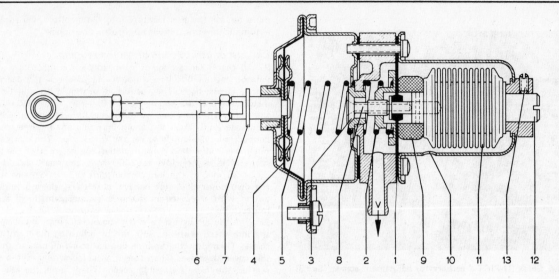

Fig. 13.3. Throttle valve positioner - cross-sectional view (Sec 3)

1	Valve diaphragm	8	Air drilling
2	Valve diaphragm spring	9	Filter
3	Valve	10	Hole
4	Pullrod diaphragm	11	Altitude corrector
5	Pullrod diaphragm spring	12	Adjusting screw
6	Pullrod	13	Locknut
7	Stop washer		

Throttle valve plate adjustment

9 If the engine has not yet been started up after overhaul, turn the throttle speed screw out until there is a gap between the end of the screw and the fast idle cam. Now turn the screw in until it just contacts the fast idle cam, and screw it in a further ¼ turn.

10 Once the engine has started, run it to normal operating temperature and let it idle.

11 Disconnect the distributor vacuum pipe from the carburettor and connect a vacuum gauge in its place.

12 Screw in the throttle speed screw until vacuum pressure is indicated on the gauge, and then unscrew the screw until the needle on the gauge drops to zero; then unscrew a further ¼ turn.

Mixture adjustment

13 Ideally, an exhaust gas analyser should now be connected to the tailpipe in accordance with the manufacturer's instructions and the mixture screw adjusted to bring the CO level within specified tolerance (2 to 4%).

14 Where an exhaust gas analyser is not available, turn the mixture control screw in to the point where the idle speed drops slightly (50 rpm).

Idle speed adjustment

15 Turn the idle speed screw in or out to bring the speed within the specified level.

16 Fit new sealing caps to the adjusting screws if they had to be broken off.

Carburettor - modification of choke cover

17 To overcome certain problems which may cause difficult cold starting or rough idle during the warming-up period, a modified choke cover (Part No 113 129 227A) may be fitted to enable the setting of the choke valve plate to be altered as follows.

18 With the automatic choke housing cover removed, press the vacuum diaphragm operating rod as far as it will go in the direction of arrow A in Fig. 13.5. Close the choke valve plate with the fingers and check the gap between the edge of the

valve plate and the wall of the carburettor throat. This should be between 1.8 and 2.2 mm. Use a twist drill of suitable diameter to test the gap.

19 Where necessary, adjust the gap by means of screw B (Fig. 13.5).

Exhaust emission control - description

20 With an eye to anticipated legislation with regard to exhaust gas pollution of the atmosphere, particularly in the United States, engines in the 1500 range starting at H 5,000,001 in 1967 were fitted with different carburettors and distributors for certain markets.

21 The cause of most of the pollutants in exhaust gas is unburnt fuel. All carburettors are a compromise to provide an acceptable and flexible performance over a wide range of engine revolutions. Consequently the air to fuel ratio is constantly changing and in certain circumstances is considerably over-rich. Such instances are, for example, during rapid acceleration when neat fuel is pumped direct into the carburettor choke tube, to overcome flat spots, or during over-run when the throttle is closed and the manifold depression draws fully on the fuel jets.

22 Development work is still going on with ways and means of finding an answer to the problem without affecting the engines' performance.

23 The devices fitted to the VW 1500 Beetle were early versions and many changes have since taken place.

24 It must be borne in mind that no amount of devices can compensate for a worn engine. It would be futile to even contemplate fitting emission control equipment to anything other than an engine in first class condition.

25 Make sure that the carburettor and distributor are matched. Any VW dealer will give the correct serial designation for your vehicle. We do not generally quote parts numbers in this manual because they have a habit of changing from time to time, and it is always best to get the most up to date information. This is particularly so when modifications can be retrospective.

26 The only outward sign of the presence of exhaust emission control on the H series engines is an automatic throttle positioner mounted on the back of the carburettor. This device prevents complete closure of the throttle on the over-run thus allowing

Fig. 13.4. Solex 31-PICT-4 carburettor adjustment screws (Sec 3)

1   Throttle speed screw   3   Idle speed screw
2   Mixture screw

Fig. 13.5. Adjusting choke valve plate gap - see text (Sec 3)

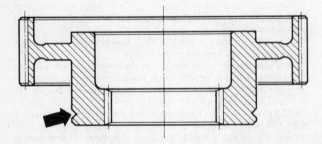

**Fig. 13.6. Modified 1st/2nd synchro hub - identification groove
arrowed (Sec 4)**

more air for the fuel mixture into the manifold. On stick-shift
automatic versions there is no throttle positioner.

Exhaust emission control - engine tuning
27 All the H series engines with emission control have a basic
ignition setting 0°. It is a good idea to check the distributor
with a strobe light. The vacuum hose should be pulled off the
distributor and the engine run at 850 rpm. The TDC mark on
the pulley (the left one of the three) should line up with the
crankcase joint. With the engine running at the same speed reconnect the vacuum hose on the distributor. The mark should
not move more than 4 mm relative to the joint. If the engine
speed is then increased to 3000 rpm, the mark should move
50 – 55 mm to the left of the joint (32 – 35° advance). If
the distributor does not behave in this way there is something
wrong with the vacuum advance or the centrifugal advance
respectively.
28 With the ignition set and the engine fully warmed up see that
the idle speed is still at 850 rpm by adjusting the throttle stop
screw. Then turn the volume control screw clockwise until the
idle speed decreases. Then turn it anti-clockwise until the engine
reaches the fastest possible speed. Then re-set the idle speed
again if necessary.
29 The throttle positioner is also adjustable. It incorporates an
altitude corrector for those who drive at a variety of heights.
To adjust the device run the engine and turn the adjusting
screw on the end (unlock the grub screw first) until the stop
washer on the plunger comes up against the housing. The engine
speed should now be 1700 to 1800 rpm. If the engine speed
is outside these limits undo the pullrod locknuts - one end is a
left-hand thread - and rotate the pullrod to lengthen it or shorten
it. Lengthening it reduces the engine speed and vice versa.
Tighten the pullrod locknuts and then re-adjust the screw on
the positioner to give the correct idle speed of 850 rpm.
30 Speed up the engine to about 3000 rpm with the accelerator
pedal and release the pedal quickly. The engine speed should
drop to 1000 rpm in 3 to 4 seconds. If it takes longer than this,
turn the adjusting screw anti-clockwise and vice versa. Obviously
this final adjustment of the screw must be minimal otherwise
the previous setting will be upset again. If, therefore, this last
adjustment exceeds 1/8 of a turn to achieve the necessary
results, there must be something wrong with the device. Parts
for repair are not normally available and a new unit may be
needed.

---

4   Manual transmission

Modified 1st/2nd gear synchro hub
1   The replacement synchro hub has been modified by increasing the hub depth. A groove is now machined into the hub for
identification purposes.
2   If a gearbox built before July 1975 is being overhauled,
and one of the modified synchro hubs is being installed as a
replacement, then any shims originally located between the
mainshaft slotted (ring) nut and the 1st/2nd synchro hub should
be discarded (refer to Chapter 6, Section 3).
3   The need for 1st gear endfloat adjustment (refer to Chapter
6, Section 5B) no longer applies once the new type of synchro
hub has been fitted.

Gearchange lever - reassembly and adjustment
4   Grease should be applied to the entire length of the gearchange rod before sliding it into the bodyframe tunnel.
5   Grease and fix the guide sleeve into the front guide bracket
and fit the retaining ring. Make sure that the slot in the sleeve
is at the side.
6   Push the gearchange rod through the front guide, moving it
towards the rear until the ball socket is centred in the hole in
the frame tunnel. Fit the gasket and cover plates.
7   Fit the gearchange rod coupling and its bolt.
8   Later models use a gearchange rod coupling bolt which has

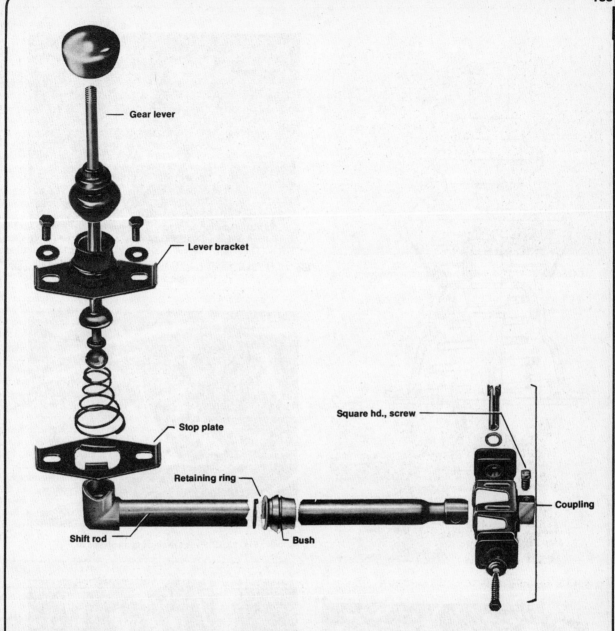

Gear lever

Lever bracket

Square hd., screw

Stop plate

Retaining ring

Coupling

Shift rod

Bush

Fig. 13.7. Gearchange lever components (Sec 4)

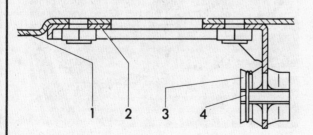

Fig. 13.8. Gearchange rod bracket in bodyframe tunnel (Sec 4)

1 Tunnel
2 Reinforcement bracket
3 Sleeve
4 Retaining ring

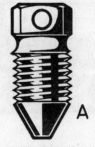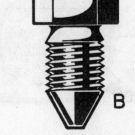

Fig. 13.9. Gearchange rod coupling bolts (Sec 4)

A Early type   B Later type

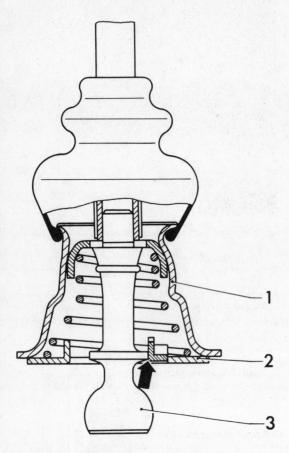

Fig. 13.10. Sectional view of gearchange lever (Sec 4)

1 Bracket   3 Gear lever
2 Stop plate

Fig. 13.11. Gearchange lever bracket showing elongated bolt holes (Sec 4)

Fig. 13.12. Front mounting nuts (Sec 4)

Fig. 13.13. Prising engine/transmission towards rear of car (Sec 4)

Fig. 13.14. Front suspension camber adjusting bush (arrowed) (Sec 6)

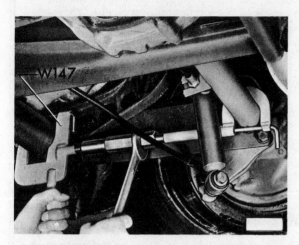

Fig. 13.15. Using special tool to adjust rear wheel toe (Sec 6)

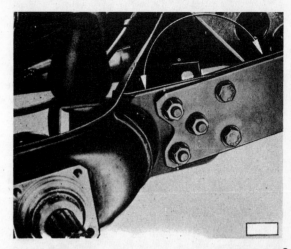

Fig. 13.16. Rear suspension arm-to-flange angle (less than 180°) (Sec 6)

thread-locking compound applied to its threads instead of the earlier type bolt, which is locked in position with wire. Always renew the later type bolt once it has been removed.

9   Assemble the gear lever with bracket, bellows and knob. Do not tighten the bracket bolts at this stage.

10 Select 2nd gear and hold the clutch pedal depressed during the following adjustment operations.

11 Move the gear lever/bracket until, with the lever still in 2nd gear, it is exactly vertical in the transverse plane but slightly inclined (11°) rearwards at its upper end.

12 Holding the lever in this position, use a screwdriver to push the stop plate, which is located under the bracket, towards the left-hand side until the plate makes contact with the lever (arrowed in Fig. 13.10). The plate should move the lever at this stage.

13 Tighten the bracket securing bolts. If the adjustment has been carried out correctly, it should be possible to move the gearchange lever sideways (still in 2nd gear) by about 15 to 20 mm measured at the knob.

14 Test gear selection by moving the lever in an H-pattern. Check also that the reverse gear safety catch is doing its job.

Front mounting - renewal

15 It is possible to renew the front mounting with the engine/ transmission in position in the car.

16 Unscrew and remove the nuts from the mounting.

17 Using two long levers, prise the engine/transmission towards the rear of the car and then tilt the mounting forward and down and remove it.

18 Fit the new mounting by reversing the removal operations.

5   Automatic transmission

Gearchange lever - reassembly and adjustment

1   The operations are as described for the manual transmission in Section 4 of this Supplement, except that during adjustment, the lever should be in the 'L' position instead of 2nd gear.

Front mounting - renewal

2   Removal of the front mounting with the engine/automatic transmission still in the car is as described for manual transmission in Section 4 of this Supplement.

6   Suspension and steering

Steering angles and wheel alignment

1   Although it is strongly recommended that all steering and suspension angles are set and adjusted by your dealer, for those who possess suitable checking equipment, and to provide more detailed information regarding adjustment methods, the following details should be read in conjunction with Chapters 6, 8 and 11.

Front suspension and steering
Camber

2   Adjustment is by means of an eccentric bush. First slacken the nut on the upper balljoint and turn the bush as necessary. The bush incorporates a notch which, when pointing towards the front of the car, indicates the basic position. Adjustment is limited to 90° either side of this position.

Wheel alignment (toe-in)

3   This is altered by releasing the clamps on the tie-rods and turning both rods by an equal amount. The horizontal setting of the steering wheel spokes will not be altered if both tie-rods are adjusted equally. If the spokes are not horizontal the steering wheel should not be repositioned on its splines to correct the situation, but the lengths of the tie-rods altered to equalise their lengths.

Rear suspension (swing type axle - manual transmission)
Camber

4   This is altered by moving the position of the trailing arms on the torsion bars.

Wheel alignment (toe)

5   Toe adjustment is carried out by releasing the bolts which connect the axle tube flanges to the trailing arms and moving the axle tube forwards or backwards within the limits of the elongated bolt holes. For precise control during adjustment, a threaded rod with turn buckle located between the axle tube and the frame crossmember is recommended.

Rear suspension (diagonal arm type axle - automatic transmission
Camber

6   This is normally set during production, but it is possible to alter the setting very slightly in the following way. With the

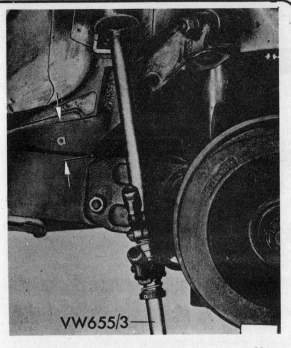

Fig. 13.17. Rear suspension arm setting angle; a = 2° 50′ (Sec 6)

Fig. 13.18. Rear suspension arm-to-stop clearance; a = 32 mm (Sec 6)

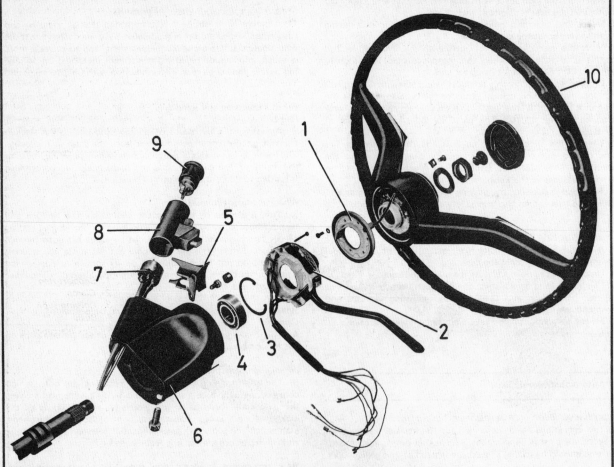

Fig. 13.19. Steering column and switch arrangement (Sec 6)

1 Slip ring	4 Bearing	7 Ignition/starter switch	9 Lock cylinder
2 Direction indicator switch	5 Retainer	8 Steering lock body	10 Steering wheel
3 Snap ring	6 Switch housing		

car standing on its roadwheels, release the bolts which connect the bearing flange and the trailing arm. This will cause the flange to move upwards to increase the positive camber setting up to a maximum of $0^o 45'$.

7 With the car raised so that the suspension is hanging free, releasing the bearing flange/trailing arm bolts will cause the flange to move downwards and increase the negative camber up to a maximum of $0^o 15'$.

Wheel alignment (toe)

8 This is adjusted just as described for swing type axles in paragraph 5. On completion, however, it is very important to set the relationship between the diagonal and trailing arms, and the arm-to-stop distance correctly. Without the proper equipment, this is definitely a job for your dealer.

Steering column switches and lock

9 On later models, the direction indicator switch is column mounted.

10 Installed on the side of the column is a steering lock combined with the ignition/starter switch.

11 To dismantle, first disconnect the battery.

12 Prise off the cap from the centre of the steering wheel and then unscrew the steering wheel retaining nut.

13 Remove the steering wheel and the slip ring noting that the switch cancelling cam is on the right-hand side.

14 Identify the electrical leads on the indicator switch, disconnect them and withdraw the switch.

15 To remove the steering lock cylinder, turn the key to the right ('Fahrt' position) and then depress the small retaining plunger and withdraw the cylinder, at the same time turning the key slightly to the right.

16 The ignition/starter switch, the retainer and the column switch housing can all be removed once their respective securing screws have been extracted.

17 Refitting is a reversal of removal but observe the following points.

18 Press the base of the lock cylinder towards the key and then turn the cylinder and key to the 'Halt' position. Withdraw the key and insert the cylinder into the lock body without its key.

19 Assemble the cylinder/lock body together with the ignition/starter switch into the switch housing.

20 Fit the retainer and check the operation of the lock. Do not fully tighten the column switch housing screws fully at this stage, but wait until the steering wheel is refitted, and adjust the position of the switch housing so that a running clearance exists between the hub of the steering wheel and the upper rim of the switch housing. Fully tighten the switch housing screws once this clearance is obtained.

21 On some models, a tubular distance piece is fitted to the top of the steering shaft and tapped down the shaft until the distance between the end of the shaft and the end face of the distance piece is 41.5 mm. This will ensure that a clearance of between 2 and 4 mm exists between the steering wheel hub and the steering column switch housing.

22 When installation is complete, reconnect the battery.

Collapsible type steering column - removal and refitting

23 Refer to Chapter 11, Section 15 for removal operations.

24 On later models, the column upper mounting is held in position by a mounting plate and two shear head bolts which must be drilled out to remove them.

25 When installing this type of steering column, observe the following points.

26 With the pinch bolt loose on the upper face of the steering shaft flexible coupling, move the shaft (with support ring in position) until there is a gap of between 6 and 8 mm as shown in Fig. 13.22. When the gap is correct, tighten the pinch bolt.

27 The steering column upper mounting plate must be fitted so that the closed sides of the slides on the plate are towards the front of the car.

28 The recess in the packing pieces must be against the column tube. Do not tighten the new shear head bolts until the column and the steering column switch housing have been moved, as necessary, to give a clearance between the lower edge of the steering wheel hub and the top edge of the column switch housing of between 2 and 4 mm. On versions with a spacer tube at the upper end of the steering shaft, this gap should be obtained automatically.

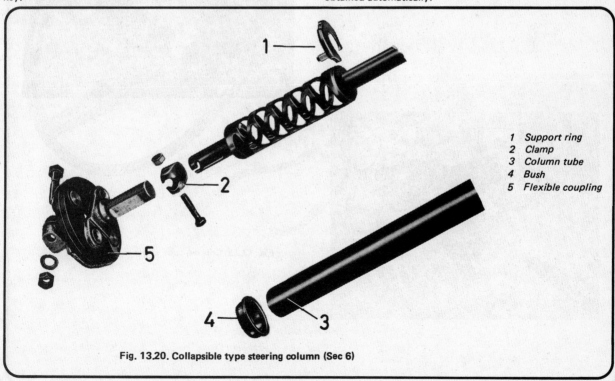

1 Support ring
2 Clamp
3 Column tube
4 Bush
5 Flexible coupling

Fig. 13.20. Collapsible type steering column (Sec 6)

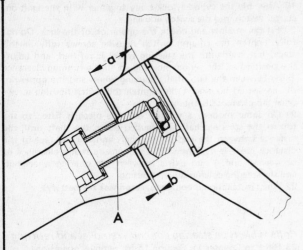

Fig. 13.21. Steering column switch housing clearance (Sec 6)

a = 41.5 mm   A = Spacer
b = 2 to 4 mm

Fig. 13.22. Steering column support ring installation (Sec 6)

a = 6 to 8 mm

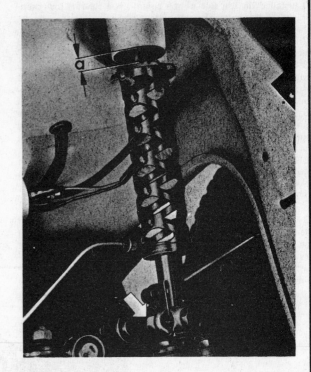

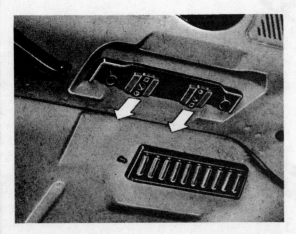

Fig. 13.23. Column tube upper mounting (Sec 6)

Fig. 13.24. Exploded view of the alternator (Sec 7)

1	Cover plate	3	Body	5	Insulator	7	Stator
2	Brush holder/voltage regulator	4	Fan end bracket	6	Diode plate	8	Rotor
						9	Drive end bracket

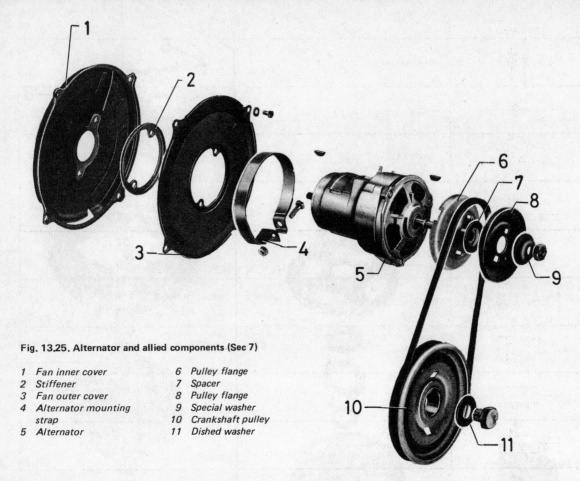

Fig. 13.25. Alternator and allied components (Sec 7)

1   Fan inner cover   6   Pulley flange
2   Stiffener   7   Spacer
3   Fan outer cover   8   Pulley flange
4   Alternator mounting   9   Special washer
    strap   10   Crankshaft pulley
5   Alternator   11   Dished washer

29 Once the gap is correct, tighten the switch housing screws and the shear head bolts at the column upper mounting until the heads break off.

7   Electrical system

Alternator - description, maintenance and precautions

1   On some of the very late models produced, an alternator was fitted instead of a dynamo.
2   A voltage regulator is integral with the alternator on this type of generator.
3   An exploded view of the alternator is given for information purposes, but it is not recommended that the unit is overhauled. A new or factory reconditioned alternator should be obtained in the event of a fault or wear developing. The exception to this is renewal of the brushes if they have worn down to 0.13 in (5.0 mm) or less.

Fault diagnosis - alternator

4   The brush holder is accessible after removal of the cover plate.
5   Where an alternator is fitted, certain precautions must be observed if damage to the unit is to be avoided.
6   Never stop a running engine by pulling off a battery lead.
7   Disconnect both battery leads before connecting a mains charger to it.
8   Always disconnect both battery leads before using an electric arc welder on the car.
9   If using a stroboscope for checking the ignition timing which is connected to the car battery, keep the stroboscope leads well away from the alternator or its leads and preferably connect it to an independent battery remote from the engine compartment.
10 Maintenance consists of keeping the drivebelt correctly tensioned, the outside of the alternator clean and the electrical wiring securely connected.
11 The mounting of the alternator and the fan and drive pulley arrangement is very similar to that for a dynamo type generator.

Symptom	Reason(s)
Ignition warning lamp does not light up when key turned	Bulb blown Open circuit in wire from D+ terminal on alternator Worn carbon brushes Fault in diode plate, rotor or stator
Ignition warning lamp does not go out when engine speed increased	Wire from alternator D+ terminal to warning lamp earthed Fault in voltage regulator Internal fault in alternator

SYMBOL	EXPLANATION	Sample use
	TRANSFORMER, IRON CORE	Ignition coil
	DIODE	Alternator
	TRANSISTOR	Voltage regulator
	MECHANICAL CONNECTION MECHANICAL CONNECTION SPRING LOADED	Double switch Oil pressure switch
	RELAY, COIL	
	RELAY, ELECTRO MAGNETIC	(a) Headlamp (b) Cut off valve (carburettor)
	HORN	
	RESISTOR	
	POTENTIOMETER	
	THERMAL RESISTOR AUTOMATIC REGULATING	Temperature sender
	HEATING ELEMENT	Rear window heater
	BATTERY 12 volt	
	MEASURING GAUGE	Fuel gauge Temperature gauge
	SUPPRESSION WIRE	
	DYNAMO	
	MECHANICAL PRESSURE SWITCH	Door switch for interior light

H 5350

13.26. Symbols used in current flow diagrams

SYMBOL	EXPLANATION	Sample use
 (G)	ALTERNATOR WITH DIODE RECTIFIERS	Alternator
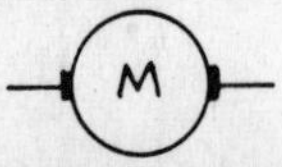 (M)	MOTOR	Radiator fan
 ▬▬▬ ▬ 10 ▬	EXTERNAL WIRING WIRE 10 mm^2 sectional area	
 ●	WIRE JUNCTION FIXED (SOLDERED)	Relay plate, dash board printed circuit
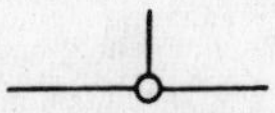 ○	WIRE JUNCTION SEPARABLE	Screw on terminals and eyelets
 ▭	PLUG, SINGLE OR MULTIPIN	T10 written by the side means a 10 pin plug
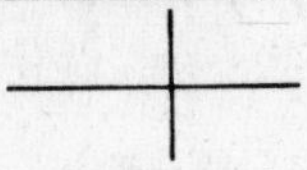 ┼	WIRE CROSSING, NOT JOINED	
 ⊥	GROUND, OR EARTH	
─┤├─	SWITCH CLOSED	
 ─/─	SWITCH OPEN	
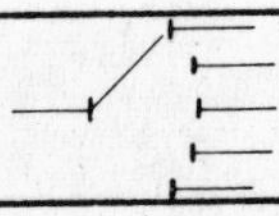	MULTI CONTACT SWITCH	
 1 2 3	SWITCH, MANUALLY OPERATED	
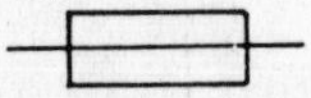 ▭	FUSE	
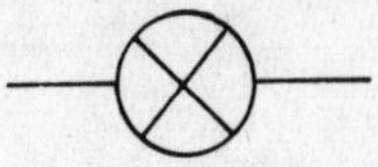 ⊗	BULB	
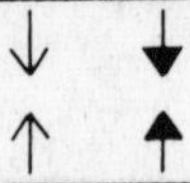 ↓ ↓ ↑ ↑	SPARK GAP	Spark plugs Distributor points
 ─┤├─	CONDENSER	Distributor

H 5550

Fig. 13.26. Symbols used in current flow diagrams - continued

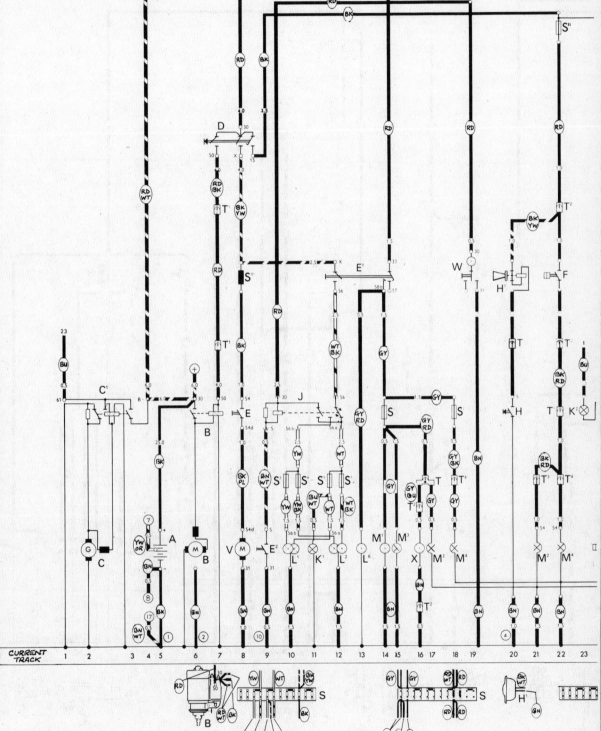

13.27. Current flow diagram - 1300 from August 1974 (see page 198 for key)

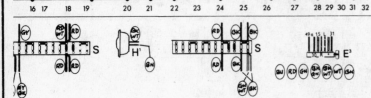

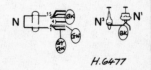

13.27. Current flow diagram - 1300 from August 1974 (continued)

H.6477

Key to wiring diagram 13.27. Current flow diagram - 1300 from August 1974

Designation		In current track
A	- Battery	5
B	- Starter	6, 7
C	- Dynamo	2
C1	- Regulator	1, 2, 3
D	- Ignition/starter switch	7, 8
E	- Windscreen wiper switch	8
E1	- Lighting switch	12, 14
E2	- Turn signal switch with contact for dip and headlight flasher	9, 29, 30
E3	- Hazard light switch	26, 28, 30, 32, 33
F	- Brake light switch	22
F1	- Oil pressure switch	24
F4	- Switch for reversing light	34
H	- Horn button	20
H1	- Horn	20
J	- Relay for dip and headlight flasher	9, 10, 12
J2	- Turn signal — hazard light relay	26, 27
K1	- High beam warning lamp	11
K2	- Ignition warning lamp	23
K3	- Oil pressure warning lamp	24
K5	- Turn signal warning lamp	25

Designation		In current track
K6	- Hazard light warning lamp	33
L1	- Left headlight	10
L2	- Right headlight	12
L6	- Speedometer light	13
M1	- Left parking light	14
M2	- Right tail light	17
M2	- Right brake light	21
M3	- Right parking light	15
M4	- Left tail light	18
M4	- Left brake light	22
M5	- Left turn signal, front	28
M6	- Left turn signal, rear	29
M7	- Right turn signal, front	31
M8	- Right turn signal, rear	32
M16	- Left reversing light	34
M17	- Right reversing light	35
N	- Ignition coil	37
N1	- Automatic choke	39
N3	- Electromagnetic cut-off valve	40
O	- Distributor	37, 38
P	- Plug connector	38
Q	- Spark plugs	38

Designation		In current track
S1)		8, 10, 12,
to)	- Fuses in fuse box	14, 18, 19,
S12)		22, 25, 26
S13	- Separate fuse for reversing lights (8 amp)	34
T	- Cable adaptor behind dashboard in engine compartment	
T1	- Cable connector, single under rear seat behind dashboard	
T2	- Cable connector, 2 pin in luggage compartment	
T3	- Cable connector, 4 pin behind engine compartment lining, left	
T20	- Central socket	36
V	- Wiper motor	8
W	- Interior light	19
X	- Number plate light	16
1	- Earth strap from battery to frame	
2	- Earth strap from gearbox to frame	
4	- Earth wire (steering column coupling)	
10	- Earth point (dashboard)	
11	- Earth point (speedometer)	

Colour code

BK	- Black	YW	- Yellow	
BU	- Blue	OR	- Orange	
BN	- Brown	GN	- Green	
PL	- Purple	GY	- Grey	
WT	- White	RD	- Red	

Note that where two colours are shown together, the upper is the main colour and the lower the tracer colour

Key to wiring diagram 13.28. Supplementary current flow diagram - 1300 from August 1974

Note: This diagram contains details of intermittent wipers, selector automatic transmission and trailer socket

Designation		In current track
B	- Starter	19, 20
B1	- To starter terminal 30	25
D	- Ignition switch	20
E17	- Starter inhibitor switch	18, 20
E21	- Selector lever contact	17
E22	- Wiper switch for intermittent operation	13, 14
J11	- Relay for intermittent operation	15, 16

Designation		In current track
J20	- Turn signal emergency light relay for trailer towing	21, 22
K18	- Trailer warning lamp	22
M2	- Tail and brake light, right	27
M4	- Tail and brake light, left	23
M6	- Turn signal rear, left	24
M8	- Turn signal rear, right	26

Designation		In current track
N7	- Control valve	18
S10	- Fuses in fuse box	11
S11		18
S22	- Separate fuse for trailer equipment	25
U	- Trailer socket	25
V	- Wiper motor	10, 13
X	- Number plate light	28

Key to wiring diagram 13.29 - USA models from August 1969

A	- Battery		K1	- High beam warning light
B	- Starter		K2	- Generator charging warning light
C	- Generator		K3	- Oil pressure warning light
C1	- Regulator		K5	- Turn signal warning light
D	- Ignition/starter switch		K6	- Emergency flasher warning light
E	- Windshield wiper switch		K7	- Dual circuit brake system warning light
E1	- Light switch		L1	- Sealed beam unit, left headlight
E2	- Turn signal and headlight dimmer switch		L2	- Sealed beam unit, right headlight
E3	- Emergency flasher switch		L10	- Instrument panel light
F	- Brake light switch with warning switch		M2	- Tail and brake light, right
F1	- Oil pressure switch		M4	- Tail and brake light, left
F2	- Door contact switch, left with contact for buzzer H5		M5	- Turn signal and parking light, front, left
F3	- Door contact switch, right		M6	- Turn signal, rear, left
F4	- Back-up light switch		M7	- Turn signal and parking light, front, right
G	- Fuel gauge sending unit		M8	- Turn signal, rear, right
G1	- Fuel gauge		M11	- Side marker light, front
H	- Horn button		N	- Ignition coil
H1	- Horn		N1	- Automatic choke
H5	- Ignition key warning buzzer		N3	- Electro-magnetic pilot jet
J	- Dimmer relay		O	- Ignition distributor
J2	- Emergency flasher relay		P1	- Spark plug connector, No 1 cylinder
J6	- Vibrator for fuel gauge		P2	- Spark plug connector, No 2 cylinder

P3	- Spark plug connector, No 3 cylinder
P4	- Spark plug connector, No 4 cylinder
Q1	- Spark plug, No 1 cylinder
Q2	- Spark plug, No 2 cylinder
Q3	- Spark plug, No 3 cylinder
Q4	- Spark plug, No 4 cylinder
R	- Radio connection
S	- Fuse box
S1	- Back-up light fuse
T	- Cable adaptor
T1	- Cable connector, single
T2	- Cable connector, double
T3	- Cable connector, triple
T4	- Cable connector (four connections)
V	- Windshield wiper motor
W	- Interior light
X	- License plate light
X1	- Back-up light, left
X2	- Back-up light, right
1	- Battery to frame ground strap
2	- Transmission to frame ground strap

Colour code

BK	Black	YW	Yellow	GY	Grey
BR	Brown	GN	Green	WH	White
RD	Red	BL	Blue	PUR	Purple
OR	Orange	VT	Violet		

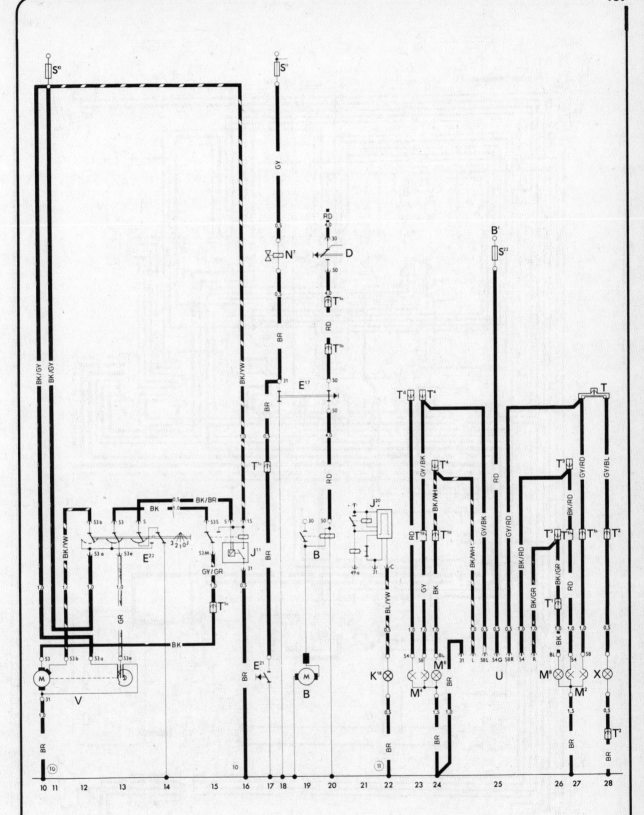

13.28. Supplementary current flow diagram - 1300 from August 1974 (see page 199 for key)

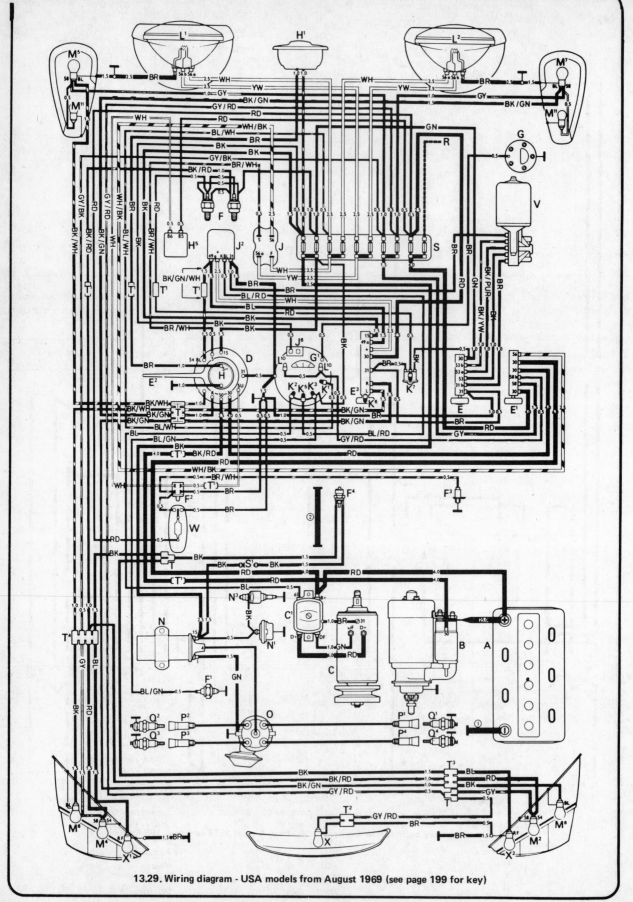

13.29. Wiring diagram - USA models from August 1969 (see page 199 for key)

Use of English

As this book has been written in England, it uses the appropriate English component names, phrases, and spelling. Some of these differ from those used in America. Normally, these cause no difficulty, but to make sure, a glossary is printed below. In ordering spare parts remember the parts list may use some of these words:

English	American	English	American
Accelerator	Gas pedal	Locks	Latches
Aerial	Antenna	Methylated spirit	Denatured alcohol
Anti-roll bar	Stabiliser or sway bar	Motorway	Freeway, turnpike etc
Big-end bearing	Rod bearing	Number plate	License plate
Bonnet (engine cover)	Hood	Paraffin	Kerosene
Boot (luggage compartment)	Trunk	Petrol	Gasoline (gas)
Bulkhead	Firewall	Petrol tank	Gas tank
Bush	Bushing	'Pinking'	'Pinging'
Cam follower or tappet	Valve lifter or tappet	Prise (force apart)	Pry
Carburettor	Carburetor	Propeller shaft	Driveshaft
Catch	Latch	Quarterlight	Quarter window
Choke/venturi	Barrel	Retread	Recap
Circlip	Snap-ring	Reverse	Back-up
Clearance	Lash	Rocker cover	Valve cover
Crownwheel	Ring gear (of differential)	Saloon	Sedan
Damper	Shock absorber, shock	Seized	Frozen
Disc (brake)	Rotor/disk	Sidelight	Parking light
Distance piece	Spacer	Silencer	Muffler
Drop arm	Pitman arm	Sill panel (beneath doors)	Rocker panel
Drop head coupe	Convertible	Small end, little end	Piston pin or wrist pin
Dynamo	Generator (DC)	Spanner	Wrench
Earth (electrical)	Ground	Split cotter (for valve spring cap)	Lock (for valve spring retainer)
Engineer's blue	Prussian blue	Split pin	Cotter pin
Estate car	Station wagon	Steering arm	Spindle arm
Exhaust manifold	Header	Sump	Oil pan
Fault finding/diagnosis	Troubleshooting	Swarf	Metal chips or debris
Float chamber	Float bowl	Tab washer	Tang or lock
Free-play	Lash	Tappet	Valve lifter
Freewheel	Coast	Thrust bearing	Throw-out bearing
Gearbox	Transmission	Top gear	High
Gearchange	Shift	Torch	Flashlight
Grub screw	Setscrew, Allen screw	Trackrod (of steering)	Tie-rod (or connecting rod)
Gudgeon pin	Piston pin or wrist pin	Trailing shoe (of brake)	Secondary shoe
Halfshaft	Axleshaft	Transmission	Whole drive line
Handbrake	Parking brake	Tyre	Tire
Hood	Soft top	Van	Panel wagon/van
Hot spot	Heat riser	Vice	Vise
Indicator	Turn signal	Wheel nut	Lug nut
Interior light	Dome lamp	Windscreen	Windshield
Layshaft (of gearbox)	Countershaft	Wing/mudguard	Fender
Leading shoe (of brake)	Primary shoe		

Safety first!

Professional motor mechanics are trained in safe working procedures. However enthusiastic you may be about getting on with the job in hand, do take the time to ensure that your safety is not put at risk. A moment's lack of attention can result in an accident, as can failure to observe certain elementary precautions.

There will always be new ways of having accidents, and the following points do not pretend to be a comprehensive list of all dangers; they are intended rather to make you aware of the risks and to encourage a safety-conscious approach to all work you carry out on your vehicle.

Essential DOs and DON'Ts

DON'T rely on a single jack when working underneath the vehicle. Always use reliable additional means of support, such as axle stands, securely placed under a part of the vehicle that you know will not give way.

DON'T attempt to loosen or tighten high-torque nuts (e.g. wheel hub nuts) while the vehicle is on a jack; it may be pulled off.

DON'T start the engine without first ascertaining that the transmission is in neutral (or 'Park' where applicable) and the parking brake applied.

DON'T suddenly remove the filler cap from a hot cooling system – cover it with a cloth and release the pressure gradually first, or you may get scalded by escaping coolant.

DON'T attempt to drain oil until you are sure it has cooled sufficiently to avoid scalding you.

DON'T grasp any part of the engine, exhaust or catalytic converter without first ascertaining that it is sufficiently cool to avoid burning you.

DON'T allow brake fluid or antifreeze to contact vehicle paintwork.

DON'T syphon toxic liquids such as fuel, brake fluid or antifreeze by mouth, or allow them to remain on your skin.

DON'T inhale dust – it may be injurious to health (see *Asbestos* below).

DON'T allow any spilt oil or grease to remain on the floor – wipe it up straight away, before someone slips on it.

DON'T use ill-fitting spanners or other tools which may slip and cause injury.

DON'T attempt to lift a heavy component which may be beyond your capability – get assistance.

DON'T rush to finish a job, or take unverified short cuts.

DON'T allow children or animals in or around an unattended vehicle.

DO wear eye protection when using power tools such as drill, sander, bench grinder etc, and when working under the vehicle.

DO use a barrier cream on your hands prior to undertaking dirty jobs – it will protect your skin from infection as well as making the dirt easier to remove afterwards; but make sure your hands aren't left slippery. Note that long-term contact with used engine oil can be a health hazard.

DO keep loose clothing (cuffs, tie etc) and long hair well out of the way of moving mechanical parts.

DO remove rings, wristwatch etc, before working on the vehicle – especially the electrical system.

DO ensure that any lifting tackle used has a safe working load rating adequate for the job.

DO keep your work area tidy – it is only too easy to fall over articles left lying around.

DO get someone to check periodically that all is well, when working alone on the vehicle.

DO carry out work in a logical sequence and check that everything is correctly assembled and tightened afterwards.

DO remember that your vehicle's safety affects that of yourself and others. If in doubt on any point, get specialist advice.

IF, in spite of following these precautions, you are unfortunate enough to injure yourself, seek medical attention as soon as possible.

Asbestos

Certain friction, insulating, sealing, and other products – such as brake linings, brake bands, clutch linings, torque converters, gaskets, etc – contain asbestos. *Extreme care must be taken to avoid inhalation of dust from such products since it is hazardous to health.* If in doubt, assume that they *do* contain asbestos.

Fire

Remember at all times that petrol (gasoline) is highly flammable. Never smoke, or have any kind of naked flame around, when working on the vehicle. But the risk does not end there – a spark caused by an electrical short-circuit, by two metal surfaces contacting each other, by careless use of tools, or even by static electricity built up in your body under certain conditions, can ignite petrol vapour, which in a confined space is highly explosive.

Always disconnect the battery earth (ground) terminal before working on any part of the fuel or electrical system, and never risk spilling fuel on to a hot engine or exhaust.

It is recommended that a fire extinguisher of a type suitable for fuel and electrical fires is kept handy in the garage or workplace at all times. Never try to extinguish a fuel or electrical fire with water.

Note: *Any reference to a 'torch' appearing in this manual should always be taken to mean a hand-held battery-operated electric lamp or flashlight. It does NOT mean a welding/gas torch or blowlamp.*

Fumes

Certain fumes are highly toxic and can quickly cause unconsciousness and even death if inhaled to any extent. Petrol (gasoline) vapour comes into this category, as do the vapours from certain solvents such as trichloroethylene. Any draining or pouring of such volatile fluids should be done in a well ventilated area.

When using cleaning fluids and solvents, read the instructions carefully. Never use materials from unmarked containers – they may give off poisonous vapours.

Never run the engine of a motor vehicle in an enclosed space such as a garage. Exhaust fumes contain carbon monoxide which is extremely poisonous; if you need to run the engine, always do so in the open air or at least have the rear of the vehicle outside the workplace.

If you are fortunate enough to have the use of an inspection pit, never drain or pour petrol, and never run the engine, while the vehicle is standing over it; the fumes, being heavier than air, will concentrate in the pit with possibly lethal results.

The battery

Never cause a spark, or allow a naked light, near the vehicle's battery. It will normally be giving off a certain amount of hydrogen gas, which is highly explosive.

Always disconnect the battery earth (ground) terminal before working on the fuel or electrical systems.

If possible, loosen the filler plugs or cover when charging the battery from an external source. Do not charge at an excessive rate or the battery may burst.

Take care when topping up and when carrying the battery. The acid electrolyte, even when diluted, is very corrosive and should not be allowed to contact the eyes or skin.

If you ever need to prepare electrolyte yourself, always add the acid slowly to the water, and never the other way round. Protect against splashes by wearing rubber gloves and goggles.

When jump starting a car using a booster battery, for negative earth (ground) vehicles, connect the jump leads in the following sequence: First connect one jump lead between the positive (+) terminals of the two batteries. Then connect the other jump lead first to the negative (–) terminal of the booster battery, and then to a good earthing (ground) point on the vehicle to be started, at least 18 in (45 cm) from the battery if possible. Ensure that hands and jump leads are clear of any moving parts, and that the two vehicles do not touch. Disconnect the leads in the reverse order.

Mains electricity and electrical equipment

When using an electric power tool, inspection light etc, always ensure that the appliance is correctly connected to its plug and that, where necessary, it is properly earthed (grounded). Do not use such appliances in damp conditions and, again, beware of creating a spark or applying excessive heat in the vicinity of fuel or fuel vapour. Also ensure that the appliances meet the relevant national safety standards.

Ignition HT voltage

A severe electric shock can result from touching certain parts of the ignition system, such as the HT leads, when the engine is running or being cranked, particularly if components are damp or the insulation is defective. Where an electronic ignition system is fitted, the HT voltage is much higher and could prove fatal.

Dimensions, weights and capacities

Dimensions

Overall length:	1965/67	160 in (4064 mm)
	1968/74	158.6 in (4028 mm)
	1975	163.4 in (4153 mm)
Overall width:	1965/68	60.6 in (1539 mm)
	1969 on	61.0 in (1549 mm)
Wheelbase ...	... ...	94.5 in (2400 mm)
Front track:	1965/67	51.4 in (1305 mm)
	1968/74	51.6 in (1311 mm)
	1975 (drum brakes)	51.5 in (1308 mm)
	1975 (disc brakes)	51.8 in (1316 mm)
Rear track:	1965/67	51.2 in (1300 mm)
	1968/74	53.2 in (1351 mm)
	1975	53.1 in (1349 mm)
Ground clearance (fully laden)	6.0 in (152 mm)

Kerb weight

	1965/66	1967	1968	1969	1970/74	1975
Saloon	1720 lb (780 kg)	1764 lb (800 kg)	1812 lb (822 kg)	1809 lb (820 kg)	1808 lb (820 kg)	1973 lb (895 kg)
Convertible ...	1808 lb (820 kg)	1852 lb (840 kg)	1922 lb (872 kg)	1918 lb (870 kg)	2028 lb (920 kg)	2127 lb (895 kg)

Capacities

Engine oil	4.4 Imp pt (2.5 litres/5.3 US pt)
Manual transmission:	(initial fill)	5.3 Imp pt (3.0 litres/6.4 US pt)
	(oil change)	4.4 Imp pt (2.5 litres/5.3 US pt)
Automatic transmission:	(casing)	6.25 Imp pt (3.0 litres/8.5 US pt)
	(converter)	7.5 Imp pt (3.6 litres/9.00 US pt)
Fuel tank	8.8 Imp gal (40 litres/10.6 US gal)

Index